Enterprise Resource Planning

Enterprise Resource Planning

Implementation and Management Accounting Change in a Transitional Country

by

Ahmed O. Kholeif
Lecturer in Accounting and Auditing, School of Accounting, Finance and Management, University of Essex, UK

Magdy G. Abdel-Kader
Senior Lecturer in Accounting, Brunel Business School, Brunel University, UK

and

Michael J. Sherer
Professor in Accounting and Auditing, School of Accounting, Finance and Management, University of Essex, UK

First published 2008 by
PALGRAVE MACMILLAN
Houndmills, Basingstoke, Hampshire RG21 6XS and
175 Fifth Avenue, New York, N.Y. 10010
Companies and representatives throughout the world

PALGRAVE MACMILLAN is the global academic imprint of the Palgrave
Macmillan division of St. Martin's Press, LLC and of Palgrave Macmillan Ltd.
Macmillan® is a registered trademark in the United States, United Kingdom
and other countries. Palgrave is a registered trademark in the European
Union and other countries.

ISBN-13: 978–0–230–51601–4   hardback

This book is printed on paper suitable for recycling and made from fully
managed and sustained forest sources. Logging, pulping and manufacturing
processes are expected to conform to the environmental regulations of the
country of origin.

A catalogue record for this book is available from the British Library.

A catalogue record for this book is available from the Library of Congress.

This book is dedicated to ...

My Mother, Aml, Aida, Mayada, and Gaber
Magda Abou-Seada and Mohamed Abdel-Kader
Denise Sherer

Contents

List of Tables

List of Figures

List of Abbreviations

ABB	Activity-Based Budgeting
ABC	Activity-Based Costing
ABCM	Activity-Based Cost Management
ABM	Activity-Based Management
AQF	Abu Qir Fertilisers Co.
BoB	Best of Breed
BPR	Business Process Re-engineering
BRCs	Business Resource Centres
BSC	Balanced Scorecard
C. A.	Central Administration
CAA	Central Agency for Accountancy
CAPMS	Central Agency for Public Mobilisation and Statistics
CEO	Chief Executive Officer
CIMA	The Chartered Institute of Management Accountants
CMA	Capital Market Authority
COQ	Cost of Quality
CPA	Certified Public Accountant
CT	Computed Tomography
EC	European Commission
EIB	European Investment Bank
ERP	Enterprise Resource Planning
ESA	Employee Shareholders Associations
ESTD	Egyptian Sales Tax Department
EU	European Union
EVA	Economic Value Added
G.A.	General Administration/General Accounts
GATT	General Agreement for Trade and Tariff
GD	General Director
GDP	Gross Domestic Product
GEIN	Government Expenditure Information Network
GLS	General Lighting and Special
GM	General Manager
GOE	Government of Egypt
GST	General Sales Tax
GSTACS	General Sales Tax Administration Computer System
H.S.	Head Sector
IAP	Integrated Automation Project
IASs	International Accounting Standards
IFAC	International Federation of Accountants

IMA	Institute of Management Accountants
IMC	Industrial Modernisation Centre
IMF	International Monetary Fund
IMP	Industrial Modernisation Programme
IPO	Initial Public Offerings
IS	Information Systems
IT	Information Technology
JIT	Just-in Time
MAS	Management Accounting Systems
MCTC	Model Customs and Tax Centre
MIS	Management Information Systems
MITD	Ministry of Industry and Technological Development
MOF	Ministry of Finance
MRP II	Manufacturing Resource Planning
MRP1	Material Resource Planning
NEEASAE	El Naser Electric and Electronic Apparatus Co
OPT	Optimised Production Technology
PDD	Product Development Department
PEO	Public Enterprise Office
PMS	Performance Measurement System
SCM	Supply Chain Management
SFA	Specific Financing Agreement
SMEs	Small and Medium Enterprises
SOEs	State-Owned Enterprises
TOC	Theory of Constraints
TQM	Total Quality Management
VAT	Value-Added-Tax

Preface

This book examines the processes of management accounting change triggered by information technology (IT) (ERP vs. custom software) implementation and use in Egyptian organisations, especially government agencies and state-owned enterprises. It analytically and empirically compares Enterprise Resource Planning (ERP) with custom software in relation to change in management accounting rules (systems) and routines (practices) as well as change in management accountants' roles and relationships with other organisational members, especially IT specialists and line managers, in highly regularised Egyptian organisations that have been influenced by recent institutional transformation in Egypt. The review of appropriate literature on ERP and management accounting change and stability revealed several important research issues that had been neglected and underresearched. A theoretical framework is developed to address management accounting change triggered by IT (ERP vs. custom software) implementation and use. This framework draws primarily on the applications and extensions of structuration theory in both management accounting and IS literatures, especially Burns and Scapens' (2000) institutional framework, Orlikowski's (1992) structurational model of technology and Barley's (1986) model of technology as a trigger of structural change, as well as some concepts of new institutional sociology theory from DiMaggio and Powell (1983).

This book adopts an interpretive methodology and uses a case study method. To help in replicating and extending the theoretical framework, this book utilises a multiple-case design that includes selecting four organisations to address the research issues on IT (custom vs. ERP software) implementation and management accounting change. The book employs multiple data collection methods: semi-structured interviews, background questionnaire, documentary evidence and websites.

Key findings in this book revealed that IT, whether ERP or custom software, is not a driver of change in management accounting systems and practices in highly regularised organisations such as state-owned enterprises and government agencies. Other institutional forces are more significant at introducing change in management accounting rules and routines in Egyptian organisations. Such findings could be expected in the case of custom software. However, they are observed in the case of ERP software as well.

Based on the concept of the operation of the dialectic of control, the analysis is conducted at two levels, the hierarchical level and the professional level. The hierarchical level examines the role of extra-organisational institutions in enabling or constraining IT projects and associated management accounting change and stability. The key findings at this level revealed that the operation of the dialectic of control between extra-organisational institutions and organisational members is much more obvious in ERP cases than in custom software cases. In the case of ERP implementations, the findings revealed that there are many conflicts and contradictions between extra-organisational institutions and organisational members. On the other hand, there is little, if any, conflict between extra-organisational institutions and organisational members in the case of custom software implementations. This supports the view that the implementation of ERP is associated with crisis situations whereas the implementation of custom software is associated with routine situations.

The second, professional level, of analysis examined the changing power relations of management accountants with IT specialists and line managers due to implementing IT projects and associated management accounting change. It focuses on the hybridisation phenomenon or the transfer of knowledge from one professional group to another. At this level, the case studies' findings revealed that there is evidence that management accountants in Egyptian organisations maintained control over their accounting knowledge and, in some cases, have unintentionally expanded their roles into other functional areas such as IT and operations management after the introduction of IT projects.

This book is organised in eight chapters. Chapters 1 and 2 are introductory chapters, which give an overview of the area and review the relevant literature on ERP and management accounting change. The theoretical framework of this research is developed in Chapter 3. This framework draws on structuration theory, 'old' institutional economics, and 'new' institutional sociology theory. In particular, a modified version of Burns and Scapens' (2000) institutional framework is adopted.

The research methodology and methods used to collect empirical data are described and justified in Chapter 4. The empirical data are analysed and discussed in Chapters 5, 6 and 7. Then, Chapter 8 concludes the book with a set of general implications and recommendations for practice and education. This chapter also discusses the book's contributions to knowledge and further opportunities for research.

Ahmed Kholeif, Magdy Abdel-Kader and Michael Sherer
Authors

1
Introduction

1.1 Introduction

An Enterprise Resource Planning (ERP) system is an advanced modern complex technology that integrates and co-ordinates almost all functional areas in the modern organisations. ERP implementation and its impact on organisations differ from the implementation and impact of custom software systems. This book investigates the processes of management accounting change triggered by the implementation and use of these two types of information technology (IT) in four Egyptian organisations, two government agencies and two state-owned enterprises. In particular, the study compares ERP with customised software in relation to change in management accounting systems and practices and change in management accountants' role and relationships with other organisational members in highly regularised Egyptian organisations that have been influenced by recent institutional transformations. On the one hand customised software, which is designed to satisfy the organisation's specific needs, tends to reinforce existing management accounting practices. On the other hand ERP systems are a special type of packaged software. Their implementation is characterised by complexity and cross-functional nature. ERP systems, with their built-in 'best' management accounting practices, promise radical change in the way of doing things, especially in developing countries.

This chapter gives an overview of the book and its contents. It is divided into seven sections. The next section provides a critical review of recent literature and research on ERP systems and management accounting change. The section concludes by identifying the most significant gaps in the literature and then outlining the principal objectives and research questions of this study. This is followed by a discussion of the theoretical framework for the research and the research methodology and methods used. The following sections describe the potential impact of ERP systems on accounting systems and practices in Egyptian organisations and the contribution that the study has made to our understanding of technical and organisational change in a developing country.

1.2 Management accounting change and ERP

In recent years there has been an increasing interest in management accounting change and stability. For example, Burns and Scapens (2000: 3) state that:

> Management accounting change has become a topic of much debate in recent years. Whether management accounting has not changed, has changed, or should change, have all been discussed.

The current debate on management accounting change and stability can be traced to Johnson and Kaplan's (1987) seminal work that presented their arguments on the relevance lost in management accounting systems and practices. They observed that management accounting techniques used in US industries had not changed since 1925 despite radical changes in manufacturing methods and environment. Kaplan (1984) claimed that management accounting systems lag far behind innovations in advanced manufacturing techniques such as materials requirements planning, Just-in-Time (JIT) purchasing and production, numerical control machines, computer-aided design and manufacturing, total quality management (TQM), and flexible manufacturing systems. Gurd *et al.* (2002) argues that the absence of innovations in management accounting to reflect the changing nature of operating systems has inhibited improvements in the performance of the organisation because 'traditional' management accounting systems are not well suited to meet planning and control needs in the new manufacturing environments.

Kaplan (1986) suggested that 'traditional' management accounting practices will, at best, imperfectly reflect changes in manufacturing performance arising from improved TQM, JIT inventory systems and computer controlled manufacturing processes. He argued that management accounting systems and practices must change to reflect changes in innovative production systems and advanced manufacturing technologies. Since the publication of the 'relevance lost' thesis there has been a burgeoning of new management accounting practices for improved decision-making such as activity-based costing and management, the balanced scorecard, quality costs and benchmarking.

Advanced manufacturing technologies such as Material Resource Planning (MRPI) and Manufacturing Resource Planning (MRPII) systems appear to be the predecessors of ERP systems[1] (Aghazadeh, 2003). In addition to operations management ERP systems have been extended to include other functional areas such as accounting, human resources, logistics, sales and marketing (Booth *et al.*, 2000). Granlund and Malmi (2002) described ERP systems as 'a change agent'. These systems, with built-in best practices, support 'modern' management accounting techniques, address many of the traditional criticisms of management accounting systems raised by Kaplan

(1984, 1986) and his colleagues (Johnson and Kaplan, 1987) and realise the dreams of management accounting researchers. For example, Anthony (1988: 123) expressed his concerns about the inability to obtain integrated and real-time information in the 1980s as follows:

> Except in organisation with simple activities, this ideal is not now achievable. The problem of making the pieces fit together, and especially, being able to revise the system as the need changes, is beyond the capability of humans.

In 1990s many commentators on management accounting identified the potential for modern software systems to revolutionise accounting practices.[2] For instance, Bjornenak and Olson (1999: 33) used the following argument in support of the balanced scorecard technology:

> Today, the use of modern database technology makes it possible to link many data sources together, including external and non-financial data. This development has diluted the one system thinking of management accounting ... Thus the technological development has made it difficult to define a management accounting system per se.

Scapens *et al.* (1996) also argue that with modern database technology it is quite feasible to have a single system of data capture for both management accounting and external reporting, with data selected, analysed, aggregated and reported in different ways for different purposes. They suggest that the increasing availability of computer technology at all levels in the firms and the integration of operating control systems with management information systems mean that managers can have on-line access to the information they need to control all aspects, including the costs, of their operations.

In the same vein, other accounting researchers identified the potential impact of ERP systems on management accounting practices and management accountants' work (Sutton, 2000; Chapman and Chua, 2000). They expected that the introduction of ERP systems to replace legacy custom developed systems would radically change management accounting systems and practices and have a significant effect on management accountants' roles and relationships with other organisational members. Thus the critical question is whether ERP systems have overcome management accounting stability and changed management accounting practices and management accountants' work and roles.

There has been some research that has attempted to address this question in the context of Anglo-American countries. With respect to change in management accounting systems and practices, previous studies tend to reveal stability or minor modifications to existing management accounting techniques after implementing ERP systems. However, they disagree on the reasons for this phenomenon. Some studies[3] find that modern management accounting techniques, like those built into ERP, have been implemented in separate systems before the introduction of ERP. They interpret this stability in functional-economic terms (i.e. long project times, scarce resources and system complexity).

Other studies observe that companies choose ERP systems to replace existing accounting systems with other very similar systems (Scapens and Jazayeri, 2003) or use Best of Breed (BoB[4]) systems that closely align the selected software with the business processes of the organisation (Hyvonen, 2003). They interpret this phenomenon in terms of institutionalised management accounting practices. In addition to these interpretations it is also the case that ERP built-in best practices are derived from existing practices actually implemented in companies working in different industries in developed countries. This can partially account for the stability phenomenon of management accounting practices after introducing ERP systems.

Concerning the issue of change in management accountants' role and relationships, prior studies tend to agree on the occurrence of change but not the direction of change. The results of these studies reveal inconsistencies in experiences between organisations. Some studies find that management accountants have lost control of their traditional role as information providers because this role is now built into IT and their accounting knowledge has become easily transferable to Information Systems (IS) staff and line managers as they can access timely real-time information (McCosh, 1986; Scapens *et al.*, 1998). Others suggest that management accountants not only continue to be the principal providers of information to management but are also expanding their role into other functional areas such as IT and production (King *et al.*, 1991; Caglio, 2003).

The above discussion indicates that there is an emerging and growing interest in the impact of ERP systems on accounting practices and accountants' role and relationships with other organisational members. However, the insights gained to date should be interpreted in the light of a number of limitations. Firstly, there have been no previous studies that address ERP impacts on accounting in less developed countries' contexts.

Secondly, previous studies ignore the fact that ERP built-in best practices, including accounting practices, are derived from companies working in Anglo-American developed countries. Hence, it is not necessarily the case that the best practices from other contexts, especially from Anglo-American developed countries, are appropriate for developing countries. Instead the introduction of ERP systems developed elsewhere may, intentionally or not, become a catalyst for changes in management accounting practices in developing countries. Thus there is the issue as to whether these changes are benign or detrimental to the organisations that implement ERP.

Thirdly, only a few exploratory, survey-based studies have been conducted to compare ERP users' views with non-ERP users', especially BoB systems' users. These latter systems usually mix ERP components with custom software. As a consequence, their impacts on management accounting may be the same as ERP systems' impacts. To avoid any effects of ERP systems on management accounting practices and to explore their relative merits, it is better to use custom software (part of BoB systems without any standard packages) as a benchmark instead of BoB systems.

Fourthly, prior research suffers from either not using an analytic framework or focusing on only one aspect of ERP impacts, that is, changes to accounting methods or changes to accountants' role. None of the past studies have used the same analytic framework to address the two perceived impacts of ERP systems.

Finally, none of the past studies looking at ERP impacts on accounting have been conducted in public sector enterprises.

1.3 Research objectives and questions

This research contributes to the debate on ERP and management accounting change in the context of a less developed country, Egypt. It extends the emerging research in three main areas:

1. It develops an analytic framework for comparing ERP's impacts on management accounting with standalone custom software's impacts;
2. It conducts a cross-sectional, qualitative case study; and
3. It considers not only ERP users' views but also the experiences of non-ERP users, that is, organisations adopting only standalone custom software.

More specifically, two main objectives are central to this research. The first objective is to develop a theoretical framework to understand the nature of management accounting changes associated with ERP systems compared with custom software. This framework draws mainly on structuration theory (Giddens, 1979, 1984) and institutional theory, especially Burns and Scapens' (2000) institutional framework and 'new' institutional sociology theory, as they have been used in a number of recent studies in the IT and accounting literatures.[5] The second objective is to provide detailed empirical evidence of actual change processes by means of cross-sectional, qualitative case studies in four Egyptian organisations, two ERP adopters (a governmental unit and a state-owned enterprise) and two non-ERP adopters (a governmental unit and a state-owned enterprise adopting standalone custom software).

To achieve these objectives, this study addresses the following two groups of research questions:

The first group deals mainly with stability and change in management accounting practices, the conditions under which stability and/or change can occur and the role of IT in their occurrence. More specifically, the research asks: why and how are institutionalised accounting practices persisted (reproduced) and/or transformed in the IT (ERP vs. custom software) environment? And what is the role of IT (ERP vs. custom software) in their persistence or transformation?

In this regard, there are two competing views concerning management accounting change and stability and the role of IT in their occurrence. The first view advocates that management accounting practices must change to cope with changes in advanced technologies. Under this view, ERP systems may be considered as a change driver where best practices, including management accounting practices are built into the software. The other view encourages the stability of management accounting practices, as this stability is a necessary condition for managing organisations in uncertain environments. Under this view, custom software may contribute to stabilising management accounting practices. This research investigates which of these forecast outcomes work in practice.

The second group focuses mainly on the changing role and relationships of management accountants due to the introduction of IT (ERP vs. custom software). The specific questions posed by this research include: how does IT (ERP vs. custom software) maintain or change the relationship of management accountants with different members (IS staff and line managers) within the organisation? And what is the role of management accountants in the IT (ERP vs. custom software) environment as perceived by management accountants themselves and other members of the organisation?

In this regard, there are also two competing views concerning the role of management accountants in the IT environment. The first view considers that management accountants have relinquished control over their mainstream responsibilities because most of their traditional role as information provider is embedded into automated IT systems and, as a consequence, their accounting knowledge has become easily transferable to IS staff and line managers who can access timely real-time information. Supporters of this view start searching for a new role for management accountants in the IT environment.

The second view is more optimistic and considers that management accountants not only have retained control over their mainstream responsibilities but also are expanding their role into other functional areas such as IT and operations management. Actually, it is difficult to relate either of these views to a particular type of IT (ERP or custom software) as custom software may be associated with networked computing. Therefore, there may be no clear-cut answer about which of these views will dominate in practice.

1.4 Theoretical framework – selection and justification

1.4.1 The selection of theoretical framework

Covaleski *et al.* (1996) identified three main approaches to examine management accounting phenomena namely, positivistic, interpretive, and critical perspectives. Each of these paradigms has different beliefs about knowledge, physical and social reality, and relationship between theory and practice (Chua, 1986; Laughlin, 1995). Prior research on management accounting change and stability include examples of all these theoretical approaches including positivistic approach such as contingency theory perspective (e.g. Williams and Seaman, 2001); interpretive perspectives such as social construction perspective (e.g. Perren and Grant, 2000), 'old' institutional theory (e.g. Soin *et al.*, 2002), and 'new' institutional theory (e.g. Modell, 2001); and critical perspectives like the Foucauldian perspective (e.g. Hopwood, 1990; Ezzamel, 1994) and labour theory processes (Uddin and Hopper, 1999, 2001).

In this regard, we share Saunders *et al.*'s (2003: 85) view that 'it would be easy to fall into the trap of thinking that one research approach is "better" than another. This would miss the point. They are "better" at doing different things'. We argue that all research approaches complement each other. However, caution should be exercised in choosing and combining different theories together as these syntheses may overcome some difficulties of these theories and, however, create others by losing sight of their key features. This research draws on structuration theory, new institutional sociology theory and old institutional economics theory to understand management accounting change induced by the implementation of IT (ERP vs. custom software) in Egyptian organisations.

Giddens' structuration theory has been proposed as a useful framework for understanding the social context of management accounting in organisations (Robert and Scapens, 1985; Macintosh and Scapens, 1990). Despite its contribution to solving the objective (positivistic) – subjective (interpretive) dualism, structuration theory has been criticised, as it does not take into account historical time. Archer (1995: 65) argued 'that structure and agency can only be linked by examining the interplay between them over time, and without the proper incorporation of time the problem of structure and agency can never be satisfactorily resolved'. Following Archer (1995), Burns and Scapens (2000) introduced their institutional model as an attempt to overcome some of these limitations in dealing with management accounting change.

This framework is mainly grounded in both structuration theory and old institutional economics theory. In their framework, Burns and Scapens (2000), drawing on old institutional economics, conceptualise management accounting systems and practices as organisational rules and routines respectively. They also conceptualise management accounting change as change in organisational rules and routines. On the other hand, Burns and Scapens (2000) draw on structuration theory to argue that there are meanings, norms and powers embedded in new and ongoing routines; all of which are shaped by prevailing institutions and the new routines could be institutionalised over time.

However, Burns and Scapens' (2000) framework is primarily concerned with management accounting change within individual organisations, that is, intra-organisational processes of change. Therefore, it does not take into account (extra-organisational) macro institutional pressures such as social, economic and political institutions of the organisational field and the society, which actually differ from one country to another. As a result, an extension of Burns and Scapens' (2000) model is to employ new institutional theory. In addition, Burns and Scapens (2000) do not address the issue of information technology in their framework. The incorporation of IT in Burns and Scapens' (2000) model is another extension.

Burns and Scapens' (2000) framework is based, principally, on the work of Barley and Tolbert (1997). The latter work is a combination of structuration theory and new institutional theory. Although Burns and Scapens' (2000) model does not explicitly incorporate new institutional theory into their work, it does recognise the importance of extra-organisational institutional pressures in affecting management accounting practices. In this research study Burns and Scapens' (2000) model is complemented by new institutional theory to address the effect of extra-organisational institutional pressures on IT-triggered management accounting change.

Furthermore, three IT models in the information systems literature, grounded in structuration theory, are introduced to explore their potentialities to be integrated with Burns and Scapens' (2000) framework. The first model, DeSanctis and Pool's (1994) adaptive structuration theory, has been criticised because it is highly deterministic and adopts a positivistic approach, as against the interpretive approach adopted in this study. The second model, Barley's (1986) work, has been extended by Barley and Tolbert (1997) to combine new institutional theory with structuration theory. This latter work forms the basis for Burns and Scapens' (2000) framework for conceptualising management accounting change.

However, Burns and Scapens (2000) replace the notion of scripts in Barley and Tolbert's (1997) model with rules and routines to link structuration theory to old institutional economics theory. Therefore, the current research benefits from the work of Barley (1986) as the implementation of ERP or customised software can be conceptualised as an 'occasion for structuring'. This concept is consistent with what Giddens (1984: 13) calls 'the cumulation of events deriving from an initiating circumstance without which that cumulation would not have been found'. Furthermore, the introduction of ERP or customised software is similar to the introduction of rules in Burns and Scapens' (2000: 7) framework, where 'rules are normally changed only at discrete intervals; but routines have the potential to be in a cumulative process of change as they continue to be reproduced'.

This research study also draws on some concepts of Orlikowski (1992), the third IT model. Orlikowski (1992) distinguishes between two iterative modes: the design mode and the use mode. This distinction, coupled with the interpretive flexibility view of technology, seems particularly appropriate for both custom software and ERP, as a configurable software package, and strongly suggests the applicability of structuration theory to the study of IT implementation and use. Unlike Barley (1986), who considers IT as an action, Orlikowski (1992) treats IT as a structure. However, both views are consistent with Burns and Scapens' (2000) model. Burns and Scapens (2000: 10) treat rules (or IT-embedded rules as will be used here) as modalities and argue that the position of rules could be closer either to actions or to structures. In this study, the new IT-embedded rules are regarded as an action in the implementation phase and the new emergent routines as modalities in the use phase.

1.4.2   Justification of selected theoretical framework

The stabilisation behaviour of management accounting practice normally has been observed when highly customised legacy systems have been the dominant information systems and most recently, when ERP systems have become the dominant ones. For example, Hedberg and Jonsson (1978: 47) argued that:

> Current information – and accounting – systems do more to stabilise organisations than to destabilise them. They filter away conflicts, ambiguities, overlaps, uncertainty etc. and they suppress many relevant change signals and kill initiatives to act on early warnings.

They attributed this tendency to using standard operating procedures, which make the behaviour of organisations more consistent over time, due to the limited information processing capacity of humans. Recently, Granlund and Malmi (2002) and Scapens and Jazayeri (2003) have recognised the stabilising role of ERP systems. For instance, Granlund and Malmi (2002: 314), in trying to interpret the results of their study showing the relative stability of management accounting practices, stated that:

> Another interpretation for our observations, taking a different perspective on change and continuity, suggests that ERPs may actually have had a stabilising effect on management accounting practice and its development. Instead of analysing effects only in terms of changes, we can also identify effects in terms of whether the new technology maintains prevailing practices.

In this regard, Weick (1969) argue that organisational members form an image of the environment, that is, enacted environment, and respond to the enacted environment rather than to objective environment. This view is consistent with Angyal (1941) who argued that 'environmental stimuli' need to be interpreted not as objective conditions in the environment but as conditions relative to the system. It seems that information and accounting systems actively contribute to creating this enacted environment by filtering away conflicts, ambiguities, overlaps, and uncertainty (Hedberg and Jonsson, 1978).

'Old' institutional theory was applied to accounting practices to explain both the stabilising role of information systems and the possibility of evolutionary change (Scapens, 1994; Burns and Scapens, 2000). Ahmed and Scapens (2000), for example, argue that despite the tendency of rules, routines and institutions to create the stability necessary for ongoing organisational activity, new ways of working can emerge from day-to-day activities as agents modify their behaviours to deal with new problems and opportunities. Therefore, 'old' institutional theory was selected to address the research problem because of its ability to explain the evolutionary nature of accounting that is widely acknowledged in the accounting literature in general and ERP in particular (Kaplan, 1984; Bromwich and Bhimani, 1989; Chenhall and Langfield Smith, 1998a, 1998b; Sharma, 2000). However, 'old' institutional theory is primarily concerned with intra-organisational behaviours. It does not consider extra-organisational institutions.

The new institutional sociology theory overcomes this limitation. It explores the role of macroeconomic, political and social institutions in shaping organisational structures, policies and procedures (Scott, 2001). Organisations respond to such external, macro pressures in order to receive support and legitimacy. Therefore, this theory has been chosen to address extra-organisational institutions that affect Egyptian organisations. In particular, coercive pressures play a major role in the Egyptian organisations under study, government agencies and state-owned enterprises.

Structuration theory has been selected because it takes account of the social context of management accounting, relates macro institutional context to micro organisational context, and emphasises the importance of the dialectic of control in social relations. It can also reconcile the polarities between technological and social determinism of information technology in IS literature and to interpret stability in management accounting practices (Granlund, 2001). Furthermore, structuration theory is capable of explaining revolutionary change in crisis situations and evolutionary change in routine situations.

1.5 Research methodology and methods

Prior research on management accounting change and stability has used a number of different methodologies, that is, qualitative and quantitative, and methods, that is, case studies (e.g. Cobb *et al.*, 1995; Vaivio, 1999), field studies (e.g. Innes and Mitchell, 1990), and surveys (e.g. Libby and Waterhouse, 1996). This study uses a qualitative methodology with a case study method. The qualitative methodology and method are consistent with structuration theory, which is used as a meta-theory in this research, and institutional theories. As Bryant and Jary (1991) note, Giddens adopts a post-empiricist and anti-positivist stance. This denies the existence of universal laws of human activity and emphasises the centrality of the interpretative endeavour, describing social science as 'irretrievably hermeneutic' (Giddens, 1979: 13), that is, interpretative.

In recent years there have been calls for detailed interpretive case studies of ERP implementations (Caglio, 2003; Scapens and Jazayeri, 2003). Scapens and Jazayeri (2003: 201), for example called for longitudinal case studies of the implementation of ERP systems to study the 'processes of management accounting change'. In response to this call, this study conducts a cross-sectional case study that compares management accounting practices in ERP adopters and ERP non-adopters. This type of case studies has been selected as little research has adopted this method in accounting domain in general and ERP studies in particular. For example, Humphrey and Scapens (1996) noted the lack of case studies that explored similarities and differences across organisations. As a consequence, they advise undertaking meaningful comparisons across cases to provide theoretically informed explanations for management accounting practices.

Interpretive case study research has been undertaken because it promises a rich description of social, cultural and political contexts. The role of case studies within the interpretive methodology, which is based on a belief that accounting practices are socially constructed, is to locate practice in its historical, as well as its economic, social and organisational contexts in order to help us to understand the social structures which shape current practice. In this regard, Scapens (1990) believes that explanatory case studies are an essential part of the interpretive approach and that other, more evaluative case studies, can also be useful within this approach.

As the purpose of the research is to compare ERP systems with custom software systems with respect to their impacts on management accounting practices and accountants' roles and relationships, two state-owned enterprises and two government agencies influenced by the recent institutional transformations in Egypt were selected for the empirical study. The two state-owned enterprises are NEEASAE (ERP software) and AQF (custom software) and the two government agencies selected are IMC (ERP software) and ESTD (custom software). The choice of four organisations was made for several reasons. Firstly, it satisfies the criteria suggested by Yin (1994) for selecting multiple case studies. The selected organisations comprise both similar and dissimilar cases. Therefore, this selection achieves both theoretical replications and theoretical extensions and, ultimately, provides a rich theoretical framework, capable of understanding management accounting change in widely differing circumstances. Secondly, the multiple-case design and site selection overcomes some limitations of prior research such as the difficulty in differentiating between ERP adopters and non-adopters and the lack of attention paid to ERP adoption in governmental units. Thirdly, the four organisations are illustrative of the economic transition in Egypt because they are highly influenced by economic and structural programmes that have been undertaken to transform Egypt from a centrally planned economy to a free market-oriented economy. For instance, AQF and NEEASAE were affected by a privatisation programme in their implementation of IT projects. Finally, the selection of organisations reflects the level of access gained during the course of conducting empirical work.

Multiple data collection methods are typically used in case study research in order to obtain a rich set of data surrounding the specific research issue, as well as to capture the contextual complexity (Benbasat *et al.*, 1987). In this study, multiple sources of empirical evidence included semi-structured interviews, background questionnaire and documentary evidence. Reference is also made to publicly available data sources such as the organisations' published accounts, DataStream and newspaper articles. These multiple methods are deliberately selected as one method can complement the others. This triangulation helps to improve the internal validity of research.

In interpretive research, the validity of evidence can only be assessed in the context of the particular case, what Scapens (1990) called 'contextual validity'. In this regard, Scapens (1990) suggests triangulation of evidence by collecting different evidence on the same research issue, collecting other evidence from the same source and working in teams in order to reach an agreed interpretation of a particular case. As a consequence, the use of multiple sources of evidence in this study is justifiable on the grounds of increasing the contextual validity of research evidence. In addition, the sources of data collection are selected to elicit the type of data required to answer each research question.

1.6   Egypt as a transitional country and ERP

Egypt has undergone fundamental economic and structural changes over the past few decades. The economic system in Egypt changed in the late 1950s when socialist policies were implemented and the economy became centrally planned. During the socialism period most Egyptian companies were owned by the Egyptian government and these companies adopted a Uniform Accounting System as a means of providing the government with information suitable for economic planning and control (Briston and El-Ashker, 1984).

By the beginning of the 1990s the shift from a central planning economy to a market-oriented economy and the implementation of structural and privatisation programmes required changes in accounting systems and practices and, in particular new management accounting systems and practices for organisations operating in the new Egyptian economy. Mostafa (1989), for example, investigates financial planning and control systems in Egypt Air and

British Airways. He concludes that the Uniform Accounting System, which is applied in Egypt Air, is inadequate to provide the information needed for planning and control purposes in the airlines industry.

The introduction of ERP systems, which are usually associated with business process re-engineering, into Egyptian companies may facilitate radical change in financial and management accounting systems and practices. As previously mentioned, ERP built-in-best practices are grounded in capitalist thinking. These practices are totally different from socialist practices, which had been adopted for decades in Egypt. Thus ERP systems promise rapid growth for the Egyptian economy and the integration of Egyptian companies into global markets. The next section addresses the importance of the study.

1.7 The significance of the research

As stated earlier, this research develops and uses an analytic framework to compare the impacts of ERP systems and custom software systems on management accounting practices and management accountants' roles and relationships in Egyptian organisations. The study is significant for a number of reasons. First, in recent years there has been growing increase in using ERP systems developed by a range of commercial companies, for example SAP, Oracle, Baan, Peoplesoft, and JD Edwards as a business information system software platform for large companies and government bodies in developed countries such as the USA, the UK, Canada, and Australia (Davenport, 1998). While there is a wide adoption of ERP systems in Anglo-American countries, developing countries lag far behind. However, due to economic growth, developing countries such as Egypt are recently becoming major targets of big ERP vendors (El Sayed and Westrup, 2003). There is an urgent need to understand ERP implementation issues in developing countries and in Egypt in particular as there is little experience of implementing and using these systems in these countries. For example, Huang and Palvia (2001: 276) argue that 'ERP technology faces additional challenges in developing countries related to economic, cultural, and basic infrastructure issues'.

Second, despite the widespread use of ERP systems in developed countries and the promising benefits of these systems for management accounting, little research has been conducted to assess these benefits in practice (Granlund and Malmi, 2002; Scapens and Jazayeri, 2003). For example, Booth *et al.* (2000) argue that '[g]iven the potential significance of ERP systems for accounting issues, it is surprising that so little research has addressed the impact of ERP systems on this domain'. Furthermore, this study provides the first systematic evaluation of the impact of ERP systems on management accounting in Egypt.

Third, the implementation of ERP systems in Egypt raises a unique accounting problem for developing countries that has not been addressed in previous studies, that is, the relevance of Anglo-American management accounting techniques in developing countries context. ERP systems have been designed to suit, among others, organisations' accounting needs in developed countries context. For example, Hedberg and Jonsson (1978: 56) argue that '[t]he way in which organizations' information (and accounting) systems reflect the world depends on the designers' assumptions about important characteristics of organizations and their environments'. In the context of ERP systems, Scapens *et al.* (1998: 48) observed this phenomenon. They stated that '...the British subsidiary of a US multinational, which was implementing SAP world-wide, found considerable difficulty in adapting SAP to its operating needs. Market conditions and structures in Britain are different from those in the US. But SAP was configured for the US operations and this led to inflexibility for the British subsidiary'.

While there is a claim that 'current management accounting practices are strongly framed and driven by factors at macro level, at which various and considerable global pressures of convergence currently at work' (Granlund and Lukka, 1998: 170), there is extensive literature that stresses the particularities of management accounting practices within each country and the difficulties of transporting Anglo-American accounting practices to developing countries.[6] Wallace (1997: 393), for example, states that '[m]uch of the literature on accounting is not designed to deal with African problems and some of it is totally irrelevant to African conditions and problems'. This research contributes to this controversial issue on the conflict between the globalisation and localisation of management accounting practices. ERP systems with built-in management accounting practices express the tendency towards globalisation, while in-house legacy systems with customised management accounting practices refer to the localisation approach.

Fourth, the implementation of ERP systems sharply differs from the implementation of traditional IT systems, especially custom software and other packaged software (Volkoff, 2001). For custom software, the software producers and software customers are, in most cases, the same or the producers are tightly controlled with the customers and the software is especially built to satisfy the consumers' specific needs. Therefore, from expected change perspective, custom software is expected to reinforce existing management accounting routines. For packaged software, the software vendors and software purchasers are different organisations, where the vendors develop software to suit generic requirements of a set of organisations.

ERP systems are a special type of packaged software, whose implementation is characterised by complexity and cross-functional nature of the software itself. Often there is a gap between the ERP's generic requirements and the specific requirements the organisation desires. When the software cannot be made to fit exactly the way the organisation had planned to operate, changes may be made to organisational business processes to fit with the best practices embedded in the software. Therefore, it is expected that ERP will radically change the way of doing things, that is, existing management accounting routines. As a consequence, the comparison between custom software's effects on accounting practices with ERP's may highlight the potential differences and changes in management accounting practices and management accountants' role and relationships.

Fifth, most previous studies focus only on ERP users' experiences (e.g. Spathis and Constantinides, 2002) or implicitly compare ERP systems with legacy systems within the same organisation over time (e.g. Scapens and Jazayeri, 2003). Only two studies (Booth *et al.*, 2000; Hyvonen, 2003) have considered comparing ERP users with non-ERP users in the accounting field, but as stated earlier they suffer from two limitations. First, they are exploratory, cross-sectional, quantitative surveys of ERP impacts that limit a rich description of social, cultural and political contexts. Second, they have difficulties in distinguishing ERP adopters from ERP non-adopters. This research attempts to avoid these limitations by focusing on comparing ERP adopters (companies adopting ERP as a special type of packaged software) with ERP non-adopters (companies adopting custom software) and on conducting exploratory-explanatory, cross-sectional, qualitative case study.

Finally, different social, economic, and technological changes put tremendous pressures on governments to become more effective, efficient and accountable for the use of public funds (Hoque, 2001). ERP systems, as one of the most recent technological changes, are widely used in government bodies in Anglo-American countries (Davenport, 1998; Booth *et al.*, 2000). However, it is surprising that none of the past studies have been conducted to address ERP systems' impacts on management accounting in governmental contexts. This research contributes to filling this gap by collecting empirical evidence on this issue from some Egyptian governmental units.

1.8   The structure of the book

This book consists of seven further chapters as follows:

Chapter 2 reviews the relevant literature on ERP and management accounting change, including positivist, interpretive, and critical approaches to management accounting change and stability and the effect of information technology on the roles and responsibilities of management accountants. It discusses assumptions and criticisms of each approach and identifies the tendency towards integrating multiple approaches to overcome their individual limitations.

Chapter 3 develops a theoretical framework that will be used to analyse empirical data. This framework draws on structuration theory, 'old' institutional economics, and 'new' institutional sociology theory. It uses structuration theory as a meta-theory to integrate the other two theories and to complement the details that are absent in both approaches. In particular, a modified version of Burns and Scapens' (2000) institutional framework is adopted.

Chapter 4 details the research methodology and methods used to collect empirical data. It discusses alternative methodologies and methods and selects the most suitable methodology and methods to address the research questions.

Chapter 5 explores the extra-organisational institutions affecting management accounting in Egypt. The focus in this chapter is on analysing coercive pressures influencing on management accounting practices and their relation with IT. This chapter focuses on recent institutional transformations in Egypt and its impact on Egyptian organisations, especially government agencies and state-owned enterprises.

Chapter 6 discusses the comparative impacts of ERP vs. custom software on management accounting systems and practices by drawing on the interplay between actions and institutions in routine and crisis situations in order to explain how institutions are reproduced, modified or changed.

Chapter 7 introduces the comparative impacts of ERP vs. custom software on management accountants' roles and relationships by drawing on the dialectic of control concept.

Chapter 8 provides conclusions to the study, explains the main findings and highlights future research opportunities.

Notes

1 ERP systems can be defined as 'packages of computer applications that support many, even most aspects of a company's ...information needs' (Davenport, 2000: 2), and these packages are single-vendor based (Light *et al.*, 2001). More details are in Chapter 2.
2 See, for example, FMAC (1994); Atkinson *et al.* (1997); Foster and Young (1997); ICAEW (1997).
3 See, for example, Booth *et al.* (2000); Granlund and Malmi (2002); Spathis and Constantinides (2002).
4 BoB is an IT system that 'integrates components of standard package and/or custom software' (Light *et al.*, 2001: 216). We should note that standard packages might be ERP packages or might not. 'The aim is for enterprise integration and a process orientation' (Light *et al.*, 2001: 217).
5 Macintosh and Scapens (1990); Orlikowski (1992); Dillard and Yuthas (1997); Caglio (2003); Scapens and Jazayeri (2003).
6 See, for example, Mensah (1981); Ndubizu (1984); Hove (1989); Wallace (1993); Larson (1993); Larson and Kenny (1995); Longden *et al.* (2001).

2
Literature Review

2.1 Introduction

The revolution in computing and information technology has facilitated the design and implementation of effective management accounting systems. ERP systems, as one of today's popular information technologies in the changing business environment, support 'modern' management accounting techniques such as activity-based costing (ABC), activity-based budgeting (ABB), product lifecycle costing and balanced scorecard (BSC). In addition, the promise of integrated, flexible, real-time financial and operating information offered by these systems addresses many of the traditional criticisms of management accounting systems raised by Kaplan (1984; 1986) and his colleagues (Johnson and Kaplan, 1987; Cooper and Kaplan, 1992). For instance, Johnson (1994: 261) argues that traditional management accounting information became 'too distorted, too aggregated and too late to help managers control operations'. Accordingly, implementation of ERP system can be described as 'a change agent' (Granlund and Malmi, 2002).

This chapter reviews the literature on management accounting change and stability, particularly the role of ERP systems in changing or stabilising management accounting systems and practices. The remainder of the chapter is divided into five sections. The next section introduces ERP systems; in particular their definition, history, scope, lifecycle, benefits and limitations. This is followed by a discussion on how ERP systems support and/or hinder management accounting innovations. The fourth section presents and evaluates various theoretical and philosophical approaches that inform management accounting change studies in general. Then, the fifth section specifically reviews the literature on ERP and management accounting change and stability in order to identify gaps in this literature and to articulate the research questions. The final section provides a brief summary of the chapter.

2.2 Enterprise Resource Planning (ERP) systems

The term Enterprise Resource Planning (ERP) was first introduced by the Gartner Group of Stamford, Connecticut, in the early 1990s (Cullen *et al.*,

2001). ERP systems can be defined as 'packages of computer applications that support many, even most aspects of a company's...information needs' (Davenport, 2000: 2), and these software packages are single-vendor based (Light *et al.*, 2001). These systems span most functional areas such as accounting, operations management and logistics, human resources, sales and marketing. Therefore, they promise a seamless integration of all the information flowing throughout a company. They use integrated client-server technology and draw on a single database, which integrates underlying relational databases across all business functions, where all data are entered only once, typically where the data originate (see Figure 2.1). The marketplace for ERP software packages is dominated by a number of global vendors such as Baan, SAP, PeopleSoft, JD Edwards and Oracle, who account for over half of all industry licence revenue (Chung and Snyder, 2000). A list of ERP vendors and their products is shown in Table 2.1.

ERP systems are considered an extension of earlier MRPI (Material Resource Planning) systems in the 1970s and MRPII (Manufacturing Resource Planning) systems in the 1980s. MRPI has been developed to replace traditional order-based information systems that support production planning and control (Cooper and Zmud, 1990). MRPI aims to control materials and uses the bill of material data, inventory data, and the master production schedule to compute timed requirements for materials. It takes requirements for finished products and works back through to materials to produce production and

Figure 2.1 ERP Components

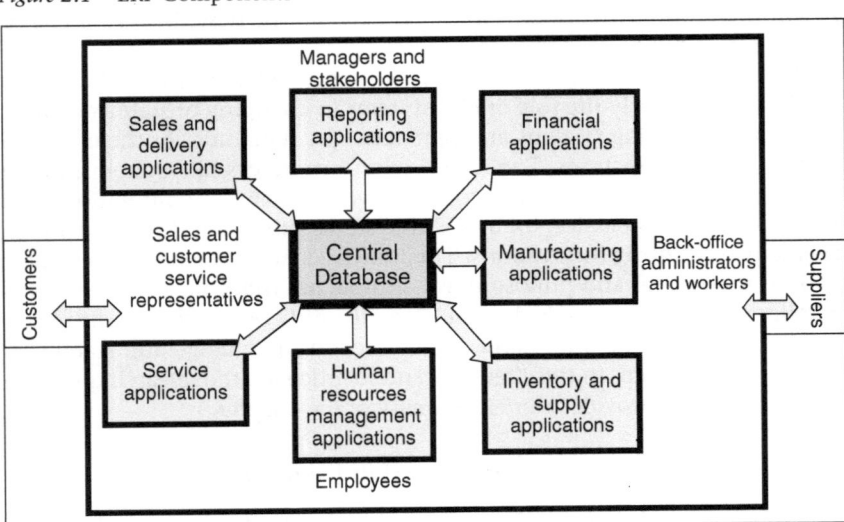

Adapted from Davenport (1998: 124).

Table 2.1   ERP Vendors and their Products

ERP Vendors	Software
Baan	Baan IV
Computer Associates International	CAS, Manman/X, PRMS
Cincom Systems	Control
IFS	IFS
Intentia	Movex
Interactive	Infoflo, JIT
JBA International	System 21
J. D. Edwards	Genesis, OneWorld, World/World Vision
Made2Manage	Made2Manage
MAI Systems	Cimpro
Marcam	MAPICS, Prism, Protean
McDonnell Information Systems	Chess
Oracle	GEMMS, Manufacturing
PeopleSoft	PeopleSoft
PivotPoint	Point.Man
PowerCerv	Adaptlications
QAD	Mfg/Pro
ROI Systems	Manage 2000
Ross Systems	Renaissance C/S
SAP	R/3
Systems and Computer Technology	Adage
System Software Associates	BPCS
Symix Computer Systems	Syteline
Tetra International	CS3

Source: Fahy and Lynch (1999: 4).

purchase orders. It was also originally run on an IBM mainframe computer (Scott, 1994). MRPI is the heart of an MRPII system (Parker, 1996).

MRPII is a company-wide manufacturing control system, which integrates all aspects of manufacturing such as production planning, scheduling, material control, purchasing and distribution planning. It aims to control all manufacturing and some commercial functions. Unlike MRPI of the 1970s, the MRPII system could be installed on a variety of IT platforms (Peteroff, 1993). A trend has been for MRPII to be run on PCs, while the organisation's IT is based around a mainframe computer. Typically, MRPII systems have been procured separately and without regard for the need to communicate across the traditional functional areas. As such, some functions of the firm lay outside the integrated set.

ERP evolved from MRPII systems in the 1990s. It has been argued that the observed limitations of MRPI and MRPII have been addressed with solutions in the ERP system. Like MRPII, ERP utilises MRPI but it integrates other functions with MRPII modules to bridge the islands of automation existing in some functions such as finance and management. In this regard, ERP systems cover the entire spectrum of business activities and support the necessary centralisation and standardisation within the organisation's own notional boundaries. Porter (2000), describing ERP evolution in relation to supply chain planning, claims that the 'post-ERP' stage starts when ERP extends beyond the organisation's business activity boundaries within the supply chain (see Figure 2.2). However, Aghazadeh (2003) considers this extension as the real beginning of ERP systems, arguing that ERP systems started when MRPII systems evolved to include supply chains and customers using electronic data interchange and advanced shipping notice. In fact, it is difficult to draw sharp boundaries between different stages of the evolutionary process of ERP systems.

2.2.1 Scope of ERP systems

ERP systems can be described as 'multi-everything' systems because they are multi-company, multi-site, multi-currency, multi-platform, multi-level, multi-stage, multi-period, multi-function and multi-industry (Gould, 1997; Davenport, 1998; Porter, 2000; Miltenburg, 2001). Multi-company means that the ERP boundary now goes beyond the boundaries of the organisation and has opened up the possibility of establishing an electronic supply chain. Multi-site refers to the fact that ERP systems could be used to manage the organisation's operations in different geographical locations, which may be at the same country or at different countries. Multi-currency refers to the number of countries' currencies which ERP systems support.

Multi-platform means that ERP systems could be installed on a variety of IT platforms.[1] ERP systems are likely to operate within a multi-user network and are considered as two-tier architecture. Multi-level means that end-

Figure 2.2 ERP and Supply Chain Planning

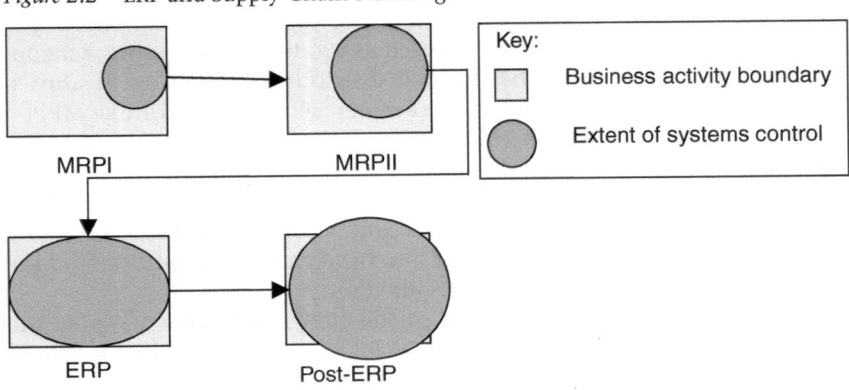

Adapted from Porter (2000).

products are made of sub-assemblies, which are made from manufactured parts. Multi-stage refers to the different manufacturing operations required to produce a product. Multi-period refers to the number of time periods for which business plans are made. As stated above, ERP systems are multi-function because they integrate all the information about the company's functions, such as financials, operations and logistics. Furthermore, ERP systems are multi-industry since, in addition to manufacturing, they are expanding into other industries such as wholesale, service, maintenance and repairs, project industry, finance, banking and insurance.

ERP systems should be differentiated from both legacy systems and 'best of breed' (BoB) systems. On the one hand, legacy systems can be defined as 'systems inherited from the past and in large groups, which have grown through mergers and acquisitions, such systems are often acquired along the way' (Scapens *et al.*, 1998: 46). These systems have dominated MRPII stage. As indicated above, early MRPII was run on client/server technology, while the remaining traditional functional areas were based around main-frame systems. On the other hand, BoB is an IT system that 'integrates components of standard packages and/or custom software' (Light *et al.*, 2001: 216). The standard packages comprise a wide range of software such as legacy packages, ERP packages and/or any recent third-party module-based software packages. But BoB systems usually mix some modules of ERP packages with other packages and/or custom software. Like ERP systems, BoB systems aim at enterprise integration and process orientation. However, they achieve this integration by linking separate software together.

2.2.2 Life cycle of ERP systems

The ERP systems development lifecycle[2] differs from that of any custom developed systems (Satzinger *et al.*, 2002). An ERP system is a special type of packaged software, where it is of cross-functional nature. It is designed by vendor organisations and is used by customer organisations, two sets of players who are independent of each other. As a consequence, when the vendor and customer come together at the point of purchase, the ERP soft-ware is already a semi-finished product.[3] The customer organisation exam-ines the ERP software to see how it can be made to fulfil its requirements. Otherwise, changes may need to be made to business processes. In addi-tion, ERP systems have a much greater scope than any typical packaged or custom software, involving virtually every function in the organisation. As such, these important differences affect ERP lifecycle in many ways (Markus and Tanis, 2000; Ross and Vitale, 2000). For example, Ross and Vitale (2000) describe five stages in the ERP 'journey': (1) design; (2) implementation; (3) stabilisation; (4) continuous improvement; and (5) transformation.

In the ERP design stage, organisations decide whether or not to accept the process assumptions embedded in the ERP software and whether to stand-ardise the entire organisations' processes or only certain processes. The ERP implementation stage refers to implementing the decisions taken in the previous stage. It involves implementing the new system and the new processes and training users on this system. The stabilisation stage includes activities such as cleaning up existing data and processes, adjusting to the new integrated environment, and eliminating bugs in the software. Following stabilisation, organisations continuously improve their ERP systems by adding new modules or third-party software such as bar-coding and sales forecasting. The last ERP stage is the transformation of organisations by changing their boundaries, that is, extending ERP applications to include customer and supplier systems.

2.2.3 Benefits and limitations of ERP systems

There are a number of perceived benefits of ERP adoption and use. ERP systems integrate all functions by replacing legacy systems, improve communication inside (different sites) and outside businesses (customers and suppliers) by providing real-time information, and standardise procedures within a business and across a specific industry by including best of practices solutions. In addition, these systems increase flexibility, where IT infrastructure allows the company to use software produced by different vendors such as BoB, and provide operational (non-financial) and financial information.[4]

Despite these advantages, ERP systems suffer from some limitations (Davenport, 1998; Spathis and Constantinides, 2002). ERP systems take a long period to be implemented, usually more than expected due to complex configurations and business process re-engineering. They also do not solve the fragmentation problem. This is evident especially in the case of implementing BoB solutions or due to the fact that an organisation may prefer functionalities that are not included or can not be included in ERP systems such as some traditional practices which the business insists on using them. Furthermore, ERP systems do not solve the trust problem between the business and its suppliers and customers. However, the different levels of security built into these systems may contribute to solving part of this problem. In addition, these systems may lead to business bankruptcy due to the large amount of investment required and the changes required in business operations. The next section discusses the expected benefits and pitfalls of ERP systems for 'modern' management accounting techniques.

2.3 ERP and management accounting innovations: opportunities and limitations

Traditionally, management accounting comprises a coherent set of techniques that provides information appropriate to internal users – especially managers (Ryan *et al.*, 1992). The use of the term management accounting is relatively new. Before the Second World War, the emphasis was on cost accounting, especially cost determination. This concern resulted in the emergence of different cost methods cf cost identification and allocation such as absorption costing, which seeks to determine the full cost of units produced. After the Second World War, a significant shift from cost accounting to management accounting occurred where management accounting has been regarded as a useful tool for providing the relevant information for managers to assist their decision-making, especially planning and control decisions.

During the 1980s, criticisms were levelled at traditional management accounting practices and new techniques emerged such as activity-based costing and management, which are more in tune with today's competitive and business environment. For example, Johnson and Kaplan (1987) argue that management accounting practices have failed to adapt quickly to the needs of the 'new' manufacturing environment. They attribute this failure partially to the dominance of 'financial accounting mentality' among US management during the twentieth century. They advocate the use of cost management principles, independent of financial accounting rules, and a 'Japanese style' approach to operations management. These new techniques seek to reduce costs and to create value for customers. Recently, the International Federation of Accountants (IFAC) (1998: 99) defined management accounting as 'the process of identification, measurement, accumulation, analysis, preparation, interpretation, and communication of information (both financial and operating) used by management to plan, evaluate, and control within an organisation and to assure use of and accountability for its resources'. Therefore, management accounting is an integral part of the management process. It focuses on adding value to organisations by attaining the effective use of resources by people in dynamic and competitive environments.

Drury (2000) divides management accounting practices into traditional cost control practices and cost management practices. Traditional cost control practices, grounded in financial accounting principles, differ from cost management practices in a number of aspects. The focus of the former is on cost containment and the preservation of the *status-quo* and is routinely applied on a continuous basis while the latter emphasises on cost reduction and continuous improvement and is applied on an *ad hoc* basis. Based on the purpose of management accounting in each stage, IFAC identifies four stages for the development of management accounting practices. These stages are cost determination and financial control, provision of information for management planning and control, reduction of resources waste in business processes, and creation of value through effective resources use (IFAC, 1998). The first two stages refer to traditional cost control practices while the last two stages refer to cost management practices.

Furthermore, Kaplan and Cooper (1998) present the development of management accounting systems as a journey that consists of four sequential stages: inadequate for financial reporting; financial reporting-driven; customised, managerially relevant, standalone; and integrated cost management

Table 2.2   The Development Stages of Management Accounting and ERP

		Prior to 1950	By 1965	By 1985	By 1995
Management accounting stages	Drury (2000)	Traditional cost control practices		Cost management practices	
	IFAC (1998)	Cost determination and financial control	Provision of information for management planning and control	Reduction of resources waste in business processes	Creation of value through effective resources use
	Kaplan and Cooper (1998)	Inadequate for financial reporting	Financial reporting-driven	Customised, managerially relevant, standalone	Integrated cost management and financial reporting

		Prior to 1970s	1970s	1980s	1990s
ERP stages		Traditional IT software (legacy/custom systems)			Integration
		Traditional order-based information systems	Material Resources Planning (MRPI)	Manufacturing Resources Planning (MRPII)	Enterprise Resource Planning (ERP)

and financial reporting. Traditional cost control practices dominate the first two stages while cost management practices occupy the last two stages. IFAC (1998) describes the change process from one stage to another as an evolutionary process, where each stage is a combination of the old and the new, with the old re-shaped to fit with the new in addressing a new set of environmental conditions. Table 2.2 depicts the evolution stages of management accounting coupled with ERP evolution stages identified in the previous section.

As Table 2.2 shows ERP systems coexist with 'modern' management accounting techniques. Below we introduce some 'modern' management accounting practices to see how ERP systems support or hinder these practices. In particular, the focus is on cost management practices. Drury (2000) argues that some cost management practices do not involve the use of accounting techniques. As a result, cost management practices cover both management accounting innovations and operations management innovations. In this regard, almost each operations management innovation has an associated management accounting innovation. For example, the cost of quality is an accounting technique used to measure the costs and benefits of total quality management (TQM) programs.

2.3.1 Business Process Re-engineering

A business process is a collection of activities that are related to each other in a co-ordinated manner in order to achieve a particular objective. For instance, material handling is a business process which consists of interrelated activities such as scheduling production, storing materials, and processing purchase orders Business Process Re-engineering (BPR) refers to 'a radical redesign of business processes to achieve dramatic improvements in critical areas of performance, such as cost, quality, delivery and flexibility' (Schniederjans and Kim, 2003: 419). BPR aims to improve the main business processes in an organisation by focusing on simplification, cost reduction, improved quality and enhanced customer satisfaction. It involves making radical changes to how the work is currently done. The adoption of a Just-in-Time (JIT) philosophy is an illustration of business process re-engineering as it involves moving from a functional plant layout to a cellular product layout (Drury, 2000).

The advancement in information technology and the capabilities provided by new information systems are one of the primary enablers of BPR, that is, IT-driven BPR (Satzinger *et al.*, 2002). Seeking to radically alter existing business practices, BPR is a key concept in the ERP implementation. It can be described as a pre-planning phase of the ERP and can be done by ERP software vendors, consultants or an organisation's own in-house team (Keller and Teufel, 1998). These analysts carefully examine existing business procedures and practices in order to propose information systems solutions that can have a radical impact. As such, BPR supports the implementation of ERP, that is, companies use BPR for change preparation of an ERP system. However, there are many barriers to the success of BPR such as resistance to change, lack of top management support and lack of cross-functional project teams (Greenberg, 1996).

2.3.2 Total Quality Management and the cost of quality

Total Quality Management (TQM), as originally applied by Japanese companies, is a term used to refer to a situation in which all business functions participate in a process of continuous quality improvement (Drury, 2000). TQM focuses on achieving a zero-defect level by designing and building quality into products and by continuous quality improvement (Crosby, 1979; Deming, 1982). Despite focusing on small incremental continuous improvement, the implementation of TQM is a powerful catalyst for change on productive improvements of the organisation and has impact on the entire organisation and its supply chain partners. This approach totally differs from traditional quality control practices adopted by most European and American companies in the 1980s.

Traditionally, western manufacturers have been guided by the economic conformance level model (Daniel and Reitsperger, 1992). According to this model, a cost minimising quality level is achieved by balancing prevention and appraisal costs (conformance costs) against failure costs (non-conformance costs). As a consequence, the optimal quality level cannot occur at a zero-defect level because this model emphasises a quality inspecting philosophy, implemented by quality control or quality assurance departments, rather than designing quality into products.

Traditional cost accounting systems have supported the acceptance of poor quality through the use of standards for labour, materials and overhead costs which institutionalise allowances for scrap and the added labour and equipment needed to produce at defect levels greater than zero (Morse *et al.*, 1987). Since these standards are considered optimal, there is no focus on continuous improvement (Daniel and Reitsperger, 1992). In addition, detailed information for the monitoring of quality cost elements is not generally available in traditional standard cost reports.

In the 1980s, academics and practitioners began to focus on how traditional management accounting systems could be modified to encourage the pursuit of quality costs (Howell and Soucy, 1987; Morse *et al.*, 1987). For example, Howell and Soucy (1987) advocate that cost accounting systems should be modified to accumulate and separately report non-conformance costs such as scrap, rework, warranty claims, etc. However, it is difficult to collect prevention and appraisal costs as it is buried in several cost classifications. To overcome this difficulty, Ito (1995) suggests such costs are measured by responsibility centres and the company as a whole. However, this requires extensive data processing. Fortunately, advances in computer technology and networking assist companies to process such extensive data and make them available for users when they are needed (Ito, 1995).

Modern information technology such as ERP systems, which spans all functional areas and keeps managers informed about what is happening in real-time throughout an organisation, can help companies assess the costs and benefits gained from implementing TQM programs by providing a variety of financial (accounting-based) and non-financial (operational-based) measures. ERP systems can supply almost all the needed data. For example, the ERP-based accounting systems can capture the financial data such as field service expense, prevention costs and other quality cost elements. Operational systems, such as MRPI production planning, can deliver most of the operational data such as defect rates, yields, downtime, and idle capacity. Finally, sales and marketing data, such as on-time delivery and the number of customers and complains, captured at the point of sale or return need to be included. Therefore, ERP systems provide a comprehensive set of TQM measures. In this regard, they have a positive impact on the ability of organisations to implement TQM.

2.3.3 Activity-based costing and management

Traditional costing systems have been criticised as they assume that products consume all resources in proportion to their production volumes

(Cooper and Kaplan, 1992). However, many resources such as material handling, setups and inspection activities do not vary directly with the volume of units produced. As a consequence, these allocation practices may result in distorted product costs. Activity-Based Costing (ABC) has been proposed to overcome this problem. ABC assumes that activities cause costs and that cost objects such as products and customers create the demand for activities. Then, costs are assigned to products based on individual products' consumption for each activity. Costs are traced from resources to activities, and then to specific products and other cost objects.

ABC has evolved into Activity-Based Management (ABM) that focuses on the management side of ABC. ABM may be non-financial or of a strategic cost nature (Johnson, 1988). It focuses managers' attention on the underlying drivers of cost and profit on the assumption that people cannot manage costs; they can only manage activities that cause costs. ABM views the business as a set of linked activities that ultimately adds value to the customer. So it gives relevant information about activities across the entire chain of value-adding business processes such as design, production, marketing and after-sales services. ABM seeks to enable organisations to satisfy customer needs while making fewer demands on organisational resources, which must deliver the highest value at the lowest total cost. It analyses costs by activities and by sub-activities that cross departmental boundaries whereas traditional budget and control reports analyse costs by responsibility centres and by types of expense.

Activity-Based Cost Management (ABCM), which includes both ABC and ABM, is typically an in-built standard solution for costing and managing costs in ERP systems (Shaw, 1998; Washington, 2000; Granlund and Malmi, 2002). ABC focuses on more accurate cost objects while ABM focuses on the use of information on sub-activities to identify process improvement opportunities. Cooper and Kaplan (1998) examine the peril and the promise of an ABCM system, running on an ERP platform. They are particularly concerned with the use of real-time, on-line ERP system cost information and non-financial measures in the ABCM. With real-time updating of cost, capacity, and activity cost driver rates; activity costs, activity driver rates, and product costs would vary daily and even hourly. To avoid these short-term fluctuations, Cooper and Kaplan (1998) suggest the use of standard ABC cost driver rates in calculating product and customer costs. In addition, they identify the promise of integrating operational, ABC, and financial reporting systems. They argue that the ABC and operational control systems can be used to generate cost of goods and inventory valuations for financial reporting purposes.

2.3.4   Benchmarking

Viewed as a natural evolution from the TQM concept, benchmarking, which originated at Rank Xerox in 1979, is another tool that can be used to help companies improve their business processes and performance. It refers to 'the search for industry best practices that an organisation can utilise to improve its performance and productivity' (Themistocleous and Irani, 2001: 318). Benchmarking aims at finding and implementing best practices, that is, the best way of performing business processes, which lead to superior performance (Drury, 2000). It is broader than traditional competitive analysis. The latter focuses on performance indicators, strategic choices and products or services within a given industry while the former is an ongoing process of measuring and improving business practices against the best.

There are three types of benchmarking: internal benchmarking, external benchmarking and best practice benchmarking (Hoque, 2001). Internal benchmarking focuses on comparing performance within one's own organisation. External benchmarking is concerned with external comparisons with other businesses in similar situations. Finally, best practice benchmarking compares performance with an undisputed leader in a critical business process regardless of sector, industry and location.

Benchmarking analysis makes use of management accounting systems in order to obtain required data for comparisons. However, traditional management accounting systems such as conventional standard costing and variance analysis are not sufficient for this analysis. In addition to internal, financial data, benchmarking analysis requires external data on customers, suppliers and competitors. Therefore, both financial and non-financial data are required for benchmarking analysis and modern management accounting systems can play an essential role in supplying such data.

As stated above, ERP systems, on the one hand, supply a wide range of financial and non-financial data that can be useful in performing benchmarking analysis. On the other hand, ERP systems have world-class best practices in a certain industry. In this regard, ERP implementation can be viewed as best practice benchmarking, the third type of benchmarking, as ERP adopters need to compare their existing business practices with ERP embodied best practices, the world-wide best practices, in order to identify possible improvements for the organisations' current practices. So benchmarking is a cornerstone of business process re-engineering that is normally associated with ERP implementation.

2.3.5 Strategic management accounting and balanced scorecard

Strategic management accounting was first introduced by Simmonds (1981) to extend traditional management accounting's internal focus to include external information about competitors. Traditional management accounting has been criticised for its focus on providing financial, *ex post*, internal information that supports routine operating decisions (Gordon, 1998; Murphy *et al.*, 1992). Strategic management accounting overcomes most of these limitations. It refers to 'the process of identifying, gathering, choosing and analysing accounting data for helping the management team to make strategic decisions and to assess organisational effectiveness' (Hoque, 2001: 2). It provides information to support the strategic decisions in organisations.

To satisfy the information's needs of senior management in the long term, strategic management accounting focuses on managing strategies and the competitive advantage of the organisation. Porter (1985) suggests three generic strategies, namely cost leadership, product differentiation and market focus, which can be used to achieve sustainable competitive advantage. In this regard, Shank (1989) argues that standard costs are a very useful tool for companies pursuing a cost leadership strategy while they are less important for companies following a product differentiation strategy. In a similar vein, Miles and Snow (1978) identify two strategies, defenders and prospectors. Defenders are operating in relatively stable environmental conditions, while prospectors are operating in changing environmental conditions. Simons (1987) finds that companies using defender strategy tend to use financial measures to evaluate managers' performance. Furthermore, Ittner *et al.* (1997) finds that there is a tendency for using non-financial measures in companies following prospector strategy.

Traditional financial performance measures such as operating income and return on investment do not consistently support the competitive strategy in today's fierce competitive environment (Kaplan and Norton, 1992; Hoque, 2001). No business decision should depend solely on financial information. Both financial information and non-financial information are necessary in managing day-to-day business operations. The balanced scorecard has been introduced to link financial and non-financial measures of performance. It is a set of measures that gives senior management a fast but comprehensive view of the organisation. The balanced scorecard aims at translating the organisation's strategy into a coherent set of performance measures. These measures look at four different perspectives; namely financial perspective, customer perspective, internal business process perspective, and learning and growth perspective. These comprehensive measures are flexible and dynamic and enable the organisation to establish long-term improvement as they focus on customers, processes and innovations.

Davenport (1998) argues that ERP systems provide support for strategic planning in the form of tighter integration of functions to support process orientation. Fahy and Lynch (1999) point out that there is a trend among ERP vendors towards adding new application areas to their products mainly in the form of front office applications, business intelligence and decision support capability. These capabilities are designed to extend the reach of ERP systems beyond transaction processing and process management to a more strategic role in decision-making. Trends such as balanced scorecard have prompted vendors such as SAP to focus on analytical applications that are designed to support top managers in their decision-making. For example, PWC and SAP have jointly developed strategic enterprise management tool to support top managers facing strategic management problems.

ERP systems can supply both financial information and non-financial information that are required for strategic management accounting analyses and balanced scorecard. For example, Silk (1998: 44) states that '[m]ost organisations have significant investments in ... ERP systems such as SAP, People-Soft, and Baan. These back office systems are the primary source of much of the data collected within an enterprise. A Balanced Scorecard solution should work in harmony with ERP... systems, extracting and using data from these systems and delivering them to the users' desktop.' In the same vein, Fahy and Lynch (1999) find that ERP systems contribute in improving the provision of transaction data for strategic management accounting purposes. However, these systems typically cause disruption to the existing decision support capability of the firm as they may inhibit the strategic learning and may result in losing the strategic thinking and problem-solving capacity in the long term.

2.3.6 Value chain analysis and supply chain management

Value chain analysis, proposed by Porter (1985), aims to find linkages within the company or between the company and its suppliers and customers in order to gain competitive advantage by lowering costs and/or enhancing product differentiation. Porter (1985: 33–34) states that '... the value chain disaggregates a firm into its strategically relevant activities... A firm gains competitive advantage by performing these strategically important activities more cheaply or better than its competitors'. The value chain model by Porter comprises two main types of activities, primary and support activities. Primary activities are involved in the physical creation of the product as well as its sale, transfer to the customer and after-sale services. These activities are of five types, namely inbound logistics, operations, outbound logistics, marketing and sales, and service. The support activities exist to support primary activities by providing purchased inputs, technology, human resources, and firm infrastructure. Each link in the value chain can be viewed as a supplier-customer relationship.

Shank and Govindarajan (1992) advocate the use of value chain analysis as a strategic approach to cost management. They criticise traditional management accounting systems because these systems adopt an internal focus which starts with purchases and stops at the point of sale. As a consequence, traditional management accounting systems miss the opportunities for exploiting linkages with suppliers and result in eliminating all opportunities for exploiting linkages with customers. In this regard, Shank (1989) found that an American automobile company, adopting traditional management accounting thinking, failed to exploit links with its suppliers as price increases from suppliers more than offset internal cost savings achieved from adopting JIT systems.

Many activities of value chain may involve a number of independently owned companies. When a firm owns more than one of these activities in the entire value chain, it is said that it follows a policy of vertical integration. As firms outsource more and more of their activities, the Supply Chain Management (SCM) become a topic of central importance (Venkatesan, 1992). Some types of supply chain management seek to develop close relationships with suppliers and customers known as strategic partnerships. In this regard, management accounting has an important role in sharing accounting information such as cost data. For example, Seal *et al.* (1999) describe the attempt at a strategic supply partnership between two UK companies as an attempt to apply cost management throughout the entire value chain.

Porter and Miller (1985: 156) states that 'information technology has had a particularly strong impact on bargaining relationships between suppliers and buyers since it affects the linkages between companies and their suppliers, channels, and buyers. Information systems that cross company lines are becoming common'. ERP systems are one of a number of recent information technology developments that help organisations analyse and manage their value chains and supply chains. During the last decade, innovative business software companies such as SAP, Baan, Oracle and PeopleSoft, have developed flexible and multi-functional modular packages. Initially, ERP packages focused on optimising internal business processes across the value-added chain. Currently, ERP vendors are also offering data warehouse and supply chain management software. Demand forecasting and supply chain optimising application can be integrated into standard ERP modules such as finance, sales and distribution, human resources and manufacturing.

2.3.7 Theory of constraint and throughput accounting

During the 1980s Goldratt and Cox (1984) introduced an approach called Optimised Production Technology (OPT). This approach aims at expanding profits by distinguishing between bottleneck and non-bottleneck resources. Goldratt and Cox (1984) argue that bottleneck resources should be identified and removed in order to increase the throughput of the whole production process while non-bottleneck resources should be scheduled and operated based on the bottlenecks within the production system. Goldratt and Cox (1993) extend OPT philosophy to what they called the Theory of Constraints (TOC), which describes the process of maximising profits when organisations face constraints. TOC supports continuous improvement process by identifying and eliminating constraints. This process consists of five steps:

1. Identify the production system's constraints.
2. Decide how to exploit the constraints.
3. Subordinate everything to the above decision.

4. Elevate the constraints.
5. If, in the previous steps, a constraint has been broken return to step 1.

Galloway and Waldron (1988) introduced the idea of throughput accounting to apply TOC philosophy. This idea depends on calculating the throughput accounting ratio as the return per factor hour divided by the cost per factor hour. In this regard, Goldratt and Cox (1993) call for accountants to learn and adapt TOC ideas for their own uses. Dugdale and Jones (1995) describe the experience of one UK firm that apply TOC concepts. They conclude that '[t]he challenge of TOC to accounting not only calls for revisions to accounting practices, but also for a rethinking of the assumptions on which they are based' (p. 124). However, Drury (2000) argues that traditional management accounting techniques such as linear programming can be considered an application of TOC ideas. Interestingly, Kaplan and Cooper (1998) argue that both TOC and ABC complement each other, where TOC seeks to maximise short-term profits while ABC provides a dynamic theory of constraints for long-term profitability.

Goldratt (2000) believes that ERP systems have an incredible power to store, transfer and retrieve information. He argues that ERP can bring benefits if, and only if, it diminishes a limitation, which is the necessity of any manager to make decisions without having all relevant information. However, Goldratt criticises ERP systems as they still provide the old product cost data. He argues that the old rules that preceded ERP were the rules that helped make decisions without all of the relevant information. Instead, he suggests the use of throughput accounting as the new rules that should be followed now (Stenzel and Stenzel, 2002: 11).

2.3.8 Just-in-Time systems and materials resource planning

Just-in-Time (JIT) systems, first used by Japanese companies, seek to eliminate non-value-added activities, to reduce inventory, defects, breakdowns and set-up times to near-zero levels, and to achieve a 100% on-time delivery service (Drury, 2000). They represent a radical change in manufacturing philosophy from the traditional push to a pull system.[5] According to JIT philosophy, companies purchase materials and produce products only as needed to meet actual customer demand. Traditional management accounting systems do not support JIT philosophy, as they do not provide information on supplier reliability, set-up times, throughput cycle times, on-time deliveries and defect rates. Modern management accounting systems such as balanced scorecard and ABC provide all these measures. For example, ABC supports JIT by measuring its benefits such as cost savings through reduced set-ups.

At the core of ERP systems is a Material Resource Planning (MRPI) system, first introduced by IBM in 1970. It does not represent radical change in manufacturing philosophy as it is grounded in the traditional push system. MRPI aims at minimising inventory levels, production run disruptions, storage costs and other extra expenses related to accepting rush orders and at providing forecasts of the production status of specific products (Bromwich and Bhimani, 1989). MRPI systems, which may not be incompatible with traditional cost accounting techniques, affect budgeting, control and short-term decisions. It can be used to provide financial cost data that are not previously part of traditional cost systems. As Campbell and Porcano (1979: 34) note, '[t]he integration of the MRPI system with the cost accounting system will enable the firm to produce information (reports) that will allow management to control operations closely and plan for the future'.

Like JIT systems, MRPI systems are developed for the same type of production, that is, discrete parts that are manufactured and assembled into complex products. However, Miltenburg (2001) finds that the algorithms used to solve production planning problems in MRPI systems are more complex than those used in JIT systems. He concludes that '...MRP [I] can struggle to find a feasible material plan, even when one exists...Compared to MRPI, JIT has almost no difficulty with the material plan. Companies that use JIT "simplify first" and then plan and execute.' (p. 208).

In sum, ERP systems seem to support and facilitate a wide range of management accounting innovations. As a consequence, they promise radical change in traditional management accounting techniques. However, caution should be exercised when choosing and using management accounting techniques built into ERP systems because these techniques may be inconsistent with some operations management techniques that are not included in ERP systems.

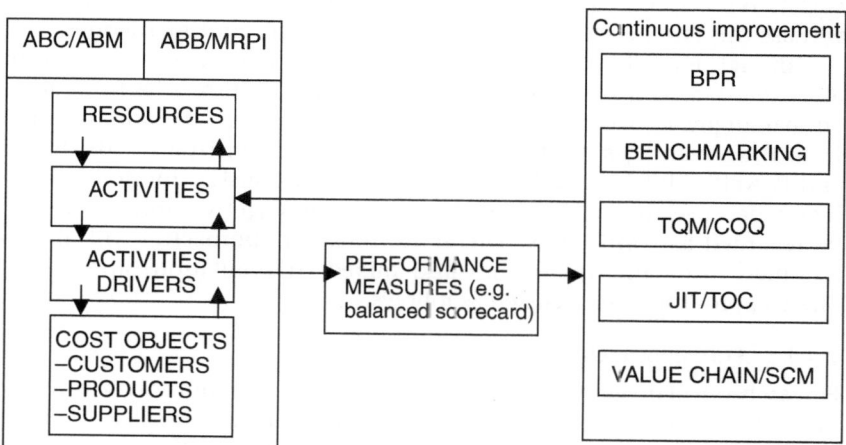

Figure 2.3 Modern Management Accounting Techniques Discussed in their Relation to ERP

Figure 2.3 summarises the management accounting practices/techniques discussed above. The next section presents the theoretical and philosophical approaches applied in studying management accounting change.

2.4   Philosophical and theoretical approaches to management accounting change

Over the years, different theoretical frameworks have been used in studying management accounting change and stability. These theories can be classified into a number of research approaches according to their philosophical and theoretical assumptions. For example, Burrell and Morgan (1979) state that 'all theories of organisation are based upon a philosophy of science (the subjective-objective dimension) and a theory of sociology (the regulation-radical change dimension)'. According to these two dimensions, they classify social and organisational theories into four paradigms[6] that are, allegedly, mutually exclusive; namely functionalist, interpretive, radical humanist and radical structuralist.

A number of accounting researchers have used Burrell and Morgan's (1979) classification in order to classify accounting theories (e.g. Cooper, 1983; Hopper and Powell, 1985; Chua, 1986). However, they tend to reduce the four paradigms proposed by Burrell and Morgan (1979) into three, namely positivist (or functionalist), interpretive and critical perspectives[7] (e.g. Hopper and Powell, 1985; Chua, 1986; Covaleski *et al.*, 1996). The latter approach focuses on the role of interest, conflicts and unequal distribution of power in providing the potential for radical change while the former two approaches are concerned with the role of regulation, order and stability in explaining why society tends to hold together (Hopper and Powell, 1985: 432). This study will use this latter classification for management accounting theories.

Although Burrell and Morgan (1979) describe their paradigms as mutually exclusive,[8] some researchers have mixed different theories from different paradigms to overcome the limitations of some theories and to benefit from the advantages of others. This is somehow consistent with Hopper and Powell's (1985) rejection of the mutually exclusive division of paradigms because they argue that the subjective-objective dimension is to be regarded as continuous. Therefore, research approaches will also be classified into pure approaches and mixed (triangulation) approaches. These approaches are discussed as follows.

2.4.1   Pure approaches

Research on management accounting change and stability has utilised a number of different perspectives, including positivistic theories (e.g. Anderson and Young, 1999; Williams and Seaman, 2001), interpretive theories (e.g. Perren and Grant, 2000; Modell, 2001; Soin *et al.*, 2002) and critical theories (Hopwood, 1990; Ezzamel, 1994; Uddin and Hopper, 2001). Each paradigm has its own ontological, epistemological and methodological positions. Ontology refers to 'the very essence of the phenomenon under investigation' (Burrell and Morgan, 1979: 1). It is concerned with the nature of reality, that is, whether reality exists as an objective, external, reality or is in fact the product of individual consciousness and hence is subjective. Epistemology is about the grounds or nature of knowledge. It concerns what is accepted as being valid knowledge. Last but not least, methodology focuses on the process of research. It indicates, among others, 'the research methods deemed appropriate for the gathering of valid evidence' (Chua, 1986: 604). The assumptions, theories and criticisms of positivist, interpretive and critical paradigms will be explored in more detailed in the next sub-sections.

2.4.1.1 Positivistic (mainstream) paradigm: assumptions, theories and criticisms

Accounting researchers became increasingly interested in the positivist approach during the 1970s and 1980s (Ryan *et al.*, 1992). Ontologically, this perspective takes an objective view of social reality, treated the same as the physical or natural world. Researchers, using this approach, believe that the reality exists 'out there' and is independent of the observer. As a result, epistemologically, observable and measurable phenomena can be regarded as valid knowledge about this external reality. Trying to maintain an independent and objective stance, researchers methodologically use the methods applied in the natural sciences to explain and predict social phenomena. Hence, they often use standard research instruments, such as questionnaires, to collect data and analyse these data using statistical techniques to test hypotheses derived from prior theories. This refers to a separation of observations from scientific theories and researchers are expected to add to an existing body of knowledge by acting as remote observers and gathering quantitative data to possibly deduce universal laws to explain and predict social reality.

Over the years, different positivistic theories have emerged and used in accounting literature such as neo-classical economic theory, agency theory, open system theory, and contingency theory. Neo-classical economic theory emerged in the second half of the nineteenth century. It presumes management accounting as a computational decision-making tool that helps maximise the goal of the organisation (Anthony, 1965). Due to its unrealistic core assumptions, especially rationality and equilibrium, neo-classical economic theory has been criticised as being irrelevant for addressing management accounting change. For example, Burns and Scapens (2000) argue that this theory focuses on management accounting change as rational outcomes rather than change processes from one equilibrium state to another. As a result of their rejection of the neo-classical economics' assumptions, accounting researchers move away to the use of alternative theories such as agency theory.

The agency theory of management accounting is concerned with agency relationship as a contract between a principal (e.g. an owner) and an agent (e.g. a manager). Under this contract, the principal delegates decision-making authority to the agent, who then takes actions on behalf of the principal (Macintosh, 1994). In this regard, agency theory can be useful in predicting management accounting practices as these practices are the tools used by the owner to limit the agent's actions that are not in the principal's best interests. However, Tiessen and Waterhouse (1983) argue that it can be used to understand management accounting systems in the conditions of environmental and technological stability. Agency theory adopts the core assumptions of neo-classical economics, that is, utility maximisation and market mechanism. Like neo-classical economics, agency theory helps in predicting rather than in explaining the agent's behaviour (Ryan *et al.*, 1992).

The use of open system theory in organisational analysis started flourishing during the 1960s. According to open system approach an organisation is profoundly affected by, dependent upon, and able to adapt to its environment in order to survive. The contingency theory of organisation is based upon this approach and subsequently management accounting. The contingency approach to management accounting is based on the premise that there is no universally 'best' design for a management accounting system, but it will depend upon the specific circumstances in which an organisation finds itself (Otley, 1980). Next, we will focus on contingency theory that exemplifies the positivistic paradigm.

The contingency theory of management accounting change.   The contingency theory of organisation is based upon open systems approach that studies the organisation and its subsystems by reference to its wider environment (Emmanuel *et al.*, 1990). Burrell and Morgan (1979: 176) state that 'contingency theory postulates that the effectiveness of the organisation in coping with the demands of its environments is contingent upon the elements of the various subsystems which comprise the organisation being designed in accordance with the demands of the environment (or, more accurately, sub-environments) with which they interact'. An organisation's management accounting system is one of such subsystems.

The three basic approaches to studying the factors affecting management accounting change are the universalistic, contingency, and situation-specific approaches (Hambrick and Lei, 1985). The universalistic view is that optimal management accounting system design holds to some extent in all settings, that is, there is only one contingency setting (Fisher, 1995). This approach can be best exemplified by Hofstede's (1968) study of budgetary control. The movement away from this approach towards the contingency approach in management accounting occurred during the 1970s (Otley, 1980).

The second contingency view is that the design of Management Accounting Systems (MAS) depends upon the specific circumstances in which an organisation finds itself (Jones, 1985). Therefore, there is no universally appropriate management accounting system that applies equally to all organisations in all circumstances. Proponents of this view tend to do cross-sectional research to make generalisation to other firms or situations (Otley, 1980).

The third – situation-specific – approach began flourishing in the 1980s. The rationale of this view is that the factors affecting each management accounting system design are unique. So, general rules and models cannot be applied. Kaplan (1986: 198), for instance, states that 'accounting systems must serve the objectives of the firm. We do not have a universal model that works well in all circumstances'. Therefore, management accounting researchers should study each system and each firm individually. The supporters of this approach tend to conduct case studies and field studies to understand the unique factors affecting management accounting system design (Fisher, 1995).

If the three approaches to studying the factors affecting management accounting change are put in a continuum where the universalistic and situation-specific approaches represent the two extremes, the contingency perspective would locate somewhere between these two extremes (Hambrick and Lei, 1985). This sub-section aims at exploring and evaluating the role of both contingency and situation-specific approaches in addressing management accounting change.

Contingency approach: cross-sectional studies and management accounting change. From a contingency perspective management accounting change literature can be classified into two categories according to the level of analysis complexity. At the first level of analysis, one contingent factor is correlated with management accounting change. Different internal and external forces such as changes in manufacturing systems and competition put tremendous pressures on MAS to change (Spicer, 1992). Manufacturing firms striving for continuous improvement often adopt manufacturing initiatives such as TQM and JIT. The adoption of such techniques requires changes in MAS. Ittner and Larcker (1995) describe these changes as gathering new information, dissemination of information across the organisational hierarchy and changes in reward systems.

Increasing competition in the market makes decision-makers use of MAS more important. Mia and Clarke (1999) examine the relationship between the intensity of market competition and business unit performance, by incorporating into the model manager's use of the information provided by the MAS using a sample of 61 business unit managers. They conclude that the intensity of market competition is a determinant of the use of the information that, in turn, is a determinant of business unit performance.

At the second level of analysis, multiple contingent factors are correlated with management accounting change. A strand of studies has used cross-sectional survey-based studies in order to understand the multiple contingent factors influencing management accounting change (Libby and Waterhouse, 1996; Williams and Seaman, 2001). Libby and Waterhouse (1996) present a review of organisational literature that is relevant to changes in MAS at the organisational level. They identify four economic and organisational factors associated with the adoption of changes in MAS: the intensity of competition, the degree of decentralisation, size, and organisational capacity to learn. The relationship between these factors and changes in MAS is tested using a sample of 24 Canadian manufacturing firms. The measures of dependent and independent variables are collected *via* a telephone interview and a facsimile of the questionnaire. The collected data are analysed by multiple regression. The results reveal that about one-third of MAS in the sampled firms changed in the 1991–1993 period. Organisational capacity to learn is the best predictor of change. Other variables do not predict changes in MAS.

Williams and Seaman (2001) replicate and extend the study of Libby and Waterhouse (1996) using a sample of 121 manufacturing firms from different economic sectors in Singapore and Hofstede's (1991) cultural framework. Williams and Seaman (2001) use almost all variables, measures, research method, and statistical analysis applied by Libby and Waterhouse (1996). The results show that centralisation, the only modified variable, is the best predictor of changes in MAS over the period January 1995 to end-June 1997. The other variables show mixed effects and do not consistently support the research hypotheses. Williams and Seaman (2001) conclude that the determinants of management accounting change are affected by cross-cultural differences and that the predictive model is not generalisable to all economic sectors.

A number of cross-sectional survey-based studies began using the factors identified in the case studies and field studies conducted by researchers such as Innes and Mitchell (1990) and Cobb *et al.* (1995) to generate their hypotheses. In the context of developing and transition countries, Luther and Longden (2001) address the extent to which South African MAS has changed with the fundamental political, structural and economic shifts over the last decade. They also compare management accounting changes and their causes in South Africa against a benchmark of UK company practices. Their results show significant changes in the perceived benefits derived from MAS in South Africa over the period 1996–2001 and that these benefits differ from the UK equivalents. The results also show that some factors causing management accounting change in South Africa are different from those at work in the UK.

Laitinen (2001) conducted a survey in 93 small Finnish technology firms to explain management accounting change over a five-year period in terms of their organisational characteristics and motivation patterns. Using factor analysis, he identifies four types of companies called 'change-oriented', 'stable and conservative', 'performance-contented', and 'discontent resourceless' organisations. A mathematical model of the technology firm is developed to obtain expectations for the differences in management accounting change between the four types of firms. These expectations are supported by correlation and regression analyses in order to explore the relationship of the four types to management accounting change.

Haldma and Laats (2002) examined management accounting change in Estonian manufacturing companies over the period 1996–1999 and explore contingent factors that influence it. They analyse 62 responses to a questionnaire survey using one-way analysis, two-way analysis and Fisher's exact test. They conclude that there are changes in cost and management accounting practices that are associated with shifts in the business and accounting environment as external contingences, and with those in technology and organisational aspects as internal contingencies.

Sulaiman (2002) investigated management accounting change in Malaysian companies over a five-year period (1997–2001) and demonstrates causes of these changes. She replicates and extends the studies of Libby and Waterhouse (1996) and Williams and Seaman (2001). She concludes that most changes in MAS are evolutionary rather than revolutionary and that the introduction of new variables improves the model developed by Libby and Waterhouse (1996).

The contingency perspective of management accounting has mainly been criticised because it provides only a static comparative analysis of accounting systems, it does not attempt to evaluate and possibly change an institutional structure and the contingent variables do not represent a comprehensive set of the factors determining management accounting change (Chua, 1986; Innes and Mitchell, 1990; Otley, 1995). To overcome these limitations, Otley (1980: 425) suggests using longitudinal case studies. These case studies involve a small number of firms and the close involvement of researchers within organisations to give a range of values on chosen contingent variables, where the interaction of variables over time may be observed. Responding to these recommendations, a number of case studies have addressed management accounting change phenomenon (Innes and Mitchell, 1990; Cobb *et al.*, 1995; Kasurinen, 2002). The use of case studies within the positivistic approach to study management accounting change will be explored in the next sub-section.

Situation-specific approach: case studies and field studies and management accounting change. There has been strong advocacy for much more extensive use of field studies and case studies[9] to study management accounting phenomena in the 1980s (Kaplan, 1983, 1986; Bruns, 1989). Kaplan (1986), for instance, conducted four case studies in US industrial firms to explore the factors impacting on accounting lag. He finds that changes in management accounting systems lag far behind changes in manufacturing techniques such as TQM, JIT inventory systems, and computer-integrated manufacturing processes. He concludes that there are four factors which contribute to the observed stability in MAS, namely the lack of adequate innovative accounting models, the prevalence of computer-based accounting systems, the emphasis on financial accounting even among management accountants, and the lack of top executives' emphasis on the need to improve the relevance and responsiveness of MAS.

Based on seven field studies in the electronics sector, Innes and Mitchell (1990) conclude that management accounting change categories are market-orientated practices, costing practice, and performance measurement. They also divide the factors associated with management accounting change within firms into three categories on the basis of the nature and timing of their influence. Motivators are related to management accounting change in a general manner such as the competitive market, organisational structure and production technology. Catalysts are directly associated with management accounting change like poor financial performance, the loss of market share, and the launch of a competing product. Finally, facilitators are necessary but not sufficient, *per se*, to result in management accounting change, for example, accounting staff resources, accounting computing resources and the degree of autonomy from the parent company. The motivators and catalysts interact positively to generate change but in the existence of facilitators.

Cobb *et al.* (1995) conducted a longitudinal case study in a division of a large multinational bank to study changes in management accounting reports over time. They further develop the accounting change model of Innes and Mitchell (1990) to include barriers to change, leaders, and momentum. The barriers to change refer to the factors that hinder, delay or even prevent change such as the changing priorities, accounting staff turnover and staff attitudes. Moreover, the expectation of continuing change is referred to as momentum, and the role of individuals in management accounting change as leaders. Motivators, catalysts and facilitators are necessary to create a potential for change. But leaders are needed to overcome the barriers to change and momentum for change is also needed to maintain the peace of change.

Kasurinen (2002) has extended the accounting change model of Cobb *et al.* (1995) by specifying the types of barriers that may hinder, delay, or even prevent management accounting change in practice. He conducted a longitudinal case study in a strategic business unit of a multinational Finnish-based metals group to study the barriers to balanced scorecard implementation. He concludes that the barriers to change can be divided into three subcategories, titled confusers, frustrators, and delayers. Gurd *et al.* (2002) examined the responses of MAS to TQM adoptions at six manufacturing sites in South Australia. Drawing on Argyris and Kaplan (1994), Gurd *et al.* (2002) identify three processes necessary to overcome the barriers to change, namely education and training, the sponsorship of the change process and the alignment of incentives.

Although the longitudinal case studies within the positivistic approach overcome some limitations of cross-sectional survey-based studies, they still suffer some problems. They share the same weakness as surveys; the factors identified in longitudinal case studies do not also represent a comprehensive set. Therefore, the case study's view is similar to the contingency perspective, but the number of possible combinations of contingent factors is very large. Scapens (1990) argues that the role of case studies within the positive research methodology is 'to generate hypotheses which will be tested by other empirical research methods (i.e. surveys)' (p. 267). These studies also ignore the socio-political aspects of organisational life and the way in which these affect management accounting practices (Otley, 1978, 1980; Alam, 1997; Gupta *et al.*, 1994). Scapens (1990), for example, argues that such studies provide a type of predictive theory but fail to locate management accounting practices in its historical, economic and social context. This view reflects the UK approach to management accounting case studies that are usually informed by social interpretive and critical theories (Ryan *et al.*, 1992). The interpretive paradigm is in the next sub-section.

2.4.1.2   *Interpretive paradigm: assumptions, theories and criticisms*

Unlike the positivistic approach, the interpretive approach is interested in making sense of the social reality through understanding how people understand the behaviour of each other (Puxty. 1993). It focuses on 'the role of language, interpretation, and understanding in social science' (Chua, 1986: 613). From an ontological standpoint, the interpretive perspective adopts a subjective view of social reality that considers the world as socially constructed and can only be understood by examining the perceptions of human actors. Therefore, each individual has a unique view of the world that can be partially communicated. In the epistemological view of interpretive approach, researchers interact with that being researched. This epistemology does not try to find generalised explanations or make predictions but instead aims at allowing interpretation and hence, ideally, understanding of particular situations. As Smith (cited in Hussey and Hussey, 1997: 49) put it, '[i]n quantitative research facts act to constrain our beliefs; while in interpretive research beliefs determine what should count as facts.' Methodologically, the interpretive approach normally uses qualitative methods such as in-depth interviews, participative observations, action research, etc. It focuses on small samples, possibly over a period of time.

Change and stability in management accounting practices have been interpreted and analysed by a number of interpretive perspectives such as social construction perspective and institutional theories. The social construction perspective addresses the central question: 'how is it possible that subjective meaning became objective facts?' (Covaleski *et al.*, 1996: 200). Berger and Luckmann (1966) argue that social order is based mainly on a shared social reality that, in turn, is a human construction, being created in social interaction. They state that 'man is capable of producing a world that he then experiences as something other than a human product' (p. 61). This perspective has been used by a number of researchers to explain management accounting change and stability (Neimark and Tinker, 1986; Bhimani, 1993; Perren and Grant, 2000; Vamosi, 2000). For example, Vamosi (2000), addressing stability and change in MAS during processes of transition, concludes that changes in MAS to a large extent are consequences of changes in the environment.

Institutional theories have received an increasing interest in recent years in economics, political science and sociology (Scott, 2001). So far three such theories have contributed to accounting research, namely 'new' institutional economics, 'old' institutional economics and 'new' institutional sociology (Ahmed and Scapens, 2000; Burns and Scapens, 2000). We critically evaluate institutional theories applied in studying management accounting change in the following sub-sections.

Transaction cost economics theory.   The transaction cost economics perspective was first introduced by Williamson (1975) to explain the characteristics of governance structures such as markets, hybrids and hierarchies as well as the transaction costs[10] associated with each organisational form. According to this theory, change from one organisational form to another occurs when transaction costs in that form becomes too high, that is, prohibitive. Scott (2001) describes two conditions under which the increase in transaction costs occurs; namely individual bounded rationality in complex and uncertain conditions and individual opportunism in the absence of alternative exchange partners. On the other hand, the continuity of a particular organisational form such as the bureaucratic hierarchy occurs because it is able to perform its function at a lower cost, thus increasing profitability. The transaction cost approach has been used in the accounting literature to explain the development of management accounting (e.g. Johnson, 1981, 1983, 1994; Johnson and Kaplan, 1987).

The transaction cost theory, in particular the work of Coase (1937) and Williamson (1975), is the theoretical basis for the relevance lost thesis introduced by Johnson and Kaplan (1987). According to Johnson and Kaplan (1987: 88), 'a firm will grow until the marginal cost of discovering opportunities for gain within the firm exceeds the marginal cost of discovering opportunities for gain in the market'. Based on this logic, they trace the evolution of management accounting practices from the middle of the nineteenth century until the 1980s. They explain the development of management accounting systems in terms of the relative gains of internal co-ordination of economic activities by management over external co-ordination by market, where the role of management accounting practices is to evaluate a company's internalised processes (Johnson and Kaplan, 1987: 42).

For instance, Johnson and Kaplan (1987) describe the development of some innovative accounting techniques such as budgets and the return on investment in the US in the early decades of the twentieth century as the means of improving the efficiency of individual processes and the overall profitability of the company. They argue that these accounting techniques have been introduced in order to manage new forms of economic organisation such as vertically integrated companies and diversified multi-divisional companies that emerged due to the intense competition and the wave of mergers during this era. However, Johnson and Kaplan (1987) observe that by 1925 virtually all management accounting techniques used today have been developed. In the years to 1980s there has been relative stability in management accounting, where management accounting practices failed to meet the information needs of the 'new' manufacturing environment.

Johnson and Kaplan (1987) attribute the decline of American industry competitiveness in the 1980s to the use of inappropriate management accounting practices. They identify two primary reasons for the failure of management accounting practices (Johnson and Kaplan, 1987; Johnson, 1994). The first reason is 'the rigidity of financial reporting rules enforced by the accounting profession after World War I' (Johnson, 1994: 260). These rules carried a high compliance cost that prohibited the development of management accounting systems for more effective decision-making. The second reason is that 'the implied endorsement accounting educators gave to financial accounting after World War II' (Johnson, 1994: 260). During this period, accounting educators increasingly encouraged the use of financial accounting information for managerial decision-making. This resulted in a 'financial accounting mentality' among future US managers.

The relevance lost thesis and its theoretical basis have been criticised from the viewpoint of rival perspectives such as the Foucauldian perspective (Ezzamel *et al.*, 1990), the labour process perspective (Hopper and Armstrong, 1991) and old institutional economics (Ahmed and Scapens, 2000). From the Foucauldian perspective, Ezzamel *et al.* (1990) introduce an alternative view to Johnson and Kaplan's (1987). They argue that different management accounting practices developed in the US/UK and in Japan from the nineteenth century until the 1980s could be attributed to the different alignments of power/knowledge relations that reflect differences in their unique cultural history.

Hopper and Armstrong (1991: 413) also provide an alternative labour process view of the evolution of the early factory organisations in the mid-nineteenth century. They state that 'much of the gain in profitability from the early factory organisation of production came ... from the ability of owners/entrepreneurs to intensify labour through close disciplinary control and to extend the working day'. Therefore, some of the accounting and cost information was used to intensify the extraction of labour from labour force. Hopper and Armstrong (1991) attribute the presence and even subsequent absence of management accounting practices to the changing forms of control over the labour process. The shift in the relative bargaining power of entrepreneurs and workers explain the rise and fall of management accounting practices. Furthermore, Ahmed and Scapens (2000) use old institutional economics as an alternative to the transaction cost approach to identify the roles of social institutions such as trade unions and government ministries in the processes of structuring and implementing cost allocation practices in the UK.

In sum, the use of the transaction cost approach in understanding management accounting change has been criticised on the ground that it is based on neo-classical economic assumptions, that is, rationality and equilibrium (Ryan *et al.*, 1992). Transaction cost theory does not explain the processes of change from one equilibrium state or an organisational form to another. It pays little attention to the processes by which varying equilibrium states arise or are transformed (Scott, 2001). Furthermore, it does not take into account the effect of macro institutional frameworks on the development of accounting practices and ignores the impact of emerging organisational forms on the environment (Ahmed and Scapens, 2000). Scapens (1994) suggests old institutional economics can be utilised to understand change in management accounting practices. Old institutional economics theory is the topic of next sub-section.

Old institutional economics theory.   Old institutional economics theory, as an evolutionary theory of the firm, has been developed by Nelson and Winter (1982). They argue that an organisation's routines, which are made up of the conscious and tacit knowledge and skills held by organisational members, are the equivalent of genes in a plant or animal. In order to survive, the organisation must reproduce, adapt and change its routines in the face of uncertain environmental conditions (Scott, 2001). However, Nelson and Winter (1982) point out that change in organisational routines is endogenous, path dependency rather than convergence to some external optimum.

Old institutional economics theory focuses 'on studying economic activities and the production and reproduction of life's day-to-day processes as part of a holistic ongoing process of change' (Ahmed and Scapens, 2000: 166). This approach has been introduced into accounting literature in the 1990s (e.g. Ahmed, 1992; Scapens, 1994). It has been used to address management accounting change in a number of recent works (e.g. Ahmed and Scapens, 2000; Burns, 2000; Burns and Scapens, 2000; Soin *et al.*, 2002). For example, Burns and Scapens (2000: 3) introduce an institutional framework that 'explores the complex and ongoing relationship between actions and institutions, and to demonstrate the importance of organisational routines and institutions in shaping the processes of management accounting change.' More about old institutional economics theory and Burns and Scapens' (2000) framework will be presented in the next chapter.

Old institutional economics theory is not without its limitations. It de-emphasises the role of technical environment in institutional change. For example, major contextual change such as take-over crisis or advances in technology may introduce revolutionary change, which radically changes existing routines and primarily challenges the existing institutions (Burns and Scapens, 2000). However, the response to such technical changes is likely to follow evolutionary, path-dependency, that is, present and future choices and trends depend on prior history. Therefore, instrumental change, which seeks to achieve efficiency and effectiveness, may become ceremonial change, that is, the de-coupling of the symbolic use of management accounting system for legitimation from the operating control in order to keep vested interests. In addition, old institutional economics pays little attention to the effect of the broader extra-organisational institutions of the organisational field and the society. Ahmed and Scapens (2000: 166) argue that 'old' institutional theory, which is primarily concerned with intra-organisational behaviours, is not designed to achieve conformity with extra-organisational institutions. As a result, 'old' institutional theory focuses on the role of agency in constructing institutions at the expense of conformity with macro institutional rules, beliefs and myths. The new institutional sociology theory, presented in the next sub-section, overcomes this latter limitation.

New institutional sociology theory. The new institutional sociology perspective explores the role of extra-organisational institutions in shaping organisational structures, policies and procedures (Scott, 2001). Organisations respond to such external, macro pressures in order to receive support and legitimacy (Modell, 2002). The general theme of new institutional theory is that organisations' conformity to the social norms and expectations, that is, institutionalised structures, policies and procedures, is required in order to survive and continually gain society's support or gain legitimacy (Covaleski *et al.*, 1996). Drawing on the work of Berger and Luckmann (1966), Meyer and Rowan (1977) discuss institutionalisation as a process whereby institutional structures are legitimated without regard to the effectiveness of those structures and of the organisational members' feelings about the efficacy of those structures. DiMaggio and Powell (1983), addressing the question of organisational structure and institutionalisation, state that 'in the long run, organizational actors making rational decisions construct around themselves an environment that constrains their ability to change in future years' (p. 148). The two articles written by Meyer and Rowan (1977) and DiMaggio and Powell (1983) are considered the classic articles of 'new' institutional sociology theory (Bowring, 2000). Some details about DiMaggio and Powell's (1983) work will be given in the next chapter.

The new institutional theory has been used by a number of accounting researchers to explain management accounting change and stability (Amat *et al.*, 1994; Granlund and Lukka, 1998; Hoque and Alam, 1999; Modell, 2001; Granlund and Malmi, 2002). Modell (2001), for example, highlights how managers proactively designed and implemented new systems for performance measurement in the context of recent reforms within the Norwegian public health sector. Amat *et al.* (1994), using this theory in the context of Spanish companies, also conclude that there is a dualism in the environment inside and outside the organisation which should be taken into consideration when explaining the process of design, implementation and change of MAS.

Many criticisms have been launched at the new institutional sociology approach over the years. The new institutional theory de-emphasises the de-institutionalisation of institutionalised practices, that is, 'the processes by which institutions weaken and disappear' (Scott, 2001: 182). Oliver (1992) identifies three pressures for deinstitutionalisation; functional, political and social pressures. Functional pressures result from poor performance levels or benefits gained from institutions and routines. Political pressures arise from shifts in the interests and power distributions that have supported and legitimated existing institutions and routines. Finally, social pressures such as the differentiation of groups, the existence of heterogeneous institutions and routines, and changes in laws or social expectations that might hinder the persistence of an institution or routine may impact on deinstitutionalisation. Greenwood *et al.* (2002) also argue that deinstitutionalisation occurs as a result of factors such as social upheaval, technological disruptions, competitive discontinuities, or regulatory change. These changes may lead to disturbing the taken-for-granted assumptions by introducing new ideas and thus the possibility of change.

In addition, new institutional sociology theory focuses on explaining homogeneity (or convergent change processes) and persistence (or stability) (Dacin *et al.*, 2002). It is largely used to explain the persistence or the stability of phenomena (Greenwood and Hinings, 1996; Dacin *et al.*, 2002). Ledford *et al.* (cited in Greenwood and Hinings, 1996: 1023), for example, point out that new institutional theory offers not 'much guidance regarding change'. A related significant critique of new institutional theory invokes its relative inattention to the role of pro-active agency in constructing institutions (Carruthers, 1995). Barley and Tolbert (1997), for example, argue that new institutional theory has largely focused on the role of institutions in shaping and constraining the action of actors.

Furthermore, new institutional theorists have typically considered the organisational environment in terms of symbolic practices, such as institutionalised management accounting practices, as opposed to an idea of

the environment built around market conditions and other technical pre-
requisites (Scott, 1987; Carruthers, 1995). Several authors suggest that it may
be useful to consider institutional and technical environments as two separate, but sometimes interdependent, dimensions (Carruthers, 1995; Greenwood and Hinings, 1996). This means that the striving for legitimacy does
not essentially conflict with the achievement of efficiency and effectiveness
through adjustment to competition and market-based transactions.

Gupta *et al.* (1994), for example, suggest that management may cope with
these two environments separately, carrying out a set of symbolic management accounting practices for addressing its institutional contexts and a separate set of instrumental management accounting practices for addressing its
technical environment. Greenwood and Hinings (1996) also argue that technical and institutional environments interrelate with interests and value commitments to generate pressures for change. In the existence of a reformative
commitment, that is, where all groups oppose the existing routine and prefer
an alternative one; they suggest that revolutionary change is more likely to
occur because of the absence of resistance. The critical paradigm is the topic of
the next sub-section.

2.4.1.3   Critical paradigm: assumptions, theories and criticisms

In the early 1980s accounting researchers have begun adopting different
critical theories to examine management accounting practices. In contrast
to the functionalist and interpretive perspectives, critical theories explicitly
address the issues of conflict, domination and power in their attempt to
understand accounting practices (Covaleski *et al.*, 1996). This difference is
most evident when classifying research theories using the regulation-radical
change dimension of Burrell and Morgan's (1979) classification. However,
from the subjective-objective dimension, critical theories ideally have mixed
ontological, epistemological and methodological assumptions of positivistic
and interpretive perspectives. In fact, the critical paradigm comprises both
radical structuralism and radical humanism. The former tends to treat the
social reality as being composed of external objects independent of any certain
person whereas the latter tends to focus on individual perceptions and interpretations (Hopper and Powell, 1985: 451).

There is a wide range of critical theories within the critical paradigm that
have influenced management accounting research such as the political economy, labour process perspective, Habermas' critical theory perspective,
Foucauldian perspective, actor-network theory, and structuration theory.
The work of Karl Marx (1818–1883) has had a great influence on management accounting literature. Within the Marxist theory it is possible to identify three different approaches, namely the political economy, labour process
perspective, and Habermas' critical theory perspective. The political economy
perspective is based on the belief that accounting affects the distribution of
income, power and wealth in society. In this regard, Cooper and Sherer (1984)

argue that researchers using this approach should be normative, descriptive and critical.

In contrast to the political economy perspective, the labour process theory focuses only on the labour process, that is, the social relations of production in capitalist economic systems. Unlike both the political economy and the labour process perspectives, Habermas' critical theory is more radical humanistic in orientation. Laughlin (1987) argues that this perspective should be used to understand the interplay between the social roots of accounting and its more technical aspects. The three Marxist perspectives represent modernism beliefs that the *status quo* can be improved through radical critique. Postmodernism perspectives such as the Foucauldian perspective and actor-network theory argue against modernism's beliefs.

The Foucauldian perspective focuses on the ways in which knowledge and power are interrelated. It emphasises not only how knowledge enables the exercising of power but also how power itself can generate systems that produces knowledge. Drawing from the Foucauldian notion of power-knowledge, the actor-network theory, especially the sociology of translation concept, links translation with the objective of achieving action at a distance. Like the Foucauldian perspective, structuration theory focuses on the interplay between knowledge (signification and legitimation) and power (domination). However, this theory differs from the Foucauldian perspective, which argues for discontinuity, as it emphasises the continuity of social life. Having given a very brief overview about the aforementioned critical theories, the labour process perspective, Foucauldian perspective, and structuration theory will be presented in more detail below. The labour process perspective represents modernism and the Foucauldian perspective exemplifies the postmodernism movement.[11] In addition, structuration theory, which will be discussed in the next chapter, is one of the chosen theories for the current book.

The labour process perspective.   The labour process perspective was first introduced by Braverman (1974). It focuses on labour-capital relations and the extraction of surplus from labour as a source of profit. Braverman (1974) argues that, in modern capitalist economies, treating workers as a commodity, that is, the purchase and sale of labour power, set the stage for their exploitation and expropriation by capital. Accordingly, there are class-based distributional conflicts between owners and workers within capitalist enterprises. Based on these assumed conflicts in the capitalist relations of production, Hopper *et al.* (1987) introduced this approach to management accounting. They argue that accounting, as an instrument of exploitation, provides control mechanisms by which surplus is extracted from labour by owners. Many other accounting researchers have used this approach to explain management accounting practices (e.g. Hopper and Armstrong, 1991; Uddin and Hopper, 2001).

However, the labour process perspective suffers from some shortcomings. Luft (1997: 174) argue that the labour process perspective is similar to neo-classical economics in some aspects such as treating labour-capital relations, in which actors with superior bargaining power can exploit their position to secure larger shares of the economic surplus, as 'a game-theory proposition'. In the same vein, Ahmed and Scapens (2000) claim that this approach shares the transaction cost perspective the deterministic and universalistic orientation. They state that '[t]he labour process approach links the historical development of accounting systems to a preconceived universal goal; the control of labour... [and assumes] that management accounting systems exist because they are the best solution for the function they serve; ... controlling the labour process ...' (p. 165). In contrast to the labour process perspective, the Foucauldian perspective is postmodernist in orientation.

The Foucauldian perspective. Michel Foucault (1926–1984) was a French philosopher whose writings have been applied to critical management accounting studies since the 1980s. As an historian of the present, he developed an alternative postmodern approach to historical analysis. One of his major contributions is the emphasis on the interdependence of bodies of knowledge and power relations. For Foucault, 'the exercise of power perpetually creates knowledge and, conversely, knowledge constantly induces effects of power' (1980: 52). He argues that power and knowledge are two sides of the same coin. Power informs knowledge and produces discourse. It unintentionally achieves strategic effects through methods of discipline and surveillance. These methods are a form of knowledge constituted in both texts and definite institutional and organisational practices. As a result, disciplinary practices are discursive practices. Ezzamel (1994: 216) states that '[k]nowledge constitutes discipline, and discipline is an effective constitution of power'.

Accounting in the Foucauldian perspective is seen as a system of surveillance rather than an aid, which helps managers in planning, control and decision-making. Foucauldian accounting historians are concerned with the exercising of power within the historical context on which accounting systems operate (Napier, 1989). Accounting as a disciplinary power creates particular visibilities that render people subject to measurement and control. Foucauldian accounting historians reject the evolutionary model to explain the emergence and change in management accounting practices (Miller and Napier, 1993). They focus on discontinuity in history with the aim to explore the hidden relations that contribute to the emergence of certain systems. In this regard, they employ what Foucault called episteme in order to identify different periods of thought featuring different discursive practices.

The Foucauldian perspective has its weaknesses in understanding change in management accounting practices. This approach does not explain why historical events happened but it provides a description or a typology of such events. For instance, the Foucauldian approach can describe the occurrence of management accounting innovations by comparing management accounting techniques in different periods but it cannot know why such innovations arose (Luft, 1997). Foucauldian approach also suffers from other limitations in management accounting literature. For example, Armstrong (1994) criticises Foucauldian accounting historians who use the Foucauldian concepts of discipline and surveillance and questions their applicability to management accounting research. Comparing Foucauldian concepts with accounting controls, he points out that disciplinary regimes involve a continuous and comprehensive surveillance of individual behaviour, while accounting controls shift the emphasis away from behavioural details to economic outcomes.

2.4.2 Mixing research approaches (Triangulation)

As stated earlier, there are three main approaches to examining management accounting change, namely positivistic, interpretive and critical perspectives. Each of these paradigms has different ontological, epistemological and methodological positions. However, a number of writers believe that all these approaches are complementary since no single approach is capable of giving a complete understanding of management accounting phenomena (Leong, 1985; Mouck, 1990; Lee, 1991; Neu, 1992; Mangos and Lewis, 1995). Covaleski *et al.* (1996: 24), for example, state that 'we offer the various paradigms not as competing perspectives but in some sense as alternative ways of understanding the multiple roles played by management accounting in organisations and society'. In addressing management accounting phenomena, there have been a number of attempts to mix different research approaches together.

Some researchers have made attempts to combine some positivistic theories with other positivistic, interpretive and critical theories. For example, contingency theory has been combined with new institutional sociology theory to understand budgetary process, co-ordination and control problems (Gupta *et al.*, 1994; Alam, 1997; Lee and Modell, 2000). Moreover, it has been used with both agency theory and transactions cost theory to understand management accounting systems in the conditions of environmental and technological stability and uncertainty (Tiessen and Waterhouse, 1983). Contingency theory has also been used with labour process theory to address the relationship between budgeting characteristics and a set of environmental factors such as industrial relations and political climate (Hoque and Hopper, 1997).

In addition, agency theory has been used with new institutional sociology theory to evaluate alternative incentive systems (Eisenhardt, 1988). Furthermore, new institutional sociology theory has been combined with other positivistic theories such as resource dependence theory to address the issue of agency (Oliver, 1991) and economic theory to take into account the technical environment in understanding organisational change (Granlund and Lukka, 1998). However, such combinations are epistemologically and ontologically problematic. In this regard, Hoque and Hopper (1997: 126) state that '...integration of theories and results based on "interpretive" theories and allegedly "scientific" research, such as contingency theory, is probably philosophically impossible'.

Other researchers have tried to link some interpretive theories with other interpretive and critical theories. For instance, Jones and Dugdale (2002) draw on actor-network theory and Giddens' concepts of modernity to explain the rise of ABC. Ezzamel (1994) uses the Foucauldian perspective of power/knowledge relations and the concept of sociology of translation from actor-network theory to study the dynamic processes of organisational change in a UK university that supplant an incremental budget by a comprehensive budget. Burns and Scapens (2000) utilise old institutional economics theory and structuration theory to propose a framework for studying management accounting change. Combining interpretive and critical perspectives is less problematic than mixing the positivistic approach with the other two approaches as interpretive and critical approaches are consistent in much of their ontological, epistemological and methodological positions, however, they are still different in the view of society as being ordered or in conflict.

In sum, the authors share Saunders *et al.*'s (2003: 85) view that 'it would be easy to fall into the trap of thinking that one research approach is "better" than another. This would miss the point. They are "better" at doing different things'. The authors believe that different research approaches can complement each other. However, caution should be exercised in choosing and combining different theories together as these syntheses may overcome some difficulties of these theories and, however, create others by losing sight of their key features.

In this book, the authors draw on structuration theory, new institutional sociology theory and old institutional economics theory to understand management accounting change induced by the implementation of IT (ERP vs. custom software) in the Egyptian environment. Research issues on ERP - systems and management accounting change are discussed in the next section.

2.5   Research issues on ERP and management accounting change

2.5.1   ERP systems as a change agent

Kaplan (1984) claims that management accounting systems lag far behind advanced manufacturing techniques. This lack in management accounting innovations in the new manufacturing environments can hold back the improving performance of the organisation. Kaplan (1986) argues that management accounting systems must change to reflect changes in innovative production systems and advanced manufacturing technology.

This refers to a simple cause-effect relationship between accounting change and advanced manufacturing technologies (Granlund, 2001). The concept of innovation has been proposed in order to address this perceived causal relation and accounting lag.

An innovation can be defined 'as an idea, practice, or material artefact perceived to be new by the relevant unit of adoption' (Dewar and Dutton, 1986: 1422). Drawing on the theory of organisational lag and innovation theory, Dunk (1989) conceptualised accounting lag by differentiating two types of innovations in organisations; technical and administrative. Technical innovations, on the one hand, are the implementation of new products, processes and services. These innovations are directly related to the basic work activity or mission of the organisation such as advanced manufacturing technology (Damanpour and Evan, 1984; Dunk, 1989). On the other hand, administrative innovations take place in an organisation's social system (Damanpour and Evan, 1984). They include the implementation of new rules, procedures, roles and structures associated with the communication and exchange between people and their environment, as well as new policies, procedures and organisational structures (Van de Ven, 1986; Dunk, 1989). This type of innovations is only indirectly related to the basic work activity of the organisation and is more immediately related to its management such as electronic data processing and accounting systems (Kimberly and Evanisko, 1981).

It has been stated earlier that advanced manufacturing technologies such as MRPI and MRPII systems are the predecessors of ERP systems. In addition to operations, ERP systems have been extended to include other functional areas such as accounting, human resources, logistics, sales and marketing (Booth *et al.*, 2000). Therefore, ERP systems, as an information technology[12] (IT), include both technical and administrative innovations. Hence, the implementation of ERP systems can contribute largely in reducing or removing accounting lag. This is because it can be associated with both technical change such as MRPI and accounting change such as ABC simultaneously. Therefore, ERP innovations[13] can be divided into: (1) technical innovations (operations module) that include new manufacturing technologies such as MRPI and (2) administrative innovations (other modules such as accounting and marketing) that comprise innovations in all other functional areas.

ERP systems contain best practices in all functional areas in a certain industry. For the purpose of this research, the authors tend to separate IT (as hardware and software) from its use in a particular function (for example in manufacturing or accounting) as this separation provides some implications for the type and content of change induced by ERP systems. For instance, the implementation of an ERP system may reflect only the introduction of advanced information technology (change in IT knowledge, that is, a new method for processing and communicating data) but it does not change accounting techniques used in practice (no change in existing accounting knowledge) (for example Granlund and Malmi, 2002). Hence, this change is technological change rather than accounting change. However, this technological change could have indirect effects on accounting practices such as improving the quality and timing of accounting reports. As a result, this separation can shed light on how ERP capacities can add value to management accounting techniques whether or not these techniques have been changed.

Dewar and Dutton (1986) distinguish between radical and incremental innovations on the basis of the level or degree of new knowledge embedded in an innovation. Radical innovations represent a clear departure from existing practices in an organisation, that is, fundamental or revolutionary change. Revolutionary change is 'so great that it must be considered a fresh start rather than an extension of what preceded it' (Kanter *et al.*, 1992: 173). It is 'a fundamental disruption to existing routines and institutions' (Burns and Scapens, 2000: 20). It is both quantum, that is, many things change together or when structures change in a concerted way, and dramatic, that is, elements change a great deal (Miller and Friesen, 1984). As a result, revolutionary change occurs when implementing multiple ERP modules that sharply contain a different set of practices at the same time in multiple divisions – a 'big-bang' approach (Schneider, 1999).

On the other hand, incremental innovations refer to minor improvements or adjustments of current practices in the adopting organisation, that is, evolutionary change. Evolutionary change is 'incremental with only minor disruption to existing routines and institutions' (Burns and Scapens, 2000: 20). Therefore, it refers to selecting a limited number of modules to be implemented that incrementally contain a different set of practices – a 'small-bang' approach (Bancroft *et al.*, 1998). Hence, there are multiple dimensions, which can be used to differentiate revolutionary change from evolutionary change, such as the scale of change (the number of modules implemented/the number of sites effected), the timing of change (at the same time or at discrete periods) and the knowledge component of change. But the authors believe that the last dimension is the critical factor in determining revolutionary-evolutionary change.

Some commentators on management accounting change have recently identified the potential for ERP systems to revolutionary change accounting practices and management accountants' role such as:

> ERP systems radically change the way accounting and businesses information exists within organisations and the effects are likely to be quite significant (Sutton, 2000: 5).

> ... [A]utomation and integration that characterise ERP-type technology dramatically reduces the necessity for employing management

accountants to collect information, prepare reports, and police adherence to agreed standards and operational procedures (Chapman and Chua, 2000: 204).

Then, the question now is that: have ERP systems overcome management accounting stability and changed management accounting practices and management accountants' work and role? In the next sub-section we address this question in Anglo-American research and discuss the gap in the literature.

2.5.2   Empirical evidence on ERP and management accounting change and stability

As the aim is to explore the impacts ERP systems have on management accounting practices, the next section draws on the recent literature on management accounting change and stability. In particular, it mainly addresses two issues. First, whether the implementation of ERP systems has somehow changed management accounting methods or management control procedures used in organisations. Second, whether the implementation of ERP systems, as an information technology (IT), has implications for the management accounting profession. In particular, it discusses how ERP systems have changed the responsibilities and work of management accountants within the organisation, including the organisation of management accounting function, the autonomy of accountants, the quality of information provided, the cross-functional communication, and the time spent on routine versus non-routine activities.

2.5.2.1   *Change and stability in management accounting methods: the role of ERP systems*

Different internal and external factors such as information technology, advanced manufacturing technology and privatisation put tremendous pressures on management accounting systems and practices to change (Spicer, 1992; Burns *et al.*, 1999; Hoque and Alam, 1999; Uddin and Hopper, 1999, 2001). However, it is often observed that management accounting practices are difficult or slow to change (Scapens, 1994; Granlund, 2001). For instance, Kaplan (1986: 175), addressing accounting lag, states that 'while it was obvious that each of the firms visited was making significant changes in its manufacturing operations, it seems equally clear that comparable changes were not being made in its accounting and control systems'.

It has been expected that the introduction of ERP systems to replace legacy systems would radically change management accounting practices (Davenport, 1998; Sutton, 2000; Chapman and Chua, 2000). But the available evidence is disappointing. It is found that ERP systems reinforce rather than change existing management accounting practices (Granlund and Malmi, 2002; Scapens and Jazayeri, 2003). In this regard, ERP may play the same expected role of in-house-developed legacy systems.

In the 1990s ERP systems have been introduced to replace in-house-developed legacy systems, thereby mainly solving integration problems. However, they have been criticised for being inflexible and not meeting specific organisation and industry requirements (Davenport, 1998; Scapens *et al.*, 1998; Booth *et al.*, 2000). Unlike highly customised legacy systems, ERP systems require the organisation to adapt to the software rather than modify the software to suit the organisation's established practices. Davenport (1998: 122), for example, argues that 'an enterprise system, by its very nature, imposes its own logic on a company's strategy, organisation and culture'. In particular, these systems are sometimes seen as embodying a technological imperative that enforces a standardised model to which organisations must adapt. Ross and Vitale (2000) report that, in a company they studied 'the daily experience of persons actually using the system was that a computer was dictating how they would do things.' 'We are slaves to the systems,' said the company's CEO, 'and we have accepted the technological imperative that that implies.' In the context of management accounting, Granlund and Malmi (2002) argue that there is a unidirectional relationship between ERP systems and management accounting practices as these systems are commonly difficult to modify. Therefore, it is the management accounting practices that are typically changed to fit the new technology, not *vice versa*. Based on this logic, Granlund and Malmi (2002) described ERP systems as a 'change agent'. Therefore, these systems promise a radical change in the way of doing things in the field of accounting.

However, the empirical evidence does not support this radical change in management accounting practices (Spathis and Constantinides, 2002; Scapens and Jazayeri, 2003). In some cases, ERP systems have produced no change in management accounting practices (Granlund, 2001) and, in other cases, there was evolutionary change in management accounting practices, that is, both traditional and advanced management accounting techniques are operated in separate systems (Granlund and Malmi, 2002). Many companies implementing ERP systems as a basic platform have not abandoned some or all of their previous legacy systems (Hyvonen, 2003) or have used ERP modules from different vendors in different functions (Themistocleous *et al.*, 2001). This latter IT strategy is known as BoB. The promise is greater flexibility and closer alignment of software with the business processes of the organisation (Light *et al.*, 2001). Unlike ERP systems, highly customised legacy systems as well as BoB allow the organisation to modify the software to satisfy the organisation's established practices rather than adapt to the software. Therefore, existing management accounting practices are easily built into the custom software or chosen standalone package. It seems that companies try to overcome the technological imperative of ERP systems by partially returning to social determinism. In the former, technology is viewed as imposing itself upon a powerless organisation (it is the technology that acts on organisations) whereas, in the latter, technology is seen to be shaped by the inexorable requirements of the organisation (humans that determine how technology is used). The empirical evidence found that there was no relationship between the groups of BoB or ERP adopters and the adoption of advanced management accounting techniques (Hyvonen, 2003). It seems that both systems tend to stabilise management accounting practices.

While the above studies tend to reveal stability or minor modifications of existing management accounting techniques after implementing ERP systems, they disagree on the reasons for this phenomenon. Some studies find that modern management accounting techniques, like those built into ERP, have been implemented in separate systems before the introduction of ERP (Booth *et al.*, 2000; Granlund and Malmi, 2002; Spathis and Constantinides, 2002). They interpret this stability in functional-economic terms (i.e. long project times, scarce resources and system complexity).

Other studies observe that companies choose ERP systems that replace existing accounting systems with other very similar systems (Scapens and Jazayeri, 2003) or use BoB systems that closely align the selected software with the business processes of the organisation (Hyvonen, 2003). They interpret this phenomenon in terms of institutionalised management accounting practices. In addition to these interpretations, we cannot ignore the fact that ERP built-in best practices are derived from existing practices actually implemented in companies working in different industries in developed countries. Therefore, this fact can partially account for the stability phenomenon of management accounting practices after introducing ERP systems.

2.5.2.2   *Changes in accountants' role and relationships due to IT adoption and use: the role of ERP systems*

There has always been major interaction between accounting and information technology (IT) in operating an organisation's financial ledgers and reporting systems (Granlund and Mouritsen, 2003). For example, the first commercial computer-based information systems application was payroll at the General Electric Co., implemented in 1954 (George and King, 1991). Carr (1985) also notes that accounting was the first areas computerised and benefited from financial modelling packages which become available in the 1970s.

The automation or computerisation of accountants' work significantly affects accountants' role within organisations (Bromwich and Bhimani, 1989; Wilson and Sangster, 1992). Collier (1984), for instance, finds that the role of management accountants is changing from accumulation, analysis, and preparation to interpretation, evaluation, control and involvement in decision-making. McCosh (1986) calls for change in the management accountants' role from interpretative to consultative. King *et al.* (1991) argue that IT facilitates changing the role of management accountants from the historian to a role combining book-keeping and decision support.

The use of IT also affects the relationship between accounting and other functions. Traditionally, many IS departments in organisations have reported to the controller or vice president of finance (Shields, 2001). Managers also looked to management accountants as providers of information service. With the introduction of IT, many organisations are realigning accounting and processing functions separated by centralisation of data processing (Carr, 1985). McCosh (1986) observes that IT enables non-accountants to inform top managers and line managers to inform themselves. However, King *et al.* (1991) find that IT developments increase the power of accountants over information systems and user managers.

Recently, the adoption and use of ERP systems have heated the debate on the changing role and relationships of management accountants in the IT environment. Scapens *et al.* (1998) are pessimistic in their expectations for the effects of ERP systems on management accountants' role and relationships. They argue that the use of ERP systems may reduce or eliminate the role of management accountants as information suppliers because line managers can directly access the information they require. They expect educational and interpretative roles for management accountants in the ERP environment. However, other information specialists could even play these roles. Granlund and Malmi (2002) expect that ERP will change the role of management accountants from 'bean-counting' to business process orientation. They find that ERP systems have freed accountants from routine tasks in the organisations in which these systems have been implemented for relatively longer periods of time.

In a similar vein, Scapens and Jazayeri (2003) find changes in accountants' roles in the ERP environment, particularly the elimination of routine tasks, the decentralisation of accounting knowledge, the expansion of accountants' roles, and more forward-looking information. Caglio (2003) also finds that management accountants have broadened their role and expertise in positions traditionally pertaining to financial accountants and IT staff.

Despite their agreement on change occurrence in accountants' roles and relationships, prior studies have not agreed on the direction of change. Analysing the results of the above studies reveals inconsistencies in experiences between organisations. Some studies find that management accountants have lost their control over their works because most of their traditional role as information providers is built into IT and their accounting knowledge has become easily transferable to IS staff and line managers as they can access timely real-time information. Other studies suggest that management accountants not only have control over their works but also are expanding their traditional role into other functional areas such as IT and production.

2.5.3   Gaps in literature and research questions

The discussion above indicates that there is an emerging and growing interest in the impacts of ERP systems on organisations, particularly the changes to accounting practices and accountants' role and relationships. However, the insights gained to date should be interpreted in the light of a number of limitations. First, as far as is known, there is no study that has been conducted in less developed countries' contexts, particularly Egypt, to address ERP impacts on accounting. Despite the fact that some works have recently started to emerge to address the impact of ERP systems on accounting in developed countries, there is no equivalent interest in this issue in less developed contexts. ERP systems promise potential benefits for economic growth in less developed countries as best organisational practices, including management accounting practices, in developed countries are built into these systems. This study attempts to avoid this limitation by meeting this challenge in the context of Egypt.

Second, previous studies ignore the fact that ERP built-in best practices, including accounting practices, are derived from companies working in Anglo-American developed countries. Hence, these practices may differ somehow from best practices in developing countries. As a result, ERP systems may become a change driver in these countries. For example, Egypt has been implementing socialist policies, with less emphasis on management accounting practices, for a long period of its recent history. ERP systems, with their capitalism content, differ significantly from socialism practices that have dominated for decades in Egyptian organisations.

Third, only a few exploratory, survey-based studies have been conducted to compare ERP users' views with non-ERP users', especially BoB systems' users. These latter systems usually mix ERP components with custom software. Consequently, their impacts on management accounting may be the same as ERP systems' impacts. The previous studies have found difficulties in differentiating ERP systems from BoB systems, which include ERP components, as the two could do the same job, that is, the integration of business processes. For example, Booth *et al.* (2000: 5) observed that '[i]n practice, it can be difficult to classify software as either "ERP" or "non-ERP"'. To avoid any effects of ERP systems on management accounting practices and to explore their relative merits, it is better to use custom software (part of BoB systems without any standard packages) as a benchmark instead of BoB systems. Unlike previous studies, this research focuses on comparing custom software's (legacy systems or not) impacts on management accounting practices and accountants' work with ERP systems' (single vendor-based/automation of accounting function and any other functional areas). None of the previous studies have explicitly compared custom software's impacts on accounting practices with ERP's.

Fourth, prior research also suffers from either not using an analytic framework or focusing on only one aspect of ERP impacts, that is, changes to accounting methods or changes to accountants' role. None of past studies have used the same analytic framework to address the two perceived impacts of ERP systems. This research extends existing studies by using Burns and Scapens' (2000) framework supplemented by some concepts from structuration theory and 'new' institutional sociology theory. Burns and Scapens' (2000) framework is micro level in orientation. It focuses on management accounting practices within organisations. Therefore, it needs to be complemented with a macro level analysis to take into account the coercive, mimetic and normative differences affecting on management accounting practices and profession in each country. This is the role of 'new' institutional sociology theory. Then, structuration theory relates the micro and macro analyses together and gives more detailed analysis of human agents' behaviours and relations, which is absent in Burns and Scapens' (2000) framework. This issue will be explored in detail in the next chapter.

Finally, none of past studies that address the impact of ERP on accounting have been conducted in public sector enterprises. Recently, there is an international movement towards reforming public sector practices, with the direction of adopting private sector practices in public sector. Despite this apparent trend, there is no research that has addressed ERP's impacts on accounting practices in governmental contexts so far.

The literature reviewed above highlights issues that warrant further considerations with respect to the changes to accounting practices and accountants' role. This study aims at overcoming some of the aforementioned limitations. As stated earlier, the purpose of the study is to compare analytically and empirically the adoption and use of ERP and custom software systems in practice, dealing especially with the management accounting function in Egyptian organisations. Specifically, this study considers the following research questions, divided into two groups of questions.

The first group includes why and how are institutionalised accounting practices persisted (reproduced) and/or transformed in the IT (ERP vs. custom software) environment? It also addresses the role of IT (ERP vs. custom software) in their persistence or transformation. These questions deal mainly with stability and change in management accounting practices, the conditions under which the stability and/or change can occur and the role of IT (ERP vs. custom software) in their occurrence.

The second group includes the question of how IT (ERP vs. custom software) maintains or changes the relationship of management accountants with different members (IS staff and line managers) within the organisation. It also explores the roles of management accountants in the IT (ERP vs. custom software) environment as perceived by management accountants themselves and other members of the organisation. These questions focus mainly on the changing roles and relationships of management accountants due to the introduction of IT (ERP vs. custom software).

2.6 Summary and conclusions

This chapter reviewed the literature on ERP systems and management accounting change. Based on this review, it seems that ERP systems have evolved from earlier MRPI systems in the 1970s and MRPII systems in the 1980s. The legacy systems that preceded ERP systems integrated manufacturing and some commercial functions. However, some other functions of the firm lay outside the integrated set. ERP software packages span most functional areas such as accounting, operations and logistics, human resources, sales and marketing. Accordingly, they promise the seamless integration of all the information flowing throughout a company. ERP systems support and facilitate a wide range of management accounting innovations. As a consequence, they promise radical change in traditional management accounting techniques.

ERP systems, with built-in best practices for business processes, support 'modern' management accounting techniques such as activity-based costing, activity-based budgeting, product lifecycle costing, and balanced scorecard. In addition, the promise of integrated, flexible, real-time financial and operating information offered by these systems addresses many of the traditional criticisms of management accounting systems. As a result, ERP systems can be described as a change agent of management accounting practices.

In recent years there has been an increasing interest in management accounting change. Different positivistic, interpretive and critical theories have been used in studying management accounting change and stability. However, it seems that there is a tendency for combining research theories to understand management accounting change. It has been found that ERP systems evolutionarily change and/or stabilise management accounting methods and change the roles and relationships of management accountants.

The next chapter develops a theoretical framework that will inform the empirical study on ERP and management accounting change in Egyptian companies. This framework will be based mainly on three theories, namely structuration theory, old institutional economics and new institutional sociology theory.

Notes

1   The term platform refers to the basic client/server configuration. The client/server systems take six forms: central system, distributed presentation, remote database access, three-layer client/server, web-based client/server and multi-layer co-operative client/server (see Buck-Emden, 2000 for more details).

2   The systems development lifecycle consists of a number of stages, namely project planning phase, analysis phase, design phase, implementation phase and support phase.

3   ERP is a semi-finished product with tables and parameters that user organisations and their implementation partners configure to their business needs.

4   See, for example, Davenport (1998), Granlund and Malmi (2002), and Scapens and Jazayeri (2003).

5   The former is based on forecasts and orders are released to the shop as planned by the master production schedule. While, for the latter, individual parts are not manufactured until pulled by the succeeding department, or by a sales order to start production in the last cell (Mackey and Thomas, 1995).

6 The term paradigm was introduced by Kuhn (1962: viii) to refer to 'universally recognised scientific achievements that for a time provide model problems and solutions to a community of practitioners'. It provides 'a framework including an accepted set of theories, methods and ways of defining data' (Hussey and Hussey, 1997: 47).

7 Critical perspectives combine the two radical paradigms.

8 This means that each paradigm has its own assumptions about ontology, epistemology, humane nature, methodology, and social order.

9 We use the terms 'field studies' and 'case studies' interchangeably in this section.

10 Transaction costs refer to 'the costs of negotiating and concluding a separate contract for each exchange transaction which takes place in a market' (Coase, 1937: 389).

11 Modernism believes that humanity has the capacity to progress, to better itself and to do so on the basis of rational thought whereas postmodernism argues that there is no higher state, no better worlds, no such thing as progress or the control of nature (Boslender, 1995: 78).

12 The term information technology (IT) in its broad sense can be defined as 'any artifact whose underlying technological base is comprised of computer or communications hardware and software' (Cooper and Zmud, 1990: 123).

13 We should note that the classification of IT depends on its application in a specific job. IT acquires its identity from its use in performing a certain task (see Cooper and Zmud, 1990; Dewar and Dutton, 1986, for IT applications as a technical innovation; Kimberly and Evanisko, 1981, for IT applications as an administrative innovation).

3
Theoretical Framework

3.1 Introduction

In the previous chapter we reviewed prior studies on ERP and management accounting change to evaluate various research approaches and to identify research issues. Our review revealed that there is a recent and increasing interest in studying management accounting change, including ERP-driven change. Different research perspectives, including positivistic, interpretive and critical approaches, have informed research on management accounting change. However, each approach on its own gives only part of the picture and needs to be complemented by other approaches to get a better understanding of management accounting change as a complex phenomenon. This study draws upon Giddens' structuration theory, as a critical meta-theory, and institutional theories, as interpretive theories, for the theoretical framework informing the current study.

As stated earlier the purpose of this study is to examine management accounting change triggered by IT (ERP vs. custom software) implementation and use, this chapter draws mainly upon the applications of structuration theory and its extensions in both management accounting and information systems (IS) literatures. The chapter is divided into five further sections. The next section introduces the main concepts of structuration theory. This is followed by two sections to examine the applications and extensions of structuration theory in management accounting and IS literatures respectively. Then the implications of the previous applications and models are discussed. The final section summarises and concludes the chapter.

3.2 Structuration theory: core concepts

Anthony Giddens introduced structuration theory to replace the dualism nature of traditional approaches to the relationship between social structure and human agency with the notion of the duality of structure (Giddens, 1976, 1977, 1979, 1982, 1984). He emphasises this fact when stating '[t]he concept of structuration involves that of the *duality of structure*, which relates to the *fundamentally recursive character of social life, and expresses the mutual dependence of structure and agency'* (Giddens, 1979: 69, emphasis added in the original). The concept of structuration involves thinking of objectivity and subjectivity with respect to the constitution of social structure, as constitutive of each other, and hence as not being mutually exclusive. In this regard, the relation between structure and agency is one of duality, not dualism. Giddens (1982: 8) argues that neither the subject (the individual) nor object (society or institutions) should be regarded as having primacy. But each is constituted in, and through recurrent practices.

Giddens (1984) distinguishes between social systems and social structures. Social systems refer to 'reproduced relations between actors or collectivities, organised as regular social practices' (Giddens, 1984: 25). They include regularised relations of interdependence between individuals or groups, as recurrent social practices. They also exist in time and space and are constituted by situated social practices. These systems exhibit structures, or structural properties, which are 'rules and resources, or sets of transformation relations, organised as properties of social systems' (Giddens, 1984: 25) or collectivities. These structures are recursively implicated in social systems, are out of time and space and are characterised by the absence of the subject. Social structure exists out of time and space or, more accurately, in virtual time and space and can be instantiated by agents during interaction in specific time-space settings (Macintosh, 1994). In this regard, they are more internal than external to agents, as memory traces and as instantiated in social practices. Social structures do not exist independent of the knowledge of agents about what they do in their daily life.

Social structure, the first half of Giddens' duality, consists of two interrelated components: rules and resources. The rules of social life refer to the 'techniques or generalisable procedures applied in the enactment/reproduction of social practices' (Giddens, 1984: 21). They can be seen as being either normative or interpretive (Dillard and Yuthas, 1997). Normative rules represent legitimation structure. These are translated and verbalised by actors as norms, specific rights and obligations, which are associated by sanctions/ rewards in interaction. Interpretive rules create signification structure or symbolic systems that provide techniques for agents to interpret social events. Agents reflexively employ interpretive schemes, as stocks of knowledge, to communicate with others.

Resources are the media through which power is exercised and domination structure is reproduced. Domination structure involves asymmetries of resources employed in the sustaining of power relations in social practices. Resources are of two types: allocative and authoritative (Giddens, 1979). Allocative resources are material or economic resources that result from human domination over nature such as raw materials. Authoritative resources are non-material resources and result from human domination over other human actors. These resources provide facilities for reaching specific outcomes. The achievement of such outcomes results in the manifestations of power by those actors controlling the resources. Power itself is not a resource (Giddens, 1979). Resources are the bases or vehicles of power. The exercise of power is not a unidirectional relation (Macintosh and Scapens, 1990). All social relations involve both autonomy and dependence, or what Giddens (1984) called the dialectic of control. In this regard, power relations are two-way: the most autonomous agent is in some degree dependent and the most dependent actor in a relation retains some autonomy. These relations are important in the situations where reaching the agent's outcomes depends upon the doings of others.

Agency, the other half of Giddens' duality, is the actions taken by individual members or agents of a social system in time-space. It expresses the activities of agents as a continuous flow of conduct rather than a series of discrete acts combined together. According to Giddens (1984: 9), '[a]gency concerns events of which an individual is the perpetrator, in the sense that the individual could, at any phase in a given sequence of conduct, have acted differently. Whatever happened would not have if that individual had not intervened'. Giddens (1979, 1984) introduces the stratification model of the agent or the self-acting to interpret the personality of the human agent as in Figure 3.1. According to this model, there are three dimensions of the agent's personality: practical consciousness (reflexive monitoring of action), discursive consciousness (rationalisation of action) and the unconscious (basic security system/motivation of action). In addition, this model describes the unintended consequences of action and the unacknowledged conditions of action.

According to the theory of structuration, the knowledgeability, or consciousness, of human agents, or what actors know about the conditions of

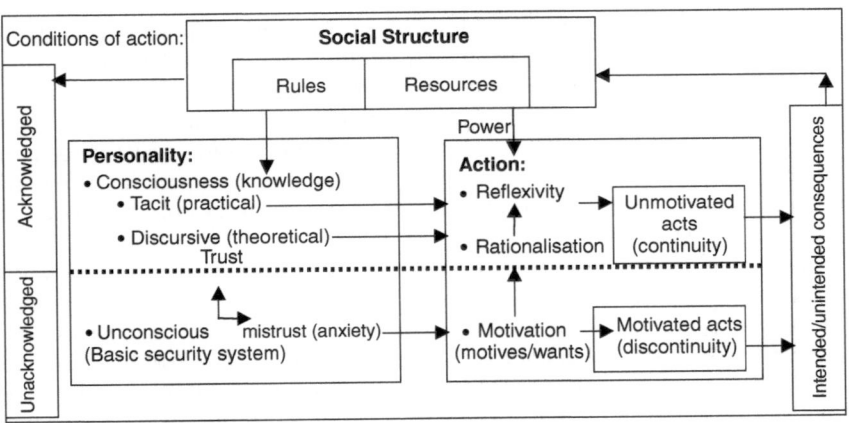

Figure 3.1 Agents' Personality, Agency and Structure

their action and that of others, is of two types: practical or tacit consciousness and theoretical or discursive consciousness. The division between the two can be altered by the agents' socialisation and learning exper-iences (Giddens, 1984). Practical consciousness refers to the tacit knowledge that actors have about social conditions, including the conditions of their own action, but cannot express verbally. It is not directly access-ible to the (discursive) con-sciousness and represents the vast bulk of the stocks of knowledge employed by actors in the production of social activities.

Discursive consciousness is the discursively available knowledge that actors are able to speak about social conditions, including the conditions of their own action. This type of knowledge provides actors with the reasons for their activities or the grounds for their actions. The rationalisation of action, as a process, means that 'actors – also routinely and for the most part without fuss – maintain a continuing "theoretical understanding" of the grounds of their activity' (Giddens, 1984: 5). It is an inherent characteristic of human beings: '[t]o be a human being is to be a purposive agent, who both has reasons for his or her activities and is able, if asked, to elaborate discursively upon those reasons (including laying about them)' (Giddens, 1984: 3). The reflexive mon-itoring of action operates against the background of the rationalisation of action, where the agent abstracts from the reflexive monitoring process when giving reasons and depends upon it. The rationalisation of action is considered the main criterion, applied by others, for evaluating generalised competence of actors.

The knowledgeability of human actors is always bounded, on the one hand, by the unconscious motivation of action and, on the other hand, by unacknowledged conditions/unintended consequences of action (Giddens, 1984). The unconscious motives refer to the wants that prompt the action. They refer to the potential for action, as they supply overall plans or pro-grammes within which a range of behaviour is enacted, and have a direct effect on action only in the unusual situations in which the routinised character or the continuity of social life is highly disrupted. According to the stratification model, actors' wants remain rooted in a basic security system, largely unconscious and established in the first years of life. The basic security system involves the deep-lying modes of tension management to principally minimise and control anxiety (Giddens, 1979).

All intentional actions have unintended consequences because of the unacknowledged conditions of interaction, which is out the range of self-understanding of the agent and of which the unconscious is one set (Macin-tosh, 1994). Unintended consequences of action are systemically incorporated in the process of institutions' reproduction, as they may become the un-acknowledged conditions of further actions (Giddens, 1984). For instance, unintended consequences occur where the intended outcome is not achieved, and instead the action of the agent results in another outcome(s). Another example is where the achievement of the intended outcome(s) has produced other consequences. The unacknowledged conditions refer to the new state of affairs that come into being as a result of the unintended consequences. These are unintended outcomes that reflect the inability of human agents to fully control the results of their actions.

The modalities of structuration relate agency to social structure. They represent the main dimensions of the duality of structure in the production of interaction (Giddens, 1984). There are three basic dimensions of this action/ structure duality: the communication of meaning (paired with signification structure); the exercise of power (paired with domination structure); and the application of moral sanctions (paired with legitimation structure). Action and structures interact with one another along each of these dimensions through three modalities: interpretive schemes, facilities and norms (see Figure 3.2), whereby concepts, embedded in the structure, are given specificity by social agents through the application of their stocks of knowledge. The interpretive schemes are the shared stocks of knowledge drawn upon in processes of meaning (re)production. Similarly, resources represent the facilities through which actors draw upon the domination structure in the exercise of power. Norms also refers to the actualisation of rights and the enactment of obligations.

3.3 Structuration theory and management accounting change and stability

In this section we critically discuss how structuration theory deals with social change or discontinuity; explore the applications of structuration theory in addressing management accounting stability; and present Burns and Scapens' (2000) institutional framework as an extension of structuration theory to overcome some of its limitations, including the applications and evaluation of this framework.

Figure 3.2   Structure, Interaction and Modalities

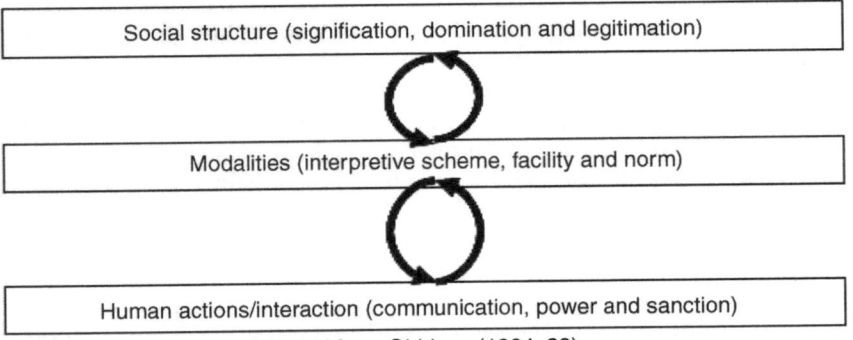

Social structure (signification, domination and legitimation)

Modalities (interpretive scheme, facility and norm)

Human actions/interaction (communication, power and sanction)

Adapted from Giddens (1984: 29)

3.3.1 Social change and stability in structuration theory: critical evaluation

For Giddens (1979: 66) structuration can be defined as the 'conditions governing the continuity or transformation of structures, and therefore the reproduction of (social) systems'. It is the process whereby social systems sometimes work to almost automatically reproduce the *status quo*, while at other times they undergo revolutionary change. This process normally occurs *via* the duality of structure, the recursive (re)production of institutional structures through the ongoing daily social practices of actors.

Social structure both enables and constrains the daily activities of agents, but does not wholly determine them, as there are some unacknowledged conditions of actions as well as unintended consequences of actions (Giddens, 1984). At the same time, while agents can choose to act in a way that will either reinforce or modify this structure, their choices are not independent of the structure within which they take their actions. This duality, then, allows change to emerge in ways that are not wholly predictable. Changes will emerge through actors' actions, and while some of the outcomes may be planned, others are unanticipated as the knowledgeability of those actors is bounded by the unconscious, unacknowledged conditions of actions and unintended consequences of actions. In this regard, the role of both structure and actions in changing the *status quo* in interaction are situationally oriented. Giddens (1979, 1984) identifies two situations under which change may occur, namely routine situations and critical situations. The possibility of change in each of these situations is discussed below.

3.3.1.1 Routine situations and the possibility of stability or evolutionary change

In routine situations agents do not consciously think and speak about their actions because social structures have primacy. Giddens (1984) argues that these situations are characterised by the tendency of social structures to dominate agency and much of agents' actions are at practical level of consciousness. Therefore, actors do things in a regular manner but cannot give them discursive expression. As such, routines are economical for agents in some senses as agents do not need to device or negotiate new practices each time they pursue in their day-to-day life (Macintosh, 1994). Routines give individuals a sense of ontological security through enabling the feeling of trust and the reproductions of social structures can be said to be automatic and chances of significant changes to existing system are rather limited.

However, incremental or gradual change occurs as an unintended outcome of social reproduction itself. The typical example of this is change in language. According to Giddens (1976: 128), 'every act which contributes to the reproduction of a structure is also an act of production ... and as such may initiate change by altering that structure at the time as it produces it'.

Therefore, this social change is part of an incremental and unintended process as the institutionalised social order is reproduced in daily life. It is unplanned, possibly unintended, and is not the result of any conscious attempt to mobilise the collective to pursue a particular interest.

3.3.1.2   *Critical situations and the possibility of revolutionary change*

According to Giddens (1979: 124), critical or crisis situations are 'a set of circumstances which – for whatever reason – radically disrupt accustomed routines of daily life'. During these situations the institutionalised social order can be drastically disrupted and routines are suspended while agents consciously attempt to change their circumstances in order to cope with the new situation. Agents operate at a discursive level of consciousness and can produce a new social structure and discard the old ones through structuration process. Critical situations unlock the possibilities for radical change, where this type of change affects a large number of people in the social system (Macintosh, 1994). This social change can be sudden and discontinuous. Therefore, structuration theory works differently. Conventions or social codes may be abandoned and new ones produced on the spot. Under crisis, agency comes to the fore; often reshaping prevailing social structures (Giddens, 1984).

3.3.1.3   *Criticisms of Giddens' treatment of change and stability*

Several criticisms have been launched on structuration theory over the years. Most of these criticisms focus on the imbalanced treatment between subjectivity (e.g. interpretive approach) and objectivity (e.g. positivistic approach) in structuration theory. For example, Layder (1987) argues that Giddens' treatment of structure as having virtual existence in the minds of agents   suggests that Giddens is anti-objectivisim and that is both unnecessary and theoretically problematic, implying that structuration theory need not be incompatible with realism. He claims that structural power is 'not simply a negotiable outcome of routine and concrete interactions and relationships' (Layder, 1985: 146). So Layder (1987) suggests that some structural constraints may be 'relatively independent'. In the same vein, Storper (1985) argues that all aspects of structure may not be equally amendable to agency.

Of particular importance to this study is the conflation problem that focuses on the problem of reducing structure to action, or *vice versa*, and the difficulty of documenting the existence of the structure apart from social activities (Archer, 1982, 1995; Layder, 1987; Mouzelis, 1991). Giddens (1984) argues that structure exists only to the degree that it is instantiated in day-to-day activities, leading to conflating structure with action. Unless structure and action are analytically and temporally separated, it is difficult to understand their mutual effects. Archer (1995: 65), for example, argues 'that structure and agency can only be linked by exam-

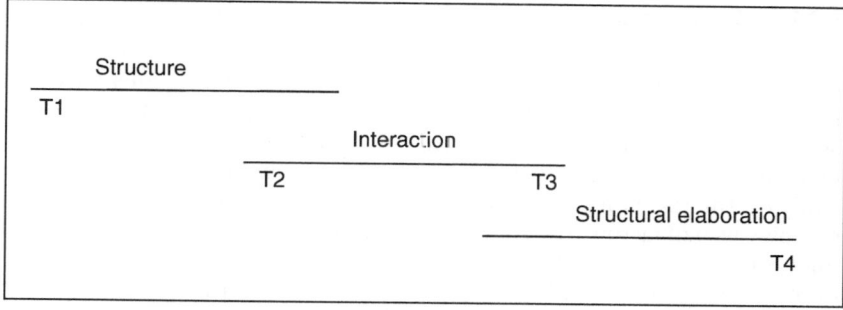

Figure 3.3   The Sequential Model of Structure and Action

ining the interplay between them over time, and without the proper incorporation of time the problem of structure and agency can never be satisfactorily resolved'.

To overcome this problem, Archer (1995: 76) suggests a model in which structure and action operate sequentially in which structure necessarily predates the action(s) which transform it and structural elaboration necessarily post-dates those actions (see Figure 3.3). This proposal argues for the analytical dualism, realism, synchrony/diachrony distinction, and pre-existence of structure separated from action. Most of these aspects are inconsistent with structuration theory. However, this solution might contribute to reducing the conflation problem and, at the same time, draws mainly on many concepts of structuration theory. A less problematic solution can be found in Barley and Tolbert (1997). They suggest complementing structuration theory with new institutional sociology theory, where Archer's (1995) proposal is more consistent with the latter than the former. According to Barley and Tolbert (1997), there is a need to observe humans' behaviours to extract the structures constraining and enabling their actions at two points of time, before and after a particular event.

In this regard, the authors believe that combining structuration theory with new institutional theory is a reasonable solution for both theories' problems. It contributes in subjectivising new institutional theory and, at the same time, in objectivising structuration theory without losing much of their tenets. The new institutional theory has been recently accused of a tendency towards the positivistic approach. For example, Bowring (2000: 258) states that the purpose of his study is 'to illustrate how (new) institutional theory, with its interpretive beginnings, has become a structuralist positivist vehicle'. Therefore, this drawback can be overcome by structuration theory that has also been criticised as it gives primacy to the interpretive approach as indicated above. As will be seen in section 3.5.3, one of the classical studies of new institutional theory, DiMaggio and Powell (1983), is grounded in structuration theory.

3.3.2 Structuration theory and management accounting stability

Structuration theory has successfully been used in accounting literature to inform a number of case studies which tend to address management accounting stability or continuity (Ouibrahim and Scapens, 1989; Macintosh and Scapens, 1990; Scapens and Roberts, 1993; Granlund, 2001). For example, Ouibrahim and Scapens (1989) draw on structuration theory to describe a case study on the resistance to management accounting change. They identify a complex web of factors that contribute to the failure of management accounting systems. The use of production language instead of accounting language as the means of communication between managers is the important failure factor. The introduction of new accounting systems poses threats to the autonomy of site managers. Therefore, they draw on a variety of resources to resist the introduction of such systems.

Granlund (2001) also identifies the potential of structuration theory, in combination with new institutional theory, for addressing stability in management accounting. He focuses on studying stability in management accounting practices and on the reasons behind the difficulty of changing existing systems. He concludes that there are different human, institutional and economic factors that intertwined in the cumulative change process or its denial. In addition, he describes the introduction of ERP systems and the resistance that follows their implementation. He explains this resistance as adherence to earlier procedures, that is, routines. This phenomenon is the major interest of Burns and Scapens' (2000) model, which is discussed next.

3.3.3 Burns and Scapens' institutional framework as an extension of structuration theory to address management accounting change

Following Archer (1995) and Barley and Tolbert (1997), who suggest solutions to the perceived difficulties of structuration theory in addressing social and organisational change, Burns and Scapens (2000) introduced their model as an attempt to overcome some of these limitations in dealing with management accounting change. This framework is mainly grounded in both structuration theory and old institutional economics theory. In their framework, Burns and Scapens (2000), drawing on old institutional economics, conceptualise management accounting systems and practices as organisational rules and routines respectively. They also conceptualise management accounting change as change in organisational rules and routines. On the other hand, Burns and Scapens (2000) draw on structuration theory to argue that there are meanings, norms and powers embedded in new and ongoing routines; all of which are shaped by prevailing institutions and the new routines could be institutionalised over time.

The main elements of Burns and Scapens' (2000) framework are illustrated in Figure 3.4. As can be seen from the figure, Burns and Scapens (2000) introduce a distinction between institutions (institutional realm) and actions (realm of action) with rules and routines linking the two realms through processes of

Figure 3.4   Burns and Scapens' (2000: 9) Institutional Framework

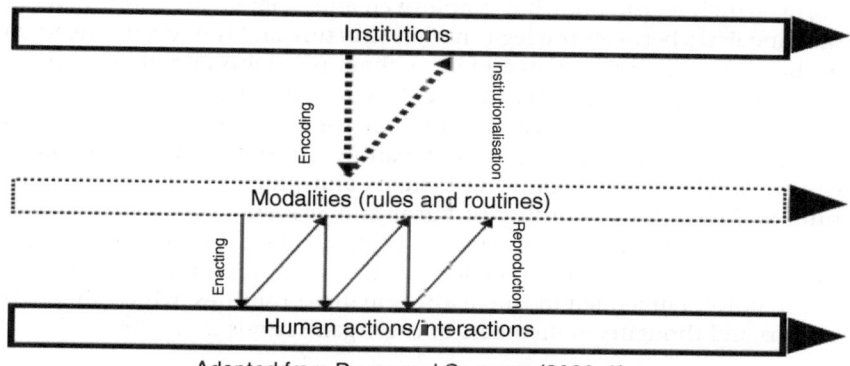

Adapted from Burns and Scapens (2000: 9)

encoding, enacting, reproduction and institutionalisation. Next, we introduce the main elements of Burns and Scapens' (2000) framework, present previous studies used in constructing this framework, explore the studies informed by this framework, and evaluate and compare it with Giddens' structuration theory to identify major similarities and differences.

3.3.3.1   An analysis of the theoretical underpinnings of Burns and Scapens' (2000) model

Burns and Scapens' framework is grounded in three main previous works, Macintosh and Scapens (1990); Scapens (1994); and Barley and Tolbert (1997). We introduce these works to identify their contributions to Burns and Scapens' model.

Macintosh and Scapens (1990) study.   Macintosh and Scapens (1990) propose structuration theory, which goes beyond the technical-efficiency focus of the traditional positivistic approach as a useful framework for studying and understanding management accounting in its organisational, social and political contexts. They describe the key idea of the theory, its limitations and its use in analysing a longitudinal case study. In structuration theory, Giddens (1984) uses the notion of modalities to link the human actions to the structural properties of social systems. He identified three interrelated modalities, namely interpretive schemes, facilities and norms, which are drawn upon in (re)production of social practices and reconstituting of social structure. Macintosh and Scapens (1990) conceptualise management accounting as modalities of structuration process in each of the three dimensions of signification, domination and legitimation.

Management accounting can be viewed as an interpretive scheme that links the signification structure to the social interaction to provide managers with a means to communicate meaningfully. Furthermore, management accounting provides facilities for the mediation of the domination structure in power relations. In addition, management accounting provides the norms which legitimate what is approved and what is disapproved and as such mediates between the legitimation structure and the social interaction in the form of a set of values and ideas about the rights and obligations.

Burns and Scapens (2000) combine the concept of management accounting as modalities with the concept of management accounting as rules and routines. They argue that there are meanings, norms, and powers embedded in management accounting systems and practices as organisational rules and routines. According to Burns and Scapens (2000), for example, '[w]hat is deemed acceptable (modes of behaviour) will be influenced by the meanings and norms embedded in the ongoing routines' (p. 12) and '...the power embedded in the institutionalised routines, which shape the actions and thoughts of members of the organisations ...' (p. 23).

Scapens (1994) study.   Scapens (1994) criticises the mainstream accounting research grounded in the neo-classical economic theory of the firm as it has difficulties in analysing management accounting change. This is due to the fact that the neo-classical economic theory is concerned with rationality and equilibrium. It predicts rational outcomes as an equilibrium state rather than a process that results in moving from one state to another. Scapens (1994) introduces old institutional economics theory as a useful alternative approach in order to tackle some of the conventional theory's problems. Based on old institutional economics theory, he conceptualises management accounting practices as organisational routines, which could be institutionalised over time.

Scapens (1994: 306) defines an institution, based on the work of Hamilton (1932: 84), as 'a way of thought or action of some prevalence and permanence, which is embedded in the habits of a group or the customs of a people'. This definition links the idea of habits and institutions. It describes the habits as components of institutions. Scapens (1994) argues that habits are personal but routines may encompass groups of individuals, that is, routines are the institutionalised habits. He regards management accounting practices as institutionalised routines that involve doing things, choosing what to do and monitoring what has been done. This concept of management accounting practices promotes studying and understanding management accounting as what is actually done rather than comparing it with what should happen or the theoretical ideas contained in current textbooks.

Burns and Scapens (2000) further develop the relationship between what should happen and what is actually done. They distinguish between rules and routines. The former refers to the formalised statement of procedures, or the way in which things should be done, whereas the latter refers to the procedures actually in use, or the way in which things are actually done. Then, Burns and Scapens (2000) use the concept of rule-based behaviour to link rules to routines. They argue that recursively following the rules may lead to a programmatic rule-based conduct, which draws heavily on tacit knowledge. This programmatic behaviour is what Burns and Scapens (2000) called routines. As such, routines may not actually replicate the rules, as there are different deliberate or unconscious modifications that could be introduced during implementing and using the rules in guiding day-to-day behaviour.

However, the relation between rules and routines is not unidirectional. The routines could be formalised in the form of rules. Burns and Scapens (2000) argue that routines may emerge which are derived either from the modifications of previously adopted rules or from the adoptions of practices without formalising them. These emergent routines may be formalised in order to retain the knowledge embedded in them, to train new organisational members, or to prevent undesired modifications. According to Burns and Scapens (2000), management accounting systems could be conceptualised as rules as they comprise the formal procedures adopted by organisations, where as management accounting practices could be conceptualised as routines because they express the procedures actually used that may be different from the original systems.

Barley and Tolbert (1997) study. Barley and Tolbert (1997) criticised new institutional sociology theory because it neglects the links between actions and institutions. They argue that the recent uses of this theory have focused on treating institutions as constraints and have paid relatively little attention to the process by which such institutions are created, modified and reproduced. To overcome the underdeveloped process view of institutionalists, Barley and Tolbert (1997) introduce structuration theory as a possible solution for this limitation. They conceptualise the institutionalisation process as a structuration process and introduce a recursive model that acknowledges the interplay between action and institutions.

This institutionalisation model consists of three interrelated components: institutional realm, realm of action and scripts. According to Barley and Tolbert (1997), the institutional realm refers to the social structure that is historically derived from repetitive actions. It comprises 'shared rules and typifications that identify categories of social actors and their appropriate activities and relationships' (p. 96). The realm of action represents the day-to-day social conduct in the form of communication, power and sanction. The scripts, which link the two realms, resemble the modalities that are in actors' stocks of practical knowledge in the form of interpretive schemes, resources and norms. However, Barley and Tolbert (1997) argue that the concept of scripts is more empirically identifiable than the concept of modalities as introduced by Giddens (1979, 1984) because it can be seen in the behaviours practised in a particular setting of interaction. Barley and Tolbert (1997: 98), drawing on

Goffman (1983), define scripts as 'observable, recurrent activities and patterns of interaction characteristic of a particular setting'.

Barley and Tolbert (1997), drawing on Giddens (1984) and Berger and Luckmann (1966), describe the relationship between actions, institutions and scripts as an institutionalisation or structuration process that comprises four stages. The first stage involves the encoding process of institutional principles that entails the internalisation of these principles into the scripts used in a particular setting during the socialisation process. Second, the enactment of scripts in social interaction, in many cases, may not involve conscious choice of action as actors behave according to the way things are. However, the modification of institutions is more likely to occur as a result of intentional actions. The third process describes the degree of replication or revision of scripts informed by social actions. Here, the existence of contextual changes such as changes in technology is essential in questioning and modifying existing scripts. The last process involves the objectification and externalisation of scripts used in a particular setting. This process includes the disassociation of patterns of behaviour from their particular setting that obscures their relationships to the interests of different actors.

Burns and Scapens (2000) draw upon the work of Barley and Tolbert (1997) in constructing their model. However, they introduce an important modification to Barley and Tolbert's (1997) model. Burns and Scapens (2000) substitute the notion of rules and routines for the notion of scripts. They argue that 'this definition (of scripts) could equally apply to the notions of rules and routines ...' (p. 9). This modification facilitates combining old institutional economics theory and structuration theory to address management accounting change.

3.3.3.2   Applications of Burns and Scapens' (2000) model

Burns and Scapens (2000) offer their framework, which is an extension of structuration theory, as a starting point for informing interpretive management accounting case studies. They illustrate the use of the framework by briefly discussing two previously published case studies. The first case is previously presented in Robert and Scapens' (1990) study. It illustrates a successful change process in which accounting practices or routines have been institutionalised over time in the Plastics Division of Ferac International, a multi-national, multi-divisional company. In this case, management accounting routines have become the mutually accepted way of doing things in the organisation. The second case is the case of the Engineering Division of Omega Plc that has been previously discussed in Scapens and Roberts (1993). This case illustrates an unsuccessful change process due to the contradictions between the new management accounting rules and the existing routines and institutions.

A number of recent case studies (Bogt and Helden, 2000; Burns, 2000; Soin *et al.*, 2002; Burns *et al.*, 2003; Granlund, 2003) have been informed by Burns and Scapens' (2000) model of institutionalisation. Some of these studies have directly applied Burns and Scapens' (2000) framework without any modifications to the original model (e.g. Soin *et al.*, 2002; Burns *et al.*, 2003). Soin *et al.* (2002), for example, use Burns and Scapens' (2000) framework to interpret the introduction of an ABC system in the Clearing Department of a UK-based multi-national bank. The implementation of this system in banking context is considered revolutionary change, as the use of this type of management accounting systems is very limited. Soin *et al.* (2002) describe the implementation of the ABC system as a successful change process in which this system as a new routine is institutionalised over time and becomes the way things are done. However, this institutionalisation process does not affect the strategic thinking of the bank's top management.

On the other hand, Burns *et al.* (2003), drawing from four previously published cases, apply Burns and Scapens' (2000) framework to interpret two successful change cases and two other unsuccessful change cases. The successful cases are Polymer and Nuovo Pignone. In the first case, management accounting change in Polymer is seen as part of, and supporting, a larger process of changing organisational culture of the organisation from a production orientation to a customer orientation to become a world-class manufacturing organisation. The new ways of thinking that underpinned the new rules and routines do not challenge but extend the existing institutions within the organisation (i.e. the production-based culture) by directing the production process towards satisfying customers' needs. As such, this change can be characterised as evolutionary change.

In the second case, an Italian organisation, Nuovo Pignone, is acquired by a US parent company, General Electric. The acquisition initiates quick revolutionary change in the ways of thinking over a period of three years, especially the redesign of accountability systems and the implementation of Six-Sigma initiative (a measurement-based quality programme). This acquisition results in considerable uncertainty and feelings of anxiety within Nuovo Pignone that things are going to change. As a result, the organisation's existing institutions are questioned and a new set of assumptions has to be introduced. This institutional change is facilitated by the accountability systems and the quality measurement system as new rules and routines. However, the change process is based on the existing ways of thinking to construct the new institutions.

In addition, they describe two cases, RatailCO and Chemicals, where management accounting change was unsuccessful. The first case study describes resistance to management accounting change in a UK-based retail organisation. An economic value-added (EVA) system is implemented to replace the previous performance measurement system that is based on profit margins. However, this new system was suspended after its implementation six months later. This failure was a reflection of the resistance to change that arises within the organisation as a result of the conflicts between accountants and managers and the contradictions between the existing (sales- and margins-based) institutions and the new rules associated with EVA. The new routines that started to emerge failed to be reproduced, as there was no corresponding institutional change.

The second example of failure arising from management accounting change is the case of the Product Development Department (PDD) of Chemicals, a small UK chemicals manufacture. This case explores the difficulties facing the accounting change that challenges existing ways of thinking. A new account-ability system is introduced to PDD. The objective of implementing this system is to make the chief chemist, the head of PDD, more result-oriented. However, the new emergent routines have a negligible impact on the ways of thinking of the chief chemist and his staff about the nature of their activities as the new accountability system is not passed down to the members of staff of PDD, except its chief.

Contrary to the above studies that used Burns and Scapens' (2000) model, there are other studies that extended the basic model of Burns and Scapens (2000) by complementing it with other theories (e.g. Bogt and Helden, 2000; Burns, 2000). For instance, Burns' (2000) case study is the case of PDD that has been included in Burns *et al.* (2003). However, Burns (2000) introduces a modification to the original model of Burns and Scapens (2000). While Burns and Scapens' (2000) framework is grounded in the concept of power developed in structuration theory, Burns (2000) uses a complementary framework of power mobilisation developed by Hardy (1996). Hardy (1996) introduces four dimensions of power: power over resources; power over decision-making pro-cesses; power over meaning; and existing institutional context. Burns (2000) interprets his case study using these dimensions of power. He finds that all the first three dimensions of power act as facilitators of the change process while the fourth dimension of power acts as a barrier against change.

Bogt and Helden (2000) is another example of a modified version of Burns and Scapens' (2000) framework. They argue that the Burns and Scapens' (2000) model is a general one, deals only vaguely with the causes and mech-anisms of accounting change and can be improved by exploring the more broadly defined patterns of organisational change. They, therefore, extend the basic model of Burns and Scapens (2000) by two complementary approaches: a pragmatic approach and a behavioural approach. The first approach is devel-oped by Shields and Young (1989) in their attempt to describe the behav-ioural and organisational factors affecting the successful implementation of cost management systems. These factors comprise seven categories: culture, champion, compensation, controls, continuous education, commitment, and continuous improvement. The second approach is the behavioural theory of the firm developed by Cyert and March (1963). This theory is about information processing, decision-making and learning in organisations. It may be useful in describing the circumstances under which accounting change could occur.

Based on Burns and Scapens' (2000) model as a starting point, Bogt and Helden (2000) develop their own model. According to Bogt and Helden's (2000) model, there are two types of accounting gaps: development gap and usage gap. The former gap refers to the ideal idea of accounting rules and their ultimate development while the latter one refers to the difference between the developed accounting rules and their use in practice. Furthermore, there are different causes and mechanisms of accounting change, including external and internal pressures, organisational culture, initiator, organisational goals, and technical and organisational enablers. Bogt and Helden (2000) use their model to interpret changes in the financial management of eight Dutch governmental organisations in Netherlands. They find that the above two gaps are caused by a lack of budgetary pressure, insufficient commitment by top management, insufficient training and irrelevant compensation schemes.

3.3.3.3 Evaluating and extending Burns and Scapens' (2000) model

As mentioned above, Burns and Scapens (2000) draw on structuration theory and old institutional economics to develop their model. In this regard, Burns and Scapens (2000) use some key concepts of structuration theory such as institutions, actions, modalities, routines, reflexivity, crisis and routine situations, consciousness and unconscious, intended and unintended actions, etc. However, that is not to say that Burns and Scapens' (2000) model is totally consistent with structuration theory. It differs with some basic ideas of structuration theory such as the analytical dualism, synchrony/diachrony distinction, and pre-existence of institutions separated from actions. In some sense, it considers a use of the essence of structuration theory.

Burns and Scapens' (2000) framework is concerned primarily with management accounting change within individual organisations, that is, intra-organisational processes of change. Therefore, it does not take into account (extra-organisational) macro institutional pressures such as social, economic and political institutions of the organisational field and the society, which actually differ from one country to another. As a result, new institutional theory offers a possible extension of Burns and Scapens' (2000) model. The details of this theory will be presented later in section 3.5.3. In addition, Burns and Scapens (2000) do not address the issue of information technology in their framework. The incorporation of IT in Burns and Scapens' (2000) model is another extension. The IT models are explored in the next section.

3.4 Structuration theory and information technology

In this section, we critically explore the position of IT within structuration theory; introduce three IT models developed in IS literature to remedy the structuration theory's limitations in this regard; and present some applications of structuration theory from accounting literature that focuses on IT issues.

3.4.1   IT status in structuration theory: a critical evaluation

Giddens does not explicitly address the issue of technology in his structuration theory. Furthermore, there are very few references to IT in his structurational writings that might be useful in determining the position of IT. Starting with Giddens' belief about social structure, he argues that structure has only virtual existence as memory traces in human agents' heads. But is that view also applicable to material allocative resources such as technology?

Giddens (1984) argues that material allocative resources such as raw materials, land and technology that might be seen to have 'real existence', that is, that have a time-space presence, become resources only when incorporated in structuration processes. As such, technology, as a material artefact, is not a structure, constraining or enabling human action, except in its instantiations in human activities. Giddens emphasises this role of technology in structuration theory by saying that '[t]echnology does nothing, except as implicated in the actions of human beings' (Giddens and Pierson, 1998: 82).

For example, technology extends human co-presence and face-to-face interaction and changes temporal and spatial character of modern organisations. In this sense, Giddens (1984: 68) states that '...mediated contacts that permit some of the intimacies of co-presence are made possible in the modern era by electronic communication ...'. He also says that '[w]riting and other media of communication (telephone, television, mechanised modes of transportation) bind much greater distances in time and space' (Giddens, 1979: 103) and that 'the invention of electronic communication...has altered the pre-existing relation between presence and the sensory media of the body' (Giddens, 1984: 174).

In addition to the moments of resources use, Giddens identifies the moments of resources accumulation. He argues that resources can be stored, rendered present but unused and the technology is the media for storing and disseminating the knowledge about other resources, including technology itself. This view of the virtual existence of material allocative resources and the storage of resources has been criticised by a number of critics (Barbalet, 1987; Layder, 1987). Parker (2000), for instance, questions the applicability of a virtual existence concept to material allocative resources such as technology in structuration theory. He argues the virtual state is appropriate for the knowledge of rules, but this does not relate to material resources, which have their own temporalities. Furthermore, Parker (2000: 62) argues that the storage of resources means that they are not necessarily reproduced as they are used, and the logical condition of recursiveness is not a guarantee of social reproduction. He concludes that 'Giddens recognises that resources (structures) are not simply internal to agency...but pre-existing, objective, socially distributed conditions of action'. (p. 62). Indeed, material allocative resources are problematic for structuration theory as it means that part of the structure can not be carried in agents' minds and is not virtual when not being used in a particular time and space. In addition, the storage of resources and the knowledge about these resources in information media means that part of social structure is external to agency and can be embedded in information technology.

In sum, information technology in structuration theory is a material allocative resource that is not only drawn upon in the moments of use but also can be stored and used in storing and disseminating knowledge about other resources and rules. This role of information technology contributes in extending time and space boundaries and human co-presence and inter-actions. However, due to the absence of a clear and satisfactory detailed treatment of information technology in structuration theory, a number of IS researchers have developed models as extensions of structuration theory that specifically address information technology in organisations. Three of the most influential models in IS literature will be discussed and evaluated next.

3.4.2   IT models in IS literature

In this section we critically review three IT models from the IS literature to explore their potentialities to be integrated with Burns and Scapens' (2000) framework and structuration theory. These models are Barley (1986), Orlikowski (1992), and DeSanctis and Pool (1994).

3.4.2.1   Model of technology as a trigger of structural change

Barley's (1986) model is one of the earliest applications of structuration theory in IS research. It is interested in technically-driven organisational change. It describes the technology as an intervention into the relationship between human actors and social structure, which potentially modifies it. The new technology disturbs the routinised processes at the level of action that event-ually leads to change in structure – but with different outcomes at different organisations. This process is called 'soft determinism', where technology is considered as an external force having effects but these effects are moderated by human agents and organisational settings. Thus the role of new techno-logy in organisations is a material trigger that occasions similar social processes that lead to anticipated and unanticipated outcomes.

Barley (1986) employs a longitudinal case study to examine the imple-mentation of similar Computed Tomography (CT) scanners, as a new tech-nology, in two radiology departments. He finds that over time the actions of the radiologists and radiological technologists affect and are affected by the institutionalised practices within the organisations and that identical machines trigger similar social processes in the two hospitals but eventually lead to different outcomes such as increased decentralisation. In order to study how actions influence and are influenced by structure, Barley (1986) uses the concept of 'scripts', as 'outlines of recurrent patterns of interaction that define, in observable and behavioural terms, the essence of actors' roles' (p. 83).

The notion of scripts links social structure to agency, thereby replacing the concept of Giddens' modalities. In his study, Barley (1986) identifies different scripts, as social processes, in the two radiology departments such as 'direct seeking', 'clandestine teaching', or 'usurping the controls'. He takes detailed notes on these patterns of interactions between radiologists and radiological technologists to see how the long-term consequences of new technology emerge from the different scripts in the two hospitals.

Barley (1986) has been criticised because he treats technology – CT scanners with fixed and standardised forms and functions – largely as a 'black box' and does not allow for the physical modification of technology during use. However, this view is not generally appropriate in the case of information technology, as there is always a possibility of physically and socially modifying the technology by different users, by different contexts and the same users over time (Orlikowski, 1992). Barley (1986) also describes structuration theory as a form of 'soft determinism'. Such a view appears to contradict Giddens' claim of indeterminacy in social processes (Jones and Karsten, 2003).

This problem appears to be related to the method applied to identify various scripts rather than the concept itself, where Barley (1986) identifies similar patterns of interactions in the two hospitals as a way for facilitating the comparisons between them. In addition, Barley's (1986) model describes sequential, recursive pattern effects of actions and institutions on each other. This view is, to some degree, is inconsistent with what Giddens (1984) believes that institutions only exist insofar as they are instantiated in day-to-day activity. However, it may be justifiable to remedy the conflation problem in Giddens' theory as referred to above.

3.4.2.2 The structurational model of technology

Orlikowski (1992) has proposed a model, called 'structurational model of technology', extending the concept of the 'duality of structure' to the 'duality of technology' (see Figure 3.5). She argues that 'technology is created and changed by human action, yet it is also used by humans to accomplish some action' (p. 405). According to this view, technology is both the outcome and the medium of human action. The technology, on the one hand, is the product of human action as it is both physically constructed by designers and socially constructed by users at a certain time and organisational context. On the other hand, technology is the medium of human action, containing rules and resources that both enable and constrain different sorts of use.

Although defining technology as 'material artefacts (various configurations of hardware and software)', Orlikowski (1992: 403) claimed that this does not imply an 'exclusive focus on technology as a physical object'. Rather, she argued that technology should be seen as 'interpretively flexible'. Orlikowski (1992) argues that the interpretive flexibility of technology works in both design and use stages. In design stage, designers build into technology certain interpretive schemes, certain facilities and certain norms. In use stage, users

Figure 3.5 Orlikowski's (1992: 410) Model

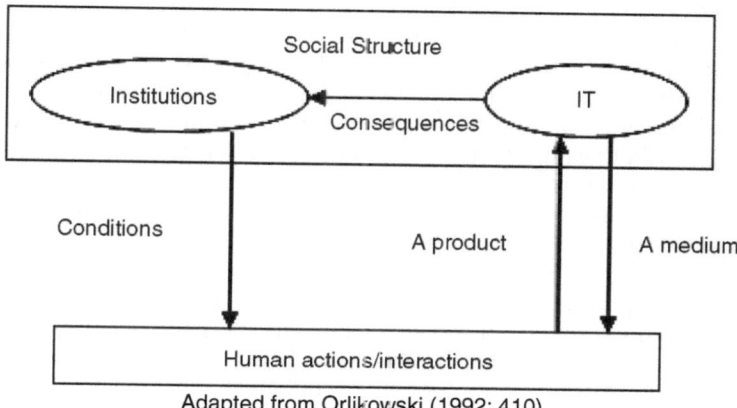

Adapted from Orlikowski (1992: 410)

interpret, appropriate and manipulate the technology's embedded rules and resources to execute their tasks. This means that technology is potentially modifiable at any time, both through deliberate redesign and through use that, accidentally or otherwise, deviates from ways intended by the developers.

Orlikowski's (1992) model overcomes some of Barley's (1986) limitations such as soft determinism and fixed technology. Nevertheless, this model still does not agree, in some aspects, with Giddens' (1984) view that structure, such as institutional properties and technology, is internal to human actors, as 'traces in the mind', drawn upon at the moment of interaction. Treating institutional properties and technology as being external to human agents leads to a dualism, the temporal separation between agency and structure, instead of a duality. In this regard, Jones and Karsten (2003: 12) states that 'to talk of structure being inscribed or embedded in artefacts is therefore inconsistent with Giddens' view, as it fixes in technology one half of the duality of action and structure, the inseparable linkage of which is a central feature of structuration theory'. However, this separation occurs in structuration theory as indicated above when addressing the storage problem of resources and knowledge. In her most recent article, Orlikowski (2000) addresses this limitation by focusing on 'technology-in-practice'. However, this separation may be necessary in order to avoid the conflation problem and the storage problem of resources and knowledge as mentioned above.

3.4.2.3   Adaptive structuration theory

DeSanctis and Pool (1994) have introduced one of the most influential technology models in IS literature, called 'adaptive structuration theory'. They suggest that their theory avoids the limitations of previous structurational models that rely on interpretive methods, give little attention to IT and focus mainly on institutional analysis. Adaptive structuration theory is based on a number of concepts. DeSanctis and Pool (1994) argue that the social structure of advanced information technologies is a template for planning and achieving tasks and can be described as structural features of the technology and the spirit of these features. The structural features are equivalent to Giddens' signification and domination structures, while the spirit of the technology's features is said to equate Giddens' legitimation structure.

Appropriation is another concept of adaptive structuration theory and refers to the 'immediate visible actions that evidence deeper structuration processes' (DeSanctis and Pool, 1994: 128). This concept is said to equate Giddens' modalities of structuration. According to DeSanctis and Pool (1994: 131), the following proposition could be developed: 'given advanced information technology and other sources of social structure and ideal appropriation processes, and decision processes that fit the task at hand, then desired outcomes of advanced information technology will result'.

There are a number of significant differences between adaptive structuration theory and Giddens' original structuration theory. For example, adaptive structuration theory is inconsistent with Giddens' ontological position. This theory takes a positivistic factor model approach rather than an interpretive process model approach. In addition, it views structure as concrete, persistent and independent of any action. This treatment violates Giddens' view that structure is virtual and is not independent of action but the two come together during interaction. As such, adaptive structuration theory is inappropriate for the current book as the authors adopt an interpretive approach, supported by Giddens, and focuses on the dynamics of change process.

3.4.3 Structuration theory and empirical evidence on IT in accounting literature

Structuration theory has been used to address the effect of IT on accounting practices (Dillard and Yuthas, 1997; Manson *et al.*, 2001; Caglio, 2003). For example, Dillard and Yuthas (1997) propose structuration theory as a tool to analyse IT and its implementation in organisations. They use a structurational framework to analyse a case study in which an IT investment decision is being taken by a large public accounting firm. The analysis attempts to make sense of the social processes working as the firm considers the implications of implementing IT to support audit, tax, and consulting partners.

Interestingly, Caglio (2003), using structuration theory, examines the role of ERP systems in changing management accountants' roles in organisations. Drawing on structuration theory, she conceptualises the potential change in accountants' roles as a structuration process and ERP systems as modalities of structuration. She concludes that ERP systems have changed management accountants' roles in organisations, leading to new hybrid positions as both IT and accounting experts. This process of hybridisation is neither predictable nor generalisable. Therefore, it depends on the circumstances surrounding change processes. The next section discusses the implications of structuration theory and its extensions for the current research.

3.5 Structuration theory and its extensions: implications for the current study

3.5.1 Structuration theory and the current study

Structuration theory has been introduced to overcome the dualism between objectivity (positivistic approach) and subjectivity (interpretive approach). It seems that Giddens adopts a post-empiricist and anti-positivist stance and emphasises the centrality of the interpretive endeavour, describing social science as 'irretrievably hermeneutic', that is, intrepretive (Giddens, 1976: 13). For instance, Layder (1987: 30 & 31) states that 'structuration theory is constantly forced to share the epistemological and ontological presuppositions of the very subjectivism that Giddens claims to have transcended'.

However, Giddens (1991: 219) does not reject the potential contribution of 'technically-sophisticated, hard-edged' research. Indeed in Giddens (1984), offering structuration theory as a critical theory, he states that 'I do not try to wield a methodological scalpel. That is to say, I do not believe that there is anything in either the logic or the substance of structuration theory which would somehow prohibit the use of ... survey methods, questionnaires or whatever' (p. xxx). He adds '... qualitative and quantitative methods should be seen as complementary rather than antagonistic aspects of social research' (p. 334). To achieve this, Giddens (1984) describes a particular use of quantitative methods. He states that 'quantitative techniques are usually likely to be demanded when a large number of "cases" of a phenomenon are to be investigated, ... But both the collection and interpretation of quantitative material depends upon procedures methodologically identical to the gathering of data of a more intensive, "qualitative" sort' (p. 333).

As such, Giddens' structuration theory can be described as a meta-theory, a way of thinking about the world rather than as empirically testable explanation of human conduct. As Archer (1990) puts it, structuration theory is 'fundamentally non-propositional', that is, it does not give us anything to test or to find out. This is acknowledged by Giddens (1989: 295) when he describes structuration theory as a generic theory. Giddens (1983: 77; 1992: 310) frequently states that structuration theory is not intended as a concrete research programme. He prefers the use of principles derived from it as 'sensitising devices' or to 'provide an explication of the logic of research into human social activities and cultural products' (Giddens, 1991: 213).

The use of structuration theory in the current study is consistent with Giddens' (1989: 294) view 'that the theory should be utilised only in a selective way in empirical work and should be seen more as a sensitising device than as providing detailed guidelines for research procedure'. This book draws on some concepts of structuration theory and uses structuration theory as a meta-theory and a sensitising tool. In addition, the authors share Giddens' interpretive stance. Therefore, the use of structuration theory, in combination with institutional theories, will focus on its interpretive standpoint.

3.5.2   IT models in IS literature and their role in the current study

Three IT models, grounded in structuration theory, have been discussed above. The first model, DeSanctis and Pool's (1994) adaptive structuration theory has been criticised because it is highly deterministic and adopts a positivistic approach, while the authors adopt an interpretive approach. The second model, Barley's (1986) work has been extended by Barley and Tolbert (1997) to combine new institutional sociology theory with structuration theory. This latter work forms the basis for Burns and Scapens' (2000) framework for conceptualising management accounting change.

As stated earlier, Burns and Scapens (2000) replace the notion of scripts in Barley and Tolbert's (1997) model with rules and routines to link structuration theory to old institutional economics theory. Therefore, the current study will benefit from the work of Barley (1986) as the implementation of ERP or customised software can be conceptualised as an 'occasion for structuring'. This concept is consistent with what Giddens (1984: 13) calls 'the cumulation of events deriving from an initiating circumstance without which that cumulation would not have been found'. Furthermore, the introduction of ERP or customised software is similar to the introduction of rules in Burns and Scapens' (2000: 7) framework, where 'rules are normally changed only at discrete intervals; but routines have the potential to be in a cumulative process of change as they continue to be reproduced'.

The current book will draw on some concepts of Orlikowski (1992), the third model. Orlikowski (1992) distinguishes between two iterative modes: the design mode and the use mode. This distinction, coupled with the interpretive flexibility view of technology, seems particularly appropriate for both custom software and ERP, as a configurable software package, and strongly suggests the applicability of structuration theory for the study of IT implementation and use. On the one hand, custom software is usually designed and used by the same organisation. It, therefore, tends to reflect the existing institutional properties of the organisation and may be easily modifiable during design and use stages. Orlikowski (1992: 409) states that 'initial designers of a technology have tended to align with managerial objectives...with the result that many technologies reinforce the institutional *status quo*, emphasising standardisation, control and efficiency'. This view may be justifiable on the ground that dominant groups in organisations tend to implement technologies in ways that sustain and reinforce their position (George and King, 1991).

ERP, on the other hand, is packaged software that is designed by vendor organisations and is used by customer organisations, two sets of players independent of each other. The institutional conditions and human actors involved in technology design are different from those involved in technology use. As a consequence, ERP, as a semi-finished product, tends to embody institutional properties in vendor organisations, which could exist in a different country with different meanings, norms and powers. However, ERP can be configured during the implementation process to match totally or partially the customer organisations' wishes. This adaptation process encodes the institutional properties of the customer organisations into the software. After the configuration process, if there is still a gap between the business process practices embedded in the software and the existing organisational processes, a decision could be made to change the organisational processes to handle certain processes outside the software or to change the base code. Each of these decisions has long-term effects on organisations. In addition, during ERP use modifications of designed systems features may occur gradually, through incremental patterns of use and non-use of these features. Notably, all these changes express the interpretive flexibility of ERP software.

Orlikowski's (1992) model bears some similarity to Burns and Scapens' (2000) model. It consists of four stages. The first stage describes the influence of institutional properties on humans' interactions with information technology (encoding stage in Burns and Scapens' model). The second stage considers information technology as a medium for human action, where IT facilitates and constrains human actions (enacting stage in Burns and Scapens' model). The third stage views information technology as a product of human action (reproduction stage in Burns and Scapens' model). The final stage reflects the influence of interaction with technology on institutional properties (institutionalisation stage in Burns and Scapens' model).

Furthermore, Orlikowski's (1992) interpretive flexibility view of technology is equivalent to the two-way relationship between rules and routines in Burns and Scapens' model. For example, according to Orlikowski (1992), custom software tends to reflect existing institutional properties of the organisation and is easily modifiable during design and use stages. In Burns and Scapens' (2000) words, this means that the 'new' IT-based rules could be a formalisation of existing routines and reinforce the institutional *status quo*.

Unlike Barley (1986), who considers IT as an action, Orlikowski (1992) treats IT as a structure. However, both views are consistent with Burns and Scapens' (2000) model. Burns and Scapens (2000) treat rules (or IT-embedded rules as will be used here) as modalities and argue that the position of rules could be closer either to actions or to structures. In this book, the new IT-embedded rules will be regarded as an action in the implementation phase and the new emergent routines as modalities in the use phase. Next, we address the use of new institutional sociology theory in the current study.

3.5.3 New institutional sociology theory and the current study

Two classical articles have introduced the concepts of 'new' institutional sociology theory. Drawing on the work of Berger and Luckmann (1966), Meyer and Rowan (1977) discuss institutionalisation as a process whereby institutional structures are legitimated without regard to the effectiveness of those structures and of the organisational members' feelings about the efficacy of those structures. In the same vein, DiMaggio and Powell (1983: 148) addressing the question of organisational structure and institutionalisation state that 'in the long run, organisational actors making rational decisions construct around themselves an environment that constrains their ability to change in future years'.

DiMaggio and Powell (1983: 148) introduce the concept of organisational fields and relate it to structuration theory, when saying '[f]ields only exist to the extent that they are institutionally defined. The process of institutional definition, or structuration, consists of four parts ...'. They define the organisational field as the organisations that constitute a recognised area of institutional life such as suppliers, customers and regulatory agencies. In structuration terms, there is a duality between the actions of organisations as actors in the field and social structure (the field). DiMaggio and Powell (1983) argue that the structuration process of an organisational field results in homogeneity within the field, where the organisations within the field tend to make organisational changes that make them very similar to each other.

There are three mechanisms (or structural properties) through which institutional isomorphic change occurs. Coercive isomorphism (domination structure) that is primarily related to the political influence exerted by institutions on which organisations depend for critical resources and long-term survival and the accompanying social expectations leading organisations to adopt particular practices to gain legitimacy. Normative isomorphism (legitimation structure) is the institutionalisation of social practices as a result of professionalisation by means of organisations such as professional bodies. Mimetic isomorphism (signification structure) stems from the tendency of organisations to imitate each other in response to symbolic uncertainty.

The work of DiMaggio and Powell (1983) has a number of applications in IT and accounting (Amat *et al.*, 1994; Hoque and Alam, 1999; Modell, 2001; Granlund and Malmi, 2002). For example, Liao (1996) suggests that organisations tend to invest in IT as a response to institutional pressures to maintain legitimacy and reduce uncertainty. In management accounting, Granlund and Lukka (1998) introduce an economic and institutional model to explain that there is a tendency towards global homogenisation of management accounting practices. They argue that economic, coercive, normative and mimetic pressures are the drivers of convergence or divergence of management accounting practices.

In addition to DiMaggio and Powell's (1983) concept of organisational field and its application to management accounting, the analysis in this book draws on the concept of deinstitutionalisation,[1] which refers to 'the processes by which institutions weaken and disappear... the weakening and disappearance of one set of beliefs and practices is likely to be associated with the arrival of new beliefs and practices' (Scott, 2001: 182 & 184). Oliver (1992) identifies three major sources of pressures for deinstitutionalisation: functional, political and social sources. Functional pressures arise from perceived problems in performance levels or the perceived utility associated with institutionalised practices. Political pressures result primarily from shifts in the interests and underlying power distributions that have supported and legitimated existing institutional arrangements. Finally, social pressures are associated with the differentiation of groups, the existence of heterogeneous divergent or discordant beliefs and practices, and change in laws or social expectations that might hinder the continuation of a practice.

Unlike deinstitutionalisation, de-structuration is unlikely to happen. In this regard, Giddens (1979: 70) argues that 'the most disruptive modes of social change, like the most rigidly stable forms, involve structuration. Hence, there is no need, nor any room, for a conception of de-structuration ...'. Instead, Giddens (1979: 220) introduces the concept of de-routinisation which refers to 'any influence that acts to counter the grip of the taken-for-granted character of day-to-day interaction'. He identifies three types of circumstances in which traditional practices, or traditions, may become undermined. The first type is the circumstances that act externally upon cold societies such as the effects of natural disasters or the establishing of dependence or conflict with societies of differing cultural composition. The second type is the emergence of diverging interpretations of established norms. The last type is the disavowal of tradition as a form of legitimation. So it can be said that deinstitutionalisation is equivalent to de-routinisation in structuration theory.

Burns and Scapens' (2000) framework is based, among others, on the work of Barley and Tolbert (1997). The latter work is a combination of structuration theory and new institutional sociology theory. However, Burns and Scapens' (2000) model does not explicitly incorporate new institutional theory into their work. But they recognise the importance of extra-organisational institutional pressures in affecting management accounting practices. In this study, Burns and Scapens' (2000) model will be complemented with new institutional theory to address the effect of extra-organisational institutional pressures on IT-triggered management accounting change. The next sub-section relates Burns and Scapens' (2000) model to the current book.

3.5.4 Burns and Scapens' (2000) framework in relation to the current study

Burns and Scapens' (2000) framework provides useful analytical tools to inform the interpretive approach adopted by this book. It is a sequential model that analytically separates the synchronic effects of institutions on actions, at a specific point in time, from the diachronic effects of actions on institutions, as a cumulative influence over time. This separation facilitates exploring change processes from the time of introducing new rules as an action, which is shaped by existing institutions, to the time of institution-alising such rules. In addition, the concept of routines, as programmatic rule-based behaviours, provides the link that explains how the new rules become institutions over time.

The model suggests that a first step in applying it is an analysis of the institutional realm with an identification of the initial set of rules and rou-tines that characterised management accounting in an organisation. Then, the analysis moves to the realm of action to identify the main actors and their relationship with the wider institutional realm. With the introduction of new IT-embedded rules, the analysis then identifies the processes of encoding and enactment as the new IT-embedded rules are introduced. One main issue in evaluating changes revolves around the issue of repro-duction. Do the changes become incorporated into new routines or are these changes simply one-shot interventions? Following that, the analysis enquires whether the new routines have implications for the wider insti-tutional realm of the organisation beyond the relatively limited domain of a particular department such as accounting department.

As stated earlier, Burns and Scapens' (2000) framework is highly related to structuration theory, IT models and new institutional theory. Therefore, it provides a co-ordinating tool for other theories and models, see Figure 3.6.

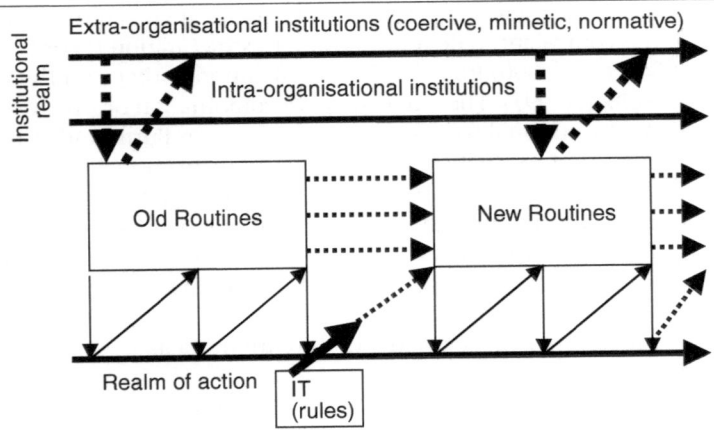

Figure 3.6   A Modified Version of Burns and Scapens' Model

3.5.5 The theoretical framework and research questions

The literature reviewed in Chapter 2 highlighted issues that warrant further considerations with respect to the changes to accounting practices and accountants' role. As stated in Chapter 1, the aim of the study is to compare analytically and empirically the adoption and use of ERP and custom software systems in practice, dealing especially with the management accounting function in Egyptian organisations. Specifically, this study addresses two groups of research questions.

The first group of questions examine stability and change in management accounting systems and practices, the conditions under which stability and/or change can occur and the role of IT in their occurrence. In addressing change in management accounting systems and practices, the authors draw on the concepts of rules and routines introduced by Burns and Scapens (2000). These concepts will be supplemented by Giddens' concepts of routine situations (trust), critical situations (anxiety) to understand the conditions and reasons for changing management accounting systems and practices.[2] In addition, the authors draw on the concept of IT-embedded knowledge supported by Orlikowski (1992, 2000), as well as Barley's (1986) concept of IT as an occasion for structuring, to explain the role of IT in management accounting change and stability. According to these concepts, ERP systems, on the one hand, may be considered as a change driver as best practices, including management accounting practices, which reflect institutional properties in advanced countries, are built into them. On the other hand, custom software may contribute in stabilising management accounting practices as it may embody existing institutional properties in a specific organisation. Furthermore, new institutional theory will be used to address the role of macro institutions such as headquarters and international agreements in inducing or impeding management accounting change associated with IT implementation and use.

The second group of questions focuses mainly on the changing role and relationships of management accountants due to the introduction of IT (ERP vs. custom software). In this regard, management accountants may lose their control over their works as most of their traditional role as information providers is built into IT and, therefore, their accounting knowledge may become easily transferable to IS staff and line managers because they can access timely real-time information. In contrast with this view, management accountants may still have control over their works and try to expand their role into other functional areas such as IT and production. In addressing the changing roles and relationships of management accountants in IT environments, the authors draw on structuration theory's concept of the dialectic of control or the relations of autonomy and dependence. In addition, new institutional theory will be used to address the role of macro institutions such as headquarters, consultants and international agreements in constraining or enabling management accountants' roles and relationships in the IT environment.

3.6 Conclusion and summary

This chapter presented the core concepts of structuration theory and its applications and extensions in accounting literature and IS literature. It identified structuration theory as a meta-theory that provides a way of thinking about the world and can be helpful in transcending objectivism and subjectivism positions. It also discussed Burns and Scapens' (2000) institutional framework as an extension of structuration theory to address management accounting change. But this model needs to be complemented, on one the hand, by IS models to deal with IT implementation and use and, on the other hand, by new institutional theory to take into account extra-organisational institutional pressures. Still, Burns and Scapens' (2000) model can not stand alone without consulting the parent theory, the structuration theory, which forms the main theoretical foundation of this model. The next chapter discusses the research methodology and methods of the empirical study.

Notes

1 The inclusion of deinstitutionalisation into the analysis overcomes a major limitation of new institutional sociology theory discussed in Chapter 2.
2 As argued in the previous chapter ERP is related to evolutionary change (routine situations) and revolutionary change (crisis situations).

4

Research Methodology and Methods

4.1 Introduction

The previous chapter discussed the theoretical framework that this study uses to analyse the empirical results. This chapter describes the design and implementation of the empirical phase of the study. It explores the research methodology and techniques used to collect empirical data. The remainder of this chapter is divided into seven sections. Section 4.2 presents different research methodologies and their relation to theory and research method selection. Section 4.3 discusses the interpretive case study as the preferred method for collecting empirical data. Section 4.4 describes the pilot case study that clarified the research issues and research design. Section 4.5 describes the design of the case study and the organisations and individuals chosen for the empirical study. Section 4.6 discusses data collection methods particularly the use of semi-structured interviews which was selected as the main method. Section 4.7 discusses the weaknesses and problems of the case study method. The last section provides a summary and conclusion.

4.2 Research methodology, theory and research method selection

A research methodology is 'a general approach to studying research topics' (Hussey and Hussey, 1997: 56), which is distinct from a research method. A research method is a tool or a technique that is used to gather data (Bailey, 1994). In contrast, a research methodology determines the important relationship between theory and method. It is associated with specific ontological and epistemological views (theory) which may help researchers to select an appropriate research method (Morgan and Smircich, 1980; Bryman, 1984; Laughlin, 1995). For example, Morgan and Smircich (1980: 491) state that '...the choice and adequacy of a method embodies a variety of assumptions regarding the nature of knowledge and the methods through which that knowledge can be obtained, as well as a set of root assumptions about the nature of the phenomena to be investigated'. This implies that the theory and methodology choices are arguably related in a simple linear way. Therefore, the research methodology may be regarded as an 'intricate set of ontological and epistemological assumptions that a researcher brings to his or her work' (Prasad, 1997: 2). Chua (1986) points out that the ontology of knowledge lies prior to and governs subsequent epistemological and methodological assumptions.

All empirical theories are rooted in an ontological assumption about the nature of the social world, that is, the very essence of the phenomena under study. With regard to this assumption, Burrell and Morgan (1979) introduce an objective-subjective dichotomy. On the one hand, the objectivist, or positivist, perspective assumes the existence of concrete, real, objects, artefacts, and relationships that can be quantified and examined through the scientific research methodology or the natural science model of social science. On the other hand, the subjectivist, or interpretive, perspective sees the social reality as 'an emergent social process which is created by the individual concerned' (Burrell and Morgan, 1979: 28). This world can be studied through the naturalistic research methodology that involves greater, if not exclusive, use of qualitative data. This implies that the nature of the social reality usefully dictates the appropriateness of research methodology and methods.[1] As Tomkins and Groves (1983: 366 & 367) put it, '...where meanings of variables are stable, the "scientific" methodology is quite appropriate...' (p. 366). In addition, '...in so far as accounting research is concerned with the effects of accounting practices upon social action whether that action relates to accounts producers, users or those affected, there is a case for examining "naturalistic" research approaches' (p. 367).

Giddens' structuration theory, which has been presented in Chapter 3, has been introduced to create a balanced treatment between objectivity (positivistic perspective) and subjectivity (interpretive perspective). However, Giddens adopts an interpretive stance. Structuration theory shares the ontological and epistemological assumptions of the very subjectivism (Layder, 1987). With regard to adopting an appropriate research method, Giddens (1984) does not dictate the use of particular research methods. Rather, he sees that '...qualitative and quantitative methods should be seen as complementary...' (p. 334). However, '[s]ome considerations brought into play are relevant to the mode of application of particular techniques to research questions and to the interpretation of results...' (p. xxx). For example, 'quantitative techniques are usually likely to be demanded when a large number of "cases" of a phenomenon are to be investigated ... But both the collection and interpretation of quantitative material depends upon procedures methodologically identical to the gathering of data of a more intensive, "qualitative" sort' (p. 333).

Most empirical management accounting studies informed by structuration theory are based on a naturalistic research methodology and a case study method (e.g. Scapens and Roberts, 1993; Granlund, 2001; Caglio, 2003). It seems that the case study method better suits the essence of structuration theory. Macintosh and Scapens (1990) propose the use of structuration theory for understanding management accounting practices in its organisational, social and political contexts. They contend that '[s]tructuration theory offers a framework with the potential to make useful contributions to management accounting research, particularly as a framework for case studies of management accounting practice' (p. 469). As stated earlier, Burns and Scapens (2000) extended structuration theory by introducing an institutional framework to explore the complex web of social processes which comprise management accounting change.

A slightly modified version of Burns and Scapens' (2000) institutional framework, which is grounded in structuration theory and is regarded as its extension, has been adopted as the theoretical framework of this study. As explained in Chapter 3, Burns and Scapens' (2000) framework needs to be complemented by IS models, new institutional theory and structuration theory. Burns and Scapens (2000) suggest using their framework for informing interpretive case studies, that is, a naturalistic research approach. They state that '[i]t should be emphasised that this framework is not intended to provide operational constructs for empirical research and hypothesis testing. Rather, its purpose is to describe and explain analytical concepts which can be used for interpretive case studies of management accounting change. These concepts will be useful in so far as they focus the attention of researchers (and also possibly practitioners) on the fundamental characteristics of change processes' (p. 9). As a consequence, an interpretive case study method has been selected for the empirical work. The case study method is discussed in the next section.

4.3 Case study method: definition and justification

A case study is 'an empirical inquiry that investigates a contemporary phenomenon within its real context when the boundaries between phenomenon and context are not clearly evident and in which multiple sources of evidence are used' (Yin, 1994: 13). This definition reflects the conditions under which a case study method is appropriate. To judge the appropriateness of the case study method, Benbasat *et al.* (1987: 372) introduce the following questions:

1. Can the phenomenon of interest be investigated outside its natural setting?
2. Must the study focus on contemporary events?
3. Is control or manipulation of subjects or events necessary?
4. Does the phenomenon of interest enjoy an established theoretical base?

According to these conditions, the case study method is useful when there is a need to study a contemporary phenomenon, which is neither controlled nor supported by a strong theoretical base, in its natural setting. This at once distinguishes case study research, not only from experiments, which seek to divorce the phenomenon under investigation from its context, but also from historical studies, which do not study contemporary events, and surveys, which attempt to limit the number of variables under study (Bergen and While, 2000). However, Spicer (1992) argues that case study research may also be exceptionally used in experimental settings where the researcher does have control over treatments.

Case study research can be categorised into five different types based on the primary objective of the research (Ryan *et al.*, 2002). Descriptive case studies aim at describing current accounting practices. Illustrative case studies seek to illustrate new and possibly innovative accounting practices used by particular companies. Experimental case studies are used to investigate the difficulties and benefits of implementing new accounting methods. Exploratory case studies are useful in areas where there are few theories to explore the reasons for particular accounting practices and can help generating hypotheses about these reasons. Finally, explanatory case studies use existing theory in order to understand and explain the reasons for observed accounting practices.

Studying a phenomenon within its context is a distinct feature of case study research. Eisenhardt (1989: 534) states that the case study focuses on understanding the dynamics present within single settings. The importance of the context is essential and Yin (1994: 13) seems clear that the case study will necessarily include data relating to that context because the researcher 'deliberately wanted to cover contextual conditions'. Furthermore, Scapens (1990: 278) argues that case study research is useful for exploring the day-to-day accounting practices of real people in the context in which they work. However, there are different meanings of the context in different research methodologies.

The context in the positivistic methodology reflects the fact that this methodology is grounded in a belief that accounting practices are natural phenomena. It refers to the technical environment where products and services are exchanged in a market situation and organisations are rewarded for effectiveness and efficiency (Otley, 1980; Alam, 1997). For example, the contingency perspective suggests that the design of management accounting systems is dependent on the specific circumstances in which an organisation operates. The technical or task environment in contingency theory is often referred to through such polarities as 'stable' versus 'dynamic' and 'simple' versus 'complex'. As discussed in Chapter 2, there are a number of case studies on management accounting change that are based on the positivistic methodology (e.g. Innes and Mitchell, 1990; Cobb *et al.*, 1995; Kasurinen, 2002).

Hopwood (1985) stresses the need to explore accounting practice in its wider context, rather than emphasise its technical aspect. From an interpretive standpoint, accounting practices are socially constructed. As a result, these practices should be located in their historical, economic, organisational, social and institutional contexts (Burns, 1996). For example, the institutional context is 'characterised by the elaboration of rules and requirements to which individual organisations must conform if they are to receive support and legitimacy' (Scott and Meyer cited in Alam, 1997: 148).

Ryan *et al.* (2002) provide a detailed comparative analysis of the role of case studies in positivist and interpretive methodologies, see Table 4.1. From the positivistic perspective, a case study is a small sample that cannot be used to make a statistical generalisation about the population from which it is drawn. However, it is useful in providing limited tests and developing hypotheses that will be tested by other research methods such as surveys. Scapens (1990) argues that case studies, informed by positivistic theories, deal with aggregates not specifics. Therefore, these theories are unable to provide suitable explanations for individual cases. According to these theories, the scientific explanation is a process of deduction in which a particular relationship is explained by deducing it from general laws. As a consequence, they fail to locate accounting practice in its historical, economic, social and institutional contexts.

On the other hand, case studies in the interpretive methodology are considered as a method by which theories are used to explain observations. They seek to provide theoretical generalisations so that theories explain the observations that have been made. Interpretive case studies adopt a holistic approach in which the relationships between various parts of the system and the system's own relationship with its context serve to explain the system. This type of explanation is called the pattern model of explanation that views case studies as a way to explain social practices in a particular set of circumstances. It is helpful in establishing a two-way relationship between theory and observation. According to this relationship, theories will be used as a means for explaining observations, and the latter will be used to modify the former. Hence, Scapens (1990) believes that explanatory case studies are an essential part of the interpretive methodology and other types of case studies can be useful in some instances.

This study takes the form of interpretive case study research to explain management accounting change triggered by IT (custom vs. ERP software) implementation. There are three reasons for adopting this research method. First, since early 1980s, several scholars have highlighted the need for more

Table 4.1 Differences in Case Study Research

Type of Research	Positive	Interpretive
View of the world	External and objective	Social construction
Types of case study	Exploratory	Explanatory
Nature of explanation	Deductive	Pattern
Nature of generalisation	Statistical	Theoretical
Role of theory	Hypothesis generation	Understanding
Nature of accounting	Economic decision-making	Object of study

Adapted from Ryan *et al.* (2002: 146).

management accounting case studies (Hopwood, 1983; Kaplan, 1983; Caglio, 2003). Otley and Berry (1994: 47), introducing the advantages of case studies, state that '... case studies are likely to be most valuable where they are clear about their initial theoretical position and where they consciously attempt to develop their own theoretical modifications, however tentative'.

Second, this type of case study has been selected since little research has adopted this method for investigating the introduction and implementation of ERP studies. In recent years there has been a call for detailed interpretive case studies of ERP implementations (Caglio, 2003; Scapens and Jazayeri, 2003). Scapens and Jazayeri (2003), for example, state that 'the paper ends with a call for further longitudinal case studies of the implementation of ERP systems to study ... [the] processes of management accounting change in other companies'. In response to this call, this study will conduct a cross-sectional case study that compares management accounting practices in ERP adopters and non-ERP adopters.

Third, interpretive case study research has been undertaken because it promises a rich description of social, cultural and political contexts. The role of case studies in interpretive methodology, which is based on a belief that accounting practices are socially constructed, is to locate practice in its historical, as well as its economic, social and organisational contexts in order to help understanding the social structures which shape current practice. In this regard, this study adopts explanatory case study research in order to understand management accounting change associated by IT (custom vs. ERP software) implementation in Egyptian social, cultural, political and institutional contexts that shape and are shaped by management accounting practices. The next section presents details of the pilot study.

4.4 Pilot study

Yin (1994) states that pilot studies can be considered as a final preparation for data collection. It helps in refining data collection plans with regard to research design and field procedures. In this regard, a pilot study differs from a pre-test in which the intended data collection plan is tested as a final test run. The pilot study is interested in substantive and methodological issues. It focuses on substantive issues when it provides considerable insight into the basic issues being studied. Methodologically, the pilot study can provide information about relevant field questions and about the logistics of the field inquiry.

In August 2003, a pilot study was conducted prior to the selection of specific information technologies for the final data collection and prior to the final articulation of the study's theoretical framework. The purpose of the pilot study was to finalise research issues and case or cases that would be included in the case study design, especially the organisations that have recently implemented ERP systems and the impacts of these systems on accounting systems and practices. Preliminary structured interview questions were developed to cover ERP implementation processes and their possible associated changes in management accounting methods and management accountants' roles and relationships.

Initially, two large companies in Egypt, AQF and NEEASAE, were visited. The choice of these organisations was based on prior knowledge that they have implemented advanced computerised systems in managing their operations. The interviews with financial executive officers and IT (IS) managers revealed that neither of these organisations currently have ERP systems. One of them, NEEASAE, which is owned by the Egyptian government and has not been privatised yet, actually started implementing an ERP system and, after a period of time, abandoned this project. The other one, AQF, which has recently been partially privatised, uses custom software developed especially to satisfy its information requirements.

As the initial objective for the pilot study was to identify organisations that had recently implemented ERP systems and exploring associated management accounting change issues, the authors sent e-mails to some international ERP vendors to ask for their help in this research and any information about their selling agents/branches in Egypt. By contacting local ERP vendors, two organisations that had recently adopted ERP systems were chosen. The interviews with financial executive officers and IT (IS) managers were conducted to explore ERP implementation processes and management accounting change. One of the two organisations, Industrial Modernisation Centre (IMC), is a governmental unit that has successfully implemented an ERP system (Baan brand) and the other one, Coca-Cola Egypt Co., is a recently privatised company that has implemented an ERP system (Oracle brand) and works as a subsidiary of the USA parent company.

The pilot data were used in conjunction with an ongoing review of relevant literature on IT implementation and management accounting change, so that the final research design could be informed by both prevailing theories and by a fresh set of empirical observations. The dual sources of information help to assure that the study to be done reflects significant theoretical issues as well as questions relevant to contemporary cases. These data have led to changes in research design and data collection plan as follows:

1. Two possible contributions can be added to accounting literature on ERP and management accounting change by:
   a) Including governmental units that have implemented ERP; and
   b) Making comparisons between custom software adopters and ERP adopters,
2. The case study design was modified from a single-case design to a multiple-case design,
3. The selection of final cases that were included in the case study design,
4. The theoretical framework was modified to allow to make comparisons between ERP (as a special type of packaged software) and custom software, and

5. The main data collection method was altered from structured interviews to semi-structure interviews to capture participants' views, perceptions and opinions about the issues raised.

4.5   Multiple-case design and site selection

Central to case study design is the decision to include one or multiple cases in the research. A researcher can use single-case designs in specific instances such as a revelatory case, a critical case, or an extreme or unique case (Yin, 1994). A revelatory case is a case that is previously inaccessible to scientific invest-igation. A critical case can be used to determine whether a well-formulated theory provides good explanations. An extreme or unique case is appropriate to extend existing theory to provide explanations in widely differing circum-stances. In situations where there is a little available theory, Scapens (1990) argues for using an exploratory case to begin the process of theory develop-ment that will be extended as additional cases are added.

Multiple case studies allow cross-case analysis to be used for building a rich theoretical framework (Perry, 1998). Rejecting representativeness, which dom-inates the positivistic perspective,[2] as the criteria for case selection, Yin (1994)

Figure 4.1   Replication Approach to Case Study Method

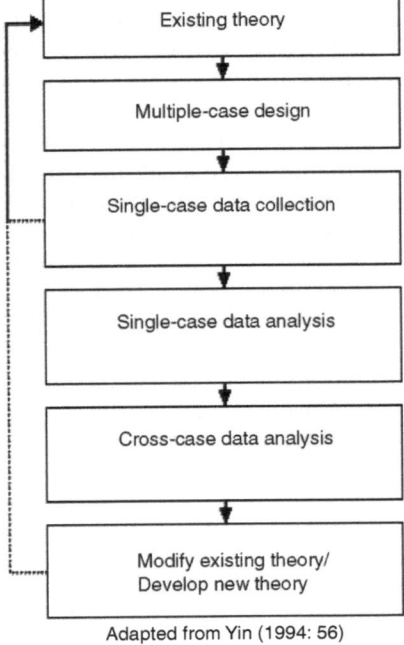

Existing theory

Multiple-case design

Single-case data collection

Single-case data analysis

Cross-case data analysis

Modify existing theory/
Develop new theory

Adapted from Yin (1994: 56)

proposes two criteria for selecting multiple case studies. First, cases where similar results are predicted for predictable reasons may be chosen for 'literal' replications. The purpose of using similar cases is to replicate the theoretical explanations. Second, cases that produce contrary results for predictable reasons may be used to pursue different patterns of 'theoretical' replications. The objective of selecting dissimilar cases is to extend the theoretical explanations. Other researchers support this method of case selection (Eisenhardt, 1989; Stake, 1994; Patton, 2002). For instance, Eisenhardt (1989: 537) states that the 'random selection of cases is neither necessary, nor even preferable'. The replication approach to multiple-case studies is illustrated in Figure 4.1.

As stated earlier, the main objective of this research is to understand the management accounting consequences of IT implementation in Egyptian organisations. The multiple-case design is considered appropriate for explaining management accounting change triggered by IT implementation. Two criteria have been used for selecting case study sites: the type of software and the type of organisation. First, two types of IT implementation are central to this research: custom software and ERP as a special type of packaged software. Second, two types of Egyptian organisations constitute case study sites: state-owned enterprises and governmental units. Based on these criteria, four case study sites have been chosen to explore two management accounting consequences: change in management accounting practices and change in management accountants' role and relationships (see Table 4.2).

The choice of four organisations is undertaken for several reasons. First, it satisfies the criteria suggested by Yin (1994) for selecting multiple case studies. The selected organisations comprise both similar and dissimilar cases. Therefore, this selection achieves both the theoretical replications and the theoretical extensions and, ultimately, provides a rich theoretical framework, capable of understanding management accounting change in widely differing circumstances. Second, a multiple-case design and site selection overcome some limitations of prior research such as the difficulty in differentiating between ERP adopters and non-ERP adopters and the inattention paid to ERP adoption by governmental units. Thirdly, the four organisations are illustrative

Table 4.2   A Multiple-Case Design and Site Selection

Type of Organisation / Type of Software	State-owned Enterprises	Governmental Units
Custom software	Abu Qir Fertilisers Co. (AQF)	General Sales Tax Organisation (ESTD)
Packaged software (ERP)	El Naser Electric and Electronic Apparatus Co. (NEEASAE)	Industrial Modernisation Centre (IMC)

of the economic transition in Egypt because they are highly influenced by economic and structural programmes that have been undertaken to transform Egypt from a centrally planned economy to a free market-oriented economy. For instance, AQF and NEEASAE were influenced by the privatisation programme in their implementation of IT projects. Finally, the selection of organisations reflects the level of access gained during the course of conducting the empirical work.

Gaining access to case study sites was achieved by two ways. First, the choice of organisations adopting ERP systems was mainly based on contacting international ERP vendors, especially SAP, Oracle and Baan. In August 2003, e-mails were sent to some key ERP vendors, asking for their help in this research and any information about their selling agents/ branches in Egypt. These vendors were helpful and provided some details on their agents/branches in Egypt. Unfortunately, the SAP branch in Egypt refused to help the authors to gain access to any of its customers. On the other hand, Baan and Oracle agents offered two organisations (one customer of each vendor), namely Coca-Cola Egypt Co. and IMC. Coca-Cola Egypt Co. is a subsidiary for the USA parent company and has recently implemented an ERP system (Oracle brand) under the pressures of its parent company to improve and control its operations in Egypt. IMC is a non-for-profit organisation (a governmental unit) that is financed by both the European Union (EU) and the Egyptian government. This organisation has recently implemented an ERP system (Baan brand) to get the support of its sponsors and satisfy their information requirements.

The above two organisations, as well as AQF and NEEASAE, formed the basis for the pilot study. In 2004 field interviews were conducted between July and September to collect the empirical evidence. However, Coca-Cola Egypt Co. was excluded because an internal auditing enquiry by the parent company was being undertaken during the planned period for interviews. Therefore, this company was replaced with NEEASAE, a public sector enterprise that failed to implement Baan software. It was decided to include two organisations, which use the same ERP brand but one organisation successfully implemented the software and the other failed in implementation, to understand the similarities and differences between their experiences and clearly demonstrate the difficulties facing ERP implementation in Egypt.

Second, the organisations adopting custom software systems were selected by visiting some companies known for their use of advanced computerised systems in managing their operations. This knowledge has been acquired through the authors' previous experience with some companies, newspapers and TV commercials. From some visited organisations, two were chosen, namely, AQF and ESTD. AQF, previously included in the pilot study, was recently partially privatised and adopted a tailored system developed especially to meet its needs. ESTD is a governmental unit that mainly collects sales tax revenues. This organisation has recently implemented custom software systems as part of a wider budget reform suggested by the World Bank.

In addition to the four organisations under study, an additional five companies were visited but the interviews and other evidence collected from these cases were not comprehensive. These companies were chosen to test the interviews' questions and to provide potential alternative sites in case of unexpected circumstances in the main selected cases. They are as follows:

1. DELTA for Construction & Rebuilding (custom software),
2. MASHREQ for Commercial Investment (ERP-Oracle brand),
3. KIRIAZI for Electric Apparatus (ERP-Baan brand), and
4. Egyptian Swedish Welding Electrodes Co (ERP-Baan brand).
5. Sea Scout Society (custom software).

Following the selection of research sites, a formal written permission was obtained from the Central Agency for Public Mobilisation and Statistics (CAPMS) to facilitate the collection of data. According to the Presidential Decree No. 2915 of 1964, CAPMS is considered as the official source of providing all the State's agencies, authorities, universities, research centres and international organisations with data, statistics and reports that serve in the activities of planning, development, evaluation, drawing policies and decision-making. It also authorises the collection of data from these organisations. Therefore, its permission was necessary for this research, taking into account the nature of organisations under study, that is, government agencies and state-owned enterprises. In fact, this formal approval was useful, especially in the case of NEEASAE. In NEEASAE, the CEO tried to limit the number of interviewees but the approval and authorisation from CAPMS was helpful in solving this matter.

In addition to this formal support, informal personal contacts were very effective in accessing and collecting a lot of evidence. For example, the selection of the organisations that implemented ERP systems was based on informal contacts with ERP vendors, internationally and locally. The ERP vendors continued their support throughout the field work. Furthermore, one of the authors was an observer at two meetings of the budget reform project team in ESTD. The access to these meetings was facilitated by some professors at Alexandria University. In addition, friendly relations were established with some staff in the selected organisations during field interviews. These relations continued and were fruitful in making some inquiries via e-mail or by phone calls during data analysis. The next section introduces data collection methods.

4.6   Data collection methods

Multiple data collection methods are typically used in case study research in order to obtain a rich set of data surrounding the specific research issues, as well as to capture the contextual complexity (Benbasat *et al.*, 1987). Typical sources of evidence that work well in case study research include interviews, documentation, direct (non-participant) observation and participant observation (Scapens, 1990; Yin, 1994). In this study, multiple sources of evidence were collected (see Table 4.3 and Appendix 5). However, the semi-structured interviews were the main vehicle of research. Other evidence included background questionnaire, documentary evidence, e-mails, phone calls, direct observation and participant observation. Reference is also made to publicly available data sources such as the organisations' published accounts, DataStream, newspaper articles and websites. These multiple methods are deliberately selected as one method can complement others. This triangulation tends to improve the validity of evidence.

From Table 4.3, it is worth noting that the use of direct and participant observations was not previously planned. It unintentionally occurred during field interviews. For instance, during a visit to IMC, the Financial Policy Manager showed the authors an e-mail received from Programme Co-ordinator to explain an occasion for transferring funds from a budget line to another. Another situation occurred in NEEASAE when a cost accountant offered a visit to a plant for manufacturing bulbs and explained the whole production processes for bulbs. In ESTD, during the period of interviews, the budget reform project team held a number of meetings. Two of these meetings were attended. During one of these meetings, the project team asked one of the authors to give his opinion about their work.

Table 4.3   Summary of Different Types of Data Sources

		Government Units		Public Sector Companies	
Data Sources		**IMC**	**ESTD**	**NEEASAE**	**AQF**
Number of	Tape Recorded	3	1	–	–
Interviews	Notes taken	4	21	7	9
Background Questionnaire		YES	YES	YES	YES
Documentary Evidence		YES	YES	YES	YES
CDs/Floppy Disks		YES	YES	NO	NO
E-mails		YES	NO	NO	NO
Phone calls		NO	YES	NO	NO
Direct and Participant Observations		YES	YES	YES	YES
Web Sites		YES	YES	YES	YES
Printed Screens from Software used		YES	YES	YES	YES
Meetings or Committees attended		NO	YES (2)	NO	NO
Publications (articles, DataStream,...etc)		YES	YES	YES	YES

– See the details of this evidence in Appendices (5 and 6).

In interpretive research, the validity of evidence can only be assessed in the context of the particular case, what Scapens (1990) called 'contextual validity'. In this regard, Scapens (1990) suggests the triangulation of evidence[3] by collecting different evidence on the same research issue, collecting other evidence from the same source and working in teams in order to reach an agreed interpretation of a particular case. As a consequence, the use of multiple sources of evidence in this study is justifiable on the grounds of increasing the contextual validity of research evidence. In addition, the sources of data collection are selected to elicit the type of data required to answer each research question.

As stated earlier, the research questions are divided into two main groups. The first group of research questions, which will be addressed in Chapter 6, focuses on change in management accounting systems (rules) and practices (routines) triggered by IT (ERP vs. custom software) projects as follows:

- Why and how are institutionalised management accounting practices persisted (reproduced) and/or transformed in the IT (ERP vs. custom software) environment? And
- What is the role of IT (ERP vs. custom software) in management accounting change and/or stability?

The second group of research questions, which will be addressed in Chapter 7, concerns change in management accountants' role and relationships with IT specialists and line managers due to the introduction of IT (ERP vs. custom software) projects as follows:

- How does IT (ERP vs. custom software) maintain or change the relationships of management accountants with different organisational members (IS staff and line managers) within the organisation? And
- What is the role of management accountants in the IT (ERP vs. custom software) environment as perceived by management accountants themselves and other members of the organisation?

The data required for the above research questions can be divided into two levels with various types of data under each level. Firstly, at the extra-organisational institutional level, the data are about the external institutional context of management accounting. The focus here is on institutions that create, facilitate or impede the need for adopting new accounting methods and IT facilities at the macro level such multinational headquarters, national laws, etc. These data were mostly extracted from literature and other documents such as laws, media reports, newspapers, government announcements and websites. Examples of websites visited are in Table 4.4.

Table 4.4　Some Important Web Sites Visited in Relation to Extra-Institutions

Organisation	Web Site Address
European Commission	http://europa.eu.int/comm/europeaid/index_en.htm
EU delegation in Egypt	http://www.eu-delegation.org.eg/EUFund.htm
Privatisation Co-ordination Support Unit	http://CARANA.COM/PCSU
OECD Development Centre	http://www.oecd.org
International Monetary Fund (IMF)	http://www.imf.org
Ministry of Finance	http://www.salestax.gov.eg/
Al-Ahram Weekly	http://weekly.ahram.org.eg/
World Bank	http://www1.worldbank.org/
Information Centre for the Cabinet in Egypt	http://www.sis.gov.eg/

Secondly, the intra-organisational institutional level focuses on the different types of data collected from the four organisations under study, particularly the following data:

a) Accounting methods and procedures adopted by organisations, changes in these methods and procedures over time and their relationships with IT. Examples of such methods and procedures are budgets and budgeting, allocation costs methods and procedures and performance evaluation systems;
b) IT facilities such as ERP or custom software and IT platform and infrastructure;
c) The interests and backgrounds of key organisational members of interest, mainly accountants, IS (IT) staff, and line managers;
d) The interactions between accountants and other organisational members and their uses of IT and accounting information; and
e) The internal context of organisations under investigations such as historical developments, organisational structure, authorities and responsibilities.

At this level semi-structured interviews were used to collect data about accounting practices, IT practices, and interactions among key organisational members. A background questionnaire was conducted to collect information from key organisational members, in particular on their education, skills, training and experiences in accounting and IT (see Appendix 4). Data about the internal context of organisations were collected from documents such as internal forms and records, published financial statements, DataStream and websites.

From the above discussion it is clear that semi-structured interviews with key organisational members would be the most appropriate data collection method for this case study research. Therefore, the next sub-section presents the design of semi-structured interview questions guided by the theoretical framework in order to address the research questions.

4.6.1 Design of interview questions and theoretical framework

Scapens (1990: 274) states that '...in any case study there will be considerable prior theory ... [that] will give an initial indication of the types of evidence which should be looked for in the case study'. According to Miles and Huberman (1994), the theoretical framework is simply the current version of the researcher's map of the territory being investigated. It involves deciding on ontological and epistemological assumptions (Laughlin, 1995). The world is normally approached with a framework (ontology) that specifies a set of questions (epistemology) that are then examined (methodology) in certain ways (Denzin and Lincoln, 1994: 9). As a consequence, the theoretical framework gives guidelines for setting research questions and collecting empirical data (sub-questions). With regard to this study, Table 4.5 presents the relation of theoretical framework to interview issues and other data sources.

As semi-structured interviews are the main data collection method, this sub-section describes the design of interview questions. Interviews are a data collection method that seeks to find out what participants do, think or feel by asking them questions (Hussey and Hussey, 1997). In the positivistic perspective, these questions take the form of structured or closed questions. On the other hand, unstructured or semi-structured interviews based on open-ended questions are essential in the interpretive perspective. Easterby-Smith *et al.* (1991) suggest that semi-structured interviews are a useful data collection method when:

1. It is necessary to understand the construct that an interviewee uses as a basis for his or her opinions and beliefs about a particular matter or situation,
2. One aim of the interview is to develop an understanding of the respondent's world so that the researcher might influence it,
3. The step-by-step logic of a situation is not clear,
4. The subject matter is highly confidential or commercially sensitive, and
5. The interviewee may be reluctant to be truthful about this issue other than confidentially in a one-to-one situation.

The authors identified 45 organisational members from the four organisations under study for interviews (see Appendix 5). They are divided into three main categories,[4] namely accountants (19), IT specialists (15) and line

Table 4.5   Theoretical Framework and Data Sources

Theoretical Framework	Data Sources
Extra-organisational Institutional Level (Institutional Analysis)	
• **Coercive pressures and deinstitutionalisation:** – Coercive pressures such as laws/ headquarters influence/international agreements that constrain and enable management accounting changes and IT projects – Reform programmes such as privatisation and IMP	– Literature review – Documentary evidence such as laws/media reports/newspapers/ government announcements/ websites
Intra-organisational Institutional Level (Strategic Conduct Analysis)	
• **Social change (management accounting change):** – Management accounting systems (rules or explicit knowledge) – Management accounting practices (routines or tacit knowledge) • **IT-embedded knowledge: IT as a trigger for change:** – The role of IT in the occurrence of management accounting change • **Routine (trust) and critical (anxiety) situations:** – Conditions and reasons for changing IT and management accounting practices within organisations	– Semi-structured interviews (with management accountants & IS staff) – Documentary evidence (manuals) – E-mails and phone calls
• **Roles and dialectical of control (autonomy and dependency)** – Management accountants' roles – Management accountants' relationships with IS staff and managers – Management accountants' control over IT facilities	– Semi-structured interview (with management accountants/ managers/IS staff) – Background questionnaire – Direct and participant observations

managers (11). Appendices 1, 2 and 3 list the semi-structured interview questions for each category of interviewees. The interview questions focus on the issues raised in the main research questions. They are divided into four groups (see Table 4.6). In the first group, interviewees (management accountants and IT staff) are asked to describe IT (custom vs. ERP software) adoption and

Table 4.6   Interview Questions Classified by Interviewees' Categories

Organisations		Management Accountants (A)	Line Managers (B)	IT (IS) Specialists (C)
State-owned	Custom ERP	Questions Groups (1), (2), (3) and (4)	Questions Group (3)	Questions Group (1)
Governmental	Custom ERP			

implementation processes. This group describes IT adoption decisions, the conditions and reasons for IT adoption and implementation stages. It also explores the roles and relationships of management accountants with IT specialists. The second group seeks to understand the current management accounting systems and how IT implementation shapes and/or is shaped by these systems. In addition, it identifies modern management accounting methods adopted by organisations, the conditions and reasons for their adoption and how they influence and/or are influenced by IT implementation. The interviewees in this group are mainly management accountants.

The third group of questions is concerned to identify changes in management accountants' roles and relationships with user managers as a result of introducing IT (custom vs. ERP software). It collects data from both management accountants and line managers about the changing roles and relationships in the IT environment. The last group is about university accounting education. It evaluates, from the perspective of management accountants, the role of accounting education in enabling and constraining change in management accounting in the IT environment. In particular, this group tries to see whether or not management accounting education is sufficient in giving management accountants the required skills and knowledge in the IT (custom vs. ERP software) environment.

It is worth noting that semi-structured interview questions were used only as a basic guideline during the interview to make sure that all relevant topics were covered, to provide direction for questioning and to help the authors conduct the interview in a systematic way. In most cases, supplementary questions were asked; particularly when initial responses needed elaboration or when new issues emerged in the course of discussions. For instance, IMC was mainly selected because it implemented an ERP system. However, during a visit to IMC, a meeting with the current Financial System Manager revealed that there is custom web-based software for managing the IMC's budget. This information initiated a number of questions that were asked to the current Financial System Manager, the ex-Financial System Manager and the current MIS manager. These questions focused on the role of both software systems in managing the IMC's budget and the possible integration between the two software systems.

Although the majority of interviews were individual interviews, a small number of group interviews were conducted as well, especially in ESTD and AQF. For instance, an interview was held with a group of four at a time in AQF. The two meetings attended in ESTD were with groups of about ten. In this regard, Hedges (1985: 89) noticed that '[t]he distinctive analysis dimension which arises with groups but not individual interviews is the identification of who said what'. In fact, this problem was at a minimum in this research because most of the interviewees in these meetings were known to the authors because, for example, the meetings in ESTD were held at the end of the visit after the authors held interviews with most of the project team that attended these meetings. In addition, extensive notes were taken and reviewed as soon as possible, directly after each meeting.

4.7   Limitations of the case study method

Although the case study method does offer significant opportunities for management accounting research, there are several problems associated with conducting case study research. Firstly, access to an appropriate organisation for the research objective is often difficult to negotiate and the whole research process can be very time-consuming (Bonoma, 1985). In fact, the authors faced this problem in the current study when the SAP[5] branch in Egypt refused to help the authors to gain access to any of its customers. A similar problem was faced in gaining access to Coca-Cola Egypt Co, which was planned to be included in the study for comparing between different ERP brands. However, it was excluded because an internal auditing investigation was being undertaken by the parent company in the USA during the period of interviews. This company was replaced with another company, NEEASAE. Another problem occurred when the CEO of NEEASAE imposed some restrictions on accessing important data for research purposes. However, this problem was solved by obtaining a written permission to collect these data from the CAPMS. NEEASAE is important for this research, as it is an illustrative case for ERP failure in Egypt.

Secondly, it is difficult to decide on the de-limitations of the subject matter of the case (Hussey and Hussey, 1997). This problem is about relating the selected case to the other parts of society. To understand the subject matter, it is important to study the interaction between the case and the rest of the social systems of which it is part (i.e. its contexts). In addition, it is often difficult to understand the events in a particular period without knowledge of history. Scapens (1990) suggests that boundaries must be placed around the area of study as this permits a detailed investigation of the selected area. In addition, limiting the research area allows other researchers to make contributions by extending the selected area of study. For example, the impact of ERP on the gap between management accounting education and actual practice was left for future research.

Thirdly, a common criticism of case study research is its inability to generalise (Burns, 1996). To overcome this limitation, Yin (1994) advises that multiple cases should be regarded as multiple experiments and not multiple respondents in a survey, and so replication logic and not sampling logic should be used for multiple-case research. In this regard, Scapens (1990) argues that such approach to case studies considers theoretical generalisations rather than statistical generalisations. Burns (1996: 50) states that 'interpretive theories can be generated only in relation to the firm being investigated. However, once a specific case study is at an end comparisons can be made with similar cases, thereby enhancing the overall picture of a problem, issue or theme being explored. Furthermore, multiple case studies can investigate phenomena from a variety of institutional contexts'. This approach is adopted in this research by selecting a multiple-case design to serve theoretical generalisations.

And finally, interpretive case studies may suffer from the problem of researcher bias in interpreting social reality (Ryan *et al.*, 2002). Data, methodological and investigator triangulation can mitigate this problem (Yin, 1994). Data triangulation involves using one method but with multiple data sources. Methodological triangulation makes use of different data collection methods (interviews, surveys, observation, records, etc.). Investigator triangulation means the use of a team of researchers with different backgrounds, research experience, etc. This study uses multiple data collection methods that may reduce this problem. For example, in NEEASAE case, planning budgets (i.e. documentary evidence) confirmed the severe financial crisis that was described by interviewees (i.e. interviews) due to fierce competition caused by General Agreement for Trade and Tariff (GATT) agreement and dumping processes. Furthermore, accountants' role in ERP failure in NEEASAE was proven by interviews with different organisational members (i.e. other evidence of the same source), especially the General Manager of Planning, the General Manager of MIS, the General Manager of Financial Accountants and a cost accountant.

4.8 Summary and conclusion

This chapter presented the design and implementation of the empirical work. It discussed how the research methodology links the theoretical framework with the research method. Two main research methodologies were discussed, namely the positivistic methodology and the interpretive methodology. The latter methodology is the one adopted by both structuration theory and Burns and Scapens' institutional framework that form the theoretical base for this study. The case study method can be used with both research methodologies. However, it is essential in the interpretive methodology as it helps in both replicating and extending interpretive theories.

The design of this study is based on a multiple-case design that includes selecting four organisations to address research issues on IT (custom vs. ERP software) implementation and management accounting change. Furthermore, it uses multiple data collection methods. Nevertheless, semi-structured interviews were considered the main method of collecting data. The design of interview questions was presented. Finally, the case study research's limitations were discussed and their solutions were recommended.

The next chapter discusses the extra-organisational institutions of management accounting practices in Egypt, with emphasis on coercive pressures.

Notes

1   Despite the usefulness of ontological position in selecting relevant research methods, other determinants exist such as the availability of prior theory, the ability to simulate phenomena in artificial settings and the degree to which phenomena can be biased by explicit control or observation (Abdel-Khalik and Ajinkya, 1983).

2   Scapens (1990) argues that a researcher, adopting the positivistic approach, seeks statistical generalisations and, therefore, sees case studies as a sample that can be used to generalise to a larger population.

3   There are different types of triangulation, including data triangulation, investigator triangulation, theory triangulation and methodological triangulation. Yin (1994) advocated what he termed data triangulation for the case study, through the commonly used term is methodological triangulation. Data triangulation implies one method but using multiple data sources, while methodological triangulation refers to the use of different data collection methods (interviews, surveys, observation, records, etc.)

4   Consultants were met in some organisations. Special questions were prepared for them.

5   SAP is acronym for Systems, Applications and Products in Data Processing.

5
Background of the Empirical Study: The Transformation of Extra-Organisational Institutions in Egypt

5.1 Introduction

Scott (2001: 182 & 184) refers to deinstitutionalisation as 'processes by which institutions weaken and disappear ... the weakening and disappearance of one set of beliefs and practices is likely to be associated with the arrival of new beliefs and practices'. Egypt is in economic transition from an inefficient command economy to an efficient and liberalised free market economy. It has adopted a number of reform programmes that transform the circumstances in which Egyptian organisations operate. These programmes create new extra-organisational institutions[1] that shape and constrain, among other things, management accounting change processes in Egyptian organisations.

The analysis in this chapter is based on the deinstitutionalisation concept as well as other concepts of new institutional sociology theory such as organisational fields and institutional isomorphic mechanisms introduced by DiMaggio and Powell (1983). Drawing on these concepts, Granlund and Lukka (1998) divide the drivers of convergence or divergence of management accounting practices into coercive pressures, normative pressures and mimetic processes. However, the focus of this chapter is on coercive pressures because of the nature of organisations under study, state-owned enterprises and government agencies. According to Granlund and Lukka (1998: 162), coercive pressures reflect the enforcing regulative aspects of certain institutions, including rule-setting and monitoring and sanctioning activities. Granlund and Lukka (1998) give examples of these pressures such as trans-national legislation, trans-national trade agreements, headquarters influence, national legislation and national institutions.

This chapter sets out the background for the empirical study and historically examines the reform programmes and the transformation of extra-organisational institutions that affect the four organisations under study, two state-owned enterprises (NEEASAE and AQF) and two governmental units (IMC and ESTD). The focus is on the privatisation programme, the industrial modernisation programme and state-budget reform programmes. In addition, a brief historical background of each of the four organisations under study is given in this chapter.

The remainder of this chapter is divided into four sections. Section 5.2 briefly describes the birth of public sector enterprises and supporting extra-organisational institutions in Egypt. It also examines the privatisation programme that privatises State-Owned Enterprises (SOEs) and transforms extra-organisational institutions governing these enterprises. In addition, this section introduces the two state-owned enterprises under study, namely AQF and NEEASAE respectively. Section 5.3 emphasises on the EU-Egypt relationship and the introduction of the industrial modernisation programme that reforms extra-organisational institutions governing industrial sector enterprises, especially Small and Medium Enterprises (SMEs). It also presents details on the first governmental unit, i.e. IMC. Section 5.4 addresses state-budget reform programmes and related extra-organisational institutions that have been introduced to support these reforms. It also provides a brief background about ESTD, the second governmental unit. The last section summarises and concludes the chapter.

5.2 The privatisation programme and the transformation of extra-organisational institutions governing public sector enterprises

5.2.1 The privatisation programme

After the revolution of July 1952, the Egyptian Government made a break with the past and moved the Egyptian economy from a free market-oriented economy to a massively state-controlled economy within just a few years. The nationalisation laws and expropriation of various private enterprises became the expression of change in Egypt. A series of nationalisation decrees was issued in 1956, 1961, and 1963 to eliminate the dominant role of both foreign and large-scale local private capital. All nationalised SOEs were organised and categorised into groups according to the nature of their main products (Briston and El-Ashker, 1984). Each group was placed under the supervision of a 'Public Organisation', established specifically for this purpose. The groups were classified into sectors on the basis of supervision by a relevant minister. Each minister was responsible for the public organisations which were working under his/her supervision. However, the activities of these public organisations were co-ordinated and supervised by the Supreme Council of Public Organisations, which was headed by the President of the state, see Figure 5.1.

Since the early 1990s, Egypt has undertaken a privatisation programme due to both the dissatisfaction of the Government of Egypt (GOE) with the failure and losses of public sector enterprises and the external pressures

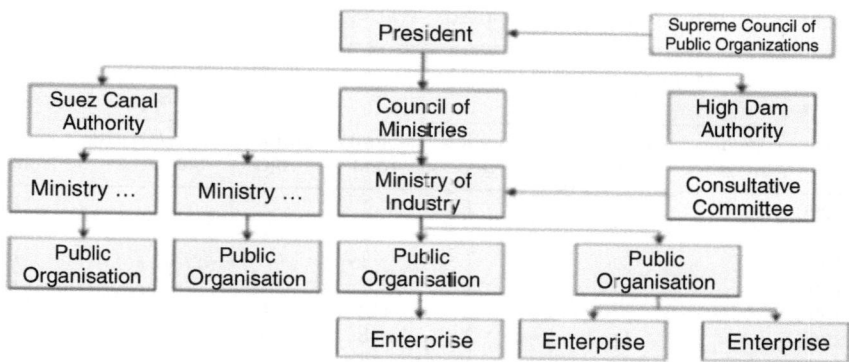

Figure 5.1   The Egyptian Centrally Planned Economy (Nour, 1969: 44)

from international donors (World Bank and IMF) in favour of privatisation. The GOE launched the privatisation programme with the Public Enterprise Law No. 203 of 1991 and its regulations, establishing the legal framework for sale of 314 public enterprises that earmarked for privatisation. This law marked the start of public enterprise reform. It was designed to eliminate the difference in treatment between public and private enterprises. The law spells out clearly the new rules of the game for SOEs as follows:

- Profit maximisation is the primary objective for all SOEs,
- No subsidies for SOEs either directly *via* transfers to losing companies, or indirectly *via* subsidised inputs,
- Non-differential terms or special interest rates on loans to SOEs,
- SOE autonomy in all decisions pertaining to their operations, and
- SOEs are affiliated to public holding companies, which monitor SOE performance and can name or change SOE management according to criteria of profitability.

Law No. 203 of 1991 solved several legal and institutional constraints that could have hindered the privatisation programme. Nonetheless, the legal and institutional frameworks were still incomplete even after Law No. 203 of 1991 was issued. The build up of the necessary legal and institutional frameworks demanded the enhancement of the capital market and its institutions. A 'new' Law No. 95 of 1992 was launched to introduce new types of institutions not known previously to the Egyptian capital market. The Law No. 95 of 1992 encourages establishing service institutions, intermediary companies such as brokerage companies, underwriters, portfolio managers and depositories. It also introduced the idea of Employee Shareholders Associations (ESA) for public and private

Table 5.1 Privatisation Achievements: Transactions Summary to 30 June 2002

Year	Majority Privatisation (> 51% sold)				Majority Total	Partial Privatisation/ Leases			Yearly Total
	Anchor Investor	Majority IPO	ESAs	Liquidation		Minority IPO	Asset Sales	Leases	
1990				1	1				1
1991				3	3				3
1992				1	1				1
1993				1	1				1
1994	3		7	2	12	1			13
1995		1	3	2	6	6			12
1996	3	14		1	18	6	1		25
1997	3	14	3	3	23	2	1	2	28
1998	2	8	12	6	28	1	3		32
1999	9		5	7	21		4	8	33
2000	5	1		3	9		6	8	23
2001	3		2	2	7		3	2	12
2002			2		2		3		5
Total	28	38	34	32	132	16	21	20	189

Majority Privatisation Total 132	Partial Privatisation/ Leases Total 57

Source: PCSU[2] (2002: 15).

enterprises. Furthermore, all restrictions that hinder easy entry to the market of foreign investors were removed.

The pace of privatisation up to 1993 was slow because time was needed to introduce the necessary legislative and regulatory arrangements. Also, the socio-economic culture of the country had not been ready to accept the concept of privatisation. Once the enabling mechanisms were in place the privatisation programme gained momentum in the second half of 1990s, after a favourable ruling by the constitutional court upholding the Government's right to privatise the public sector. As of June 30, 2002, of the 314 Law 203 portfolio of companies 189 public enterprises had been sold through various methods, including anchor investor, asset sales, sales to ESA, asset liquidations as well as long-term leases, see Table 5.1.

Appendix 7 gives more details about the Egyptian privatisation programme. In the next section we give background about the two state-owned enterprises under study, AQF and NEEASAE. They were affected by the privatisation programme and the transformation of extra-organisational institutions due to this programme.

5.2.2   Background information on state-owned enterprises under study

5.2.2.1   Abu Qir Fertilisers Co.

Abu Qir Fertilisers Co. (AQF) is a leading company in nitrogenous fertiliser production based in Egypt. It was established by the Ministerial Decree No. 374 of 1976 as one of the public sector companies. It manufactures and sells a full line of nitrogenous fertilisers including Prilled Urea, Granular Urea, and Ammonium Nitrate. Currently, the AQF's local market share is 71% Urea in both forms and 54% Ammonium Nitrate. As for the export market share, it has become 69% Urea in both forms and 89% Ammonium Nitrate. However, the company started to perceive local competition from new established companies such as Alexandria Fertilisers Co. and other possible competitors that planned to enter the local market as a result of implementing GATT agreement in 2006. Sales and operating income of AQF have increased in recent years. In 2002/2003, AQF reported sales of L.E. 1,082.7 million and operating income of L.E. 421.5 million. Total assets of the company at June 30, 2003 were L.E. 3,756.6 million. AQF has about 2,992 employees as chemical engineers, technicians and administrative staff. The organisational structure is shown in Figure 5.2.

Currently, AQF operates in three factories: Abu Qir I Plant, Abu Qir II Plant, and Abu Qir III Plant. Abu Qir I Plant started manufacturing Ammonia and Urea in two production lines in September 1979. Its production capacity is 1,100 tons/day of Ammonia and 1,550 tons/day of Urea. In December 1990, AQF introduced marine loading to export its products to international markets. Abu Qir II Plant was established in August 1991 to produce Ammonia, Nitric Acid and Ammonium Nitrate

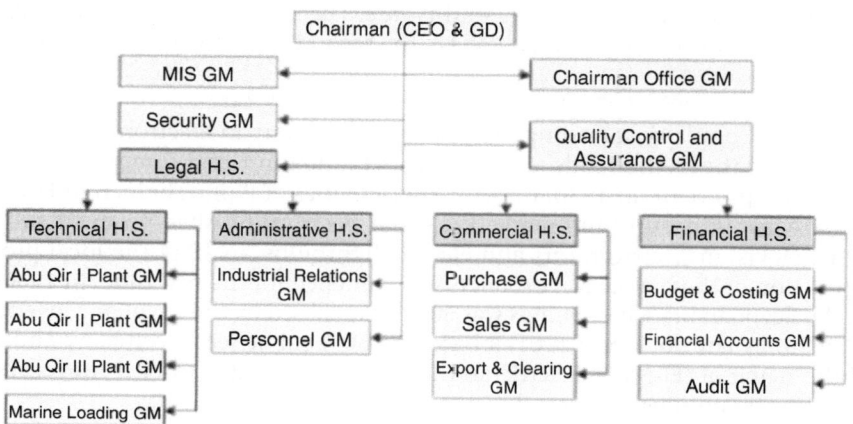

Figure 5.2   The Management Structure of AQF

with capacity of 1,000 tons/day, 1,800 tons/ day and 2,400 tons/day respectively. AQF continued its expansion and established Abu Qir III Plant in October 1998. The capacity of this plant is 1,200 tons/day of Ammonia and 2,000 tons/day of Granular Urea. In 2001, AQF introduced its most recent extension project, Abu Qir IV, to be established on a private free zone basis. However, in 2003, the Egyptian Government decided to establish this new project as a separate company known as Alexandria Fertilisers Co., which will start its production at the beginning of 2006.

According to Law No. 203 of 1991, AQF Co. has been supervised by the Holding Company for Chemical Industries to organise its gradual sale. In May 1996, 2.80% of the company' shares was sold to private sector for L.E. 20 million through the stock market. As from August 1996, AQF became one of the joint stock companies running under the Companies Law No. 159 of 1981, which organises the establishment of private sector companies. In 2002/2003, the company's shares that were sold to the public and employee share associations became 18.1%. The remaining shares are still owned by non-manufacturing public enterprises; including National Banks Sector (39.4%), National Petroleum Authority (19.1%), General Organisation for Industrialisation (12.7%), and Insurance Sector (10.7%).

Following its partial privatisation in 1996, AQF continued its expansion by introducing Abu Qir III in 1998 and participating in establishing a new company in 2001. Furthermore, AQF started to improve its information systems. The company was awarded ISO 9001:2000 certificate for the quality management system in 2001 as well as ISO 14001 certificate for the environment management system in 1999. As part of the preparation for ISO 9001 certificate, the company renewed its IT infrastructure and introduced custom developed accounting software in 1998/1999. The impact of this software on management accounting practices and management accountants' relationships is the topic of this case. The next section provides background information about NEEASAE, the second state-owned enterprise.

5.2.2.2   El-Naser Electric and Electronic Apparatus Co.

Philips Company, a leading international company in electronic industry based in the Netherlands, established its branch in Egypt under the name of 'Philips-orient' in 1930. Initially, the activities of Philips branch in Egypt were just importing and marketing some electrical finished products such as televisions, refrigerators and electric lightbulbs. In 1944 the local production of these electrical products was launched for the first time. In 1960s the Egyptian branch of Philips was 50% nationalised by the Egyptian Government. By law no. 118 of 1961, it became a 50% public sector company under the name of 'El-Naser Electric and Electronic Apparatus Co.'. However, its products continued to have the brand name of 'Philips'.

According to Law No. 203 of 1991, the ownership and management of the Government's share in the company were transferred to the Holding Com-

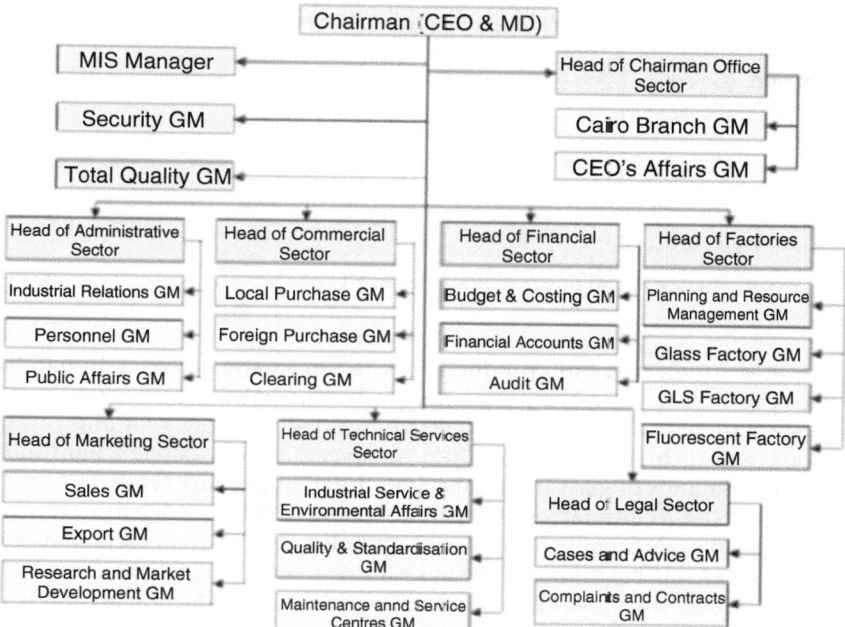

Figure 5.3 The Management Structure of NEEASAE

pany for Engineering Industries to organise its sale. In December 1997, the Egyptian Government tried to privatise the company by selling it to the Dutch company, Philips. However, negotiations failed and the Egyptian Government decided to buy the share of the Dutch partner. The company's name was changed to NEEASAE, which became a 100% public sector company. NEEASAE has about 3,300 employees as engineers, technicians and administrative staff. The organisational structure is shown in Figure 5.3.

Following its establishment in January 1998 NEEASAE Company reduced its activities to electric lightbulbs manufacturing and marketing. It currently operates in three factories: glass factory; General Lighting and Special (GLS) electric lightbulbs factory; and fluorescent tubes factory (see Figure 5.4). The glass factory started manufacturing glass shells in 1947, using the primitive methods of formation known as 'hard-blowing'. The work has continued with this style together with the continuous expansion in production capacity. In 1968, an automatic system for bulb formation had been introduced *via* the installation of a melting furnace of production capacity of 5 tons glass shells per day, with a rotating carrousel machine attached to it from the glass shells with a production capacity of 24 million balloons every year. In 1976, 1981 and 1991 successive expansion operations were

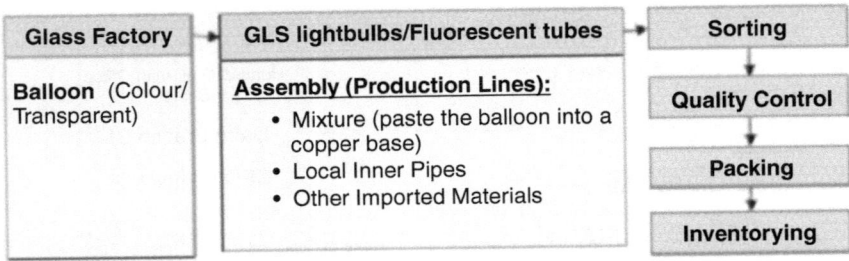

Figure 5.4 Factories and Business Processes in NEEASAE

executed for electric bulb production with automatic blowing, in parallel with the expansion in the production of electric lightbulbs. Currently, the production capacity has reached 90 million balloons per year and can be produced on three production lines to cover the incandescent lightbulbs factory demands of glass lightbulbs with different product types.

The GLS lightbulbs factory started producing GLS lightbulbs in 1947 with production capacity of three million lightbulbs per year. Since that date the GLS factory has been greatly developed. New production lines have been added to cover the market needs and renew the art of production according to the most recent universal development either in equipment or manufacturing methods, keeping quality and reducing cost. In 1990, the last developed production line with speed up to 2,500 lightbulbs per hour was installed. Nowadays, the production capacity of the GLS factory with normal operation, two-shifts system, is up to 78 million lightbulbs per year. This capacity can be increased to 117 million lightbulbs per year with a three-shifts operation system.

The manufacturing of fluorescent tubes started in 1970. Initially, it was only one production group that belonged to the GLS lightbulbs factory, where the production speed was 800 lightbulbs per hour. In 1981, fluorescent bulb production started in a new building with a separate organisation with a speed of 1,200 lightbulbs per hour. Later, the management put an improvement plan to increase the production capacity of this fluorescent tubes factory to 8.5 million lightbulbs per year by working into two shifts. This capacity could also be increased to be 12 million by working three shifts.

Following its privatisation attempt at the end of 1997, the company started to modernise its information systems. It was awarded ISO 9002 and ISO 14000 certificates. In addition, a decision was taken to adopt an ERP system in NEEASAE. As an initial stage, the company started implementing three modules of Baan software, namely Finance, Distribution and Manufacturing. The implementation processes started at the end of 1999. Three years later, the ERP project stopped and the company declared the failure of this project. The failure of ERP project in NEEASAE and the roles of institutionalised accounting practices and accountants in its failure are the topic of this case. The next section analyses the EU-Egypt relationship and the Industrial Modernisation Programme (IMP) and provides background information about IMC, the first government unit under study.

5.3 The Industrial Modernisation Programme and the transformation of extra-organisational institutions governing industrial sector enterprises

5.3.1 The Euro-Mediterranean Partnership and the Industrial Modernisation Programme

Since 1977, EU/Egypt bilateral relations have been governed by a Co-operation Agreement, which provides for economic co-operation between the parties and establishes provisions for non-reciprocal trade liberalisation and market access. In 1995, it was decided to change the system to enable the European Union (EU) and its Mediterranean Partners to adapt their development co-operation activities more clearly to the goals set out in the Barcelona Declaration of 1995 and subsequently included in the Association Agreements signed with each Partner country. The MEDA programme, which was put in place in 1996, is the principal financial instrument of the EU for the implementation of the Euro-Mediterranean Partnership (EC, 2000a). The first legal basis of the MEDA programme was 1996 MEDA I Regulation (Council Regulation No. 1488/98) for the period of 1995–1999 where the programme accounted for 3,435 million Euros. In November 2000, a new improved regulation (No. 2698/2000) establishing MEDA II for the period 2000–2006 was adopted. The funding of the new programme amounts to 5.35 billion Euros. The main areas of intervention and objectives are directly derived from those of the 1995 Barcelona Declaration (readers who seeks more details of EU-Mediterranean Partnership, EU-Egypt Association and other related topics are referred to Appendix 8 at the end of the book).

Under MEDA I (1995–1999), total funds committed for Egypt as a bilateral assistance amounted to 686 million Euros (20% of the total MEDA I funds). The following major ongoing programmes are being financed in Egypt under MEDA I regulation (1995–1999) (EC, 2000c):

1. Programmes that support economic transition in Egypt
   The EU supports economic transition in Egypt with four key programmes providing a total grant funding of about 350 million Euros, through:
   a) The Industrial Modernisation Programme (Euro 250 millions),
   b) Private Sector Development Programme (Euro 45 millions),
   c) Public Enterprise Reform and Privatisation Programme (Euro 43 millions), and
   d) Banking Sector Reform (Euro 11.7 millions).

2. Programmes that support socio-economic balancing
   The EU actively supports Egypt in promoting socio-economic balancing
   and poverty alleviation while pursuing economic modernisation and
   free trade, through:
   a) Social Fund for Development-Phase II (Euro 155 millions),
   b) Health Sector Reform Programme (Euro 110 millions), and
   c) Education Enhancement Programme (Euro 100 millions)

Among these EU programmes, the focus is on the IMP as one of MEDA I
programmes that support economic transition in Egypt. The IMP is a national
initiative jointly funded by the Government of Egypt and the EU to help
develop international competitiveness in the private manufacturing sector,
so that it can benefit from new opportunities arising from exposure to
global markets and the progressive introduction of free trade conditions. It
is the Ministry of Industry and Technological Development (MITD)'s
largest and most comprehensive programme for industrial rehabilitation.
The declared mission statement and strategic vision of the IMP is to equip
and modernise SMEs so that they can enjoy sustained international competitiveness. However, when looking closer at the constituting programmes
of the IMP, it is clear that its scope surpasses the scope of SMEs development and support to the formulation and implementation of Egypt's overall
industrial policy. This can be evident from the five sub-programmes of the
IMP displayed in Table 5.2.
    In fact, the IMP is based on three dimensions. The first dimension focuses
on about 5,000 individual firms. It is made up of three stages. The first stage
focuses on assessing the position of these firms in the market and proposing
an immediate action to improve this position. This is done at virtually no cost
to the firms. The second stage studies, if necessary, how to modernise the
firms. Such studies are financed in part by the company owner. The last stage
is about financing the required equipment and machinery through loans
offered by the European Investment Bank to the Egyptian banking sector. The
second dimension deals with industrial organisations, such as the businessmen's association and the Egyptian Federation of Industries, with the aim of
activating their involvement and co-operation to secure the modernisation of
Egyptian industry. Finally, the third dimension deals with policies required
to support industrial processes, including those to be adopted by the Egyptian
government and industrial entities.
    For the past few years, the IMP has been a topic of much controversy. The
programme, scheduled to start in 1999, was only launched in December 2001.
Approved by the Egyptian People's Assembly in December 1998, the IMP aims
at boosting Egypt's export capacity by improving industrial efficiency and
competitiveness, bringing about policy and regulatory reform and boosting
the capacity and services of both the MITD and business associations. The
sum of 250 million Euros has been earmarked by the EU for the programme,

Table 5.2   IMP Sub-programmes and their Objectives

Sub-programmes	Objectives
1) Policy Change	• Work with the MITD to modernise its management and organisational skills to function more effectively in a changing global economy, • Assist MITD in the formulation and implementation of a comprehensive industrial policy, and • Assist in improving the Egyptian business environment to attract more foreign direct investment.
2) Integrated Technical Assistance	• Provide business upgrading services, • Provide training through the Egyptian-European Management Development Centre, • Provide export development services through strategic partners and counterparts for SMEs to access European, African, Middle East and US markets and match makers with qualified buyers, and • Increase attraction for foreign direct investment through the General Authority for Investment and other partners.
3) Business Resource Centres	• Act as an entry point for SMEs seeking assistance, • Provide consultancy, technical assistance, specialised advisory services, as well as information and training to the private manufacturing sector, and • Host the European Information Correspondence Centre that is one of approximately 300 such centres located throughout Europe and the Mediterranean Region.
4) National Quality and Institutional Support	• Support institutions in achieving international acceptance with regards to quality (accreditation, standardisation, testing and certification), • Link research and development institutions with industry, and • Launch industrial initiatives through business representative organisations (the Federation of Egyptian Industries, Chambers of Commerce and Industry and Business and Investors Associations).
5) Financial Policy	• Increase access to finance for SMEs on suitable terms through partner banks.

Source: IMC website (http://www.imc-egypt.org/, accessed on 08 February 2007).

in addition to 103 million Euros to be mobilised by the Egyptian government and 73 million Euros to be provided by Egyptian private sector industrialists or beneficiaries as cost sharing contributions.

The failure of the programme to materialise until December 2001, despite the availability of the fund, had the European Commission (EC) threatening to withdraw its support. President Hosni Mobarak intervened in December 2000, issuing a presidential decree establishing the organisational structure for the programme. The decree stipulated that four entities were created for its implementation. First, the Industrial Modernisation Council is headed by the Minister of Industry and Technological Development and includes representatives from the ministries of international co-ordination, trade, finance and public sector. Six private sector businessmen and two university professors are also present on the Council. Second, the Industrial Modernisation Centre (IMC) is the executive body for the programme. The general director and eight other directors of IMC were recruited internationally. Third, the IMC Consultancy Board is headed by the Minister of Industry and Technological Development and is made up of members with an industrial or economic development background. Finally, the Interim Committee was composed of the members of the board of directors with an additional member to represent the Ministry of Foreign Affairs. The mandate of the Interim Committee was to take the necessary measures to establish the executive body for the programme. It has been dissolved the day it created IMC.

The specific financing agreement, signed in December 1998, that launched the programme set a time frame of 54 months for the programme, which was due to expire in June 2003. The three-year delay means that only one and a half years of the programme are left. To cover the lost time, the Minister of Industry and Technological Development has announced in April 2002 that the ministry arranged with the EC for the programme to extend until 2006. The executive director of IMC commented:

> to be able to do our job properly we need long-term planning. A year and a half is not enough. It's like taking off to land again...We have given the green light by the EC to go ahead and make a one-year plan that starts in June 2002, which means that, in principle, the programme will extended beyond its deadline. (Al-Ahram Weekly, 2002).

The final details of the IMP are presented in Table 5.3. IMC is the topic of the next sub-section.

5.3.2   Background information about government agencies under study: Industrial Modernisation Centre

As previously stated, the main objectives of the IMP are to promote Gross Domestic Product (GDP) growth and competitiveness of the private manufacturing sector, with special emphasis on SMEs in the context of continued economic liberation. Moreover, the programme will foster employment and entrepreneurial spirit. The specific programme objectives are to assist private enterprises in their development, strengthen business associations, support institutions and services, improve the sector policy framework and strengthen

Table 5.3   Some Details of the IMP

EC financing	250 million Euros
Egyptian Government Commitment	103 million Euros
Private Sector Companies	73 million Euros
Financial Agreement Signed	1 December 1998
Starting Date	1 December 2001
Implementation Period	54 months
End of the Programme	31 May 2006
Project Authority	Industrial Modernisation Centre, Cairo
Main Consultancy Services	Provided by European, Egyptian and MEDA-based service providers

Source: IMC website (http://www.imc-egypt.org/, accessed on 08 February 2007).

the MITD. Therefore, the IMP is designed to become a permanent structure in the long term. The IMP is managed by the IMC, providing demand-driven services for the private sector companies and institutions and support to the MITD, notably in the policy-making area.

The role of IMC needs to be carefully distinguished from the role of the MITD to avoid duplication and ensure consistency. The history of the MITD was characterised by passivity and inability to cope with the demands of the industrial sector. To overcome some weaknesses of the MITD, the IMP was introduced as the MITD's largest and the most comprehensive programme for industrial development. The sub-programmes of the IMP entail a crucial and influential role for IMC in the process of industrial development. However, the role of IMC is transitional with the aim of helping in the layout of a sustainable framework that provides the basis for devising Egypt's industrial development plan and also helping with implementation issues. Therefore, after the termination of the IMP, the MITD should become more efficient and be able to carry over the IMC initiatives and programmes.

In 2001, the legal basis of IMC was established. The IMC Consultancy Board was set up and a Council for Industrial Modernisation was appointed with members from both the private and public sectors. Furthermore, the management team of IMC was selected and appointed, comprising both European and Egyptian Executives. The IMC Consultancy Board comprises donors and representatives from the public and private sectors and provides advice to IMC on work plans, procedures manuals and donor requirements. The Industrial Modernisation Council comprises members drawn from the Egyptian government and a majority from the private industrial and financial sector and academia. The Minister of Industry and Technological Development acts as chairman and reports to the Prime Minister and the President.

The senior management team structure of IMC is made up of the Excutive Director, the Programme Co-ordinator/Monitor, the Contracts/Log-frame Controller and the Financial Controller as well as five Component Managers. The Executive Director has overall responsibility for managing the activities, staff and budget of the Centre. He reports to the Industrial Modernisation Council, chaired by the Minister of Industry and Technological Development, which in turn reports to the Prime Minister, the Cabinet and the President. The Programme Co-ordinator/Monitor is responsible for co-ordinating and overseeing the range of support sub-programmes operated under the Centre. In addition, he is responsible for monitoring the implementation progress of the range of sub-programmes under the Centre and providing regular feedback to other executive staff and to financiers. He reports to the Executive Director and deputises for the Executive Director in his absence.

The Contracts and Log-frame Controller is responsible for contract procedures and Management Information Systems (MIS). He reports to the Executive Director. The Financial Controller is responsible for receiving funds allocated to the Centre and ensuring that they are dispersed in an approved manner. He reports to the Executive Director. The five Component Managers are responsible for directly supervising the implementation of a range of sub-programmes of assistance to help upgrade and modernise the Egyptian industry. These sub-programmes include Technical Assistance, Policy Support Unit, Financial Policy, Business Resource Centres and National Quality. The Component Managers report to the Programme Co-ordinator/Monitor. The management structure of IMC is shown in Figure 5.5.

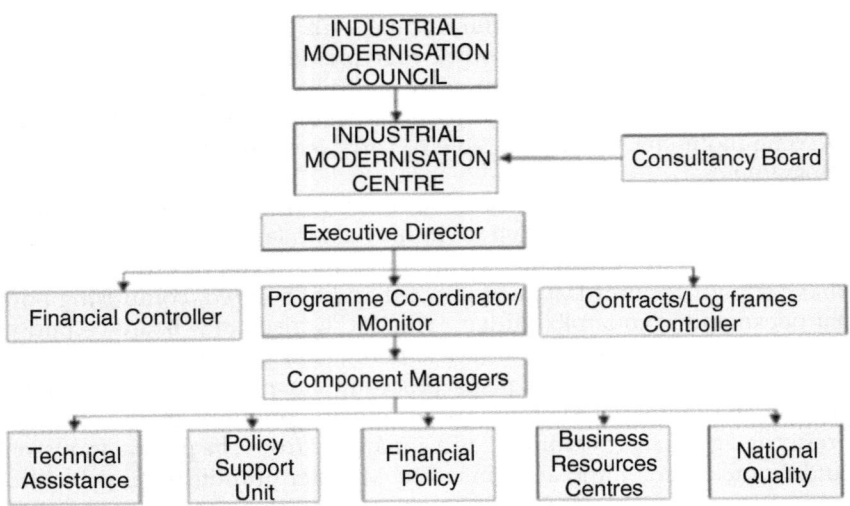

Figure 5.5   The Management Structure of IMC

A closer look at this organisational chart reveals that there are two types of the IMC departments: five operating departments and two support departments. The operating departments are called 'components' that are mainly responsible for implementing the IMP's sub-programmes. The support departments are the Finance Department and the MIS and Contracting Department. Furthermore, the IMC's structure consists of Egyptians and Foreigners. Generally speaking, the foreigners occupy top, senior and line-managerial positions. For example, the current Executive Director is Algerian, the current Financial Controller is Italian and the Financial Policy Manager is French. The Egyptians mainly occupy lower management and most staff positions. Examples of such positions are the Financial Manager, the Financial Systems Manager and the MIS manager.

Interestingly, there are two groups of IT specialists in the organisational structure. IT specialists in the MIS and Contracting Department are responsible for developing and managing the IMC's web site and its Intranet network. The network connects the IMC's branches or the Business Resource Centres (BRCs) in other districts with the headquarters in Cairo. It is mainly used to collect modernisation requests from beneficiaries. Furthermore, MIS staff has developed web-based custom software to help components' managers in managing their budgets. Another IT specialist in the Finance Department is the Financial Systems Manager who manages and maintains a Baan ERP system. The Finance Department uses the ERP software to record the IMC's budget estimates at the beginning of the accounting period, contracts and other transactions and to prepare monthly reports and annual reports to show how budget lines have been used and remaining balances. The reports extracted from the ERP system are subject to customisation in order to meet the needs of component managers. Moreover, the Finance Department is responsible for feeding the financial data to the web-based custom software.

IMC has been designed to act primarily as an incubator of sub-programmes of support demand-driven services for private sector enterprises and institutions. It provides industrial assistance to companies and institutions in Egypt by way of sponsoring various sub-programmes, see Table 5.2. The companies and institutions, which benefit through these sub-programmes, are called 'Beneficiaries'. Enterprises eligible for technical assistance should fulfil the following conditions:

a) Be fully privately owned or with majority private share,
b) Show potential for growth and profit,
c) Operate in the industry or industry related service sectors,
d) Be an enterprise of more than ten full-time employees, and
e) Be commercially registered in Egypt.

Third parties called 'Consultants', who carry out the services on behalf of IMC, are involved. Main consultancy services are provided by European,

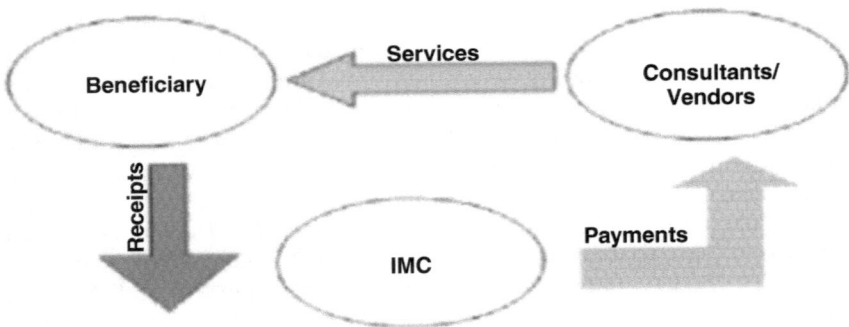

Figure 5.6   Business Processes for IMC

Egyptian and MEDA-based service providers. These consultants get paid by IMC for services rendered to the beneficiaries. The beneficiaries in turn pay IMC a percentage of the total project cost. This share is on average 25% in the first and second years of the IMP duration, rising to 30% and 40% in the third and fourth year respectively. Under this IMP, no beneficiary shall get benefited by more than Euro 100,000 over the duration of the programme. The following figure summarises these processes.

Normally, there is a contract between the parities involved under various sub-programmes. In some cases, there would not be any contract between IMC and the consultants. The consultants can carry out any number of projects, to any number of beneficiaries at any point of time. There is no limit specified for the business that can be done with the consultants. Furthermore, there are no terms of payments specified for the payments made by the parties involved. No taxes are involved in any of these transactions.

In 2002, the IMC's management decided to adopt an ERP system, Baan software, especially Finance and Distribution modules. The implementation processes were gradual over a period of time. Different forces have shaped the implementation processes. The purpose of this case is to analyse the IMC's experience in implementing and using Baan software. In particular, the focus is on change in management accounting practices and management accountants' relationships associated with ERP implementation in IMC. The next section is about state-budget reform programmes and ESTD.

5.4   State-budget reform programmes and the transformation of extra-organisational institutions governing governmental units

5.4.1   The Egyptian Ministry of Finance and state budget reform programmes

The Egyptian Ministry of Finance (MOF) is mainly responsible for planning and implementing the Government's overall fiscal policy. The Ministry pre-

Figure 5.7 The Ministry of Finance's Organisational Chart

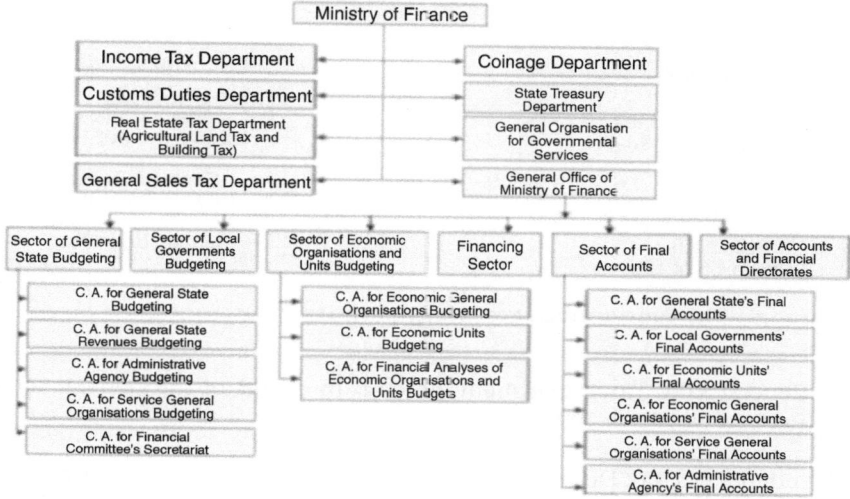

N.B.: C. A. refers to Central Administration.

pares the draft state budget to be approved by the People's Assembly, monitors the implementation of the approved budget, and manages state revenues as well as collects direct and indirect taxes. It also manages the external and internal public debt and achieves integration between the fiscal policy and the monetary policy to serve the national economy through co-ordination and co-operation with the Central Bank of Egypt and other related public agencies. The following departments are currently linked to the Ministry of Finance: Income Tax Department, Customs Department, Real Estate (Property) Tax Department, General Sales Tax Department, Governmental Services, Coinage Department, Treasury Central Department and Minister' Office, see Figure 5.7.

The MOF is also in charge of the enforcement of various tax laws *via* its independent tax departments (see the current structure of the Egyptian tax system in Figure 5.8. These departments are also involved in amending, designing and drafting tax laws, which are then submitted to the legislature for ratification. These departments are as follows:

- General Income Tax Department which is in charge of Unified Income Tax Law No. 187 of 1993, Stamp Duties Law No. 111 of 1980 and Development Fees Law,
- Customs Department which is responsible for Custom Duties Law No. 66 of 1963,
- Real Estate Tax Department which is in charge of the Agricultural Land Law No. 113 of 1939 and Building Tax Law No. 56 of 1954, and

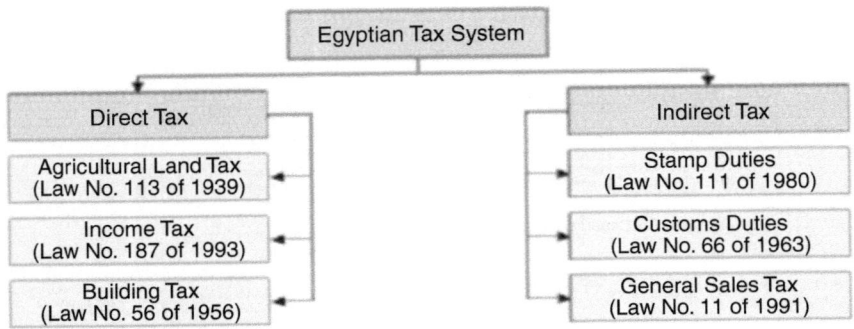

Figure 5.8   The Current Structure of the Egyptian Tax System

- General Sales Tax Department which is in charge of the General Sales Tax Law No. 11 of 1991.

Egyptian Sales Tax Department (ESTD) is the second government agency under study. But before introducing the background information about ESTD, this sub-section presents the fiscal crisis that led to the establishment of ESTD as one of the most important tax reform of the Egyptian tax system in the early 1990s. This revenue-side reform was followed by another reform that addressed the expenditure-side of the state budget, that is, the performance-based budgeting at the beginning of 2000. ESTD, as one of the MOF's departments, started implementing the performance-based budgeting. The introduction of performance-based budgeting was associated with automating almost all information systems in ESTD.

Towards the latter part of the 1980s the Egyptian authorities were faced with the unenviable convergence of major economic and fiscal imbalances, a growing budget deficit, high inflation, low savings, low investments, high debt and deteriorating local currency. At that time, the Egyptian economy was not in a good state. Economic growth had fallen sharply; the rate of inflation was high; and both the balance of payments deficit and the state budget deficit had expanded enormously. In 1986, for example, Egypt's debt to GDP ratio was one of the highest in the world and the consolidated budget deficit had reached 23% of GDP (Licari, 1997).

In 1991 the Egyptian government signed two economic reform and structural adjustment agreements with the World Bank and the International Monetary Fund (IMF) to stabilise the economy *via* a package of speedy-recovery reforms and guarantee fiscal sustainability by balancing public revenues and expenditures. A tax reform programme began in the early 1990s as part of the Economic Reform and Structural Adjustment Programme that emerged from discussions between 1987 and 1991 with IMF and also, in 1991,

Table 5.4   Major Revenue-Side Reforms

Reform Description

- Tax Reforms: improving tax administration, automation and new income tax law, sales tax law and property tax law.
- Customs reforms: administrative and procedural, legislative, tariff structure, duty-relief, customs valuation and release span, human resources and risk management, automation, ex ante goods release, web site and one-stop shop.
- Model Customs Tax Centre: One-stop shop; pilot basis

Source: Based on Hassanein (2004: 9).

with the World Bank. A number of revenue-side reforms have been introduced, see Table 5.4.

Since the beginning of the 1990s USAID has provided about $60 million in assistance to the Egyptian government to assist in reforming its tax system, strengthening its institutional capacity to administer taxes, and building analytic capacity for the design of fiscal, and especially tax, policy (Ramos, 2002). From a policy perspective, two of the most important achievements have been the enactment of the General Sales Tax in 1991 and the Global Income Tax in 1993. Both led to transformations in the Egyptian tax system, and to the establishment of a new institution and the modernisation of the country's tax administration.

The reform programme adopted during the 1990s was successful. However, with the termination of the economic reform and structural adjustment programmes towards the end of 1990s a lax attitude towards growth

Table 5.5   Major Expenditures-Side Reforms

Reform Description

- Performance-based budgeting and public-expenditure review using pilot-navigation approach.
- Cash-flow management: sustainability, primary dealers and treasury management.
- Government procurement, inventory and asset management: encoding; bulk purchases, procurement from SMEs, e-procurement and public assets registry.
- Public debt management: rolling over high cost for cheap debt and debt-to-equity swaps.
- Corporatisation of public economic authorities: financial restructuring and preparation for planning, programming and performance.
- Pensions reforms: sustainability and effective actuarial calculations.
- National investment bank: administrative and financial restructuring, project appraisal, portfolio management, human resource development and automation.

Source: Based on Hassanein (2004: 10–11).

in many of the key economic sectors and activities was witnessed. This coincided with a series of internal and external shocks, such as South East Asian crisis, that were an obstacle to progress and had multiple effects on overall performance and economic outlook. As a consequence, a number of expenditure-side reforms have been introduced, see Table 5.5. However, the focus here is on one of these reforms: performance-based budgeting.[3]

In September 2000 the World Bank suggested a budget reform programme to the Government of Egypt. It recommended replacing the current traditional line-item budgeting with a performance-based or results-oriented budgeting system. In November 2002 the Egyptian People's Assembly approved an agreement with the World Bank to design and implement a performance-based budgeting system for the purpose of fiscal reform, expenditure control and enhanced quality public service delivery. Presidential Decree No. 275 of 2002 was issued to regulate the experimental application of performance-based budgeting in Egyptian governmental units. Under this decree, the Government of Egypt began experimenting with performance-based budgeting in five ministries – the Ministry of Finance, the Ministry of Planning, the Ministry of Industry and Technological Development, the Ministry of Electricity and Energy and the Ministry of Information and Communication. This innovation was among the first of its kind in the Arab world and ESTD was among the governmental units that achieved a good progress in implementing the performance-based budgeting.

5.4.2   Background information about government agencies under study: Egyptian sales tax department

The ESTD, with headquarters in Cairo, is one of the revenue departments affiliated to the Ministry of Finance. It is mainly responsible for collecting sales tax levied on local, imported and exported goods and services. In 2003/2004, ESTD reported sales tax revenues of more than L.E. 22 milliard (approximately more than $3.5 billion). In 2004/2005, it is planned to collect L.E. 26 milliard (about $4.2 billion). ESTD is organised into 23 Regions, with Districts and Offices in each Region. There are 81 Districts and 25 Offices. For example, Sales Tax Region-Middle of Alexandria consists of three districts, namely SEDY-GABER district, MOHARM BAK district and ATAREIN district. The organisational chart of ESTD is diagrammed in Figure 5.9.

Several points should be noted about Figure 5.9. There are two types of central administrations: functional central administrations and regional central administrations. The functional central administrations, located in the headquarters in Cairo, are responsible for drawing up policies and providing support, co-ordination, and planning for different functional areas in regions and districts. Examples of such central administrations are the central administration for tax operations, the central administration for registrant assistance and the central administration for training. Each functional administration has branches in each region and each district. On the

Figure 5.9 The Organisational Chart of ESTD

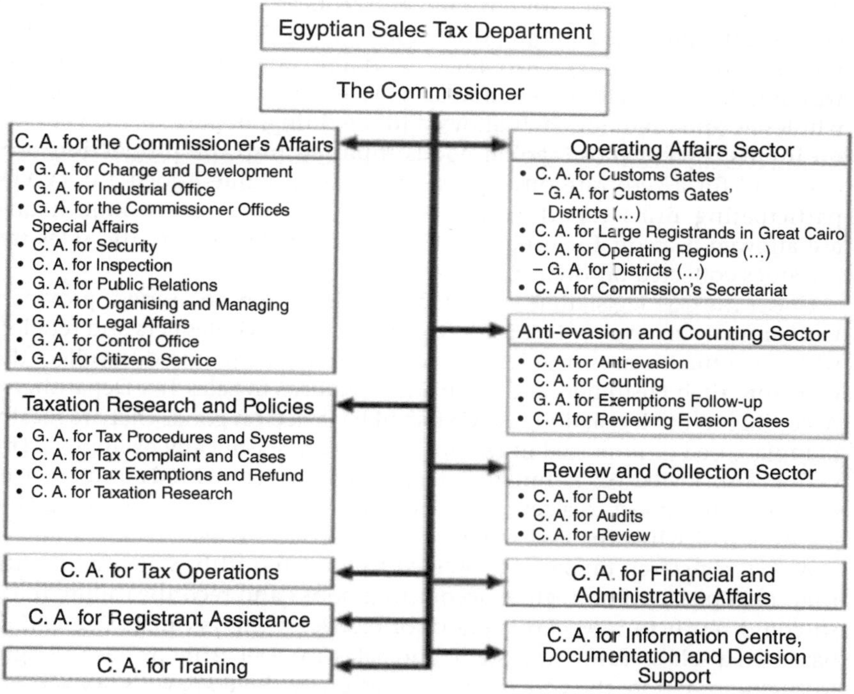

| Egyptian Sales Tax Department |
| The Commissioner |

C. A. for the Commissioner's Affairs
- G. A. for Change and Development
- G. A. for Industrial Office
- G. A. for the Commissioner Offices Special Affairs
- C. A. for Security
- C. A. for Inspection
- G. A. for Public Relations
- G. A. for Organising and Managing
- G. A. for Legal Affairs
- G. A. for Control Office
- G. A. for Citizens Service

Taxation Research and Policies
- G. A. for Tax Procedures and Systems
- C. A. for Tax Complaint and Cases
- C. A. for Tax Exemptions and Refund
- C. A. for Taxation Research

C. A. for Tax Operations

C. A. for Registrant Assistance

C. A. for Training

Operating Affairs Sector
- C. A. for Customs Gates
  - G. A. for Customs Gates' Districts (...)
- C. A. for Large Registrands in Great Cairo
- C. A. for Operating Regions (...)
  - G. A. for Districts (...)
- C. A. for Commission's Secretariat

Anti-evasion and Counting Sector
- C. A. for Anti-evasion
- C. A. for Counting
- G. A. for Exemptions Follow-up
- C. A. for Reviewing Evasion Cases

Review and Collection Sector
- C. A. for Debt
- C. A. for Audits
- C. A. for Review

C. A. for Financial and Administrative Affairs

C. A. for Information Centre, Documentation and Decision Support

Note: C. A. refers to Central Administration and G. A. refers to General Administration

other hand, the regional central administrations, located in different regions in different governorates, are responsible for providing support, direction, supervision, and follow-up for their affiliated districts in implementing the long-term and short-term plans. One key feature of the above organisational chart was the establishment of the general administration for change and development in 2004. This administration is responsible for managing change processes and the move to performance-based budgeting.

The ESTD first applied the General Sales Tax (GST) on 3rd May 1991 as part of the overarching Economic Reform and Structural Adjustment Programme sponsored by the World Bank and the IMF. The GST replaced the old Consumption Tax in 1991. Before introducing the GST, Egypt had roughly 150 different consumption taxes, essentially excise taxes collected from about 4,000 different firms and from imports. The consumption taxes not only discriminated against foreign competition, its application was also unclear and its rates highly varied.

The Egyptian government consolidated this set of taxes, moving toward more uniform taxation with few rates and reduced discrimination between domestically produced and imported goods. The GST replaced myriad rates, imposed mainly at the factory level, with a broader tax on sales. This tax was initially levied at the manufacturing level but was later extended to the wholesale and retail levels. It allowed for crediting, in part, of the tax paid on inputs, except most capital goods inputted into the production process, and for a zero rate on exports. As under a Value-Added Tax (VAT), participating firms report their sales and purchases every month and are allowed a credit for inputs to their production, against the sales tax revenues collected on their final sales.

Under the GST legislation, manufacturers, importers and service providers with annual turnover of L.E. 54,000 or more, while wholesalers and retailers with an annual turnover of L.E. 150,000 or more, are required to collect the GST from their customers and remit such amounts to Sales Tax Department. According to the legislation, the GST shall be levied on goods that are locally manufactured or imported unless such goods are specifically exempted. The GST is also levied on a number of specified services. Goods and services exported are subject to a zero rate. The standard GST rate levied on taxable goods is 10% while the GST rate for taxable services is 5%.

A GST registered taxpayer is obliged to file a monthly Sales Tax Return that must be based on regular accounting books and records. Failure to do so could result in a weekly penalty of 0.05% of the tax due. The GST is based on a self-assessment system, and Sales Tax Department has the right to amend or ignore the GST return, and estimate the taxpayer's tax liability based on available information. In such instances, the burden of proof rests on Sales Tax Department. The ESTD has the right to conduct tax audits that are usually based on the invoice system.

The GST was originally applied only at the level of importer and manufacturer as well as to some specified services. In the first year of operations, the Sales Tax Department registered about 25,000 firms. On 24th May 2001, the GST was extended to include wholesale and retail sales. With the extension of the tax to the wholesale and retail level, more than 140,000 firms have become active sales tax participants. This broadening of the base was essential not only to generate revenues, but also to increase fairness and enhance tax compliance.

However, the multiplicity of registrant numbers, coupled with the divergence of the geographical distribution of the Regional and District Offices, was expected to cause a lot of complexities in the tax administration. Examples of these problems are the shortage of the trained qualified labour required for extending the tax application, the lack of facilities concerning work locations and circumstances and the lack of tax awareness at the wholesale and retail level. To face the expected expansion problems, the ESTD approved the experimental implementation of the performance-based budgeting, offered by the World Bank, to allow for comprehensive development in all work fields. One important aspect of this development has been computerising the work systems and integrating the information systems of the Department. The introduction of custom software systems in the ESTD as part of wider budget system reform and their impact on management accounting practices and management accountants' relationships are the main issue of this case.

5.5 Conclusion

Drawing on the concepts of new institutional sociology theory such as deinstitutionalisation, organisational fields and institutional isomorphic mechanisms, particularly coercive pressures, this chapter provided a description and, to some extent, an historical analysis of the transformation of extra-organisational institutions that have had influences on state-owned enterprises and government agencies due to the change of economic orientation from a centrally planned economy to a free market-oriented economy in Egypt. Various forces have played vital roles in the institutional transformation through reform programmes. The chapter focused on the privatisation programme, the Industrial Modernisation Programme and state-budget reforms because they have major influences on the four cases under study.

This chapter also gave a brief historical background to each of the four organisations under study. The two state-owned enterprises are AQF and NEEASAE. AQF, a leading company in nitrogenous fertiliser production based in Egypt, renewed its IT infrastructure and introduced custom developed accounting software in 1998/99. The impact of this software on management accounting practices and management accountants' relationships is the focus of this case. NEEASAE, previously known as Philips, failed to implement Baan software. The topic of this case is the failure of ERP project and the roles of institutionalised accounting practices and accountants in its failure. The two government agencies selected are IMC and ESTD. The IMC, the executive arm of the IMP as one of the economic transition programmes sponsored by the EU, adopted an ERP system in 2002. This case focuses on change in management accounting practices and management accountants' relationships associated with ERP implementation. The ESTD, one of the revenue departments affiliated to the Ministry of Finance, started implementing the performance-based budgeting offered by the World Bank. The introduction of custom software systems as part of the wider budget system reform and their impact on management accounting in the ESTD is the topic of this case. The next chapter analyses change and stability in management accounting rules and routines following IT (ERP vs. custom software) implementations in the four selected organisations.

Notes

1 Burns and Scapens (2000: 8) define institutions as the taken-for-granted assumptions that identify specific groups and their appropriate activities and relationships.
2 PCSU is a co-ordination unit formed by CARANA Corporation that is implementing USAID's three year (1999–2002) Monitoring and Co-ordination Services Project under the 'Partnership for Competitiveness' agreement between the GOE and the United States.
3 For more details about state budget reforms see Appendix 9.

6

ERP vs. Custom Software and Change (Transformation) and Stability (Continuity) in Management Accounting Rules and Routines

6.1 Introduction

The previous chapter described the extra-organisational institutions of management accounting practices in Egypt. Drawing on the theoretical framework developed in Chapter 3, this chapter aims at making sense of change and stability in management accounting rules (systems) and routines (practices) associated with IT (ERP vs. custom software) implementation and use in the four Egyptian organisations under study. The analysis in this chapter addresses the first group of research questions. It is based on the use of different theoretical concepts such as path-dependent change processes and interpretive flexibility of technology in interpreting the empirical evidence. It is also conducted at different levels, including action, routines, intra-institutionalisation and extra-institutionalisation.

The reminder of this chapter is divided into four sections. Section 6.2 analyses the experiences of IMC and NEEASAE in implementing ERP projects and their association with management accounting change and stability. It starts with the processes of ERP implementation and use in IMC and their association with the institutionalisation processes of management accounting rules and routines. It then compares the NEEASAE's experience with the IMC's experience. Section 6.3 examines the implementation processes of custom software systems and their association with change and stability in management accounting rules and routines in ESTD and AQF. It analyses the ESTD's experience and compares it with the AQF's experience. Section 6.4 compares IT implementations and the associated change and stability in management accounting in both groups of organisations presented in the previous two sections and relates the case studies' findings to our research questions and previous studies' results. Section 6.5 sets out some conclusions.

6.2   ERP and change and stability in management accounting rules and routines

6.2.1   ERP and management accounting change in IMC as path-dependent processes: action, routines and institutionalisation

IMC is the executive arm of the Industrial Modernisation Programme (IMP), a jointly funded initiative of the GOE and the EU. It was legally established in December 2001 although it started its activities in June 2002. Since its early beginnings, IMC applies the programme and performance-based budget that is used by the EU. Even the organisational structure of IMC is based on the programme budget concept. Actually, this budgeting technique is different from budgeting and government accounting practices that are used in other Egyptian government agencies. In June 2002, Baan software was introduced to IMC. It was customised to fit programme and performance budgeting practices used by IMC.

Burns and Scapens (2000: 13) describe change processes as evolutionary processes that comprise a combination of random, systematic and inertial forces, which together create the context out of which new practices emerge. The ERP implementation and its associated management accounting change in IMC were path-dependent. Random elements, systematic mechanisms and inertial forces have shaped the implementation processes. In this section we describe ERP implementation and the associated management accounting change in IMC and the forces that shaped these processes. More details on IMC's experience will be presented in the next chapter.

6.2.1.1   *ERP implementation and customisation processes: the interpretive flexibility of technology and ERP project as an action that encodes institutional principles*

Following the selection of Baan software an ERP project team was formed (see Table 6.1). The team was composed of a project leader (the ex-Financial Controller), a project manager (the ex-Financial System Manager), three key users and two IT specialists from the Baan vendor in Egypt. From the IMC side, only the Finance Department's members had been represented in the project team. The project team began the implementation process. The ERP implementation started with the definition of business requirements, especially with respect to the finance area. A number of meetings were held with the component departments' members, especially senior level managers, to know what each department does. Based on these meetings, the workflow and the business processes that ought to be done were developed.

The definition of business requirements led to encoding EU institutional principles into the ERP software because the IMC's executives were selected

Table 6.1 ERP Project Team

From the IMC side: mainly all Finance Department's members:
Financial Controller as a project leader Financial Systems Manager as a project manager Two senior accountants and one junior accountant as key users
From the Baan vendor side:
Finance Consultant (an Indian expert) Technical Manager

on the basis of their experiences in the EU programmes and projects. For example, one qualification that formed the basis for selecting the Financial Controller was that the candidate should possess a detailed knowledge of at least one international donor organisation's financial and disbursement procedures, and knowledge of EU contract procedures in particular would be an advantage. The ERP Project Manager described this encoding process:

> Frankly, before ERP installation, we developed a cycle as business logic and this cycle has been applied as it is to the ERP system. We let other people apply it as a part of the consultation or the implementation. We were working according to the business-wise without application-wise or system-wise. Firstly, we established the business-wise, which is the workflow required according to EU procedures. We understood it and taught it to other departments. Then, we applied the business-wise as it is to the ERP system. For example, according to EU purchase procedures; there are three types of contracts. Each contract has specific conditions and procedures for its use. The first contract, which has the highest value, requires doing an international tender if the contract value has exceeded a certain amount. The second contract, with the middle value, requires launching a local tender. The last one, with the lowest value, requires the use of direct order provided that three offers have to be submitted to choose among them.

The Baan software has been customised to suit the IMC's needs, earlier identified through the business analysis. A senior accountant stated:

> The ERP software has been modified several times. The ERP vendor has been called in to modify the software to satisfy the

basic needs of the Centre and the increasing demands of managers for information.

According to the interpretive flexibility view of technology (Orlikowski, 1992), ERP is a configurable software package that can be configured during the implementation process to match totally or partially the way the customer organisation desires. During this adaptation process, certain interpretive schemes, certain facilities and certain norms can be built into ERP. This happened in IMC. For example, the programme budget concept as certain interpretive schemes has been built into the ERP.

Programmes in IMC are the main classification of the modernisation schemes. Budgets for the programmes are set annually. In some cases, the periods are revised in order to suit the requirements. So, there may be overlapping between the budgets for various programmes. Each programme consists of projects that are specific to it. For some programmes, there are sub-projects within a project that are unique to it. The budget lines are the last lines of activity that are specific to a project/sub-project. The limit of spending is set at a programme level and at the budget line level within the programme. Figure 6.1 illustrates the hierarchy of various programmes.

This concept of programme budget was built into the ERP system and is drawn upon in the day-to-day interactions. The ERP Project Manager explained this process of customisation:

> There is no module for government units in Baan software. This is something in the implementation. Something we call work around which means that something the system does not normally do, you turn around the system because you know functions in the system that can handle this thing. For example ... The word 'budget' in IMC .... means activities for which money will be allocated. Therefore, the

Figure 6.1 The Hierarchy of Various Programmes

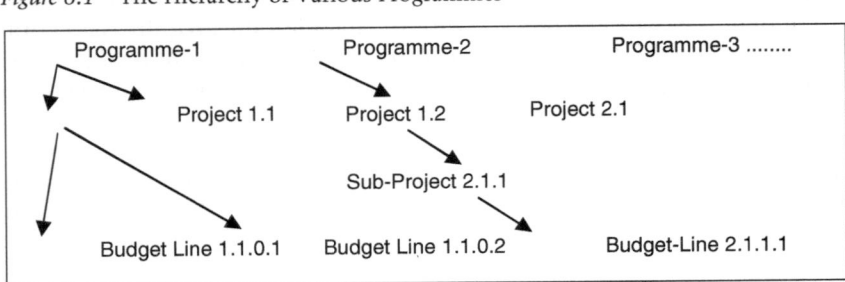

Source: IMC Business Process Summary.

business lines in the budget have been treated as expense accounts. Each account has been connected to a budget in the system. It is a different concept. The word 'budget' in any application is a group of accounts. The word 'budget' in IMC is another thing. It is a group of activities or lines of activities... There is an ability to open more than one budget at the same time. There is a budget called 'IWP'; another one called 'IEWP' and another one called 'takeoff'. At the same time, there are three budgets opened one for each different source of fund, that is, EU, Egyptian government and private sector... The budget in IMC, this is confusing, is not the same as the budget in the system....

For example, the IMC operation is based on work plans, which does not have fixed time duration. To accommodate this requirement, 20 fiscal periods are defined in Baan. If any particular work plan is going to exceed 20 months, the end dates for the year need to be changed in advance, see Figure 6.2.

Furthermore, there are certain facilities built into the ERP that are drawn upon in the exercise of power. Macintosh and Scapens (1990) argue that management accounting knowledge is a key element in the process of accountability in organisations. In this regard, the ERP Project Manager pointed out:

Component managers take pride in what, or what is the performance measure, how much money a manager has disbursed. The larger he/she disburses, the more work he/she does. Therefore, in order to show he/she is working hardly, a component manager says that, for example, I have a certain budget line amounted to Euro 100,000 and I have disbursed Euro 70,000. When the Finance Department examines his/her budget lines, it reveals that the actual expenditures are Euro 40,000 and

Figure 6.2 Customising Baan to Deal with the Work Plan Concept

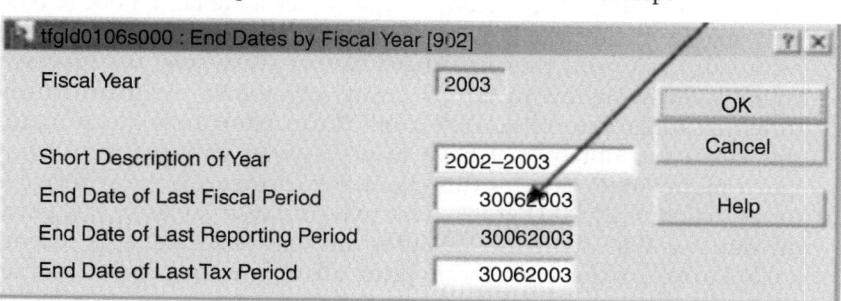

Source: IMC Baan Process Manual.

the rest is requisitions in progress. The Finance Department does not know any thing about the requisitions until the Executive Director, the IMC's chairman, approves them because sometime some requisitions are not approved.

The likelihood that component managers will under-perform is very high due to several factors, some of which are out of control such as some environmental uncertainties. Drawing upon accounting information, the Financial Policy Manager expressed his concern about the consequences of uncertainties on accountability issue:

> It is very important for us to make what is called the budget management or budget control to analyse the gaps between what was forecasted and the actual figures...my problem is more where we miss something, what happened, what was our vision when you go and what change since then. Ok, because we are facing a high degree of change in the entire environment. As you know, the government changed recently, for instance, and so the orientation may change. So, I might have, five million Euros, in a foreign exchange heritage fund. This assumes that there will be a strong political support because it is very sensitive instruments...If a minister comes and says this is not a priority I will have to change it to stop it to stop this project, but the budget will still be there...Meaning that there could be a gap. I am not interested to see this gap.

Moreover, certain norms have been built into the ERP system. The ERP Project Manager described a customisation process that aimed at setting a certain norm, that is, a single enterprise or beneficiary shall not exceed the sum of Euro 100,000 over the duration of the IMP programme:

> A client who is eligible for the fund pays an advance as a cost share, say 3,000 Euros...I have to record this transaction on the system. I record bank 3,000 Euros (debit) and customer share Euro 3,000 (credit). This means that the client owes IMC 3,000 Euros. If this entry is recorded, I can print this customer's history. Take care; the process is complicated somehow in IMC. I mean, it is totally different concept from any other enterprise. Doing this, I can know-how much money this client has obtained. I have to do another entry to record how much money IMC pays for this client. For instance, if the service cost for this client is 27,000 Euros, I have to record receivables 27,000 Euros, discount or IMC share 24,000 Euros and customer share as revenue 3,000 Euros. In the end, I can print all discounts granted to each client. Then, I can know how much money has been assigned by IMC for each client... Let's say the purpose from the above treatment.

The funds permitted for each customer must not exceed 100,000 Euros. That's the top ceiling for each customer. As a result, when approving a requisition, I have to make sure that the customer has not obtained more than 100,000 Euros from IMC in order to approve this requisition.

A senior accountant explained the use of norms built into the ERP:

The ERP software can discover right and wrong transactions. For instance, if the ceiling of a budget line is one million Euros and you try to enter a contract amounted to 1.2 million Euros; the ERP will reject this transaction.

Therefore, the programme and performance-based budget is built into the Baan software during the implementation processes of the software. This result is consistent with Caglio (2003: 128), who finds that ERP systems embed some interpretive schemes and certain norms for action and represent a facility drawn upon in the exercise of power. The next sub-section analyses the use of ERP in the production and re-production of budgeting and budgetary accounting and reporting in IMC.

6.2.1.2 ERP use and production and reproduction of management accounting routines: stability in budgeting, budgetary accounting and budgetary reporting routines

Budgeting refers to 'the process of allocating scarce resources to unlimited demands' (Freeman and Shoulders, 1999: 70). The outcome of this process is a budget that contains the proposed fund sources and the proposed expenditures. When the legislative branch enacts the budget, the expenditure estimates become appropriations. Then, the accounting system's role comes to help the administrators in controlling the activities authorised to carry out the plans and in preparing the statements that compare actual expenditures with the budget and permit evaluating variances. IMC has a budgeting system and applies a typical governmental accounting system. The aim of this sub-section is to explore these systems and the role of ERP in budgeting, budgetary accounting and budgetary reporting.

As stated earlier, the ERP software that has been introduced to IMC is Baan. Two main modules have been implemented, Finance and Distribution. There was gradual implementation for ERP modules and sub-modules. At the beginning, the Finance module was implemented; especially Budgeting, General Ledger, Accounts Receivable and Accounts Payable. The General Ledger is used to record cash transactions (payments). The Accounts Receivable is used to record customers' transactions (beneficiaries). The Accounts Payable is used to record service providers' transactions (consultants). After a few months,

Cash Management sub-module in Finance was introduced. This was followed by the Distribution module after about six months from implementing the first module. Managers requested the second module to monitor contracts. Baan is mainly used in budgetary accounting and reporting in IMC. The current Financial Systems Manager explained:

> Budget preparation does not benefit from the ERP. The control is important because it determines the remaining balances that can be used to fund future activities and the part that has been allocated to requisitions.

The IMC's budget preparation and approval are governed by the Specific Financing Agreement (SFA) signed between the EU and the Egyptian Government. This agreement divides the IMP into a number of work plans. Each work plan is prepared to achieve specific objectives. This plan will be implemented during a certain period, e.g. 12 months or 15 months. However, the implementation of a certain work plan might be advanced or deferred. Furthermore, budget items and classifications are determined by the SFA. There is no difference in the budget format prepared for the EU or the Egyptian Government. The only difference is the items that each party is going to fund.

The budget preparation starts from bottom to top, where each department prepares its expenditure estimates for the next work plan distributed to the main budget lines. There are two types of expenditure estimates: operational expenditures and component expenditures. The operational expenditures for the Centre include items such as wages and salaries, water and electricity, rents and stationary. This type of expenditures is estimated on the basis of historical data. The Finance Department uses monthly averages of operational expenditures. The ERP system provides this type of data. The average data is modified by any expected significant adjustments during the next work plan such as renting a new building.

With regard to component expenditures, each component prepares its plan for the next period. The basis for components' estimates is the specific objectives of each component. As mentioned earlier, the plans' items are determined by the SFA. The components' plans take the form of financial estimates, aggregated amount and its particularities. These estimates are submitted to the Financial Department in order to consolidate them in the form of a budget. During the consolidation process, there is a possibility of overstated estimates or understated estimates. The Financial Manager meets each component's manager to reach fair estimates. He draws on his experience with the Egyptian market and on comparisons with previous years' expenditures. Moreover, he is guided by a number of ceilings such as budget ceiling and component ceiling.

After the negotiation process, a lead schedule is prepared. This schedule starts with aggregated items for operational expenditures and components' expenditures. This is followed by more detailed items until reaching to a zero level of activities. After aggregation, the budget is submitted to the Executive Director for approval after more discussions with component and support departments' managers.

At this point, there are some differences in budget approval procedures between the EU and the Egyptian government. The Egyptian part of the budget is approved by the Egyptian Government, mainly the Minister of Industry and Technological Development, whereas the European part is approved by EU delegation and subsequently the European Commission (EC) in Brussels. The EU can modify or cancel any budget line. The EU approval duration is about ten days. After approval of the EU and the Egyptian Government, the expenditure estimates become appropriations.

As soon as the work plan is approved the budget execution starts. The execution includes every operating decision and transaction made during the work plan period. Accounting keeps a record of the results of the transactions and permits their summarisation, reporting and comparison with plans (the budget). Much routine budgetary accounting, budgetary reporting and other information processing activities within IMC are now undertaken within Baan. When the budget or the work plan is adopted, the total appropriations are recorded in Baan. Following this process, whenever the funds are received, the bank account is debited and the contribution account is credited. Then, budget allocations or encumbrances start.

The budget allocation procedure seeks to allocate and check the availability of funds by budget line. There is a set of steps in this procedure:

1. When the component issues a requisition form (an encumbrance), the Finance Department will start to check the availability of the budget line determined by this requisition. If the funds are available, an accountant will record budget allocation entry, debiting budget line (expense) and crediting the contra contracts payable.
2. The administrator (the Financial Systems Manager) will finalise the transactions and submit the requisition with the finalised reports from the system along with the budget variance report.
3. The Financial Controller reviews the document and if approved the document will be passed to the Executive Director. If approved by the Executive Director, the Finance Executive will pass the original requisition to the initiator component. A copy of the requisition and Baan-attached reports will be kept at the Finance Department and filled on the budget allocations physical file.

When encumbrances result in expenditures, an invoices/contract recording process begins. The requisition has to be followed either by a purchase order, payment request or contract. For example, the following steps will deal with a payment request or a purchase order:

1. A reversal entry to a requisition has to be recorded by debiting contra accounts payables and crediting budget line (expense). An accountant has to record the actual amount from the invoice approved from component managers by debiting the budget line specified and crediting accounts payable, registering the document number on the invoice and writing the check.
2. A senior accountant will approve and record the payments on Baan at the same batch of payable (previous step). The accountant will print the non-finalised transaction report and deliver the check, invoice and report to the Financial Controller for approval.
3. After Financial Controller and Executive Director's approval, the Financial Executive will handle the signed checks to a junior accountant to be delivered to vendors. The administrator will finalise payables and payments after the Financial Controller's approval.

Accounting reports are prepared monthly from the trial balance extracted from the ERP system. In addition, an aggregated report is prepared for every work plan period. Accountants prepare simplified reports using Microsoft Excel sheets. In these reports, numbers are clearly explained in more details. In this regard, data extracted from the ERP software is re-presented in order to be understandable to managers. The trial balance is shown in Figure 6.3.

6.2.1.3   ERP and the institutionalisation of management accounting routines in IMC

The future of ERP in IMC: expansion or contraction.   The ERP implementation in IMC was a path-dependent process. Random elements, systematic mechanisms and inertial forces have shaped the implementation process. For example, the existence of an accountant, the ex-Financial System Manager,

Date: 27-07-04	[11:40, Eur]		BUDGET VARIANCE (PRINT SQUENCE/ LEDGER ACCOUNT)				
IMC-EU			Trial Balance for	1 2004	Home Currency	Eur	Page: 1
Ledger Account	From:	07B	Account Type	All	All Companies of Group	No	Company: 702
	To:	07B1B010601	Non Finalised Trans.	No	Budget:		
sublevel	From:	0	Print Zero Balances	Yes	Accounting Scheme	Both	
	To:	0	Print Quantities	No			

Ledger Acc.	Sublevel	Ledger Account Description	Actual Amount	Budget Amounts	Variance		Var%
07B02020102	0		0.00	0.00	0.00	0.00	
07B02020103	0		0.00	0.00	0.00		0.00
07B02020201	0		0.00	0.00	0.00	0.00	
.....	0		0.00	0.00	0.00		0.00
			0.00	0.00	0.00	0.00	

Figure 6.3   The IMC's Trial Balance

who has a lot of experience in ERP systems, was one of the most influential conditions for the successful implementation of ERP in IMC. The reliance on an Indian expert on the part of the Baan vendor in Egypt and his sudden departure threatened the termination of the implementation process and the possibility of ERP failure. However, the ex-Financial System Manager, who was the ERP Project Manager, successfully completed the implementation process and added a new sub-module in Finance, Cash Management sub-module, as well. This issue will be explored further in the next chapter. The Baan implementation has been expanded gradually to include Distribution Module. However, the ERP system has now stopped expanding any more. A number of unplanned events caused this outcome.

In 2003 the Iraq War, led by the USA to remove Saddam Hussein from power by military force, dramatically affected the IMC's expansion plans. The EU decided to re-distribute the IMC's budget to assist the Egyptian Government in addressing the economic impact of the war in Iraq. Some expansion plans have been cancelled. At the beginning, there was a plan to establish six Business Resource Centres (BRCs), which will form the basis for an eventual national network of up to 20 centres. This number has been reduced and the implementation of ERP software in these centres has been abandoned. In 2003, a network of only three BRCs was established in three cities, namely Alexandria, 6th October and 10th Ramadan, with first support services towards the regional business community. Money shortages due to the Iraq War and the transfer of part of the IMC's budget to support the Egyptian Government interrupted the intended plan for expanding the ERP implementation and use into the BRCs. The ERP Project Manager described the impact of the Iraq War on IMC:

> During the Iraq War, the Egyptian Government requested from the EU to transfer part of the IMC's budget to support the Egyptian Government's budget. This is due to the dramatic effects of the Iraq War on the Government's revenues. The EU transferred about Euro 70 million from the IMC's budget for supporting the Egyptian Government's budget. Therefore, when this transfer occurred, the EU started to re-allocate and resize the IMC's budget. For instance, it was planned to set up 20 BRCs. Until I left IMC, only five BRCs have been built, including 10th Ramadan, 6th October, Borg El-Arab, Alexandria and Assuit. The EU stated that no more BRCs would be set up because there were not enough funds for doing so.

The establishment of the MIS department is another event that happened in 2003 and shaped the future of the ERP system in IMC. The 'new' MIS and Contracting Controller decided to develop new custom software using Java language, a web-based system. He completely refused to use or integrate the Baan system with his new software. Moreover, the MIS and Contracting Controller did not accept the move of ex-Financial Systems Manager to his department. In the end, the web-based system is not a complete rival for the Baan system. Although the two have not been integrated physically, they are integrated practically. Every one of them complements the other in some aspects and replaces it in others. However, the mere existence of rival software stopped the future expansion of the ERP in the area where the web-based system has advantage.

At the end of 2003 and the beginning of 2004, the EU decided to terminate the service contracts of Executive Director, Financial Controller and Financial System Manager. The departure of the ERP sponsor, initiator and manager put an end to any future development of the ERP system. The ERP Project Manager admitted that there was not sufficient support for the ERP project because the initiator was the Financial Controller not the Executive Director.

The temporary nature of IMC also sharply affects the future of the ERP system. This has been reflected in the feelings of the IMC's staff towards this system and other systems. Current IMC members feel that their positions are not secure. They have less incentive to further develop existing systems, including the ERP system and even the web-based custom system. At the end of the day, the ERP system has not been developed since the departure of its sponsor, initiator and manager. The next sub-section addresses the intra-institutionalisation of management accounting routines in IMC.

The intra-institutionalisation of management accounting routines in IMC.   The ERP implementation has been evolutionary, an unplanned process, and has facilitated the routinisation and intra-organisational institutionalisation of EU budgetary accounting, budgetary reporting and contracting procedures used by IMC (see section 6.1.1.2). However, at the level of IMC, there have been no fundamental changes in the management accounting information used and no 'new' management accounting systems or techniques have been introduced following the introduction of Baan. The Financial Policy Manager explained:

> ... I think we have for each component the same project lifecycle. The project lifecycle is extremely standardised. It's the same as the project's manual lifecycle in every country; all institutions give this the same. So it may be the fact that the organisation (IMC) is more or less sticking to the rules but you do not start inventing and re-inventing by asking for specific reports. I think this is standard, the same, and we have to if you need to deliver. We need to have a degree of standardisation at each level actually when issuing the terms of reference, drafting the contracts, processing the invoices, every step should be standard-

ised...The ERP did not change the information but it is much quicker to get the information. Furthermore, I do not need to print out every thing and I am working on an electronic basis which is, of course, paperless.

Management accounting information is now available much more quickly and component managers can access real-time information rather than wait for accounting reports. However, the real-time information is not provided by Baan. It is provided by a rival web-based custom system. This reality has been created by a number of forces. IMC did not complete the purchasing of a sufficient number of licences to cover the component managers' needs because the EU auditors rejected the ERP project and did not support it financially. The component managers themselves also refused to take responsibility for the financial aspects of their own activities. In addition, the MIS and Contracting Controller preferred introducing new IT software to relying on the existing ERP system. This latter issue will be further explored in the next chapter.

The introduction of Baan, however, helped in organising the documentary cycle and in eliminating the duplication of work in IMC. The ERP Project Manager stated:

The system helped us in developing our documentary cycle. There was no real documentary cycle before the system implementation. I mean, the documentary cycle that existed was a limited one. During the ERP implementation process, the documentary cycle became clear...We were able to discover that there were some departments that were duplicating the work of other departments and they were not aware of that. There was no communication between them. After that, each department started to direct customers to the appropriate department. This led eventually to the elimination of work duplication. It was useful.

The Baan system contributed directly and indirectly, through the web-based system, to the intra-institutionalisation of management accounting routines within IMC. It helped in the disassociation of management accounting routines from their historical circumstances, the Finance Department. Component managers can now access real-time accounting information to check the availability of funds and analyse budget variance. That is not to say that accounting knowledge has been decentralised or transferred to component managers. This issue will be discussed in more detail in the next chapter. Although real-time access is offered by the web-based custom software, the ERP implementation played a major role in facilitating the development of the web-based software, where the workflow developed for ERP has been used to design the web-based software.

The extra-institutionalisation of management accounting routines. Despite the fact that ERP implementation has not been associated with change in management accounting rules and routines used by IMC, the IMC's use of EU budgeting, budgetary accounting and budgetary reporting rules and routines represents revolutionary change when compared with other Egyptian governmental units, especially the MITD. There are some differences in budgeting, budgetary accounting and budgetary reporting between IMC and other Egyptian government units, in particular the MITD, as follows:

1. Financial year: in Egyptian government units, the financial year starts in July and ends in June each year. In IMC, there is no clear-cut financial year but there is a work plan that may be implemented in one year or more or less.
2. The preparation of budget estimates: Egyptian government units follow the Budget Act No. 53 of 1973 in preparing budget estimates. IMC follows the procedures set in the Specific Financial Agreement between the EU and Egypt.
3. The approval of budget: in the Egyptian government units, the unit's budget must be approved by the Ministry of Finance (MOF) and, after aggregations with other units' budgets, by the Egyptian People's Assembly. In IMC, the budget must be approved by the Industrial Modernisation Council, which is headed by the Minister of Industry and Technological Development, by the EU delegation in Egypt and eventually by the EC in Brussels.
4. The budgetary accounting system: Egyptian government units use the government accounting system set by the Government Accounting Act No. 27 of 1981 and follow the law No. 89 of 1998 tilted 'Tender and Bidding Act' in tender and contracting procedures. However, IMC applies an accounting system that has been set according to EU tender and contracting procedures.
5. The accounting basis: Egyptian government units use the cash basis in accounting for revenues and expenditures every financial year. IMC uses the accrual basis in accounting for IMC revenues and expenses every work plan.
6. Reports prepared: the contents and frequency of reports in IMC are different from any other Egyptian government unit, including the MITD. For example, Egyptian government units prepare monthly report of revenues and expenditures, quarterly reports and the end-of-year final account. IMC, on the other hand, prepares monthly reports, quarterly reports and the end-of-work plan report.
7. Budget control: in Egyptian government units, the MOF and the Central Agency for Accountancy (CAA) have permanent staff in each unit to daily monitor the pre-spending and post-spending of budget items

respectively. In IMC, there are no such personnel. The Programme Co-ordinator performs the pre-spending review and the EU auditors perform the post-spending audit. For example, a senior accountant stated that:

> The EU sends its auditors every 6 months to examine the Centre's accounts. On the other hand, for the Egyptian government, the audit only needs to be performed annually. The CAA's auditors were even more tardy in auditing the Centre's accounts for the previous work plan taking more than 15 months.

This implies that IMC is not under the direct control of the CAA and clearly confirms that IMC is not of the same nature as other Egyptian governmental units. However, the use of performance-based budgeting by IMC is not expected to expand beyond the boundaries of IMC.

Management accounting routines in IMC are not expected to be extra-institutionalised or disassociated from their historical circumstances. They are not expected to be used by other Egyptian government units. This fact can be interpreted in the light of some observations. Initially, on 14 December 2000, a presidential decree was issued to establish mechanisms for the IMP. The decree established a relatively independent organisational structure of the IMP from the MITD. However, IMC is still under the supervision of the Minister of Industry and Technological Development but he does not intervene in day-to-day activities. A report of the Centre's performance is made to the Industrial Modernisation Council, which is chaired by the Minister of Industry and Technological Development, on a quarterly basis.

Furthermore, the IMP is the MITD's largest and the most comprehensive programme for industrial development. However, the role of IMC in the process of Egyptian industrial development is transitional. Its duration is only 54 months. Therefore, after the termination of the IMP, its industrial assistance sub-programmes will be placed to outside independent structures. The ERP Project Manager confirmed this information:

> The EU and the Egyptian government started to think about the legal status of the BRCs (Business Resource Centres). Should they be business societies or something else? So when IMC closes, these BRCs continue and do not stop working. They become self-funded and self-acquisition and become autonomous.

Next, we briefly analyse the failure of ERP implementation and stability in management accounting rules and routines in NEEASAE. We also compare this experience with the IMC's experience.

6.2.2 Comparison of ERP and accounting stability in NEEASAE with ERP and associated accounting change in IMC

NEEASAE is a state-owned enterprise that has applied the Uniform Accounting System to serve both financial accounting and cost accounting since 1966. It also prepares traditional planning budgets such as sales budget, production budget and commodity and service requirements budget. In 1999, the company started implementing an ERP project, Baan software. This project was not completed and ended in 2002. It failed during the customisation processes of the software to suit the requirements of the Uniform Accounting System. This sub-section aims at comparing and contrasting ERP implementation processes in NEEASAE and IMC in relation to change and stability in management accounting rules and routines.

6.2.2.1 The failure of ERP customisation processes in NEEASAE: the tension between the new rules built into the ERP and established routines and institutions

Following its 50% nationalisation in 1961, NEEASAE, previously known as Philips, has used the Uniform Accounting System to prepare its financial and cost accounts. The Dutch partner had not affected the accounting system used. However, the reports prepared were affected. Certain reports were requested to be filled by the Finance Department. These reports were specially designed to satisfy the Dutch partner's needs. Before the introduction of ERP and after its failure, NEEASAE has been using custom accounting software. The Uniform Accounting System was programmed into this software. However, the software has been run by IT staff. A Computer Engineer in the MIS Department described this software as follows:

> We currently have accounting software. It was programmed using FoxPro as a database and NOVELL as an operating system. It handles wages and accounting transactions such as general ledger, trial balance and local sales. It is a complete Uniform Accounting System.

Following ERP adoption, NEEASAE implemented three main modules of Baan as a first phase, namely Finance, Distribution and Manufacturing. These modules were simultaneously implemented in the Financial Sector (financial accounts, budgeting and costing), the Commercial Sector (purchases) and the Marketing Sector (sales), and the Factories Sector (production) respectively. The implementation progress was different from one sector to another. The Planning and Resource Management Department had the least demands and the Marketing Department requested slight modifications. But the Financial Accounts Department and the Budgeting and Costing Department insisted that the Uniform Accounting

System had to be built into the ERP software and the reports must be prepared in the same normal format. The MIS General Manager explained:

> Customisation was the main reason for ERP failure. The Finance Department is required to apply the Uniform Accounting System. This system is like the constitution. It has to be followed. Accountants have certain reports that have to be prepared...We were extremely inflexible and we have not had an ability to change the business processes.

The General Manager of Planning gave an example of the inflexibility of accountants:

> If we used the software as it is, we would complete the project. This would solve a lot of problems. A lot of modifications and customisations were done. There was no flexibility on the part of accountants at all. They even insisted on using four decimal numbers as the manual work... They wanted the ERP to be customised to reflect the Uniform Accounting System. It took a lot of efforts to customise the ERP to be in conformity with the Uniform Accounting System...The same document should be prepared by the ERP system as the manual document. Otherwise, the software was not suitable.

For example, the Uniform Accounting System dictates the chart of accounts in terms of eight numbers. To customise the ERP system to accept the chart of accounts, it took two months. However, the ERP system required changing the documents, procedures and documentary cycle between the company's departments. Accountants rejected this type of change as it contradicted with existing routines and institutions. The General Manager of Financial Accounts gave the following reason:

> We found that we should prepare and change the documentary cycle to fit the ERP system before starting implementing it. There are control authorities that accepted and recognised the procedures a lot of years ago. So it was difficult to replace and change these procedures.

He added:

> I cannot violate the rules of Uniform Accounting System. The Central Agency for Accountancy audits my compliance with these rules and disagrees with any differences. I cannot violate the rules in order to adopt the ERP system. There will be legal responsibility. If the ERP Company were able to customise the ERP system to be in

conformity with the Uniform Accounting System, the ERP system would operate.

The multiplicity of Egyptian taxes, especially on transactions between governmental units or public sector companies, represented another obstacle to implementing ERP system in NEEASAE. When NEEASAE sells goods to a governmental unit, the governmental customer deducts an income tax from the company and NEEASAE collects a sales tax from the customer. The consultants found strange that there are more than one tax that has to be collected on the same transaction. They introduced intermediate accounts to record taxes in non-tax accounts. However, the mediation of tax accounts, suggested by consultants, in the ERP system were perceived by accountants as tax evasion, which would lead to legal responsibility when tax officials examine the company's accounts. The General Manager for Financial Accounts pointed out:

> Tax officials closely monitor the invoice. I cannot tell them that the computer software requires another form for the invoice. This would cause a lot of tax problems... Tax officials examine our documents and what we reimbursed. It should be specific accounts for this purpose. If we used intermediate accounts, it would be tax evasion... I cannot change the state tax system in order to implement the ERP system but my system can be modified... As an international system, Baan should leave this part for each country. Furthermore, taxes change from year to year.

Furthermore, the division of one invoice into a number of screens led to difficulty in using the ERP system in NEEASAE. There were a lot of documents that were difficult to be entered into the ERP system using the screens designed in the system. The division of a single document into several screens was seen by accountants as impossible. For instance, there were six screens to record the fixed assets' depreciation. The General Manager for Financial Accounts explained:

> Any system opens a single screen that leads to other screens. However, in Baan, if I have not entered a screen, the system would not accept the others ... We prepare depreciation reserve for fully depreciated assets in books. This reserve requires re-evaluation of assets. For two years, we were unable to customise the ERP system to record this reserve. To prepare a compound entry (from two or more accounts to two or more accounts), the system required using intermediate accounts. The system consumed our time in preparing unnecessary intermediate accounts and entries.

The ERP caused tensions in the process of encoding existing institutions into the new rules. According to Burns and Scapens (2000: 16 & 17), it is likely to be much easier to introduce changes which do not challenge existing ways of thinking and norms of behaviours. However, change that conflicts with existing routines and institutions is likely to be much difficult to implement. In NEEASAE, the new rules built into the ERP system were incompatible with the established ways of thinking and norms of behaviours embedded in the existing routines. One major reason for ERP failure in NEEASAE was the resistance due to a 'mental allegiance' to the established ways of thinking and doing, embodied in existing routines and institutions, especially the Uniform Accounting System and local tax laws. The General Manager of Financial Accounts pointed out:

> Baan system was not suitable for the nature of our business and our work systems. We concluded that we could not change the state systems, such tax laws and the Uniform Accounting System, in order to implement the Baan system.

He added:

> The ERP offered solutions but they were not suitable for us. The software is not suitable for the Egyptian environment. It might be useful for Europe. There was a will to make the ERP system succeed; however, the system was not in conformity with our systems. The problem was that it was customisable software. It was inflexible software like a train that has to be pulled along a railway line. Tailored (custom-developed) systems would satisfy our needs.

A cost accountant agreed with the above statement:

> The user needs from financial data and tax accountability should be determined and satisfied. The computerised system should be tailored rather than imposed a software package.

He continued:

> There were a lot of difficulties in implementing the Baan system. This system is not suitable for our reality, our life and our systems that we are used to use. The software does not satisfy our needs. I personally prefer custom software to packaged software.

Other organisational members expressed similar comments to the above opinions on the irrelevance of the Baan system to NEEASAE. The General Manager of Planning said:

> The Baan system is very large. They (consultants) selected a very big system compared to our size, and we have not had any idea about it... It

is an ideal system for Philips (the international company). It is very obvious.

The General Manager for MIS department made a similar point:

The package exceeded our capacity. It should be implemented in companies achieving sales $250 million or more...Here, there is a small Local Area Network (LAN). It can be used to handle wages and accounts. We should be gradually developed step by step. Baan may be suitable for international companies.

Compared to the IMC's experience, the NEEASAE's experience in ERP implementation and its association with management accounting stability is completely different. In the case of NEEASAE, ERP modules and submodules were co-implemented at the same time. ERP consultants tried to customise the software. However, the software has challenged established accounting rules and routines. It contradicted the Uniform Accounting System, which has been used by public sector enterprises since 1966, and local tax rules during encoding existing institutional principles into the new rules built into the ERP. Unlike ERP implementation in NEEASAE, ERP implementation in IMC was gradual over a period of time. ERP software has also been customised to reflect existing routines and institutions. However, it has not challenged existing management accounting rules and routines. It reinforced EU budgeting procedures by successfully encoding EU institutional principles into the new rules built into the ERP. The next subsection focuses on the role of the financial crisis in ERP failure in NEEASAE compared to the role of scarce financial resources in limiting the use of ERP in IMC.

6.2.2.2 The severe financial crisis and the ERP failure

Following the withdrawal of Philips Company at the end of 1997, NEEASAE suffered severe successive losses over the following years. For example, reported losses in 1996/97 were L.E. 5,563,000. These losses can be attributed to a number of coincident circumstances. Firstly, some of the company's machines were fully depreciated. This means that the use of these old machines increased the production of defect products. These products incur two types of costs. The first type is the manufacturing costs associated with products that fail to meet quality standards and are identified before the product is delivered to the customer such as the costs of scrap and spoilage. The second type is the costs incurred because poor quality products are delivered to customers such as negative goodwill.

Secondly, the withdrawal of Philips Company led to changing the company's brand name from 'Philips' to 'NEEASAE'. Therefore, customers did not know the new brand name and they did not differentiate it from other available brands in the Egyptian market. Thirdly, the collapse of Soviet Union in the early 1990s facilitated importing complete electric lightbulbs factories on a large-scale from former Soviet Union countries. The phenomenon known as 'downstairs factories' started to emerge. These factories, managed by unknown producers, started to compete with NEEASAE by manufacturing and selling a diversity cf cheap untested rival electric lightbulbs. Last but not least, another scurce of rival electric lightbulbs came from the implementation of GATT agreement in 1990s in Egypt.[1] As a direct impact of this agreement, a lot of rival electric lightbulbs have been imported and sold in the Egyptian market at a much lower price, normally less than the product costs. A cost accountant said:

> GATT agreement has led to the entrance of a lot of imported products, including electric lightbulbs, to the Egyptian market, especially from China. This resulted in fierce competition and difficulties in competing with these products. For example, there is currently a dumping process, where products are sold with prices less than their costs. As a result, the local product can not be sold.

The General Manager of Budgeting and Cost Accounting Department confirmed this fact:

> We won a legal case against a company to stop cheap imported electric lightbulbs being dumped in the Egyptian market.

Due to all the above circumstances, the company lost most of its market share. Because of the marketing problems of NEEASAE's products, the company started producing and inventorying electric lightbulbs in order to continue running and find work for the company's workers. However, the ERP system did not support the policy of production for inventory and would increase the visibility of this policy. The General Manager of Financial Accounts Department described this problem as follows:

> At the end of each year, we need to increase production either to reduce losses or to make use of available materials and workforce. Therefore, we produce to put our production in warehouses until we find an opportunity for sale. But that was not available in the Baan system. The Baan system did not recognise the production for inventory purpose but the production without inventory. This was an obstacle to implementing the ERP system in the Production Planning Department.

Furthermore, the ERP project increased the degree of financial crisis in NEEASAE. The cost of Baan software was very high. So it was difficult for the company to recover the cost of this software, taking into account the previously mentioned circumstances.[2] However, NEEASAE has not been declared insolvent because there is no notion of bankruptcy in the public sector. To avoid the legal liability of cancelling ERP purchase contract, the company transferred the reason for ERP failure to the ERP vendor. This is because the ERP vendor failed to customise the software to satisfy the company's needs. Later, the ERP vendor in Egypt was declared insolvent and has withdrawn from the Egyptian market.[3] The General Manager for Planning Department said:

> There was a fear of legal responsibility from control agencies such as the Central Agency for Accountability. I refused to take responsibility for the ERP project. All had a real fear. After three years, it was found that the sound solution was to stop the project although we have approached to achieve results. We had hope. It was decided to stop the project at this extent... We stopped and liquidated the guarantee letter. For three years, the Central Agency for Accountancy was asking us. We stopped it (the ERP project). It was a fear rather than anything else. The ERP vendor in Saudi has been charged all the costs. It was a high cost. The Baan vendor in Saudi decided to close its branch in Egypt.

The ex-CEO explained:

> During the implementation process of the software in NEEASE, dramatic changes in the ownership of Baan agent in Egypt have occurred...The cost of the software was reasonable. This was because there was a good contract and the company has not been charged large costs. The implementing company (Baan company in Egypt) charged all the costs.

Scapens and Jazayeri (2003) argue that revolutionary change occurs when there are major threats to the survival of the organisation as a whole and/or to particular sub-groups within the organisation or what Giddens (1984) calls 'ontological security'. The introduction of the Baan system into NEEASAE was revolutionary change as it challenged existing routines and institutions. So this type of change has been subject to a high degree of resistance from the company's entire members, leading to the failure of ERP implementation. The severe financial crisis reinforced and legitimised the ERP failure, rather than facilitated change.

Similar to NEEASAE, IMC suffered from the lack of financial resources that limited expanding the use of ERP. IMC did not complete purchasing a sufficient number of licences to cover the component managers' needs because the EU auditors rejected the ERP project and did not support it financially. In addition, the Iraq War has dramatically affected the IMC's expansion plans. The number of BRCs has been reduced and the implementation of ERP software in these centres has been abandoned to support the Egyptian government to address the economic impact of the war in Iraq. However, this financial crisis has not resulted in the ERP failure in IMC. The next section focuses on analysing and comparing stability and change in management accounting rules and routines in the two organisations implementing custom software, ESTD and AQF.

6.3 Custom software and change and stability in management accounting rules and routines

6.3.1 Custom software and management accounting change in ESTD as a path-dependent process: action, routines and institutionalisation

ESTD is a government agency affiliated to the MOF. It prepares a line-item budget according to Law No. 53 of 1973. In 2000, the World Bank introduced a budget reform programme to the Government of Egypt, including the replacement of the current line-item budget with a performance-based budget. ESTD is one of the government agencies that have been chosen to experimentally implement this project. This project is still ongoing. It included the introduction of a number of custom software systems to support the budget reform. In ESTD, the performance-based budget reform and subsequent change in accounting and non-accounting information systems have been evolutionary and not discrete in nature, and are a continuing effort. A combination of random, systematic, and inertial forces has shaped the implementation processes of all supporting systems of the budget reform. The analysis is consistent with Burns and Scapens' (2000: 13) view that 'specific changes in management accounting could be quite revolutionary...Nevertheless, the change process will be influenced, to some extent, by the existing routines and institutions, and as such the process is still path-dependent.' This sub-section aims at describing the implementation processes of the performance-based budget reform and the systems that have been introduced and computerised to support this reform in ESTD. Further details on this issue will be introduced in the next chapter.

6.3.1.1 *Budget reform and custom software systems design and implementation: the interpretive flexibility of technology and custom software as an action that encodes institutional principles*

In 2002, the World Bank delegation met with the ESTD's officials to discuss the implementation of the performance-based budget. Following this meeting, a Steering Committee (the Principal Committee) and a project team (including six functional permanent committees) were formed. The six functional committees included Tax Systems, Organisation, Administrative and Financial Affairs, Information Systems, Planning, and Budgeting. The roles, activities and responsibilities of these committees were defined as shown in Appendix 6. The Principal Committee was composed of the Commissioner (the project leader and manager), helped by two consultants (the Minister of Finance Consultant and the World Bank Consultant); six area leaders, one of each single area in charge of co-ordinating each area project team. Each project area or functional committee had a leader who was the Head of the Central Administration or the General Manager of the related functional area. He/she was in charge of co-ordinating an area project team composed of a group of key users and an IT area developer.

The Committee of Information Systems, headed by the Head of Central Administration for Information Centre, was in charge of co-ordinating IT specialists in various functional areas, especially planning, administrative and financial affairs, and tax systems. So the information systems team was divided mainly into three sub-teams: the tax systems team; the administrative and financial affairs team; and the planning and performance budget and evaluation team. Each IT sub-team was responsible for designing and implementing custom software systems for its functional area. However, most members of the General Administration for Computing Service were involved in developing IT infrastructure and custom software systems for tax systems. Two computer engineers were sent to the Planning Department and the Administrative and Financial Department to help them in developing their custom software systems.

After forming the project team, each area project team started implementing its action plan that has been set in its committee's responsibilities. All action plans of different committees have been simultaneously implemented. This resulted in a number of automated information systems that have been customised to serve the budget reform in ESTD. These custom software systems can be divided into two types:

A) Systems that indirectly support the budget reform:
   1. Developing IT infrastructure and upgrading the General Sales Tax Administration Computer System (GSTACS).
   2. The new tax return and on-line tax return.
   3. Payment through banks and the immediate addition of tax receipts to the Central Bank using the SWIFT system.
B) Systems that directly support the budget reform:
   1. Computerising the government accounting system.
   2. Developing a computerised cost accounting system, an inventories management system and a fixed assets management system.
   3. Developing a computerised performance measures and standards system.

Clearly, almost all 'new' accounting and non-accounting information systems are computerised custom software systems. According to the interpretive flexibility view of technology (Orlikowski, 1992), custom software tends to reflect existing institutional properties of the organisation and is easily modifiable during design and use stages. In Burns and Scapens' (2000) words, this means that the 'new' IT-based rules could be a formalisation of existing routines and reinforce the institutional *status quo*. The following sub-sections describe each of the above systems and its customisation process in ESTD. More attention will be given to custom software accounting systems, especially the government accounting system, the costing system and the performance reporting system.

IT infrastructure and the new GSTACS. The Committee of Information Systems has renewed completely the IT infrastructure and its applications. It started first with introducing a new computer network that connects the headquarters in Cairo with all districts and regions in all governorates. The Committee of Information Systems, with co-operation with the Committee of Tax Systems, has also upgraded the GSTACS. The GSTACS is the tax information system in ESTD. It is mainly used to manage all sales tax operations, including registration, cancellation, counting, tax return, tax payment, audit and review, tax research, legal affairs and anti-evasion. Power builder and Sybase database were used to develop the new version of the GSTACS. The old version of the GSTACS has been introduced since the establishment of ESTD in 1991. So it became too obsolete and caused a lot of delay in handling data. The next sub-section focuses on reforming and automating the tax return.

The new tax return and the services of sending tax return by mail and filing tax return on-line. The Committee of Tax Systems has introduced a new tax return and simplified the procedures of filing and sending the tax return. The new tax return came into effect as from 1/7/2004. It includes only one page instead of four pages. It also has fewer columns. Times for filing the new tax return have not been changed. They are the times established by the Sales Tax Law. The new tax return is sent monthly to all registrants by registered mail. A registrant should fill in the new tax return according to the instructions included in the back of the return, in addition to the guide of filing distributed by ESTD. The tax return should be fully completed and sent to the concerned district by mail taking into account the time of filing stated by the law. Most registrants are currently reluctant to use the service of sending the tax return by mail. The reason for this behaviour is that if they send the return late, or if the return has been received by the district late, registrants are violating the tax law as the return should be received by the district within the time specified by the law. Registrants who fail to file the return and to pay the tax within the period specified by the law have to pay a fine amounted to a minimum of L.E. 100 up to a maximum of L.E. 2000 plus the tax due and the additional tax.

Furthermore, the Committee of Information Systems, together with the Committee of Tax Systems, has developed on-line tax return filing service. It is the most recent service to registrants. A password is assigned for each registrant and is distributed through local districts in order not to breach the confidentiality of registrants' data. The new tax return is to be submitted electronically by registrants on form (10) G.S.T specially assigned for goods and services subject to the GST and on form (100) G.S.T specially assigned for commodities of Table (1) attached to sales tax law. The use of on-line tax return filing service faces some problems. The number of registrants increased sharply. A large number of wholesalers and retailers, regardless of their educational and cultural levels, have been registered. The less educated registrants would be obstacles for using information technology in managing sales tax such as filling tax returns on-line. The next sub-section focuses on reforming and automating tax payments.

The SWIFT system and payment through banks. On 2/12/ 2001, the permanent Committee of Administrative and Financial Affairs has been formed to achieve four objectives:

1. The immediate addition of tax receipts to the ESTD's bank account in the Central Bank,
2. The automation of government accounting system,
3. Setting up a computerised cost accounting system, and
4. Setting up computerised systems for managing the use of fixed assets and inventories.

In order to achieve the first objective, the Committee of Administrative and Financial Affairs introduced new methods that ensure the immediate addition of tax receipts to the bank account of ESTD in the Central Bank. The Manager of Cost Accounting Department (the reporter of the Committee) described the reasons for these improvements:

> There were long delays in adding cash receipts and cheques to the ESTD's bank account in the Central Bank. Cash receipts were transferred to the Central Bank in 15 days through the correspondent bank. Furthermore, tax revenues collected by cheques were taken 45 days in the clearance room in the Central Bank. The alternative is to implement SWIFT service. The SWIFT service is located in Sweden and transfers money immediately. The study revealed that the savings expected would be about L.E. $\frac{1}{2}$ million.

The SWIFT system was applied to cash receipts on 1/12/2002. In addition, ESTD has benefited from the recent developments in the clearance room in the Central Bank. The clearance room was automated and the cheques are currently collected in 2–3 days. Furthermore, ESTD started to apply the

SWIFT system to monetary transfers from registrants' bank accounts in commercial banks to the ESTD's bank account in the Central Bank. Therefore, ESTD has allowed for a registrant to pay the tax by transferring the amount due from his/her own account to any of the banks all over Egypt to the Department's bank account in the Central Bank instead of remitting the tax collected to the district.

This new system of payment came into effect as from 1/7/2004. It has two steps. First, ESTD issues the registrants' cards. Each registrant has his/her own card which includes the following information: registration number, registrant's name, name of district, telephone number, number of the Department's account in the bank, postal number of the district, and the district's address. Second, the Department gives each registrant a booklet including a form of account transference through banks. A registrant should accurately fill in the form according to the attached instructions and the information of the registrant card. Still, very few registrants use the new system of payment. The next sub-section focuses on automating the existing government accounting system.

Automating the government accounting system. ESTD applies the government accounting system according to Government Accounting Act No. 27 of 1981. The automation of the government accounting system is a key objective of the Committee of Administrative and Financial Affairs. The committee has used Oracle database version (8) to automate the government accounting system. An IT developer – the computer engineer in the Committee – described the software's customisation process as follows:

> The automation seeks to speed up performance, increase accuracy, avoid human errors, and reduce time, effort and cost. The government accounting system has been analysed, designed and programmed. Form No. 75 G. A. is completely automated. This includes automating books and records such as general journal books, budget accounts, current accounts, and encumbrance records that are used in preparing monthly statements of trail balance, monthly reports of expenditures and revenues and the end of year final account. Furthermore, employees have been trained on using the computerised system. We automated the old accounting system because all people are used to use it.

The automation of the existing government accounting system reinforces rather than reforms the traditional budget system. So far the automated government accounting system is only experimentally used in the Central Accounts Unit in Cairo. So other accounts units in other regions have not yet used it. They still manually prepare journal books, general ledgers and monthly and annually reports. The details of the manual government accounting system are presented in sub-section 6.3.1.2. The

Table 6.2   Plans for Deploying the Automated Government Accounting System in ESTD

The current year plan 2004/2005:

1. Finalising all necessary reports that are going to be used to achieve the objectives of systems designed,
2. Preparing a user guide manual for government accounting software's users, and
3. Implementing some module of the software in accounts units in districts and regions in ESTD.

The medium-term plan (three years) 2004/2007:

1. Implementing government accounting software in all accounts units, where final accounts are sent from sub-units to the central unit through the computer networks (the intranet) and the consolidated final account is prepared automatically, and
2. Integrating tax information systems with financial and administrative systems.

---

plans for routinising and intra-institutionalising the automated government accounting system for next year (2004/2005) and medium term (2004–2007) are as shown in Table 6.2.

Next, we focus on introducing and automating the cost accounting system, the inventories management system and the fixed assets management system.

Developing a computerised cost accounting system, an inventories management system and a fixed assets management system.   The other objectives of the Committee of Administrative and Financial Affairs have been to develop computerised custom systems for cost accounting, inventories and fixed assets using Oracle database version (8). The introduction of these systems reforms the traditional budget system and supports the move towards the performance-based budget. However, these systems have been customised to reinforce existing institutional principles in the Egyptian environment. The Manager of Cost Accounting Department (IT developer and a member of the committee) described the difficulties that the committee has faced in setting up the costing system and the other related systems as follows:

> To set up a costing system, we started studying the problems of existing government accounting system to tackle them. We found two main problems as a direct result of using the cash basis. Firstly, fixed assets are not capitalised. Hence, depreciation is not recognised. Secondly, the inventory does not show the goods and services used during the fiscal year. So we decided to switch to accrual accounting by setting an inventory system and a fixed assets system. The Uniform Accounting System

formed the base for the move to accrual accounting. In addition, the non-existence of computing facilities was a limitation to the use of costing system.

According to the Article No. 5 of Government Accounting Act No. 127 of 1981, the cash basis is applied on the current budget[4] with respect of expenditures and revenues. The use of cash basis by the government accounting system is the result of the fact that the line-item budget is used. The nature and the requirements of the traditional budget are consistent with the implication and concept of cash basis. The traditional budget is more focused on inputs and the costs of those inputs, and cash accounting serves this orientation quite adequately. So the government accounts in ESTD are maintained on a cash disbursement basis, showing the amount of goods and services paid for during the year and the expenditures on purchases of fixed assets as current expenditures.

In the development of the cost figures that make up a performance-based budget, all costs should be included. This requires an accrual accounting system for the measurement of past programme costs and estimates on accrual basis for the budget year. In turn, this would mean that inventory should be maintained on an accrual basis and that the portion of capital expenditures used up in each fiscal year should be charged to the performance cost for that period. The introduction of performance-based budget into ESTD required the adoption of a costing system, whose role is rather limited in the traditional budget system. Drawing on the Uniform Accounting System, the Committee of Administrative and Financial Affairs has introduced computerised systems for cost accounting, inventories and fixed assets. The Egyptian Uniform Accounting System was introduced by the CAA in 1966. It is compulsory for all enterprises in the public sector, with the exception of banks and insurance companies that have different regulation. However, ESTD has voluntarily used some treatments of the Uniform Accounting System in establishing its costing system, inventory system and fixed assets system.

The Uniform Accounting System has set out the main principles of cost accounting in general terms. The importance of using the direct costing techniques has been emphasised in this system, which included a section related to the definitions of the various cost elements and the costing centres, see Table 6.3. According to the Uniform Accounting System, cost items (the uses of resources) are classified into wages, commodity requirements, service requirements, finished goods purchased for sale, current transferred expenses and current transfer. This classification of cost items has some similarities with the classification of uses (expenditures) in the general state budget. The expenditures in the general state budget are classified into wages [chapter 1], current expenditures (i.e. commodity requirements, service requirements and finished goods purchased for sale) and current transfers [chapter 2],

Table 6.3   Cost Items and Cost Centres in the Uniform Accounting System

	Analysis of Uses of Resources				
Three Uses of Resources	**Five Production Centres**	**Six Production Service Centres**	**Seven Marketing Service Centres**	**Eight Finance and Administrative Centres**	**Nine Capital Transaction Centres**
31 wages	531 wages	631 wages	731 wages	831 wages	931 wages
32 commodity requirements	532 commodity requirements	632 commodity requirements	732 commodity requirements	832 commodity requirements	932 commodity requirements
33 service acquired	533 service acquired	633 service acquired	733 service acquired	833 service acquired	933 service acquired
34 finished goods purchased for sale	534 finished goods purchased for sale	–	–	–	–
35 current transferred expenses	535 current transferred expenses	635 current transferred expenses	735 current transferred expenses	835 current transferred expenses	935 current transferred expenses
36 current transfer	–	–	–	–	–

This information is based on (Briston and El-Ashker, 1984).

investment uses [chapter 3], and capital transfers [chapter 4]. The costing accounting system in ESTD covers only cost items in chapter (1) and chapter (2).

Furthermore, the Uniform Accounting System divides responsibility centres into five cost centres, namely the production centre, the production service centre, the marketing service centre, the finance and administrative centre, and the capital transaction centre. The latter centre is used to analyse and show separately the cost of self-constructed fixed assets. Then, the Uniform Accounting System directly allocates the uses of resources to the five cost centres. ESTD uses the same classification of cost centres as follows:

1. The production centres that include Districts and Offices,
2. The production service centres that include Regions and some functional central administrations,
3. The marketing service centres that include the Central Administration for Registrants' Assistance,

4. The finance and administrative centres that include the Central Administration for the Commissioner's Affairs and the Central Administration for Financial and Administrative Affairs, and
5. The capital transaction centres that include the Central Printing Department and the Central Carpentry Department.

This classification of cost centres reflects the fact that the costing system closely follows the ESTD's existing organisational structure. Then, the expenditures in chapter 1 and chapter 2 are directly allocated to these cost centres.

The computerised inventory system in ESTD is also based on the treatment of commodity requirements in the Uniform Accounting System. According to the Uniform Accounting System, the commodity requirements consist of raw materials, fuel, spare parts and supplies, packing and wrapping materials, and salvage. This system uses the perpetual inventory system to keep a running, continuous record that tracks inventories (the commodity requirements) on a day-to-day basis. In a perpetual inventory system, detailed records of the cost of each inventory purchase and use are maintained. These records continually – perpetually – show the inventory that should be on hand for every item. The moving average method is used to calculate the cost of units used and the cost of the remaining units on hand. Under this method, a new average is computed after each purchase. The average cost is computed by dividing the cost of goods available for use by the units on hand.

Furthermore, the computerised fixed assets system in ESTD reflects the influence of Uniform Accounting System. According to the Uniform Accounting System, fixed assets are classified into lands; buildings, constructions, facilities and roads; machinery and equipment; transportation and delivery facilities; tools; furniture and fixture; animal and water resources; and deferred expenses. The fixed assets are valued at their historical cost plus any additional capital expenses. Depreciation has been defined as the accounting method for dividing the cost of the fixed asset over the lifetime of the asset using depreciation rates. For example, the depreciation rates for equipment, furniture and cars are 10%, 6% and 20% respectively.

The computerised costing system in ESTD was tested during the period from 1/5/2003 to 30/6/2003. It is centrally used as from 1/7/2003 in the Central Accounts Unit in Cairo. Other accounts units in various regions analyse their expenditures using a certain form (see Appendix 8) and send this form to the Central Accounts Unit. Currently, quarterly reports are prepared to analyse expenses and calculate the cost per collected pound in order to evaluate performance and support decision-making. However, the costing system in ESTD has not completed yet as the implementation processes of the inventory system and the fixed asset system are still in progress. Table 6.4 shows the plans for next year 2004/2005 and medium term (2004/2007).

Table 6.4   Plans for Routinising and Intra-Institutionalising the Automated Costing System, Inventory System and Fixed Assets System in ESTD

The Current Year Plan 2004/2005:	Medium-term Plan 2004/2007:
Costing System: Implementing the costing system in the following cost centres: – The Central Administration for Training Centre, and – Car Administration.	**Costing System:** Extending the use of costing system in all districts and regions to support top management's decisions in each region.
Inventory and Fixed Assets: Allocating the ESTD's fixed assets to different responsibility centres after valuing them and preparing depreciation values every three months to service cost accounting.	**Inventory and Fixed Assets:** Installing the inventory software in all warehouses and connecting them to Headquarter.

The use of the Uniform Accounting System by ESTD in setting up its costing system clearly demonstrates the relevance lost thesis introduced by Johnson and Kaplan (1987). It reflects the dominance of the financial accounting requirements on management accounting information needs. The next sub-section focuses on developing and automating the performance measures and standards system.

Developing a computerised performance measures and standards system.   The Committee of Planning and Performance Budgeting and Evaluation, headed by the head of General Administration for Planning, is mainly responsible for developing the programme and performance budgeting system in ESTD. The Planning Department in ESTD has been established over ten years ago to prepare the annual plans for all regions and districts to achieve annual estimated tax revenues. As a result, this department took the responsibility for the new budgeting system and its members became the key members of the committee set for this purpose. The use of performance-based budget term by ESTD is not accurate.[5]

In fact, what has been developed so far is a system of performance reporting rather than a system of performance budgeting. It is a system that identifies different activities and measures changes therein. Performance data are developed by management independently of the budget and control accounts, and cost figures have not been attached thereto. Performance budgeting goes beyond this. The identification of programmes and the measurement of changes therein are set forth on a cost basis so that performance costs are equal to total costs for budgetary purposes. Currently, the

Committee of Administrative and Financial Affairs develops a costing system that would overcome this limitation. However, there are difficulties in integrating the performance reporting system with the costing system due to the division of responsibility on the two systems between two committees. More details about these problems will be discussed in the next chapter.

The current performance reporting system reflects a slight development in the existing planning system adopted by ESTD before the introduction of the performance-based budget. A planner in the General Planning Department explained this point as follows:

> We have been preparing the annual plan and have been using efficiency and effectiveness measures before implementing the performance-based budget. This helped us to absorb the idea and complete its components. Furthermore, we depend on the existing organisational structure to set programmes for each region and district.

Thus the 'new' performance reporting system is based on existing planning practices. For example, ESTD has reformulated its mission, principles, strategy, policy and methodology, see Appendix 6. Furthermore, it added three new performance indicators to efficiency and effectiveness measures. ESTD has selected five performance indicators to measure the performance of each responsibility centre. For example, performance indicators for a district's manager, as a responsibility centre, are as follows:

1. Productivity = actual tax revenues collected ÷ actual labour hours in all the district's departments. This figure should be compared with (estimated tax revenues ÷ planned labour hours),
2. Effectiveness = (actual tax revenues collected: estimated tax revenues) + (achieved sub-objectives ÷ planned sub-objectives),
3. Efficiency = actual labour hours ÷ planned labour hours,
4. Quality = collecting estimated tax revenues, together with achieving 98% taxpayers' satisfaction,
5. Results = (actual tax revenues collected this period – actual tax revenues collected in the same period in the previous year) compared with actual tax revenues collected in the same period in the previous year. This percentage should be compared with the targeted growth rate.

The 'new' performance reporting system has been automated using Excel files. All districts and regions currently prepare performance reports using Excel files and use the Intranet to exchange the files between the districts and regions and the headquarters in Cairo. In addition, other custom software called 'performance standards system' has been developed using Power Builder and Sybase Database as programming tools. However, this new software has not been used yet. Commenting on this software, the IT developer – the computer engineer in the Committee of Planning – said:

> The new software has been programmed. However, it has not replaced the existing system that is based on Excel files. I have developed Excel files to automatically calculate and update performance measures.

So it can be concluded that the 'new' performance reporting system has not radically changed the existing budgeting system in ESTD. It is path-dependent change that draws on existing system and practices. The next sub-section analyses change and stability in management accounting routines following the introduction of custom software systems to reform budgeting techniques in ESTD.

6.3.1.2   *Custom software use and budgeting, budgetary accounting and budgetary reporting routines in ESTD*

As previously stated, ESTD is one of the revenue departments affiliated to the MOF. So it follows Budget Act No. 53 of 1973, which was amended by Law No. 104 of 1980, in preparing its budget. Moreover, ESTD uses the Egyptian Government Accounting System according to the Act No. 127 of 1981 in accounting for actual revenues and expenditures and in preparing financial statements. At the end of 2000, ESTD started switching to the programme-performance budgeting system. A number of 'new' accounting systems have been introduced to support the move to the performance-based budget. These systems include a costing system, inventory system, a fixed assets system and a performance measurement and reporting system. These 'new' systems are fully computerised. Custom software has been developed for each system. In addition, the traditional Government Accounting System has been computerised. Some of the computerised accounting systems have not been used yet because there are some implementation problems facing these systems as shown in section 6.3.1.3. So ESTD is still preparing its budget according to the line-item budgeting system and is still using the traditional Government Accounting System. The next sub-section examines budget preparation and approval in ESTD.

Budget preparation and approval.   The ESTD's budget is a part of the Egyptian government's budget that is governed by Budget Act No. 53 of 1973. Generally speaking, there are three steps for preparing the government's budget in Egypt. Firstly, a budgeting committee is established in each governmental unit to prepare current and capital budget proposal. Secondly, each government unit submits its budget proposal to its related ministry. Then, each ministry consolidates the budget proposals of its related government units and submits its consolidated budget proposal to the MOF before the 1st of January each year. Budget proposals of different ministries should be associated with supporting documents that justify their estimates and any changes therein from previous year appropriations. Finally, the Sector of General State Budgeting in the MOF prepares the general state budget proposal that consolidates all budget proposals of all ministries after modifying these proposals. After that, the Minister of Finance submits the general state budget proposal to the People's Assembly to approve.

The budget preparation in ESTD starts with the formation of the budgeting committee. In ESTD, there are two departments, which are permanent members of the budgeting committee, responsible for its budget proposal, the General Administration for Revenues and the General Administration for Budget and Encumbrances. The first department is in charge of preparing the estimates of sales tax revenues and following up their collection. The estimates of tax revenues are based on the previous year estimated revenues, expected growth rate and prevailing economic conditions in each industrial sector and service sector. These estimates are prepared for each individual commodity and service separately.

The second department, the General Administration for Budget and Encumbrances, is in charge of preparing the estimates of expenditures and monitoring the spending of encumbrances and changes therein. Expenditure estimates are prepared using the forms received from the MOF at the beginning of each year. These estimates are based on sending requests to all districts and regions to determine their needs for the coming year. After consolidating all these needs, the expenditure estimates are submitted to the MOF that decides certain encumbrances after the approval of the People's Assembly. Next, we examine budget execution in ESTD after the approval of the People's Assembly.

Budget execution: budgetary accounting and budgetary reporting. As stated earlier, ESTD uses the Egyptian government accounting system. The main purpose of this accounting system is to control the execution of the annual budget approved by the parliament. For this control purpose, budget and accounting numbers are continuously compared and at the end of the fiscal year variances between the budget (ex-ante) and the accounting (ex-post) figures are reported. The Egyptian government accounting system is uniform for the whole governmental sector, including all government units. It is a group of regulations and restrictions that government units have to follow in the implementation of the general state budget, in recording and classifying the financial operations and in preparing the budgetary statements of the government units.

The Egyptian government accounting system relies on a group of documents, books and records. The documents are used to record in accounting books and records in the framework of the line-item budget (the traditional budget). These documents are of two types: documents of original entry and supplementary documents. The documents of original entry are used to record the financial transactions in journals and ledger accounts. Examples of these documents are expending form (132 G.A.), reconciliation form (61 G.A.), expending form (50 G.A.) and reconciliation form (62 G.A.). The supplementary documents are enclosed in the documents of original entry in order to enhance the operations of those documents.

The books and records of government accounting consist of journal books, ledger books and statistical and controlling books. Journal books are used to record the financial transactions based on the double entry system. These books are the general journal book for expending forms (224 G.A.) and general journal book for reconciliation forms (224 G.A.). Ledger books include budget accounts [ledger book of expenditures (81 G.A.) and ledger book of revenues (81 G.A.)], ledger book of current central bank (87 G.A.), current accounts under reconciliation (39 G.A.), regular accounts (e.g. prepaid amounts), and intermediate accounts book (e.g. book of remittance and book of cheque). The statistical and controlling books complement the above fundamental accounting books to follow up some aspects that are not available in the accounting records. Examples of these books are encumbrance records (291 G.A. and 292 G.A.) and statement of daily trial balance (69 G.A.).

Based on monthly statements of trial balance, the central accounts unit in ESTD prepares both interim and annual budgetary statements. The main objective of these statements is to determine the compliance with the budget regarding the appropriations and revenues and to indicate whether these appropriations and revenues were obtained and utilised in accordance with legal and contractual requirements. According to the Executive Manual of the Government Accounting Act No. 27 of 1981, ESTD is required to prepare the following interim budgetary statements:

1. An approximate monthly follow-up report of revenues and expenditures. This report is quickly prepared to give a rough view of the ESTD's financial positions before closing the accounts,
2. Monthly report of revenues and expenditures (form no. 75 G.A.). It is prepared to show the actual financial position of ESTD, and
3. Quarterly report of revenues and expenditures (form no. 75 G.A.). This report is prepared every three months and comprises the expenditures, revenues and the balances of the financial accounts for this period. Moreover, it includes the expenditures, revenues and the balances of the financial accounts of the preceding three-quarters.

Furthermore, ESTD prepares the end of year final account (form no. 75 G.A.) to show the actual expenditures and revenues. The actual expenditures and revenues are compared with the adopted expenditures and revenues in the budget in order to demonstrate to what extend ESTD has complied with spending mandates and the financing of activities. The final account is prepared in the light of the periodical bock that is issued by the MOF. All the aforementioned budgetary statements are submitted to the MOF, Central Accounting Agency and People's Assembly.

Next, we examine the intra-institutionalisation processes of 'new' management accounting routines following the introduction of custom software systems in ESTD.

6.3.1.3 The intra-institutionalisation of performance-based budgeting in ESTD

Recently, the Government of Egypt started an attempt to switch from the traditional budget to the programme-performance budget. ESTD, among other governmental units, was chosen to implement the programme-performance budget. The implementation process of this budget reform is still in progress. Different 'new' computerised systems have been introduced to support this reform. However, these systems are still at different stages of routinisation and intra-institutionalisation and are facing some implementation problems. Consequently, preparing the performance-based budget is practically difficult at the moment. In August 2004, a number of meetings have been held to assess the progress achieved so far in implementing the performance-based budget in ESTD before the official meeting with the World Bank officials in September 2004. In one of these meeting, the Minister of Finance Consultant (a university professor) asked the following questions:

> We need to have a performance-based budget for ESTD before the World Bank meeting on 12/09/2004. Is that possible? ...The estimated revenues for 2004/2005 are L.E. 26 milliard and the appropriations (chapters 1 and 2) are L.E. 260 million. What are the programmes planned to achieve the L.E. 26 milliard? ... We need a programming and performance budget with L.E. 260 million to collect L.E. 26 milliard. If you continue using the old system, you would only achieve only L.E. 22 milliard (the previous year actual revenues). What are the means to increase the revenues by L.E. 4 milliard?

The answers on these questions revealed the problems facing the implementation of performance-based budgeting and its supporting systems. Firstly, there was a tendency to use the performance-based budget as a complementary tool to the current line-item budget. Different observations support this conclusion. According to Article No. 5 of the Budget Act No. 53 of 1973, the government units are required to set their activities in the form of programmes. This means that these units should prepare programme budgets for their activities in addition to the current and capital budgets. Bearing in mind this legal requirement, a budgeting accountant responded to the Minister of Finance Consultant's questions:

The use of performance-based budget is currently difficult because the whole government budget is a line-item budget. So it would be difficult that some government units use line-item budgets and other units use performance-based budgets.

The General Manager for Budgeting and Encumbrances said:

We currently use the line-item budget. If the Ministry of Finance wants us to implement the performance-based budget, it would send the appropriate forms to fill.

The General Manager for Planning commented:

The Ministry of Finance should itself implement the performance-based budget. If it has not implemented the budget reform, the current situation would continue for a long period and there would not be integration.

The Minister of Finance Consultant replied:

The implementation will be gradual and will take from 5 to 10 years, like Malaysia. We can not change the current budgeting system...What we need is a performance-based budget for 2004/2005, together with the state general budget before 12/09/2004... We need to re-allocate the line-item budget for 2004/2005 to programmes according to responsibility centres. What do you need to do so?

All the above comments reveal the tendency towards using the performance-based budget as a complementary tool. It is just another classification of budget items. Another observation is the automation of the traditional government accounting system that is based on the current line-item budget. The accounts maintained to control and record the distributions of money have not been established on a programme basis, sub-divided by performance units. All these mean that there is no current attitude towards replacing the current line-item budget with the performance-based budget.

Secondly, there was no general agreement on the estimation bases of the performance-based budget for 2004/2005. According to Budget Act No. 53 of 1973, the current estimation base of both revenues and expenditures depends on the results of prior three years as a base for predicting the coming year revenues and expenditures. However, there are no clear guidelines for preparing performance-based budget estimates. The Minister of Finance Consultant asked:

The estimated revenues for 2004/2005 are L.E. 26 milliard. There is a planned increase in revenues with L.E. 4 milliard this year. What are the spending requirements to achieve this increase?

The General Manager of Planning Department suggested:

We can analyse the actual expenditures for the previous year (2003/2004). The fundamental appropriations at the beginning of the year were L.E. 215 million and the actual expenditures at the end of the year were L.E. 275 million. Thus there was L.E. 60 million deficit or additional appropriations.

The Minister of Finance Consultant tried to benefit from the reasons for such additional appropriations to estimate next year expenditures. He said:

Is there a relationship for such increase with other variables such as the increase in collected revenues or the increase in the workforce? Or is it just coincidence? What were the reasons for the additional appropriations and the means used to fund them? We can assume that the increase in expenditures would be the same as the prior year (L.E. 60 million).

The General Manager of Budgeting and Encumbrances responded:

There were a lot of reasons for such increase and we cannot classify them into categories. In addition, your suggestion means that there is an official recognition of the additional appropriations and that the costs have to increase. We can use the fundamental appropriations for 2004/2005 (L.E. 260 million) as a minimum estimation.

The Minister of Finance Consultant suggested:

The budget in Egypt is based on actual basis. What is supposed to do is that the labour in Egypt is fixed cost except incentives... You can start with prior year actual expenditures (L.E. 275 million) as an initial basis for estimation and, then, add 10% the annual increase in wages and salaries as an inevitable increase.

Apparently, all these discussions reveal that the performance-based budget in ESTD will be approximate estimates at best because there is no agreement on a unified basis for preparing the performance-based budget or even the starting point for such estimates. Should these estimates be based on current year appropriations and expected additional appropriations by an amount equal to prior year additional appropriations? Or should previous year actual expenditures be modified by only inevitable increases such as the 10% annual increase in wages and salaries?

Thirdly, there are some problems in the full measurement of performance costs and the cost per unit in each responsibility centre because of the lack of co-ordination between different departments responsible for designing and implementing the supporting systems for budget reform. One problem is the differences in cost classifications between Cost Accounting Department and Budgeting and Encumbrances Department. The Minister of Finance Consultant asked:

Can you convert the line-item budget for 2004/2005 into a performance-based budget?

The General Manager for Budgeting and Encumbrances replied:

We prepared the current year budget according to the object of expenditure classification as we received the old forms from the Ministry of Finance. We do not have the functional classification of expenditures.

The Manager of Cost Accounting Department commented:

We have the functional classification of expenditures (chapter 1 and 2) on the costing system but for the previous year 2003/2004. We have not prepared the functional classification for the current year because we have not received cost data reports from some districts.

The Minister of Finance Consultant asked:

Is it possible to prepare both cost classifications together (by functions and by object of expenditure), which allow for allocating the total appropriations to different types of expenditures and different responsibility centres at the same time?

The World Bank Consultant responded:

We are interested in the costs of programmes and their activities. If we get these figures, that's enough and there is no need for relating them to the object of expenditure classification.

The Manager of Cost Accounting Department commented:

> We actually analysed the previous year expenditures according to both cost classifications. The costing software is able to do so.

Another problem of cost determination is that the costing system can only determine the cost of each responsibility centre and can not calculate the cost per output unit in each responsibility centre. This is because the Planning Department is in charge of performance measurement and reporting system and has the information on the outputs and activities of each responsibility centre. So these outputs and activities should be sent to the Cost Accounting Department. There are other features of the lack of co-ordination between the Planning Department and the Cost Accounting Department such as the use of different programming tools and databases and the different response to the change in organisational structure. These issues will be explored in the next chapter.

In general, the decision to divide the responsibility on designing and implementing the different information systems that support the budget reform resulted in this apparent lack of co-ordination. However, ESTD tried to overcome these problems by forming a new sub-committee that consists of members of the Planning Department the Cost Accounting Department and the Budgeting and Encumbrances Department. This sub-committee will be responsible for preparing the performance-based budget for 2004/2005. However, this is a temporal solution.

Fourthly, there was a debate on the issue of performance evaluation; the need for performance evaluation and who should be responsible for it. The Minister of Finance Consultant stated:

> According to the World Bank's recommendations, there should be a department responsible for evaluating performance. It must be totally independent from other departments.

The General Manager of Planning Department recommended:

> The Planning Department, which is currently in charge of performance measurement, could be responsible for performance evaluation as well. The title of the department could become 'the Planning and Performance Evaluation Department'.

A Computer Engineer commented:

> Currently, persons, who audit our work, do not understand in IT. They report only on computers' problems such as the breakdown of a printer or a network.

The General Manager of Databases said:

Performance evaluators should have sufficient knowledge with IT.

The General Manager of Computer Operating suggested:

Some current employees in the IT department could be transferred to such evaluation functions.

The World Bank Consultant said:

Auditors evaluate results. It is not necessary for auditors to understand in IT. Auditors can get help from some experts when they do not have such expertise.

He continued:

The Central Agency for Accountancy should be responsible for performance evaluation in the organisation as it has experts in different financial, administrative and technical areas.

The Minister of Finance Consultant commented:

The Central Agency for Accountancy has permanent auditors in organisations. It is a good idea for performance evaluators to live in the field. Performance evaluation should be in the field. There should be performance evaluation units in each district and each region. Moreover, there should be different experts in each functional area such as tax and information systems.

Clearly, there is an agreement on the need for evaluating performance. However, no decision has been taken as to who should be responsible for performance evaluation. Is it the Planning Department or the Central Agency for Accountancy?

Finally, a number of 'new' computerised subsystems have been introduced to support the budget reform. These include a costing system, an inventory system, a fixed assets system and a performance measurement system. These systems are at different stages of routinisation and intra-institutionalisation (see section 6.3.1.1). So far some of these systems have still had some implementation problems. For example, there is an attempt to introduce an inventory system at the level of ESTD. This system depends on the immediate update on inventory status in all the ESTD's warehouses. It also depends on the use of information networks to achieve integration and communication between different warehouses. However, this system has not been put into action because of some shortage in the IT infrastructure in the 6th of October City, where the main warehouse of ESTD is located. The next sub-section examines the possibility of extra-institutionalisation processes of 'new' management accounting routines.

6.3.1.4   The extra-institutionalisation of performance-based budgeting

The use of performance-based budgeting in ESTD is expected to be extra-institutionalised or disassociated from its historical circumstances. A number of observations support this conclusion. ESTD is a leading department in the MOF. Therefore, there will be imitation processes of the best practices adopted by this department (mimetic processes). These imitation processes are expected to occur due to at least two main reasons. Firstly, the Minister of Finance has recently moved his office to ESTD and considered the ESTD web site as the formal web site of the MOF. He manages all other departments from the ESTD's location. Therefore, the successful practices followed by ESTD are expected to influence the decisions taken by the Minister in developing and changing other departments.

Secondly and most importantly, the Model Customs and Tax Centre (MCTC) has recently been established. The MCTC combines most of the best practices of tax administration in a single, pilot project. It provides one-stop shopping for large taxpayers who have opted to participate in the new system in terms of receiving and filing tax forms, making tax payments, and visiting auditors and examiners for all their tax matters, including customs payments. The MCTC conducts joint audit of customs and taxes, maintains full current accounts of taxpayers, and has organised processes on a functional rather than tax-type basis. It has employees from Customs Department, Income Tax Department and Sales Tax Department. The Commissioner of ESTD has been appointed as MCTC general supervisor. Therefore, the best practices used in ESTD are expected to be coped by the MCTC and other tax departments. One of these practices is the implementation of performance-based budgeting, which has actually started in the MCTC. The Minister of Finance Consultant confirmed this fact by saying:

> The Sales Tax Department is the first government unit in Egypt that has implemented the programmes-and-performance-based budget to achieve expenditure efficiency and effectiveness. It has well-trained staff, innovative thinking and ability to change for better. It successfully started to experimentally implement the programmes-and-performance-based budget. This opens the door for the possible implementation in other government units. The objective of this is to provide better service at lower cost (ESTD, 2002a).

In addition to ESTD, the experimental implementation of performance-based budgeting started in other governmental units, see Table 6.5. This application of performance-based budgeting is supported by sufficient enforcement

Table 6.5 Examples of Ministries and Governmental Units that Started Performance Budgeting

Ministry	Related Governmental Units
The Ministry of Electricity and Energy	• The Parent Company for Electricity and its subsidiaries, • The General Organisation for New and Renewable Energy.
The Ministry of Finance	• The General Sales Tax Department, • The Model Customs and Tax Centre.
The Ministry of Industry and Technological Development	• The Productivity Authority, • The General Organisation for Standardisation and Quality Control.
The Ministry of Information and Communication	• The General Organisation for Post.

(coercive pressures); that is, the approval of the People's Assembly, presidential decree and ministerial decisions. For example, the Minister of Finance issued a decision No. 582 of 2002 to form a committee in the MOF that started applying a performance-based system to governmental purchases and inventories. Furthermore, in 2004, the MOF prepared and published forms and models that guide the preparation of budget according to programmes and performance budgeting. These forms and models are to be used as guidelines in preparing the draft budget for 2004/2005 (see Appendix 6).

In support for the widespread use of performance-based budgeting, the MOF has initiated and funded a project called Integrated Automation Project (IAP)[6] in January 2002. The project takes five years and consists of five annual phases. Table 6.6 presents these phases and the activities expected to be accomplished in each phase. These phases achieve seven major objectives of the project as follows:

1. Development and institutionalisation of information systems,
2. Improvement of policy formulation and implementation,
3. Improvement of public expenditure management,
4. Implementation of an outcome-oriented budgeting system,
5. Development of human resources,
6. Provision of technical tools, and
7. Development of an integrated automated system for the MOF and its entities.

As clearly evident from the above objectives and phases, the project's aim is to support the MOF in computerising its government expenditure system.

Table 6.6   The IAP Implementation Phases

Phase	Activities	2004	2005	2006	2007	2008
1	Budgeting Sectors, Finance Sector, Performance Measurement System (PMS) – Pilot, MOF portal, Data Centre (1st phase), and linking with Central Bank	■				
2	Economic Units Budgeting Sector, Auditing Units in Ministries, Governorates HQ, major entities, Data Centre (2nd phase), extension of PMS, linking with General Tax and Sales Tax Departments.		■			
3	Sector of Accounts and Financial Directorates, Account and Auditing Units in Governorates Department, Service and Economic Units, extension of PMS, linking with customs and Real Estate Tax Departments			■		
4	50% of line agencies accounting and auditing units in local governments, linking with government services authority and Treasury Department, extension of PMS.				■	
5	Completion of the rest of line agencies accounting and auditing units in local governments, extension of PMS.					■

Source: The Ministry of Finance.

This system is based on building a Government Expenditure Information Network (GEIN) that relates the different sectors of the MOF (see Figure 6.4) and linking these sectors with other MOF's departments and other related agencies (see Figure 6.5). The new system will provide a comprehensive, reliable and timely budget and financial management information and help the Government to effectively manage the budget and expenditures and control funds.

The government expenditure modernisation project as the core of IAP is an important step in implementing a series of wide ranging

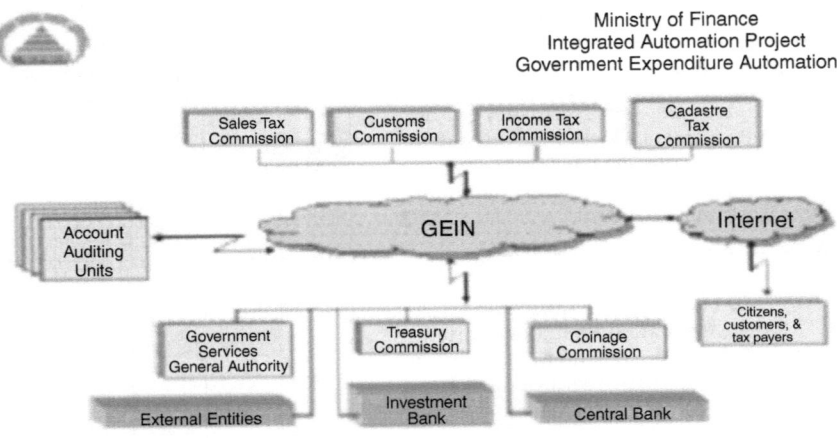

Figure 6.4   Government Expenditure Information Network (GEIN)

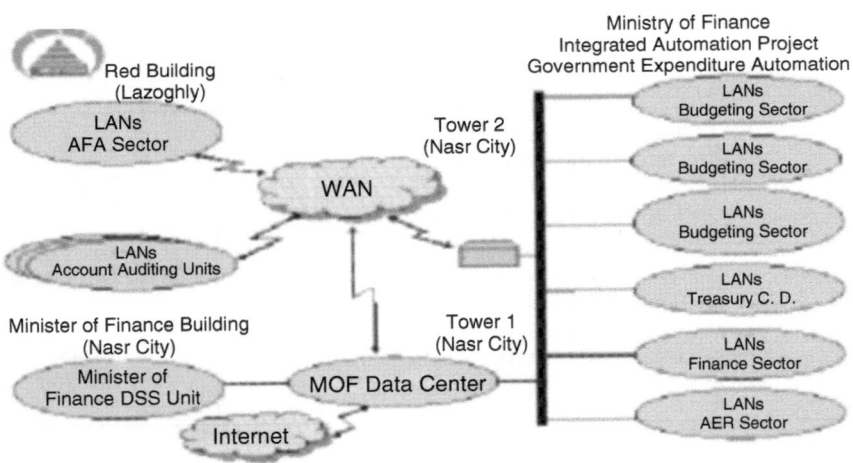

Figure 6.5   MOF Integrated Automation

public expenditure management reforms undertaken by the Government, including the gradual incorporation of the concepts of programmes and performance budgeting into the traditional budgeting system. Thus the programmes and performance-based budgeting system is expected to be extra-institutionalised and the IT will facilitate the process of extra-institutionalisation in different MOF entities.

In the next section we briefly analyse custom software and stability and change in management accounting rules and routines in AQF, the second company that implemented custom accounting software. Moreover, we compare custom software and stability and change in management accounting rules and routines in ESTD with the stability and change in AQF.

6.3.2 Comparison of custom software and accounting stability in AQF with custom software and associated accounting change in ESTD

Since its early beginnings in 1976, AQF has adopted the Uniform Accounting System to both financial accounting and cost accounting because it has been owned by non-manufacturing public enterprises. The Government's contributions in the ownership have been the main factor for using the Uniform Accounting System. In 1996, the Government started the partial privatisation of AQF. However, the majority of the company's ownership (more than 80%) is still owned by public enterprises. Therefore, the company continued using the Uniform Accounting System despite the registration in the stock exchange, which requires registered companies to adopt the Egyptian Accounting Standards, an Arabic translation of International Accounting Standards. The General Manager of Financial Accounts explained this apparent conflict as follows:

We use the account chart (account codes and names) from the Uniform Accounting System but the company applies the Egyptian Accounting Standards. The company also uses some treatments of the Uniform Accounting System such as depreciation rates. This is because accounting standards are general principles and have not determined specific depreciation rates. In addition, we disclose the methods used in notes to financial statements. With respect to the matters that were in conflict with accounting standards, we applied the accounting standards. The company applies accounting standards and is subject to Law No. 159 of 1981 and its executive regulations.

In 1989 custom accounting software based on the Uniform Accounting System was introduced to the Finance Sector in AQF. It was based on a mainframe-computerised system that used COBOL language. It had three applications: wages, inventories and purchases. These applications were isolated from each other. Moreover, there was duplication in data entry. In 1998/99 AQF adopted 'new' custom software, Oracle software, as part of the preparation for ISO 9001 certificate. Historical data were transferred into Oracle software and new applications have been introduced. The 'new' software integrates and relates different databases. It has 28 applications that cover the most important systems of the company. Examples of these applications are wages, inventories, cost accounts, purchases, suppliers and sales. However, almost all of these applications are based on the Uniform Accounting System. For example, the General Manager of Financial Accounts stated that:

> Before adopting Oracle software, the work was manual in preparing financial statements, including documentary cycle and trial balance. In 1990s...the Uniform Accounting System has been programmed. The software currently prepares the trail balance. We still try to prepare financial statements by the software. We currently use Excel files to prepare financial statements.

Similarly, a cost accountant described the role of the Oracle software in determining product costs:

> Cost centres are divided into production (Account No. 5), production service (Account No. 6), marketing service (Account No. 7), and administrative and finance service (Account No. 8). Any journal entry recorded is also directed to the related cost centre. Account No. 3 (use of resources) is first allocated to cost centres as a first stage... The costs of service centres are next allocated to production centres. Then, we calculate the unit product cost... In past, the allocation process was manual. We were spending days to perform such allocation. Currently, the allocation is very fast and accurate. The software saves efforts and time and provides high degree of accuracy.

The software supplier has been contracted to complete programming the software to meet the needs of the company in 11 months. However, the software was formally delivered in July 2001. Consultants from the vendor company conducted a survey to identify the information needs of all departments in AQF. Each department provided its documentary cycle and outputs during the survey. Then, consultants programmed some modules and a few months later they brought the software and installed it. However, this initial copy was almost not suitable for the company's circumstances. Applications designed were significantly different from reality. Consultants withdrew this copy and re-designed the current version of the software.

In fact, the Oracle software was fully customised to meet the information needs of the company. The customisability of the software was seen by the company's members as a major advantage. This is consistent with Burns and Scapens (2000) that it is easy to introduce change that does not conflict with existing routines and institutions. It is also in agreement with the interpretive flexibility of technology. The General Manager of MIS

Department explained the advantage of custom developed software over packaged software as follows:

> We conducted a feasibility study that compared between a number of packaged software to determine customisation efforts required in each one. We reached a decision that custom developed software is the best solution to the company's circumstances. We found that we would pay a large amount of money and we had to customise the purchased package. Furthermore, we would not obtain the source code for the package because its price would be unreasonable... In the case of package software, the company's organisational structure should be modified to fit the package.

He added:

> Sometimes, we have to change or modify a module in response to a law or a governmental decision. There is no problem at all in the software's flexibility because we programmed the software. Each person responsible for a module is capable of modifying it at any time and under any circumstances.

Although the custom Oracle software covers both financial accounting and cost accounting, there are still some management and financial accounting practices not included into the software. Examples of these practices are planning budget preparation, cost variance calculation and environmental disclosure. The company prepares two types of budgets: current budgets and investment budget. Current budgets include sales budget, production budget, wages budget, commodity and service requirements budget, cash flow budget, planned balance sheet, and planned current operations. All these budgets are prepared using Excel files. In addition, the company calculates cost variances that compare amounts included in budgets with actual figures using Excel files.

In 1999 the company introduced voluntary environmental reports after it was awarded ISO 14001 certificate for the environment management system. The objectives of publishing environmental data are to present the company's contributions to the environment, show how it gives up part of its profit to protect the environment and gain tax incentives and exemptions from customs duties. The environmental reports are prepared by modifying original financial statements on Excel files. With respect to the income statement, expenses spent on the environment are added to net profit to show that if the company has not spent on the environment, its profit would increase. With respect to the balance sheet, assets that are used in environment protection are excluded and the finance related to these assets is excluded from the opposite side as well.

Compared with ESTD, the AQF's experience in custom software implementation and its association with management accounting stability has some similarities and some differences. In AQF, custom Oracle software was implemented to fit the requirements of the Uniform Accounting System. It has not challenged established accounting rules and routines. The company has introduced environmental disclosures that are based on the financial statements prepared according to the Uniform Accounting System's requirements. These environmental reports are 'new' accounting routines but they are not influenced by the use of the Oracle software. Unlike custom software implementation in AQF, ESTD has implemented a number of custom software systems to supposedly reform budgeting techniques. Each of this custom software has a specific purpose. However, similar to AQF, some custom software systems tended to support existing routines and institutions, especially traditional budgeting practices. Unlike AQF, ESTD has voluntarily adopted the Uniform Accounting System to allocate cost items to different responsibility centres and account for inventories and depreciation.

6.4   Discussion

This chapter addressed the first group of research questions, which focuses on the role of IT (ERP vs. custom software) in changing management accounting rules and routines and the forces driving management accounting change and stability. It has analysed four case studies in line with the theoretical framework developed in Chapter 3. The analysis was conducted at different levels, including action, routines, intra-institutionalisation and extra-institutionalisation to understand the interplay between action and structure. Overall, this analysis indicated that IT projects, whether ERP or custom software, did not initiate change in management accounting rules (systems) and routines (practices) in highly regularised Egyptian organisations, especially government agencies and state-owned enterprises. Other institutional forces were behind introducing change in management accounting rules and routines in Egyptian organisations.

With respect to the role of IT in management accounting change, the case studies' findings revealed that IT was not a trigger for change in management accounting systems and practices as it tended to routinise and institutionalise existing accounting techniques. The term 'association' could be more suitable than the term 'driver' or 'trigger' with respect to change in accounting methods. Usually, accounting change occurs first and IT comes to support this change as in IMC and ESTD. Alternatively, IT is introduced to support existing accounting routines as in NEEASAE and AQF. This result could be expected in the case of custom software. However, it has been observed in the case of ERP software as well. This is because ERP built-in accounting knowledge has not been transferred into ERP users. This could be related to the lack of training and/or the education system.

ERP software customisation is very acceptable in practice in Egyptian organisations as it tends to reinforce existing routines and institutions. The tendency of ERP customisation supports Orlikowski's (1992) view about the interpretive flexibility of technology. It is also consistent with Burns and Scapens' (2000) view about the possibility of formalising existing organisational routines into rules. The result that ERP tended to reinforce existing routines and institutions supports previous studies' findings, especially Scapens and Jazayeri (2003) and Granlund and Malmi (2002). However, it differs from these studies in the use of customisation strategy to stabilise management accounting systems and practices.

It is fair enough to say that the forces driving change and stability in management accounting rules and routines are different from the forces driving IT projects in Egyptian organisations. In the case of state-owned enterprises, there was stability in the use of Uniform Accounting System and traditional planning budgets despite the introduction of ERP into NEEASAE and custom software into AQF. These accounting rules and routines are closely monitored by the CAA and other government agencies such as the Income Tax Department and Sales Tax Department. The ERP was introduced to NEEASAE to improve its performance and facilitate its privatisation. It was initiated by the Egyptian Holding Company for Engineering Industries, which is a state-owned enterprise and has to obey control authorities and tax departments by applying the Uniform Accounting System. The order of the holding company was less effective than the institutionalised accounting rules and routines that prevented change in management accounting to take place in NEEASAE.

The partial privatisation of AQF, coupled with its orientation towards international markets, encouraged the company to improve its information systems by adopting ISO 9001, ISO 14000, and custom accounting software. AQF was registered in the Egyptian stock exchange, which imposes the use of international accounting standards. It has introduced some voluntary environmental reports to gain tax incentives and exemptions from customs duties. However, the company still uses the Uniform Accounting System and traditional planning budgets as the majority of the company's shares are still owned by non-manufacturing state-owned enterprises. The disclosure requirements of the stock exchange were not able to overcome the institutionalised accounting rules and routines supported by control authorities and other government agencies. The extra-organisational institutions that dominated the centrally planned economy era still have the major influence on state-owned enterprises.

In the case of government agencies there was change in management accounting rules and routines. IMC and ESTD have adopted the programme and performance-based budget. However, neither ERP implemented by IMC nor custom software implemented by ESTD was the driver of this change. In the case of IMC, the EU Commission has played an essential role in selecting the 'new' management accounting system for IMC by appointing a management team that had experience in EU projects and programmes. That ensured the selection of management accounting rules and routines that were in conformity with EU budgeting (programme and performance-based budget) and EU contracting procedures. Later, the ERP project was initiated by accountants in IMC to overcome the problems of the previous software and to face expected expansion of IMC. It has been customised to reinforce EU budgeting and contracting procedures. However, the EU Commission has not given sufficient financial support for the ERP project. This situation clearly demonstrates the conflicting roles of extra-organisational institutions. The EU Commission supported the budget reform not the IT reform.

In the case of ESTD the World Bank and the MOF have introduced the programme and performance-based budget to replace the line-item budget in ESTD. Custom software systems have been introduced, supposedly, to support the budget reform. They also implemented to manage the extension of the sales tax to the wholesale and retail stages. However, these systems reinforced the *status quo* rather than reformed it. Consistent with the Budget Act No. 53 of 1973, the programme and performance-based budget was considered a complementary tool to the line-item budget. In addition, ESTD introduced both custom software that supports the line-item budget and custom software that supports the programme and performance-based budget. However, the custom software that was introduced to support the programme and performance-based budget was based on existing routines and institutions. For example, the cost accounting system introduced to ESTD was based on the Uniform Accounting System. Furthermore, some performance measures were also based on existing measures applied by ESTD. Therefore, when ESTD faced with conflicting institutional pressures, it responded by trying to compromise their requirements.

The above four Egyptian organisations faced conflicting institutional environments as a result of the move to a free market-oriented economy. The results in this chapter raise the following question: how do organisational units respond to new extra-organisational institutional demands that conflict with their traditional practices? Meyer and Rowan's (1977) view about this issue is that organisations adopt inconsistent, even conflicting, practice to gain legitimacy. However, D' Aunno *et al.* (1991) argue that organisations have limited ability to respond to conflicting demands and thus will conform to them only partially. In fact, there is no definite answer to this question; the response will depend on the circumstances of each organisation. A detailed analysis of this issue is outside the scope of this book.

6.5   Conclusion

Drawing on the theoretical framework developed in Chapter 3, this chapter examined the role of IT (ERP vs. custom software) implementation and use in management accounting change and stability and the forces behind change and stability in management accounting rules and routines in four Egyptian organisations. The analysis revealed that IT was not a driver of change in management accounting systems and practices in highly regularised organisations such as state-owned enterprises and government agencies. Other institutional forces were behind introducing change in management accounting rules and routines in Egyptian organisations.

This result could be expected in the case of custom software. However, it has been observed in the case of ERP software as well. In IMC, ERP modules and sub-modules were gradually implemented over a period of time. ERP has also been customised to reinforce EU budgeting procedures, programme and performance-based budgeting, by encoding EU institutional principles into the new rules built into the ERP. In NEEASAE, ERP modules and sub-modules were co-implemented at the same time. However, it contradicted the Uniform Accounting System and local tax rules during encoding institutional principles into the ERP. The tendency towards ERP customisation could be attributed to the fact that ERP built-in accounting knowledge has not been transferred into ERP users. This could be related to the lack of training and/or the education system.

Custom software was also not a driver of change in management accounting rules and routines in Egyptian organisations. In ESTD case, custom software systems have been introduced to support the budget reform from line-item budgeting to programme and performance-based budgeting. However, these systems reinforced the *status quo* rather than reformed it. ESTD introduced both custom software that supports the line-item budget and custom software that supports the programme and performance-based budget. However, the custom software that was introduced to support the programme and performance-based budget was based on existing routines and institutions. In AQF, custom accounting software was implemented as well. However, it reinforced existing routines, mainly the Uniform Accounting System.

The next chapter examines the operation of the dialectic of control in the four organisations under study.

Notes

1   In the planning budgets for 1998/99, the custom duties on imported electric light-bulbs were reduced from 70% to 45%. In addition, the company continued the production reduction policy followed in 1996/97 and in 1997/98 as a result of the fierce competition caused by removing the protection policy for local products and dumping processes.

2   The company expanded the use of overdraft loans from local and international banks to finance its operations. In the planning budgets for 1998/99, local overdraft loans on 30/06/1997 were L.E. 27,793,000 (total assets were L.E. 249,327,000). These loans were expected to become L.E. 40,000,000 in 1998/99 (total assets were L.E. 269,027,000).

3   Shortly after the withdrawal of the local Baan agent, another company was established to sell Baan software in the Egyptian market.

4   The accrual basis is applied on the investment budget. The operations associated with the capital projects should be recorded on the basis of what is actually achieved as soon as this achievement is fulfilled whether it was accompanied by payments or not.

5   See section 6.3.1.3 for arguments that support this view.

6   Two phone conversations were conducted with IAP Director and the Minister of Finance's consultant on 23 November 2004 to explore more details about this project.

7
ERP vs. Custom Software and the Operation of the Dialectic of Control

7.1 Introduction

Giddens (1984) argues that there is misdistribution of resources that is the basis for domination structure. He develops the concept of the dialectic of control that implies that, despite this asymmetrical distribution of resources, all power relations involve reproduced relations of autonomy and dependence in interaction in both directions. Drawing on this concept and its application in Burns and Scapens' (2000) framework, this chapter analyses extra-institutional pressures and change in management accountants' roles and relationships due to the introduction of IT in the four cases under study. The analysis is conducted at two levels. The first level examines the changing power relations between extra-organisational institutions and organisational members due to the implementation of IT projects and associated management accounting change, if any. The second level examines the changing power relations among organisational members due to the implementation of IT projects and associated management accounting change and stability. We analyse the roles of management accountants, IT specialists and line managers and their relationships within each organisation.

This chapter is structured into four sections. The next section addresses the operation of the dialectic of control in the organisations that adopted ERP systems. It presents and compares the impact of ERP implementations on management accountants' role and relationships in IMC and NEEASAE. Then, we analyse and compare the operation of the dialectic of control in ESTD and AQF, the organisations that adopted custom software systems. This is followed by a discussion section that compares the changing power relations in both groups of organisations and relates the case studies' findings to research questions and previous studies' results. The final section summaries and concludes the chapter.

7.2 ERP and the operation of dialectic of control

7.2.1 ERP and the operation of dialectic of control in IMC

In this sub-section we examine the operation of the dialectic of control in IMC after the introduction of a 'new' ERP system. It focuses on the role of IMC's members in challenging the power of EU and the changing role and relationships of management accountants with external IT specialists, internal IT specialists and Component Managers.

7.2.1.1 ERP adoption and challenging the EU power

Following the establishment of IMC in 2001, the management team was selected and appointed, comprising both European and Egyptian executives. The Finance Department consisted of five Egyptian personnel reporting to the Financial Controller. The organisational structure for the Finance Department is shown in Figure 7.1. At that time, The Finance Department was headed by an Egyptian Financial Controller, who is a Certified Public Accountant (CPA) and previously worked for more than 30 years in multinational companies in the USA. Its responsibility was to establish accounting systems within IMC.

The Financial Controller worked closely with the Financial Systems Manager[1] on developing computerised accounting systems. Initially, a software package called 'Quick Books' was selected and implemented to deal with routine transactions processing such as general ledger, accounts receivable and accounts payable. However, it suffered from some main problems. The Financial Systems Manager indicated that:

> The Quick Books software lacks users' security, has a limited database and is vulnerable to being corrupted. You could easily lose all data

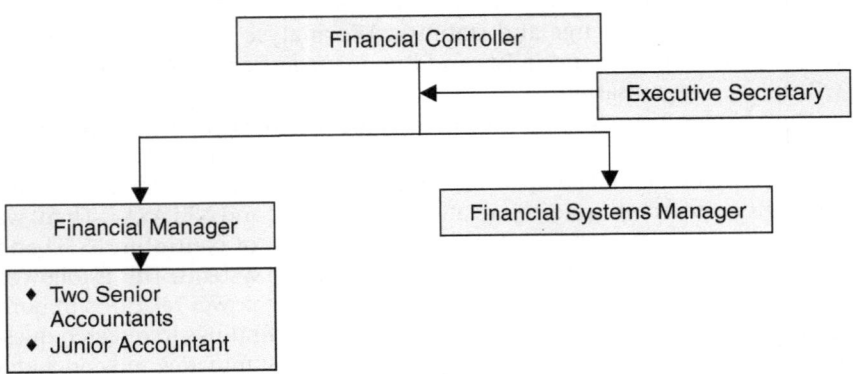

Figure 7.1   Structure of Finance Department

stored on it. It is limited software similar to a Microsoft Excel file. Furthermore, it suddenly stops working, from time to time, and does not accept any new records. It was totally unreliable.

In view of the weaknesses stated above and the planned expansion of IMC's activities to establish a number of new Business Resource Centres (BRCs),[2] the Financial Controller regarded the introduction of ERP as a legitimate and rational response to the Centre's problems and future expansion. So he proposed adopting ERP to integrate all the Centre's internal components and the BRCs and overcome the existing package's problems.

In the middle of 2002 the Executive Director of IMC, who is a close friend of the Financial Controller, made a decision to purchase an ERP system. The technical requirements of ERP software were identified. A tender for the supply of this system to IMC was prepared and advertised in newspapers. A number of ERP vendors submitted their offers. The ERP suppliers' technical offers and other supported documents were copied and distributed to the IMC's members to evaluate these offers. After a short period of time the Commission of the European Communities cancelled the ERP project as its members found out that IMC violated the EU tender procedures and published the tender without a prior written authorisation of the EU Commission. In particular, the value of the supply contract exceeded the contracting authority of IMC.

Furthermore, the members of the Commission were not convinced of the urgent need by IMC for such software. They saw that IMC did not deserve to have an ERP system because of the IMC's temporal nature and the large amount required to buy the software. As a result, the Commission's members considered the cost of ERP was very high and exceeded their budget. The Financial Systems Manager complained:

> The members of the Commission saw that a small package would satisfy the IMC's information needs. Regrettably, they did not understand what ERP means. You spoke to persons who did not understand the value of ERP. All their perceptions and believes were that ERP is accounting software. Therefore, we should purchase any small accounting software. The Commission's members cancelled the ERP project and, at the same time, they required reports and other requests that could not be prepared without the ERP system. Things could not be done manually.

Following this situation, another tender, which took into account the limits of the contracting authority of IMC, was prepared and advertised. There is a specific type of contract that does not require a prior written authorisation of the EU Commission as its value is less than the limit required for the pre-approval of the EU. The value of the tender for ERP supply was reduced to be within the contracting authority of IMC to avoid the EU pre-approval and intervention. This demonstrates Giddens' (1984) concept of reflexive monitoring of activity, where actors continuously monitor not only their actions but also the actions of others.

Baan software was selected and purchased. IMC only purchased five licences for five users. This number of licences was not enough to cover all the IMC's members. The Technical Manager of Baan vendor in Egypt described the tender procedures as follows:

> The tender included all the technical specifications for the system and we found ourselves satisfying all conditions. Therefore, we decided to participate in the tender...We submitted our offer. There were only three ERP vendors and we won the tender...What I want to confirm is that the market proved that building the business model and then configuring it on the application facilitate the implementation process and shorten the implementation period. This was what gave us the chance of success because IMC requested that the implementation period did not exceed three months. All other rival offers considered eight months at least as an implementation period. We said three months because we were very confident.

A year after implementing the ERP, the EU auditors discovered that IMC had adopted an ERP system despite their non-approval for this project. This action rendered the ERP project illegitimate. The EU auditors took a series of negative sanctions against the IMC's members. As a result of this project the service contracts of the Executive Director, the Financial Controller and subsequently the Financial System Manager were terminated. The ex-Financial Systems Manager described some of these actions:

> Subsequently, the EU Commission discovered that we adopted the ERP system. Between you and me, this was one of the main causes for terminating the service contracts of both the Executive Director and the Financial Controller. What I mean, the EU Commission rejected the ERP project and we insisted on doing it. You want me to tell you more? After a period of time, the EU Commission requested each department to submit a report about its achievements. We, as a Finance Department, included the implementation of an ERP system in Finance and Logistics as one of the Department's achievements. The EU Commission returned the report in order to omit the word 'ERP'. We modified the report and stated that we implemented an accounting package called Baan.

Burns and Scapens (2000) emphasise that the extra-organisational institutions can be challenged. The power struggle between the EU and IMC on the purchase of the ERP system is an example of strategic response of the IMC's actors to institutional pressures or resistance to the EU power, particularly the avoidance strategy (Oliver, 1991). According to this strategy organisations disguise non-conformity, loosen institutional attachments or escape from institutional rules and expectations. A more dramatic avoidance response to institutional pressures towards conformity is escape, that is, an organisation may exit the domain within which pressure is exerted or significantly alter its own goals, activities or domain to avoid the necessity of conformity altogether. That was the action taken by the IMC's members. The IMC's members challenged the EU commissioners' power by changing the amount of the ERP tender to avoid the need for their approval.

Furthermore, this situation clearly explains legitimation structure, norm and sanction (Giddens, 1979, 1984). The IMC's members worked around EU tender procedures (legitimation structure). They drew on their knowledge about different types of contracts that are acceptable for EU auditors to avoid their intervention (norms). However, EU auditors considered that the IMC's members violated their orders. So they imposed a series of negative sanctions, including the termination of service contracts of the Executive Director, the Financial Controller and the Financial System Manager (sanctions).

Next we describe the ERP implementation process which took place before the above sanctions came into force. We also examine the operation of the dialectic of control between external IT specialists and accountants.

7.2.1.2 Accountants and external IT specialists (ERP vendor)

Following the purchase of the ERP system, the Baan vendor in Egypt provided consultancy services in implementing the ERP system and in training the IMC's members. During the implementation process a number of unplanned events have occurred. An unintended consequence of these events was that accountants became relatively independent in their relationship with external IT specialists. There were several gradual implementations. At the time of the first implementation the consulting company, the Baan agent in Egypt, did not have any human resources to implement the ERP system. Thus, it recruited an Indian expert to do the implementation process.

The Indian expert implemented only some sub-modules of the Finance module, mainly Budgeting, General Ledger and a small part of both Accounts Receivables and Accounts Payable, and did not complete the implementation of these sub-modules. He had a dispute with the consulting company. He resigned and returned home. The implementation stopped and was not completed. IMC was in big trouble, 'stuck in the middle', the ERP Project Manager commented.

He added:

There were no available human resources. The man came and implemented some sub-modules and went. He left us in the middle of the implementation. Therefore, we spent a long time. The Egyptian agent did not support us at this time. No one came to help us. There were no resources. I started to study and experiment until I got the knowledge and completed the implementation. Thanks God. There was not much delay. There was an urgent need for the implementation and the time was limited. Therefore, we kept trying until we knew how to implement the remaining work.

This situation created a problem of trust between accountants and the ERP vendor and caused a lot of anxiety on the part of the ERP Project Manager. The departure of the Indian expert motivated the ERP Project Manager to complete the implementation of the receivables and payables in the Finance module. He drew on his past experience in using another ERP package in another company. After a while, IMC discovered the need for a cash management sub-module. The ERP Project Manager implemented this sub-module himself. This was an unintended consequence of the ERP vendor's failure in providing sufficient support during the first implementation of the ERP system. Commenting on this moment, the ERP Project Manager stated:

> I studied the cash management sub-module and implemented it ... All this work was done without the involvement of the consulting company. The company did not have human resources. There was nobody at all.

The Technical Manager of the ERP vendor did not deny this fact. He stated that:

> During the implementation, they did not have a need for cash management. Two or three months after finalising the implementation, the Financial Systems Manager, who was responsible for the implementation, called me and informed me that he implemented the cash management sub-module. I asked you used it, how? He told me I implemented it and we did not need you. I said to him this fosters feelings of pride for us and not for any one else that the implementation is so easy to the degree that you can do it yourself and your experience in Baan is just three months.

He continued his comments:

> The Financial System Manager has an excellent background in ERP systems. Fortunately, he was using ERP systems. But, I mean, at that time, he still had only three months experience in using Baan and was able to implement the sub-module. That was impressive.

Without the prior knowledge of the ERP Project Manager (ex-Financial Systems Manager), the ERP project would have failed. The Baan Technical

Manager in Egypt recognised that he was lucky to find such expertise and experts in IMC. He stated:

> Fortunately, the people in IMC were very well qualified. For example, accounting staff was five; three of them had CPA qualifications. Do you imagine the people who implemented like what? ... Therefore, their procedures and manuals were standard to the degree that you could apply them to the application directly. IMC's members did not take a long period. They were open-minded. We have not expensed a lot of time in their training.

The Technical Manager faced a lot of difficulties in other companies when trying to implement Baan systems such as the need to convince people of the logic of business processes, integration and benefits of shared knowledge. The Technical Manager continued:

> The real problem is ... that the ERP is built on the company's integration. This concept is totally unacceptable in our society. Everyone keeps some documents and thinks that his/her existence in the company is related to these documents. The problem is that the concept of integration is not in our courses, in our society, or in our morals. The story is that the integration, which means no one is capable of doing everything or what can be called 'one man show', is not among our habits and routines. It is a cultural problem. It is also a problem of education curriculum in our universities and educational institutions. It is behaviour of society... ERP is supposed to develop this behaviour ... Fortunately, the people in IMC were very good in their thinking. They were able to absorb the concept of integration. Most of them were (educated) abroad and some participated in big projects. I mean, all of them have good background. Therefore, the implementation of ERP was so easy.

At that time, all the Finance sub-modules, except fixed assets, were implemented, including General Ledger, Accounts Payables, Accounts Receivables and Cash Management and Budgeting as well. The Finance module did not cover all the IMC's activities. It satisfied only all the Financial Department's needs and transactions. After about six months from implementing the Finance module, IMC started to expand its business. As previously stated, the nature of the IMC's business is that there is a group of beneficiaries from the IMP. Those beneficiaries request vendors to provide services for them. Both the clients and IMC pay the costs of these services. At the beginning of IMC, the business was based on small contracts, which were paid in cash after providing consultancy services.

However, IMC started to sign long-term contracts for more than a year, two or three years, with organisations and bodies. As a result, there was a need for monitoring the progress of contracts or contract management. The IMC's managers wanted to trace the contract either according to its implementation stages, what is done so far, or according to payments, whether the IMC's share or the client's share. In order to monitor contracts, there was a need for implementing purchase orders or the Distribution module. The current Financial Systems Manager described the introduction of the Distribution module.

> The second module, Distribution, was introduced because components' managers called for more information. This demand was requested by the big boss (the ex-Executive Director). The need for monitoring contracts was the reason for such demand. The extraction of certain data on contracts was required such as paid or unpaid instalments.

Like the previous module implementation, the implementation of this module was subject to a customisation process. In this regard, the provision of service is treated as if goods are received. This means a purchase order has to be issued not for goods but for services. Each service will be delivered/provided in a specific day or certain time. The consulting company, the Baan vendor in Egypt, helped IMC in implementing and customising the Distribution module. According to the Technical Manager of the Baan vendor in Egypt,

> There was a need for contact management. What had been done, I would say, was work around the Distribution module to manage this process in terms of defining contracts and assigning contracts' payments to budget lines...Therefore, there was a need for contract management to trace contract to each component's budget.

Thus there were relations of autonomy and dependency between accountants and external IT experts during the implementation of ERP in IMC. Next we analyse the operation of the dialectic of control between internal IT specialists and accountants.

7.2.1.3   *Accountants and internal IT specialists (MIS department)*

It was the accounting function that played a prominent role in all the decisions regarding the implementation of the ERP in IMC. As stated earlier, the Finance Department's members, the ex-Financial Controller and the ex-Financial Systems Manager played a major role in purchasing and implementing the ERP system. The introduction of the ERP resulted in the intervention of EU auditors. Following the conflict between EU auditors and accountants on the legitimacy of the ERP system, the MIS and Contracting Department was established. Figure 7.2 presents the structure of this department. A British Controller had been appointed to manage this department. Accountants perceived the introduction of this department as a kind of

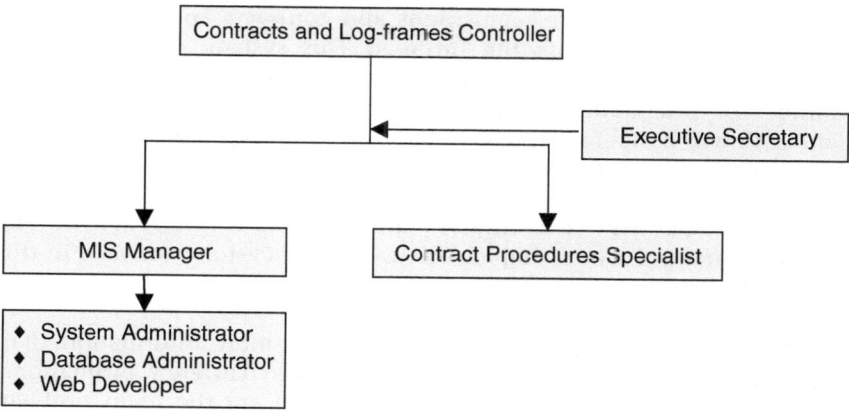

Figure 7.2 The Structure of MIS and Contracting Department

'punishment'. The ERP Project Manager tried to convince the new department's controller to take up the ERP system. However, the MIS and Contacting Controller refused this suggestion. The controversy around the ERP system affected his rejection.

Furthermore, the MIS and Contacting Controller had his own agenda. He decided to develop and implement a rival web-based custom system for managing the components' budgets from scratch. He appointed an Egyptian, who served with him in a previous EU programme, as the MIS Manager to develop and implement this software. The ERP Project Manager described this moment of conflict as follows:

> With all my appreciation, he (the MIS Manager) is a good IT developer. However, he will never be more aware of business processes than ERP designers, ready-made applications. All what he has done, all what he is intended to do and all what he will think about it are in the ERP package ... There was no need to create duplication of work. It was a stupid thing. The in-house developed system will never be at the same quality as the ERP system that provides the same reports but has been tested. Do you understand? The MIS and Contacting Controller said no. I panicked and resisted this trend. I asked 'what is the problem?' Is it in my position? I can leave the Finance Department and join the MIS and become under the supervision of the MIS and Contracting Controller. I mean, I report to him. There is no problem with me. The ERP is available and has more quality. The MIS and Contracting Controller said no. He told me keep your job.

Actually, the 'new' MIS Manager started internally developing and implementing web-based custom software supported by an electronic signature system to trace requisitions and contracts and automatically adjust budget lines using the Intranet. This system is based on the workflow prepared by the ERP project team. The MIS Manager used a number of programming languages and applications such as Visual Basic, Visual Basic for Applications, Java and SQL Server, Microsoft Word application and Microsoft Outlook-based e-mail system. Suddenly, the MIS and Contracting Controller and his friend, the MIS Manager, left IMC. Their service contracts with IMC were not renewed. The ex-MIS Manager did not complete the web-based custom software. In this regard, the current Financial System Manager stated that:

> The ERP records a lot of data and provides more information than the Java software such as banks and foreign currency evaluations. The budget allocations (tracing requisitions) are the main problem of the ERP. The Java project is experimental and is incomplete. In addition, the project has not been completed as its designer left IMC and his predecessor only operates the available part of the project.

The current MIS Manager confirmed the fact that the ERP system has not succeeded in dealing with the component managers' requisitions. He explained:

> The ERP is incomplete. For example, it is unable to trace the requisitions launched until its approval by the Executive Director. The web-based custom software is able to do so using a Java system, Microsoft Outlook e-mail, an electronic signature system and Intranet. In addition, customers and consultants in other Egyptian districts can use the web-based custom software. All information is stored on the server and the Intranet facilitates this access.

The debate about the legitimacy of the ERP system affected the possibility of integrating the ERP with the web-based system. There were three main reasons for this disintegration between the ERP and the web-based system. Firstly, it was planned to connect the ERP to the Intranet and it was agreed upon at the beginning of the ERP project. In the business model, component managers were supposed to access the system and see the information they need. However, the EU auditors' intervention led to reducing the number of licences purchased. The Technical Manager of the Baan vendor in Egypt stated that:

> This is not a shortcoming in the software (ERP software) to play this role that each manager has his/her own user name, password and business model. The software can satisfy this requirement

without any problem ... IMC only purchased five licences for five users. This number of licences was not enough to be used by all managers and their assistants. Therefore, it was a mere financial problem.

Secondly, in a later time, the ERP Project Manager suggested the integration between the ERP and the web-based system to help suppliers get tenders information and technical specifications from the web. In this regard, every supplier would have access to tenders, which he/she is eligible to participate in them, using a user name and password in order to download the technical specifications and apply on the system. A demo had been presented to the MIS and Contracting Controller. However, he refused this recommendation.

Finally, the MIS Department's members have not been trained in using the ERP system because this department has been established after the implementation of the ERP system. Therefore, they do not understand how the system operates. They do not gain relevant knowledge about the use of the Baan system. This fact coupled with the initial conflict could interpret the apparent disintegration between the ERP system and the web-based system. In this regard, the current MIS Manager expressed this difficulty as follows:

> Our system has not been integrated with the ERP system because of the ambiguity in saving and storing the data in the ERP using a number of tables. The ERP creates very large tables. We are unable to trace the data stored on them without proper documentation. Therefore, we are unable to connect our database with the ERP database.

As a consequence of these reasons, both the ERP and the web-based custom software operate separately from each other. Accountants are completely independent in their use of the ERP system from the MIS department. However, the operation of the web-based custom software depends partially on accounting staff. For instance, accountants are responsible for some data entry such as the budget lines' estimates at the beginning of each work plan and actual payments for suppliers. Other data entries come from contracting staff and component managers. The Financial Policy Manager commented on this dependency:

> The MIS manager set up the instruments, the tools, which we use as components' managers. We can go to the database and see for each other what the status of our components is. The MIS Department did just provided the infrastructure for us to do so, I mean, provided us the gate to the database. This database is technically managed by the MIS

Department but, in terms of accounting, it is managed by the accounting department.

Clearly, accountants are independent in their relationship with internal IT specialists. They also tried to control the MIS Department through offering the use of ERP by internal IT specialists. Next, we examine the operation of the dialectic of control between component managers and accountants.

7.2.1.4   Accountants and component managers

Management accountants draw upon different resources in their exercise of power in daily social relations with component managers. These resources give them independence in their interaction with component managers. First of all, management accountants are the custodians/managers of the ERP system. A senior accountant stated:

We are in the Finance Department the only persons who have the right to access the ERP software and to extract data from it. We are the only

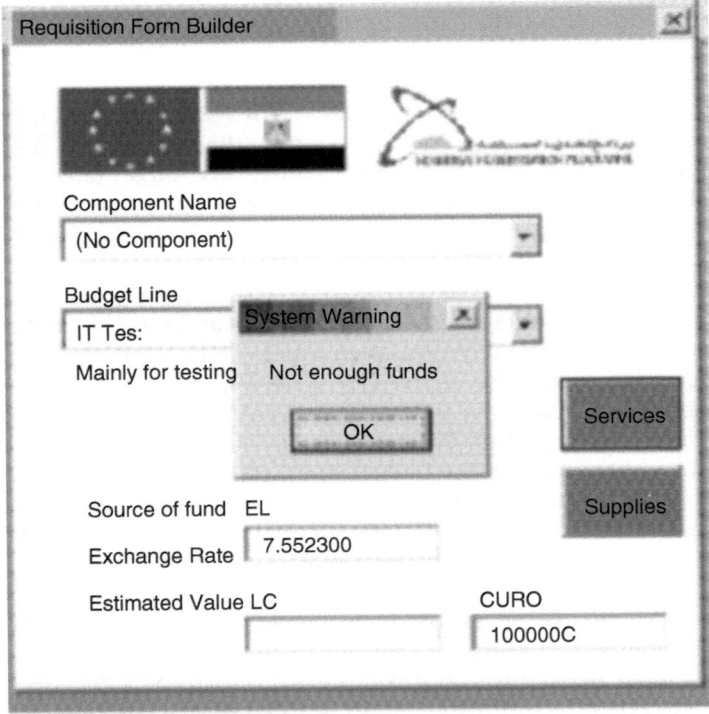

Figure 7.3   The Web-Based Custom Software and the Availability of Funds

source of information for the centre. All other departments depend on us in obtaining the information and we satisfy their needs.

The command over the ERP system is a resource that can be used in the exercise of the power of accepting or rejecting the component manager's requisitions for funds. Each component manager can launch a requisition calling for an allocation or an encumbrance for a specific amount of money to be used in a specific activity. He/ she can informally check whether there are enough funds for that activity in the budget or not by using the web-based custom system (see Figure 7.3). The Financial Policy Manager described:

> Now we have a real-time access to the status of each of our budget lines. So for each component, I mean, we can go to the Intranet and see how much money by line remains. It is available. It is a real-time.

However, managers always request accountants to formally accept or reject their requisitions because there are a number of dimensions for each requisition that accountants are aware of such as:

- Are suppliers included in the requisition registered in the approved list of IMC?
- Does the customer involved in the requisition exceed the allowable limit for each customer to benefit from IMC funds?
- Are there available funds in the budget line(s) to finance the requisition?

Accountants formally use the ERP system to query all this information. The ERP Project Manager tried to transfer this task to component managers but they refused. He stated:

> We considered not doing this step by the Finance Department. A Baan screen could become available for each component to enquire about the availability of funds. However, component managers did not accept this idea. They said that this is not our responsibility but the Finance. We said ok, as you like. You are happy with the delay.

This means that line managers within IMC refused to take responsibility for the financial aspects of their own activities. So the accounting knowledge within IMC has not been decentralised. The lack of the accounting knowledge on the part of component managers can interpret their resistance to the use of ERP system in their enquiry. The accounting knowledge is another resource of power. As a senior accountant explained,

> Managers are unable to understand the accounts codes used and their meanings. Therefore, data extracted from the ERP software is

re-presented in order to be understandable to managers. Accountants prepare simplified reports using Microsoft Excel sheets. In these simplified reports, numbers are clearly explained in more details.

The current Financial Systems Manager confirmed this fact by saying:

> Some managers request more details on the Centre. Excel files are used to provide all the details in order to facilitate the managers' understanding for such details. For example, there is something in the ERP called dimensions that help in providing more details on operational expenses of 10th Ramadan office, for instance. Further details can be given such as wages, cars...etc.

The accounting knowledge gives management accountants power in their interaction with managers. The accountants' ability to make sense of numbers gives confidence and safety to component managers. Sometimes, component managers sign a lot of requisitions at the same time to accelerate a project or launch a project. What is important for managers is to feel safe and they are still within the budget. Sometimes, component managers are lost because they actually cannot go through all their files to consolidate all requisitions that they launched to identify what they have committed, what has been disbursed and what is available. In that situation, management accountants have the ability to influence line managers. They communicate a set of values and ideals about what is approved and what is disapproved. The Financial Policy Manager, commenting on the role of management accountants, stated that:

> Of course, they advise me on when I have something that is a bit out of track or something unusual. They advise me. So I see them as functional but also as providing a kind of comfort. They comfort me on what I am doing. Meaning that, that is their responsibility to do so. I take their advice and implement it. This is because I know they have the full picture of accounting.

Despite the apparent dependence of component managers on management accountants, the component managers maintain an area of independence from management accountants and resist the full control of accountants on some of their daily activities. The ERP Project Manager pointed out:

> Among the ideas, we tried to implement the transportation management module in monitoring the IMC's cars. We have a large number of cars assigned for each manager and his/ her assistants. Do you know? We had an idea to control the use of these vehicles. Managers said there

is no need for this module. There was a lot of information that would be recorded such as trip price, maintenance costs...etc. Managers complained that the Finance Department exceeded its authority and intervened in their own affairs.

Another area of managers' independence from management accountants is the managers' technical knowledge with their components' activities. As far as the technical aspects are concerned, there are other people who provide inputs from outside IMC. For example, some component managers get some formal and informal quotations on some services to be run. Moreover, the co-ordinator is the one who has an overall perspective. He is the bridge between the accounting and the project because he is the one who approves both in terms of the reference of the technical assistance and the budget. So he has an understanding that the Finance Department does not have. As noted by The Financial Policy Manager:

> Yes...yes, of course, I ask them because they have the experience ... but when it comes to the expertise of what we are doing they do not know about it. I will not discuss private equity fund with them. I might discuss, ok, how it costs if we organise a meeting in terms of hotels and this stuff. They have experience in that.

He continued:

> As far as a financial component, it is very interesting for me to get their feedback on the instruments themselves. Because I am not Egyptian, they are Egyptians and they talk the same language as we do.

In this regard, there is a room for management accountants' intervention. The knowledge of the Egyptian circumstances is another resource that accountants draw upon in their interaction with managers. This is due to the fact that all component managers are foreigners. For example, in the preparation stage of work plan, accountants can modify the budget estimates for component managers because these managers do not have the knowledge of the prices of goods and services in the Egyptian market or the daily changes in foreign currencies. The Financial Manager stated:

> During the consolidation process of components' estimates, there is a possibility of overstated estimates or understated estimates. I meet each component's manager to reach fair estimations of activities. I draw on my experience with the Egyptian market and on comparisons with previous years' expenses. The ERP provides this historical data. In addition,

I am guided by a number of ceilings such as budget ceiling, component ceiling, operational expenses' ceiling...etc.

Undoubtedly, accountants are independent in their relationship with component managers and tried to expand their role to operations in IMC. Next, we briefly analyse the operation of the dialectic of control in NEEASAE and compare it with IMC.

7.2.2 Comparison of the operation of dialectic of control in NEEASAE and IMC

In this section we compare and contrast ERP implementation processes in NEEASAE and IMC in relation to the dialectic of control. We briefly examine the tension in NEEASAE's relationship with the holding company as a result of adopting the ERP system and compare this relationship with IMC's relationship with EU Commission. We also analyse the changing power relations of accountants with IT specialists and line managers in NEEASAE and compare these relationships with those in IMC.

7.2.2.1 ERP adoption and challenging the holding company's decision

The decision to implement an ERP system at NEEASAE was related to its privatisation attempt at the end of 1997. In 1990s, the Egyptian Government started a privatisation programme to privatise most of the public sector companies, including Philips branch in Egypt. The negotiations on selling Philips branch in Egypt started between Philips Company and the Egyptian Government in 1995. However, they failed in December 1997 and the Egyptian Government decided to buy the share of the Dutch partner. The company's name has been changed from 'Philips' to 'NEEASAE'. Therefore, NEEASAE Company became a 100% public sector company. It has become a 100% affiliated company to the Egyptian Holding Company for Engineering Industries, an Egyptian public sector company established according to Law No. 203 of 1991. The General Manager for Budgeting and Costing described this situation as follows:

> During the negotiations on selling the company at the end of 1997, it was re-evaluated. Philips Company evaluated its brand name with 60% of the company's value and was willing to pay the Government the remaining value. However, the Egyptian side rejected this deal and bought the Dutch partner's share. A new brand name, 'NEEASAE', was introduced.

However, the Egyptian Government has not given up the hope of selling NEEASAE to Philips Company or finding an alternative buyer. Following the withdrawal of Philips Company, the NEEASAE's management started improving the company's information systems by imitating the systems adopted by Philips Company, including ISO 9002, ISO 14000 and ERP systems. In this regard, the ex-Chief Executive Officer of NEEASAE (the sponsor of ERP project) stated:

> The adoption of ERP in NEEASAE was an imitation of Philips Company's systems. Philips owned 50% of the company's value and has been using an ERP system for a long period. It was an attempt to attract the attention of Philips Company and encourage it to increase its investments in NEEASAE. However, Philips Company decided to completely withdraw its investments in Egypt and transferred them to eastern Asia, especially China.

At the end of 1997, a decision to adopt an ERP system in NEEASAE was mainly taken by the Egyptian Holding Company for Engineering Industries, which started implementing an ERP system at the same time. The General Manager of MIS Department described this decision as follows:

> The ERP project came as a compulsory order from the holding company. It has not expressed our needs. We have not initiated this project. As a decision-maker, you are not able to make a decision... People, I mean financial accountants and cost accountants, rejected the project. They have not co-operated with the top management in implementing the project as they felt that it was imposed on them and they were not in need for it ... The holding company itself failed to implement the ERP software.

The General Manager of Planning emphasised this fact:

> The ERP project was a recommendation from the holding company to implement a good information system. The objective was the existence of common integrated database for the whole company to facilitate communications and the availability of information to decision-makers in real-time. However, I think that because there was a complete collapse in the company, the ERP project failed ... The holding company wanted to modernise information systems. It implemented the same system and failed.

According to Burns and Scapens (2000), if those responsible for implementing the new system possess sufficient power, they may be able to impose change, possibly with some difficulty. However, if other key individuals or groups have sufficient power, they may be able to resist or subvert the change process. That was what happened in NEEASAE. The holding company and top management imposed the ERP project on all the company's key members, in particular accountants, who resisted it through their control of resources required in the implementation process. The holding company and top management wanted to make NEEASAE attractive to investors. For that reason, the ERP caused a lot of anxiety as it was seen as a necessary step towards privatisation and, subsequently, early retirement. The General Manager of Planning described the feelings of employees towards the ERP:

> People resisted the ERP system and implemented it against their will. It was like doing your job without liking it.

So ERP was a major threat to the survival of the organisation as a whole and its constituent organisational members. The General Manager of Planning said 'there was a fear from privatisation. Would we stay working in the company or would we leave the company?' The General Manager of Financial Accounts added 'the number of employees has been reduced because of early retirement'.[3] Furthermore, the failure of ERP implementation in the holding company legitimised the failure of the same ERP package in NEEASAE. The ERP failure in NEEASAE became a logical outcome and self-explained result as a result of its failure in the holding company.

Compared to the IMC's experience, the NEEASAE's experience in challenging extra-organisational institutions is completely different. The NEEASAE's organisational members challenged the holding company's decision to implement Baan software. They resisted the ERP implementation as they felt that this software was a threat to the existence of the company as a whole and to their secured jobs. Unlike the NEEASAE's organisational members, the IMC's organisational members challenged the power of EU Commission in order to enforce implementing the ERP system. They worked around EU contracting procedures to purchase and implement the software and, consequently, those members, who participated in making this action, lost their jobs. Next, we focus on the accountants' relationships with line managers and IT specialists in NEEASAE and comparing them with those relationships in IMC.

7.2.2.2 Accountants and managers

Production engineers dominate important positions in NEEASAE because of the nature of the company's activities. So this domination was reflected in the formation of ERP project team and the steering committee. For ple, the ex-CEO (the ERP sponsor), the ex-head of Factories Sector (ERP Project Manager), the General Manager of MIS Department (a key user) and the General Manager of Planning (a key user) are all ex-line managers and production engineers. Unlike accountants in IMC, accountants in NEEASAE were absent from initiating or leading the ERP project. Rather, they negatively affected the ERP implementation and were one of the main causes of ERP failure in NEEASAE. However, accountants were not the only reason for ERP failure in NEEASAE.

An important reason for the failure of ERP system in NEEASAE can be attributed to the non-existence of well-qualified employees within the company to manage the implementation process of the system. The ERP project was supervised by the ex-head of Factories Sector (the ERP Project Manager) and the heads of administrations (the key users). All of them have not had any knowledge about the computer or the ERP software. The MIS General Manager said:

> All the company's leaders were not qualified to use the computer. They were still in A B C computer. They only trained on the beginnings of Windows and DOS ... Training was internal in MIS Department for one week. One week was not enough. It was just background information.

The ERP Project Manager was the ex-head of Factories Sector. She was far from the use of computer. She did not have any IT background or prior experience on the project. The ERP Project Manager managed the project from a managerial perspective not from a technical perspective. The mistrust of the ERP Project Manager's capability and the lack of confidence in her leadership were reflected in the comments on her performance. The General Manager for Planning said:

> The Project Manager did not know anything about the computer and has not got any training courses. She was responsible for co-ordinating people's efforts. Being understood the company's processes did not mean that she understood the ERP system. She was a reason for ERP failure... She was on retirement. The project stopped on August 2002 and she retired on December 2002.

The MIS General Manager reinforced this opinion:

> ERP project was a big burden on the Project Manager, the head of Factories Sector. She was appointed to manage the ERP and to train staff...Good intentions do not make projects succeed.

So the ERP Project Manager in NEEASAE was an important reason for the ERP failure. The ERP Project Manager in IMC, by contrast, was one of the most important reasons for the successful implementation of ERP software. He has good experience in the ERP system. This enabled him to complete the ERP implementation when the Indian expert resigned. Therefore, the knowledge with ERP software on the part of ERP Project Manager is a valuable resource that was missing in the case of NEEASAE. This implies that the proper selection of the project leader is vital for the successful implementation of the project. This leader could manage the change process and achieve the desired outcome.

The steering committee's members in NEEASAE did not also have any computer skills. Every head of a sector or administration was responsible for the co-ordination between the implementation team from the ERP Company and the company's employees. However, they were not well qualified enough to do so. The General Manager of Planning (a key user) described her skills in IT as follows:

> I do not know anything about computers at all. I am managing people and understand my work. I can prepare a flow chart for my processes. On this basis, I can interact with others. I do not know computer and I cannot use it. The only training we have got was on the use of Windows. All engineers have been trained on the use of Windows. The people have not been suitably trained.

Other ERP users did not have computer culture as well. They were not familiar with the computer. The MIS General Manager explained:

> Users were in need for upgrading their computer knowledge levels before starting ERP implementation. They took a lot of time in entering the data of only a month from a prior year. People were all upset. They always told each other 'it was a failed project'.

The lack of computer knowledge on the part of almost all organisational members (ERP Project Manager, Key Users and End users) is a missing resource in NEEASAE. On the contrary, organisational members in IMC were well qualified and well trained on the use of IT and ERP. Most of ERP users in IMC had CPAs, postgraduate qualifications and previous experiences in international companies. So these valuable resources enabled the IMC's members to successfully manage the ERP project. However, the lack of such resources in NEESASE led to losing control over internally managing the ERP project.

Like other organisational members in NEEASAE, accountants suffered from the lack of IT knowledge. Thus the ERP project has not changed their relationship with line managers. However, following the withdrawal of Philips Company, NEEASAE suffered a financial crisis due to continual losses. This crisis increased the importance of cost accountants' role in the company to control the cost of products. This was reflected in a number of observations such as the interest of both the Chief Executive Officer (CEO) and the Central Agency for Accountancy (CAA) in monitoring cost information and the move of cost accountants' location to factories.

The relationship between accountants and line managers in NEEASAE has not changed because of the failure of the ERP project and the lack of IT knowledge on the part of both sides. This relationship in IMC has not changed as well, but for different reasons. Line managers in IMC refused to take responsibility for the financial aspects of their own activities because they did not have sufficient accounting knowledge. The lack of IT knowledge on the part of accountants in NEEASAE and their relationship with internal IT specialists are discussed next.

7.2.2.3 Accountants and internal IT specialists

Compared to other ERP users accountants in NEEASAE were no exception. Before the ERP adoption and after its failure, there has been tailored accounting software. Accountants have not ever used this software. They always use manual books. IT specialists in the MIS Department, mainly computer engineers, record financial transactions using this software. They duplicate the accountants' work. This is because of the lack of IT skills among accountants. As a result, accountants depend on IT staff in using the accounting software. Bearing this fact in mind, it was not a surprise that accountants have not supported the ERP software and caused its failure by asking the ERP vendor to programme the Uniform Accounting System into the ERP. Accountants insisted on the customisation of the ERP system to totally match the Uniform Accounting System's requirements. The MIS General Manager described the resistance of accountants due to the lack of capacity to copy with IT:

> There was an attitude against the ERP project. The Finance Department totally rejected the project. Accountants were totally against it. Each time, when no correct outputs were produced from the ERP system, accountants said, 'preparing them by hand was faster'. This was the company's culture. It did not allow for the ERP implementation. We should be in need for the software.

The General Manager of Planning noticed the same point:

> The Finance Department was the main resistant. It highly resisted the software despite a lot work was done. Accountants did not like the idea (the ERP project). They used to use a paper and pen. Then, a very big process came into effect. It was worthless. Although accountants were not convinced with the idea, they worked hard.

Following ERP adoption, accountants continued their dependence on internal IT specialists in feeding their financial data into the ERP. The MIS General Manager stated:

> IT staff, not accounting department, was responsible for entering data into the ERP to avoid mistakes in data entry.

Like other ERP users, accountants did not get enough training to deal with the ERP software. Furthermore, they did not have the motive to develop their computer skills. A cost accountant explained the absence of motives to increase the accountants' knowledge with IT:

> Over-staffing, the lack of skills in using computer and the age of employees (approaching retirement age) hindered the ability to learn.

The dependence of accountants on internal IT specialists in NEEASAE was totally different from the relationship between accountants and internal IT specialists in IMC. In IMC, accountants were totally independent from internal IT specialists in using the ERP. Moreover, they tried to control the MIS Department through offering the use of the ERP system by the members of MIS Department. The relationship of accountants in NEEASAE with external IT specialists is the issue we discuss next.

7.2.2.4   Accountants and external IT specialists

Due to the lack of internal IT experts in NEEASAE, the only available and reasonable solution to implement the ERP software was to depend on external IT specialists. Consultants from the faculty of engineering, university professors, prepared all technical specifications, wrote the tender report, selected the software, received the network and continued monitoring the implementation process. The General Manager of Planning described the role of university consultants in ERP selection and implementation:

> In 1997 consultants wrote the technical specifications with the company's engineers. Then, they prepared a technical report on the system. And they selected the ERP system and gave their reasons for this. They said that Baan is the best company. They also selected the computers' hardware and software. They requested them and received the network after its installation. They were also attending all the meetings with the ERP Company. They were giving their opinions and have not solved any problem. They stayed for a time and cancelled their contracts.

The MIS General Manager expressed her lack of power and knowledge about selecting Baan software:

> It was not our choice. During the evaluation of offers, Baan was not known for us. The demo was presented to top management not to users, who did not have any knowledge about it ... There were not any criteria for selecting the ERP software. Baan was number five. It did not have any module about quality... Also, there was a problem in using Arabic

language in the system. The advantage of Baan was that it could be connected to any other package.

This situation in NEEASAE was totally different from that in IMC. In IMC, the organisation's members prepared the technical specifications and selected the ERP software. They did not rely on external consultants to help them in choosing the software. They had sufficient knowledge about the nature of ERP and its characteristics.

In addition to the university consultants, there were ERP consultants from the Baan vendor, who were responsible for defining business processes with the NEEASAE's users, installing Baan software, training users, customising the software and preparing the prototype of the new system. The critical phase of ERP implementation in NEEASAE was software customisation. The ex-CEO (the ERP sponsor) described the problems caused by software customisation:

> The software was customised to fit the company's operations. All cus-tomisation processes were done by the ERP vendor. A lot of problems occurred because of the software customisation. There was a conflict between the ERP vendor and the company about customising a lot of the software configurations. There was also non-compliance with unified characteristics. In addition, no enough data were available to design business operations.

The General Manager for Financial Accounts explained the role of Baan consultants in the customisation process:

> Consultants were explaining piece by piece even for people who did not study computer. Six from 10 persons understood at different managerial levels. We understood some stuff but there was some other stuff that we were unable to understand. The consultants were answering our questions until we encountered problems that the ERP system could not solve.

Furthermore, the customisation of the software to copy the Uniform Account-ing System led to the multiplicity of external teams. The ERP Company used four different teams to implement the software in NEEASAE. When one team failed it was replaced by another team. This happened for three years. The mastermind behind the ERP was in Saudi Arabia rather than Egypt. The man in Saudi Arabia came to Egypt three times to identify the NEEASE's problems. Furthermore, he tried to solve and customise the software from Saudi Arabia. There were always communications with him using telephone conference between NEASSA Company and Saudi Arabia to try to implement the modi-fications and customisations. One obstacle was that the people who were available in Egypt did not understand the software. The General Manager of

Planning described the lack of experience on the part of the Baan agent in Egypt as follows:

> The Baan Company in Egypt had a limited experience. It always contacted the headquarters in Saudi Arabia and held conferences. After three years of hard work without any result, we got upset. Implementation teams have been changed four times during three years and each team started from the beginning, I mean, entering the data and step by step. After preparing a report to determine something, the new team cancelled it and started from the beginning. People went and another team started. Every team set certain steps without any training. We had to implement the written steps in manuals. We could not cancel an order or even change wrong data entered.

The multiplicity of external teams and the lack of confidence in their knowledge with Baan software led to ERP failure. The use of Indian experts in implementing the ERP software as well as the reliance on the headquarters in Saudi Arabia increased the lack of confidence in the ERP vendor in Egypt. The MIS General Manager described the mistrust caused by using different teams and foreign consultants:

> There was multiplicity in consultants who offered technical support. This led to confusion on the part of our staff. There was no continuity between the internal team and consultants. There should be one well-known company responsible for the project. The consultants did not have prior experience in other companies that implemented Baan systems. They always contacted people in Saudi Arabia (the headquarters). This caused a lot of delay in obtaining results... ERP consultants wanted to help people but they could not do so. After three years, they did not have Indian consultants. The main weakness of this strategy is the software maintenance in the future. It is not just software operation and training. It should be long-term service.

The relationship of accountants with Baan consultants was very similar in both NEEASAE and IMC. Baan Company in Egypt suffered from the lack of local expertise in the software. This shortage in human resources and the use of foreign experts led to the lack of confidence in the company's future performance and exposed the customer companies to the risk of the ERP projects' failure. In addition, this lack also affected on the training given to the customer companies' members, who could save the ERP project in case of absence of external IT specialists.

The next section focuses on analysing and comparing the operation of the dialectic of control in the two organisations implementing custom software, ESTD and AQF.

7.3 Custom software and the operation of dialectic of control

7.3.1 Custom software and the operation of dialectic of control in ESTD

Drawing on the concept of dialectic of control, we examine the response of the ESTD's members to coercive pressures exerted by the World Bank and the Ministry of Finance (MOF) and the changing role and relationships of management accountants with IT specialists and managers in ESTD after the introduction of budget reform and custom software systems that support this reform.

7.3.1.1 *The adoption of performance-based budget system reform and supporting custom software systems as a response to coercive pressures*

The decision to implement the performance-based budget system and supporting custom software systems at ESTD was a response to the World Bank's recommendations to the Government of Egypt (GOE) at the end of 2000. At that time, the MOF started to study these recommendations before the formal approval at the end of 2002. In November 2000 the Minister of Finance made a decision to implement the performance-based-budget and related custom software systems in ESTD. Based on the Minister's decision, the Commissioner of ESTD made the administration decision No. 1544 of 2000 on 02/12/2000 to conduct a study on the possible implementation of the performance-based budget and supporting custom software systems in ESTD. According to this decision, seven groups were formed to conduct this study that aimed at determining the means of moving from the line-item budget to the performance-based budget. The groups covered the following areas of the comprehensive institutional reform of ESTD: administrative and financial affairs, information systems, planning, tax system, human resources, organisation, financial accounting and cost accounting, and performance indicators and incentives. A number of workshops have been held to clearly define the implementation approach of the performance-based budget and supporting custom software systems in ESTD.

At the beginning of 2002, the World Bank delegation met with the ESTD's officials. The ESTD's Commissioner pointed out that:

> Selecting the Department as one of the governmental units responsible for the experimental implementation of the programs-and-performance-based budget in the governmental sector results in the following:
> 1. Boosting confidence,
> 2. Realising transparency in evaluating performance accurately,
> 3. Providing performance programs for all the Department's activities and tasks according to responsibility centres to achieve the Department's mission,

4. Developing the Department's financial system according to the programs-and-performance-based budget by developing the financial accounting and cost accounting systems with responsibility centres, and

5. Developing the system of incentives and linking it with the system of programs-and-performance-based budget according to specific standards of efficiency, effectiveness, productivity, and quality (ESTD, 2002b).

He continued:

The implementation of the programs-and-performance-based budget at Sales Tax Department, is the first government unit in Egypt that has implemented this type of budget reform, started from the fiscal year 2002/2003. The Minister of Finance fostered feelings of pride for all the Sales Tax Department's officials. Sales Tax Department is qualified to implement this budget reform that requires well-trained employees who are capable of using modern technologies and achieving high quality (ESTD, 2002c).

The World Bank Consultant commented on selecting ESTD by saying:

Sales Tax Department was selected for implementing the programs-and-performance-based budget because it is characterised by well-qualified employees, top executives who support the budget reform and well-paid employees and the availability of integrated information system as well (ESTD, 2002c).

It is clearly evident that the implementation of the budget reform and related custom software systems in ESTD was a direct response to coercive pressures exerted by the World Bank and the MOF. ESTD accepted these pressures to gain financial support to develop its information systems to be able to manage the sales tax after extending the application to wholesalers and retailers stages in 2001. The formal implementation of the programs-and-performance-based budget and supporting custom software systems in ESTD started shortly after the World Bank delegation's meeting with the ESTD's officials. However, ESTD informally started designing and implementing some custom software systems that support the budget reform since the Commissioner's decision on 02/12/2000. This is due to the fact that extending the tax application to include wholesale and retail sales created the need for developing and integrating various information systems. So far the implementation processes of the budget reform and related information systems are still in progress.

In fact, the move from the line-item budget to the performance-based budget is a revolutionary change. However, the response to this type of coercive revolutionary change in ESTD was path-dependent. As stated earlier, the custom software systems introduced to support this budget reform were highly influenced by existing routines and institutions. For instance, there was a tendency to use the performance-based budget as a complementary tool to comply with existing Budget Act No. 53 of 1973. In addition, the proposed computerised cost accounting system was based on the Uniform Accounting System that was used by state-owned enterprises since 1966. Therefore, ESTD has responded to extra-organisational coercive pressures by producing and reproducing some existing routines and institutions. This type of change is called 'ceremonial change'. Next we analyse the relationship of accountants with IT specialists in ESTD.

7.3.1.2 Management accountants and IT specialists

Before the introduction of the budget reform into ESTD, there were not any interactions between accountants and IT specialists at all managerial levels. The General Administration for Computing Services and its branches in regions and districts are formally responsible for managing the organisation's IT capability. The General Administration for Computing Services is a part of the Central Administration for Information Centre, Documentation and Decision Support. It supervises a number of computing services departments in regions and districts, where each region has a computing services department that supervises computing services departments in its affiliated districts. IT specialists in computing centres in the headquarters, regions and districts are mainly engineers. Traditionally, IT staff in districts was in charge of the previous version of GSTACS, which focuses only on recording, processing and reporting tax operations. The government accounting system is the responsibility of accountants in accounts units in regions and the headquarters. This system is a manual system that depends on the use of standardised forms, documents, books, procedures and reports in all regions and the headquarters. Traditionally, accountants did not use IT in processing accounting transactions.

The decision to implement the budget reform in ESTD has introduced new roles for accountants as software developers and IT users and started a new era of interactions between accountants and IT specialists. This decision decentralised the responsibility on developing and implementing custom-developed software systems into the members of functional areas in the project team. The IT specialists in the General Administration for Computing Services focused on installing a new Intranet and developing and implementing computerised tax information systems (a new version of the GSTACS), and decentralised the development and implementation of other information systems to other related departments. However, the

General Administration for Computing Services sent one of its IT specialists to help other departments, especially accounting department and planning department, in developing and implementing their software systems. This resulted in the formation of three IT teams: the accounting system team, the planning system team and the tax system team.

The accounting system team was responsible for developing and implementing all computerised accounting systems, including the government accounting system, the costing system, the inventories system and the fixed assets management system. The planning system team is in charge of developing and implementing the performance measurement and reporting system. Finally, the tax system team has the responsibility for developing and implementing the new version of GSTACS. Historically, the General Administration for Computing Services in ESTD controlled computerised tax information systems (the previous version of the GSTACS). Other functional areas either did not have computerised systems (used manual systems) or used Excel files. The current role of the General Administration for Computing Services is continuity for its traditional role.

As a consequence, the General Administration for Computing Services lost control over the development and implementation processes of custom software systems in other departments despite the existence of one of its members in each IT team. This can be attributed to the fact that the General Administration for Computing Services has been busy in developing and implementing computerised tax information systems and did not have time to co-ordinate the work of other departments. IT specialists in each IT team have become loyal to other team's members and to the related departments. Therefore, the decentralisation of software systems development and implementation to other departments created independence on the part of these departments and resulted in a number of functional information systems that are difficult to be integrated.

The accounting system team has developed the accounting software systems using Oracle database but both the planning system team and tax system team have developed their software systems using Sybase database and Power Builder. The use of different programming languages in different functional areas resulted from the fact that the accounting system team started developing its software systems using Oracle database before the official approval of the World Bank's offer in 2002. The World Bank experts imposed the use of Sybase and Power Builder. Later, the other two IT teams developed their software systems using these programming tools. A member of IT staff, who is responsible for managing IT network, in Central Alexandria Region explained that:

The World Bank experts imposed the use of Power Builder to design interface forms and Sybase database to store data. These programming tools have been used to develop the ESTD's information systems. A consulting group from KPMG managed the ESTD's software development process.

The use of different programming languages, coupled with the multiplicity of design approaches, created difficulties in integrating the tax information systems with the performance measurement system to eliminate duplication of work, where tax information systems provide some performance measures such as registrant compliance rates. Furthermore, there are difficulties in integrating the performance measurement system with the cost accounting system to measure performance costs. On the one hand, both the tax information systems and the performance measurement system use the same programming language and provide some common information. However, the design approaches for both systems are different. On the other hand, both the cost accounting system and the performance measurement system use the ESTD's organisational structure as a basis for determining the responsibility centres but they have been developed using different programming languages. The computer engineer who developed the performance measurement system in the planning department stated that:

> I have developed custom software called 'performance standards system' using Sybase and Power Builder, the same programming tools used in developing the new GSTACS software. However, the IT department has not finalised yet its software. I completed my software before its software. I have not designed my software to co-operate with the GSTACS and vice versa. Both are completely independent from each other. Nevertheless, I can re-programme my software again to be compatible with the GSTACS.

The General Manager of Planning Department requested the Database Manager in the General Administration for Computing Services to integrate the performance measurement system with the GSTACS. The Database Manager stated:

> You have not submitted a formal request to our department. We built the systems for the parties who requested from us and any other department that needs our help in building its system should request that and we are able to help it.

This response reflects the desire of IT specialists in the General Administration for Computing Services to regain control over other functional information systems and to combine other functional systems to become part of their systems.

The computer engineer who developed the performance measurement system in the planning department raised the issue of integrating the performance measurement system with the costing system:

> The use of different programming languages might be an obstacle to integrating my software with cost accounting software but such integration is not impossible. Both systems use the organisational structure as a base for determining the responsibility centres.

Despite the use of the same organisational structure in designing the costing system and the performance measurement system, the recent change in the ESTD's organisational structure, which changed the number and scope of responsibility centres, resulted in different views on the responsibility centres between costing system designers and performance measurement system designers. The cost accountant who is in charge of designing, implementing and using the costing system said that:

> We modified the responsibility centres in the costing system to reflect the last change in the organisational structure.

The General Manager of Planning Department who is in charge of the performance measurement system responded by saying:

> We have not modified the responsibility centres yet because the members of the new departments have not been appointed yet and no one has set a plan for each of these departments.

So there is a time lag between the planning department and the cost department in responding to changes in organisational structure. This inevitably creates different views on responsibility centres and affects sharply on the design and integration of both the costing system and the performance measurement system. The integration problems between the costing system, the performance measurement system and the GSTACS are expected to continue in the future because of the continual use of different programming languages. The cost accountant in charge of designing, implementing and using the costing system said that:

> We are only five in ESTD who understand Oracle and its use in programming software. We need to build a base of developers who are capable of using this language within the organisation. I suggested teaching Oracle as a training course in the training programme of ESTD.

Furthermore, the dominance of the General Administration for Computing Services over the Intranet, as well as the difficulties in implementing the tax information systems, caused delays in deploying other functional areas' information systems such as accounting systems and the performance measurement system. For example, the implementation of the new GSTACS software has been delayed for more than a year. There are different causes for this delay. The Database Manager in the General Administration for Computing Services mentioned some of these problems as follows:

> The IT department has programmed the systems of other departments according to their requirements. What they said we did. The heads of Functional Central Administrations submitted signed reports that the software satisfies their needs. However, when we started to install the software in different districts and regions, problems started to emerge as the people who participated in systems design (the heads of Functional Central Administrations) were not involved in day-to-day activities. They did not have comprehensive views on the end-users' needs and expected problems.

He continued explaining the reasons for the delay in deploying the GSTACS:

> Furthermore, we have trained 20 lecturers in the new software for two days. They absorbed the new software and its functions and requested terminating the training. However, it seems that those lecturers did not transfer their acquired knowledge to end-users. We will not train all end-users in all districts and regions. This is the responsibility of the Training Centre and the lectures. Our role is limited to training lecturers.

The General Manager of Planning Department disagreed with this opinion. She said:

> It is the responsibility of IT department to train even the end-users. The IT department's role is not limited to training lecturers. If the IT department discovered the need for additional training, it should start training end-users in the field.

The IT Operating Manager in the General Administration for Computing Services welcomed this suggestion. He said:

> Ok, we will provide such additional training when we find a need for it.

The introduction of the new GSTACS software and the use of Intranet support centralisation in managing IT facilities in ESTD as the General Administration for Computing Services centrally manages IT facilities in all locations. The need for IT specialists in various districts is eliminated because their tasks have been decentralised into employees in tax operations. Therefore, a decision has been taken to re-allocate IT specialists in different districts to other jobs.

However, there is no such change in accounts units in various regions as the automated accounting systems are still in the central accounts unit in the headquarters in Cairo.

7.3.1.3   Management accountants and managers

Traditionally, the role of management accountants in Egyptian government units is very limited as the Sector of General State Budgeting (the central budget office) in the MOF centrally manages the process of preparing the government budget. ESTD is no exception. It has a budgeting committee that is represented by two departments in the ESTD's organisational structure: the General Administration for Revenues and the General Administration for Budget and Encumbrances. The first department is responsible for preparing revenue estimates and monitoring revenue collection. The second department is in charge of preparing expenditure estimates and following up actual expenditures. However, the MOF normally does not take into account such estimates. It always expects that there are an overestimation of expenditures and an underestimation of revenues submitted by government units.

So far the introduction of performance-based budgeting into ESTD has not changed the method of preparing budget estimates. The managers of regions and districts as budget programme managers have not been given greater personal freedom in preparing their budget estimates. The preparation of the ESTD's budget is still controlled by management accountants in the MOF. The head of Central Administration-Gomrok Region stated that:

> Estimated revenues are imposed on us from the top. We have no say in that. The MOF does not ask for our opinions. At the beginning of each year, we submit our needs, whether current expenditures or capital expenditures. However, appropriations sometime do not meet all our needs. Unsatisfied needs are delayed to next year(s). For example, there was a building that was intended to be built to absorb the increase in the number of employees. The employees were 800 and became 1800. However, the facilities have not been changed. To reduce expenditures, we are currently using a four-employee desk. I mean that every four persons share one desk.

The General Manager of Karmouz District made a similar complaint about budget estimates. He said:

> There is a contradiction between imposing estimated revenues on us from top to down and preparing a performance-based plan from down to top. This is not consistent with accountability principle. The heads of regions and the managers of districts should participate in setting their own budgets to be able to achieve them. The major disadvantage of performance-based budget implementation so far is that it has not been

associated with decentralising the authorities of preparing budgets to the heads of regions and the managers of districts.

He continued saying:

> Before the introduction of the sales tax, we were collecting registered companies' budgets in each district and we were using them as a basis for our estimates for tax revenues. If the companies achieved their budgets we would achieve our estimated revenues.

Interestingly, almost all heads of regions and managers of districts have accounting qualifications and, therefore, can handle their own budgets effectively.

In ESTD, the Planning Department does not participate in preparing the budget proposal. Its role comes after approving the government budget. It prepares the annual plans of districts and regions to achieve their allocated revenues. Therefore, there is a almost complete segregation between the planning system and the budgeting system in ESTD. This segregation continued after the introduction of the budget reform to ESTD. However, a new role has been added to the Planning Department in ESTD, that is, the performance measurement and reporting. Management accountants in ESTD lost this role. So far performance data are collected at the level of each district and are analysed by the Planning Department. The Planning Department uses the Intranet to exchange performance data, prepared using Excel files, with different districts and regions. However, these data have not been used in evaluating the performance of district managers because there is no department responsible for performance evaluation. Furthermore, the performance measurement has not been linked to an incentive system.

Before the introduction of the programming- and performance-based budget, there was no cost accountant position. The implementation of the performance-based budget created the need for such position. However, the new cost accountant position is not an independent position. It is subject to the supervision of traditional financial accountant position. ESTD introduced a new cost accounting department as a part of the Central Administration for Accounts. The cost accounting department is located in the headquarters in Cairo. It does not have branches in regions and districts. However, it sends forms to regional accounts units to collect cost data classified by both districts and the object of expenditure. The cost accounting department uses computerised costing software to allocate and calculate the costs of each responsibility centre. A cost accountant stated that:

> Without computer software, we would not be able to calculate the costs of responsibility centres. We prepare reports every three months for

decision-making purposes. These reports are submitted to the Commissioner and contain the costs of each district and each region, and the cost per Egyptian pound collected by each district and each region.

The use of IT facilitates the role of cost accountants in the headquarters in calculating and controlling the costs of various districts and regions. Currently, cost accountants are capable of allocating cost items to responsibility centres, determining the cost per Egyptian pound collected, and submitting detailed cost reports to the Commissioner. The change in the accountants' relationship with regional and district managers was not caused by the introduction of IT into the central accounts unit but it happened because of the new role of accountants as cost accountants. For example, the comparative cost data is useful in comparing the efficiencies of different districts in collecting sales tax. It could be used to evaluate the performance of district managers. However, the costs of each district and the cost per Egyptian pound collected by each district do not express the real costs and efficiencies of districts. There are many internal and external factors that are out of district managers' control. These factors sharply affect the costs and efficiencies of districts. The General Manager of Karmouz District gave some examples of these factors.

> There are some factors that limit the usefulness of implementing the performance-based budget in Sales Tax Department. These factors are out of our control. Examples of such factors are change in petroleum prices, sharp fluctuations in the exchange rates of foreign currencies, and the move of registrants from one district to another. Furthermore, our performance depends on the performance of other government units such as courts and police stations when solving the disputes with registrants and taxpayers. Sometimes, there is over-employment in some districts due to social reasons such as the transfer of wives to be with their husbands in the same districts.

Therefore, the costs and revenues of districts are affected by many factors that are out of their control. In addition, capital investment decisions are centrally managed. Therefore, all these factors need to be considered in evaluating the performance of district managers.

The next section analyses the operation of the dialectic of control in AQF, the second company that implemented custom accounting software. In addition, it compares the operation of the dialectic of control in ESTD with that of AQF.

7.3.2 Comparison of the operation of dialectic of control in AQF and ESTD

This section compares and contrasts custom software implementation processes in AQF and ESTD in relation to the dialectic of control. It examines the relationship of AQF with the holding company and the GOE and compares these relationships with the ESTD's relationships with the World Bank and the MOF. It also analyses the changing power relations of accountants with IT specialists and line managers in AQF and compares these relationships with those in ESTD.

7.3.2.1 The adoption of custom accounting software and the intervention of the government and the holding company

AQF is a state-owned enterprise. Since 1991, it has been supervised by the Holding Company for Chemical Industries to organise its gradual sale. However, more than 80% of its shares are still owned by non-manufacturing public enterprises. The GOE controls the pricing of AQF's products because these products affect about 90% of the public's interests. In addition, the Government intervenes in selling decisions. Sometimes, it makes a decision to deliver the whole of the company's production to the Agriculture National Bank to be sold in the local market. This kind of decisions affects the competitive advantage of the company and limits the quantities exported to international markets.

The decision to implement custom accounting software and renew IT infrastructure in 1998/99 was related to its gradual privatisation. However, this decision was not influenced by the holding company.[4] It was an initiative launched by the ex-head of Quality Control and Assurance as part of the preparation for ISO 9001:2000 certificate. So the introduction of new custom software was seen as an internal decision rather than a mandatory order. It was not subjected to resistance from the company's organisational members as it did not challenge existing routines and institutions. The software was customised to be in full conformity with the Uniform Accounting System used by the company since its establishment in 1976.

Compared to the decision to implement custom software in AQF, the decision to implement custom software systems in ESTD was an external coercive decision taken by the World Bank and the MOF as part of a wider state-budget reform. However, the ESTD's organisational members have not resisted this decision as the 'new' custom software systems have not challenged the existing way of thinking. These systems have been customised to accommodate existing routines and institutions. Next, we focus on the accountants' relationships with line managers and IT specialists in AQF and comparing them with those relationships in ESTD.

7.3.2.2 Accountants and IT specialists

Historically, the MIS Department in AQF had reported to the controller, the Head of Finance Sector. In 1998/99, following the renewal of IT infrastructure and the introduction of custom Oracle software, the company's management decided to relocate the MIS Department to become under the direct supervision of the vice-CEO of Control and Commercial Affairs.

The department has therefore become much closer to the office of the CEO. This new location gives the MIS Department the power to serve all the company's departments and sectors. It reflects the increasing importance of IT in the company.

Despite the change in the MIS Department's location in the organisational structure, the department is still dominated by accountants. The General Manager of the MIS Department and almost all its staff are accountants. This dominance of accountants over the MIS Department is the result of historical events. So, accountants are still the custodians/managers of custom Oracle software and the company's Intranet. However, they were not the initiators of the IT reform. As stated earlier, the new software and change in IT infrastructure were suggested by the ex-head of Quality Control and Assurance as part of the preparation for ISO 9001:2000 certificate.

Accountants in AQF resisted any possibility of decentralising part of their knowledge to other functional areas such as IT specialists. The General Manager of Financial Accounts said:

> Each sector has its own secrets and privacy. Specialisation is vital in interpreting figures... Does anyone in the company understand the budget? No-one that checks the budget is capable of spotting specific data. The computer operator would take a lot of time... S/he has not worked for 10–20 years in financial accounts to be sensitive to number interpretation. The data could be available but its interpretation should be left to specialists.

Therefore, accountants in AQF have not lost control over accounting knowledge but rather have expanded their knowledge into the IT field and thus have taken control of the MIS Department. Compared with the situation in AQF, accountants in ESTD also have not lost control over accounting knowledge and have developed their skills in IT. However, they are still dependent on IT specialists in deploying their accounting software as IT specialists in ESTD have control over the Intranet. The relationship of accountants in AQF with line managers is the topic of next sub-section.

7.3.2.3   Accountants and line managers

The custom Oracle software and the Intranet (LAN network), introduced in 1998/99, significantly improved the relationship between accountants and line managers. They have contributed in providing timely information for decision-makers, especially the CEO and line managers in the field. There are terminals in plants and the CEO's office. In this regard, the General Manager of the MIS Department stated:

> The company depends on Intranet (LAN network) that connects about 80 personal computers. There are also other standalone computers that are

not connected to the LAN. There are a number of terminals that present the information to the CEO and line managers. They use this information to monitor transactions such as bank transactions and sales transactions.

The Head of Technical Sector (production department-factories) confirmed this information:

> Computerised information systems were launched approximately five years ago (about 1998/99). Terminals were connected to different pants. For example, warehouses have a number of terminals. When the company started the IT project, it requested from each department to document its data inputs and information outputs. Then, IT experts designed screens for these departments. They allowed some departments to see the information produced by other departments such as warehouses and purchases... Other departments have personal computers that are not connected to the Intranet and have customised software.

Therefore, the terminals present information to organisational members such as line managers and top management to follow-up the company's status with respect to sales, purchases and inventories. However, these members are not allowed to modify this information. Only accountants have the authority to do so. This reflects the dominance of accountants on data flows throughout the company. Accountants are totally responsible for data entry in the formal information system of the company. A cost accountant explained:

> The Production Department provides us with production data. It operates at full capacity. It provides weekly and monthly reports to the Costing Department. These reports include units produced during the period, stop periods and the reasons for stop.

The Head of Technical Sector supported this information that line managers are the suppliers of production information to the Costing Department. He said:

> Generally speaking, accountants are more dependent on engineers in collecting data on production activities of the company.

The Costing Department collects production data to control the production activities. It directs the line managers' attention to some matters and provides signals about certain events. Sometimes, a conflict arises between cost accountants and line managers because of cost variances between actual figures and planned ones, especially when actual rates exceed planned rates. In particular, this situation occurs when the CAA intervenes to know the reasons for cost variances. The Head of Technical Sector gave an example for this situation:

> For example, there could be a hole in a gas tube that supplies the gas to the company. To continue production, this hole could be temporarily repaired without totally preventing the gas leak. As a consequence, the gas consumption increases and exceeds its normal rates. The Costing Department and the Central Agency for Accountancy ask about the reason for this variance. But engineers do not like this type of questions.

It seems that line managers have some independence from accountants in their informal information systems. For example, the Production Department sometimes requests a special study to be prepared by the Purchase Department to collect information about raw materials, their suppliers and their prices. This study is not conducted by the Finance Sector. Furthermore, line managers have their own custom software. The Head of Technical Sector explained:

> In 2001, when I was the General Manager of the Spare Part Planning Department, I had a personal computer and I had custom software based on MS-access. The software was used to record all the factories' orders... Any purchase order was recorded and there was a continuous update for the orders' status.

The relationship between accountants and line managers in AQF has not changed as a result of the introduction of custom Oracle software and Intranet. Accountants still have control over accounting knowledge and line managers have control over production knowledge. This relationship in ESTD has also not changed but for different reasons. Custom software systems introduced to support the budget reform in ESTD were not integrated and the responsibility for managing these systems was decentralised. The responsibility for managing the non-financial aspects of the performance-based budget, including related software, was given to planning staff not accountants. Cost accountants, a new position that was introduced to ESTD, were given the responsibility for managing the financial aspects of the performance-based budget, including relevant software. They collect cost data to evaluate the performance of line managers but the use of these data is still ineffective because of the absence of an incentive system. Line managers in ESTD have accounting knowledge because of the nature of the organisation's activities and can manage their own performance-based budgets but the MOF refused to decentralise the responsibility for the financial aspects of the budget to line managers.

7.4 Discussion

Drawing on the theoretical framework developed in Chapter 3 and the empirical data collected, this chapter addressed the second group of research questions, which focuses on the role of extra-institutional pressures in enabling or constraining IT projects and the role of IT (ERP vs. custom software) in changing management accountants' role and relationships with IT specialists and line managers. Based on the structuration theory's concept of the dialectic of control, the analysis in this chapter was conducted at two levels in four Egyptian organisations. The first level, the hierarchical level, examined the role of extra-organisational institutions in enabling or constraining IT projects and associated management accounting change, if any. The second level, the professional level, examined the changing power relations of management accountants with IT specialists and line managers due to implementing IT projects and associated management accounting change, if any. The analysis revealed that the dialectic of control operates at both levels as shown in the next sections.

7.4.1 ERP vs. custom software and the dialectic of control at the hierarchical level

Giddens (1984) uses the concept of dialectic of control in reference to power relations between subordinates and their superiors, reflecting a hierarchical relationship. In fact, the dialectic of control operates at every level in social systems, where every higher level has more authority but has less knowledge about the detailed activities of its immediate lower level. In this section we presented the four case studies' findings about the power relations between extra-organisational institutions and organisational members. These findings revealed that the operation of the dialectic of control between extra-organisational institutions and organisational members in the four Egyptian organisations is much more obvious in ERP cases than in custom software cases.

In the case of ERP implementations, there was a great deal of conflicts and contradictions between extra-organisational institutions and organisational members in IMC and NEEASAE. In the IMC case, the ERP project was initiated by the organisational members, particularly accountants. The EU Commission rejected the project as they saw that the software cost exceeded the budget limit. However, the organisational members insisted on purchasing and implementing the software. As a result, the EU Commission terminated the service contracts of those involved in the ERP project. In NEEASAE case, the ERP project was imposed by the holding company in order to facilitate the sale of the company. Hence, the organisational members resisted the ERP project as they felt that it was a threat to their secured jobs.

In the case of custom software implementations, there was little, if any, conflict between extra-organisational institutions and organisational members in ESTD and AQF. In ESTD, the decision to implement custom software systems in ESTD was an external coercive decision taken by the World Bank and the MOF as part of a wider state-budget reform. However, the organisational members have not resisted this decision as the 'new' custom software systems have not challenged existing ways of thinking. There was a similar situation in AQF. Custom accounting software was proposed by the ex-head of Quality Control and Assurance as a part of the preparation for ISO 9001 certificate. This decision was not influenced by the holding company as AQF had not requested any financial support from the holding company to implement this software. The software was not subjected to resistance from the company's organisational members as it did not challenge existing routines and institutions.

The above findings support the view that the implementation of ERP is associated with crisis situations whereas the implementation of custom software is associated with routine situations (Schneider, 1999; Orlikowski, 1992). On the one hand, the ERP implementation causes tensions and resistance as it tends to challenge existing routines and institutions. In these critical situations, Giddens (1984) argues that agents will come to the fore to radically reshape existing structure which leads to more exercise of power and a great deal of conflict. On the other hand, custom software implementation tends to reinforce existing routines and institutions. In this regard, Giddens (1984) suggests that under routine situations the interaction of agency and structure will result in the reproduction of existing structure and reasonable exercise of power and, consequently, little conflict.

7.4.2   ERP vs. custom software and the dialectic of control at the professional level

The literature reviewed in Chapter 2 provided two conflicting views about the management accountants' changing role and relationships with other professional groups in the IT (ERP vs. custom software) environment. The first view sees that management accountants lose their traditional role as information providers because this role is built into IT and, therefore, accounting knowledge becomes easily transferable to other professional groups such as IS staff and line managers. The other view considers that management accountants still have control over their accounting knowledge and try to expand their role to other functional areas such as IS and production. The transfer of knowledge from one professional group to another is known as hybridisation.

With respect to hybridisation phenomenon, the analysis of the case studies' findings revealed that there is evidence that management accountants in Egyptian organisations still control their accounting knowledge and, in some cases, have unintentionally expanded their roles into other functional areas such as IT and operations after the introduction of IT projects. This general statement equally applies to ERP cases and custom software cases. In the

IMC case, management accountants have broadened their role and expertise in positions traditionally pertaining to IT specialists. They played a prominent role in all decisions regarding the adoption and implementation of the ERP. Furthermore, the ERP has not affected the traditional role of management accountants as information suppliers in IMC. There was apparent dependence of line managers on management accountants in providing accounting information. This was due to the fact that management accountants were the custodians/managers of the ERP software. In addition, management accountants in IMC have expanded their knowledge into operations. They did so to customise the ERP during the implementation process and to inform line managers, who were foreigners, about the Egyptian market.

However, management accountants sometimes do not support ERP projects and reject expanding their knowledge to other functional areas. In the NEEASAE case, management accountants played a major role in ERP failure by requiring the ERP vendor to customise the software to a complete match to the Uniform Accounting System. This apparent resistance from accountants in NEEASAE was mainly because of the lack of IT skills among accountants. For example, before the ERP adoption, there had been tailored accounting software run by IT specialists, engineers. So some IT specialists expanded their roles into accounting area. In addition, the ERP project was managed by the head of line managers and other ex-line managers. All these managers did not have enough, if any, IT qualifications and skills to manage the process of ERP implementation. Taking this into consideration, it was not a surprise that ERP failed in NEEASAE.

The hybridisation phenomenon is not limited to ERP implementation. It could also occur in the case of custom software implementation. In ESTD, management accountants have not lost control over accounting knowledge and have developed their skills in IT. However, they are still dependent on IT specialists in deploying their accounting software because IT specialists in ESTD have control over the Intranet. Furthermore, the relationship between accountants and line managers in ESTD has not changed. The custom software systems introduced to support the budget reform in ESTD were not integrated and the responsibility for managing these systems was decentralised. The responsibility for managing the non-financial aspects of the performance-based budget, including related software, was given to planning staff not accountants. Cost accountants, a new position that was introduced to ESTD, were given the responsibility for managing the financial aspects of the performance-based budget, including relevant software. They collected cost data to evaluate the performance of line managers but the use of these data was still ineffective because of the absence of an incentive system. Line managers in ESTD have accounting knowledge because of the nature of the organisation's activities and can manage their own performance-based budgets but the MOF refused to decentralise the responsibility for the financial aspects of the budget to line managers.

In AQF, accountants have not lost control over accounting knowledge but expanded their knowledge to IT field and controlled the MIS Department. The relationship between management accountants and line managers in AQF has not changed due to the introduction of custom Oracle software and Intranet. Accountants still have control over accounting knowledge and line managers have control over production knowledge.

Generally speaking, the results of the four case studies support the view that IT, whether ERP or custom software, has not affected the traditional role of management accountants as information providers. Accounting knowledge has not been decentralised to other professional groups following the introduction of IT projects. In the case of custom software, these findings are consistent with previous studies' results that dominant groups in organisations tend to implement technologies in ways that sustain and reinforce their position (George and King, 1991). In the case of ERP, the cases' findings are consistent with Granlund and Malmi (2002), who found that management accounting tasks do not seem to be devolving to non-accountants. They are also consistent with Caglio (2003), who found that, following the introduction of ERP systems, management accountants have expanded their role and expertise into other functional positions. However, these findings may seem to be in conflict with Scapens and Jazayeri (2003) that line managers have direct knowledge of their budget and cost through the ERP system.

In this chapter, structuration theory was used to analyse the relationship between management accountants and other professional groups. This use of structuration theory could be criticised on the ground that Giddens' (1979, 1984) dependency and independence concept is related to hierarchical relationships between superiors and subordinates. Thus, it may not be relevant for analysing relations between various professional groups such as accountants and both IT specialists and line managers. However, the authors believe that Giddens' view of dependence and independence is a general concept. Giddens' structuration theory, in the first place, is a social theory rather than an organisational theory. It is equally applicable to different social relations, including relations between professional groups.[5] In support of this view, Giddens (1984) argues that the dialectic of control is in the very nature of agency, which implies power. He added:

> An agent who does not participate in the dialectic of control, in minimal fashion, ceases to be an agent...all power relations, or relations of autonomy and dependence, are reciprocal... (Giddens, 1979: 149).

The exercise of power in social relations depends on both formal sources (hierarchy of authority and responsibility) and informal sources (knowledge, mobilisation of authority, experience, significance of the institution, personal relations or connections with power holders). The social relations between various professional groups tend to depend more on informal sources than on formal sources. This is consistent with the evidence collected from the four cases. For example, the introduction of ERP software in IMC was based on the personal relations between the Financial Controller and the Executive Director of the Centre. However, knowledge, whether tacit or explicit, is the most important resource which differentiates between various professional groups. So the transfer of knowledge from one professional group to another could lead to redefining the boundaries of a certain profession. IT, especially ERP, could re-distribute the knowledge among various professional groups. In defining the generalised competence of actors, Giddens (1984) argues that the competent agents are the persons who are usually able to explain most of what they do, if asked. It is the knowledge with social conventions which differentiates a competent or knowledgeable agent from a non-competent agent.

7.5 Conclusion

This chapter analysed the role of extra-institutional pressures in enabling or constraining IT projects (ERP vs. custom software) and the role of IT in changing management accountants' role and relationships with IT specialists and line managers in four Egyptian organisations, IMC, NEEASAE, ESTD and AQF. Drawing on the structuration theory's concept of the dialectic of control and its application in Burns and Scapens' (2000) framework, the analysis in this chapter was conducted at two levels. The first level, the hierarchical level, examined the role of extra-organisational institutions in enabling or constraining IT projects and associated management accounting change and stability. The findings at this level revealed that the operation of the dialectic of control between extra-organisational institutions and organisational members in the four Egyptian organisations is much more obvious in ERP cases than in custom software cases.

In the case of ERP implementations, there was a great deal of conflict and contradiction between extra-organisational institutions and organisational members in IMC and NEEASAE. The ERP implementation caused tensions and resistance as it tended to challenge existing routines and institutions. In the case of custom software implementations, there was little, if any, conflict between extra-organisational institutions and organisational members in ESTD and AQF. Custom software implementation tended to reinforce existing routines and institutions.

The second level, the professional level, examined the changing power relations of management accountants with IT specialists and line managers due to implementing IT projects and associated management accounting change. It focused on the hybridisation phenomenon or the transfer of knowledge from one professional group to another. At this level of analysis, the case studies' findings revealed that there was evidence that management accountants in Egyptian organisations maintained the control over their accounting knowledge and, in some cases, have unintentionally expanded their roles into other functional areas such as IT and operations after the introduction of IT projects. This general statement equally applies to ERP cases and custom software cases. In the IMC case, management accountants have broadened their role and expertise in positions traditionally pertaining to IT specialists. In addition, management accountants in IMC have expanded their knowledge into operations. In the NEEASAE case, management accountants have not supported the ERP project and refused expanding their knowledge to other functional areas.

The hybridisation phenomenon is not limited to ERP implementation. It could also occur in the case of custom software implementation. In ESTD, management accountants have not lost control over accounting knowledge and have developed their skills in IT. Furthermore, the relationship between accountants and line managers in ESTD has not changed. In AQF, accountants have not lost control over accounting knowledge but expanded their knowledge to IT field and controlled the MIS Department. The relationship between management accountants and line managers in AQF has not changed due to the introduction of custom Oracle software and Intranet.

Notes

1   The Financial Systems Manager had been recruited from another large company in 2001 and has substantial expertise in the use of IT and in particular ERP systems.

2   BRCs represent branches of IMC in a number of Egyptian industrial cities. Their role is to act as a catalyst for modernising industry in Egypt and encourage entrepreneurship.

3   In the planning budgets for 1998/99, the number of employees was 3,630 on 31/12/1997. This number was planned to be reduced to 3,360 employees due to the use of early retirement policy.

4   AQF is a wealthy company. It controls the majority of Egyptian local market of fertilisers. Furthermore, it recently participated in establishing a new fertiliser company.

5   See Sibanda-Ndiweni (2002) and Caglio (2003) for applications of structuration theory to the power relations between various professional groups.

8
Summary and Conclusions

8.1 Introduction

This chapter summarises the main findings of the study, provides some recommendations, sets out research contributions, shows research limitations, and identifies future research opportunities. The first section summarises the main findings from this study and draws relevant conclusions. The following section presents the main implications and recommendations for companies that initiate IT projects and accounting educators. The next section sets out the contributions this study makes to our understanding of the interaction of new technology and management accounting. Specifically, it compares the experiences of ERP implementations in Egypt and developed countries to shed light on the additional challenges facing ERP projects in Egypt. The final two sections in the chapter discuss respectively the limitations of the study and possible areas for future research.

8.2 Summary of research findings

This study examined management accounting change triggered by IT (ERP vs. custom software) implementation and use in four Egyptian organisations. It analytically and empirically compared ERP with custom software in relation to change in management accounting rules and routines as well as change in management accountants' roles and relationships with other organisational members, especially IT specialists and line managers, in highly regularised Egyptian organisations that have been influenced by recent institutional transformation. To address this issue, two groups of research questions were developed. The first group of questions deals with change and stability in management accounting rules and routines due to the introduction of IT (ERP vs. custom software). This group of questions includes the following:

- Why and how are institutionalised accounting practices persisted (reproduced) and/or transformed in the IT (ERP vs. custom software) environment? These questions deal mainly with stability and change in management accounting practices and the conditions under which stability and/or change can occur.

- What is the role of IT (ERP vs. custom software) in their persistence or transformation? This question focuses on the role of IT in initiating change or stabilising existing accounting rules and routines.

The second group of questions deals with change in management accountants' roles and relationships due to the introduction of IT (ERP vs. custom software). This group of questions includes the following:

- How does IT (ERP vs. custom software) maintain or change the relationship of management accountants with different members (IS staff and line managers) within the organisation? This question focuses mainly on the changing relationships of management accountants arising from the introduction of IT (ERP vs. custom software).
- What is the role of management accountants in the IT (ERP vs. custom software) environment as perceived by management accountants themselves and other members of the organisation? This question focuses on the changing role of management accountants arising from the introduction of IT (ERP vs. custom software).

To address the above questions this book was organised into eight chapters. Chapter 1 provided a brief overview of the research objectives, theoretical framework, and research methodology and method. The chapter introduced several motives for conducting this study. Firstly, no previous studies that address the impact of ERP implementation on management accounting change, have been conducted in Egypt, as an example of a developing country in transition from a centrally planned economy to a free-market-oriented economy. It is also the case that Egyptian organisations paid little attention to management accounting techniques in the socialist period. Secondly, previous studies tended to compare the experiences of ERP implementation and 'Best of Breed' (BoB) systems implementation. The latter systems could have similar impacts on management accounting because they include different modules of various ERP packages. This study compared ERP with custom software instead of BoB systems to avoid any impact of ERP systems. Thirdly, there have been very few previous studies that use analytical frameworks for interpreting accounting change induced by ERP. Finally, none of previous studies have been conducted in public sector or state-controlled organisations. Accordingly, this study was conducted to address the above gaps in the literature on ERP and management accounting change.

Chapter 2 reviewed the previous literature on ERP systems and management accounting change. Based on this review, it seems that ERP systems have evolved from earlier MRPI systems in the 1970s and MRPII systems in the 1980s. ERP systems addressed the limitations of these legacy systems by spanning most functional areas such as accounting, operations, logistics, human resources, and sales and marketing. ERP systems support and facilitate a wide range of modern management accounting techniques such as Activity-Based Costing (ABC) and Balanced Scorecard (BSC). Thus, these systems promise radical change in management accounting practices and management accountants' roles and relationships. Previous studies provided empirical evidence that ERP systems tended to evolutionarily change or stabilise management accounting rules and routines as well as change the role and relationships of management accountants. Different positivistic, interpretive and critical theories have been used to address management accounting change and stability. However, there has been a tendency towards combining different research theories to understand management accounting change as a complex phenomenon.

Accordingly, Chapter 3 developed a theoretical framework to address management accounting change triggered by IT (ERP vs. custom software) implementation and use. This framework drew primarily upon the applications and extensions of structuration theory in both the management accounting literature and the IS literature. This chapter identified structuration theory as a meta-theory that provides a way of thinking about the world and can be helpful in transcending objectivism and subjectivism positions. It also discussed Burns and Scapens' (2000) institutional framework as an extension to structuration theory to overcome its limitations in addressing management accounting change. However, Burns and Scapens' model needed to be complemented, on the one hand, by IS models to deal with IT implementation and use and, on the other hand, by new institutional sociology theory to take into account extra-organisational institutions. Furthermore, Burns and Scapens' framework could not stand alone without considering structuration theory. In sum, the theoretical framework in this study was based mainly on three theories, namely structuration theory, old institutional economics theory and new institutional sociology theory.

Chapter 4 discussed the design and implementation of the empirical work. It discussed how the research methodology links the theoretical framework with the research method. Two main research methodologies were introduced, namely the positivistic methodology and the interpretive methodology. The latter methodology was the one adopted by both structuration theory and Burns and Scapens' institutional framework that formed the theoretical base for this study. The case study method can be used with both research methodologies. However, it is essential in interpretive methodology as it helps in both replicating and extending interpretive theories. The design of this study was based on a multiple-case design that compared four organisations to address research issues on IT (custom vs.

ERP software) implementation and management accounting change. Furthermore, although it used multiple data collection methods, semi-structured interviews were considered the main method of collecting data. Finally, the chapter discussed the case study research's limitations and how their effects can be minimised.

Drawing on the concepts of deinstitutionalisation, organisational fields and coercive pressures, Chapter 5 provided a description and, to some extent, an historical analysis of the transformation of extra-organisational institutions that have had influences on state-owned enterprises and government agencies due to the change of economic orientation from a centrally planned economy to a market-oriented economy in Egypt. Various forces have played vital roles in the institutional transformation through reform programmes. The chapter focused on the privatisation pro-gramme, industrial modernisation programmes and state-budget reforms because they have major influences on the four cases under study; two state-owned enterprises (AQF and NEEASAE) and two government agencies (IMC and ESTD). This chapter also gave a brief historical background of each of the four organisations under study.

In order to address the first group of questions Chapter 6 analysed the four case studies in line with the theoretical framework developed in Chapter 3. The analysis provided empirical evidence of the role of IT (ERP vs. custom software) implementation and use in management accounting change and stability and the forces behind change and stability in manage-ment accounting rules and routines in four Egyptian organisations. The analysis was based on the use of different theoretical concepts such as path-dependence and interpretive flexibility in interpreting empirical evidence collected. This analysis indicated that IT, whether ERP or custom software, was not a driver of change in management accounting systems and prac-tices in highly regularised organisations such as state-owned enterprises and government agencies. Other institutional forces were behind introduc-ing change in management accounting rules and routines in Egyptian organisations.

The above findings could be expected in the case of custom software. However, they have been observed in the case of ERP software as well. In IMC, ERP modules and sub-modules were gradually implemented over a period of time. ERP has also been customised to reinforce EU budgeting procedures and programme and performance-based budgeting by encoding EU institutional principles into the new rules built into the ERP. In NEEASAE, ERP modules and sub-modules were co-implemented at the same time. However, it contradicted the Uniform Accounting System and local tax rules during encoding institutional principles into the ERP. The ten-dency towards ERP customisation could be attributed to the fact that ERP built-in accounting knowledge had not been transferred into ERP users. This could be related to the lack of training and/or the education system.

Another finding was that custom software was not a driver of change in management accounting rules and routines in Egyptian organisations. In ESTD case, custom software systems have been introduced to support the budget reform from line-item budgeting to programme and performance-based budgeting. However, these systems reinforced the *status quo* rather than reformed it. ESTD introduced both custom software that supported line-item budgeting and custom software that supported programme and performance-based budgeting. However, the custom software that was introduced to support programme and performance-based budgeting was based on existing routines and institutions. In AQF, custom accounting software was implemented as well. However, it reinforced existing routines, mainly the Uniform Accounting System and local tax laws.

In order to address the second group of questions, Chapter 7 analysed the four case studies in line with the theoretical framework developed in Chapter 3. The analysis provided empirical evidence of the operation of the dialectic of control, as developed in structuration theory and applied in Burns and Scapens' institutional framework, in the four organisations under study that implemented IT (ERP vs. custom software) projects. It was conducted at two levels. The first level, the hierarchical level, examined the role of extra-organisational institutions in enabling or constraining IT projects and associated management accounting change and stability. The key findings at this level were that the operation of the dialectic of control between extra-organisational institutions and organisational members in the four Egyptian organisations was much more obvious in ERP cases than in custom software cases.

In the case of ERP implementations, the analysis revealed that there were many conflicts and contradictions between extra-organisational institutions and organisational members in IMC and NEEASAE. The ERP implementation caused tensions and resistance as it tended to challenge existing routines and institutions. In the case of custom software implementations, there was little, if any, conflict between extra-organisational institutions and organisational members in ESTD and AQF. Custom software implementation tended to reinforce existing routines and institutions. The findings in this chapter support the view that the implementation of ERP is associated with crisis situations whereas the implementation of custom software is associated with routine situations.

The second level of analysis in Chapter 7, the professional level, examined the changing power relations of management accountants with IT specialists and line managers due to implementing IT projects and associated management accounting change. It focused on the hybridisation phenomenon or the transfer of knowledge from one professional group to another. At this level of analysis the case studies' findings provide evidence that management accountants in Egyptian organisations maintained control over their accounting knowledge and, in some cases, have unintentionally expanded their roles into other functional areas such as IT and operations after the introduction of IT projects. This conclusion equally applied to ERP cases and custom software cases. In the case of IMC management accountants have broadened their role and expertise in positions traditionally pertaining to IT specialists. In addition, management accountants in IMC have expanded their knowledge into operations. In NEEASAE case, management accountants have not supported the ERP project and rejected expanding their knowledge to other functional areas.

An important finding in Chapter 7 was that the hybridisation phenomenon was not limited to ERP implementation. It could also occur in the case of custom software implementation. In ESTD management accountants have also not lost control over accounting knowledge and have developed their skills in IT. Furthermore, the relationship between accountants and line managers in ESTD has not changed. In AQF, accountants have not lost control over accounting knowledge but expanded their knowledge to IT field and controlled the MIS department. The relationship between management accountants and line managers in AQF has not changed due to the introduction of custom Oracle software and Intranet.

8.3   Implications and recommendations

This section provides some implications and recommendations that might be of interest and assistance to companies that initiate IT projects, with special emphasis on ERP projects, as well as accounting educators. The implications and recommendations can be summarised as follows.

First, the findings of this study revealed that the capacity to cope with IT in general and, ERP in particular, was a critical factor for the success or failure of ERP projects. For example, the ERP project in IMC was successfully implemented because of the existence of a well-trained and qualified team. On the other hand, one of the main reasons for ERP failure in NEEASAE was the lack of basic computer skills and the lack of capacity to cope with ERP on the part of not only the project team but also almost all organisational members. In this regard, Burns and Scapens (2000) argue that the lack of capacity (knowledge and experience) is a major source of resistance to change. To alleviate this resistance, Argyris and Kaplan (1994) identify three processes necessary to implement innovative technical initiatives by overcoming the barriers to change that exist at individual, group, inter-group and organisational levels. These processes are education and training, the sponsorship of the change process, and the alignment of incentives.

In order to increase the possibility of ERP success in Egyptian organisations, there is a need for improving the education system in Egyptian universities as well as developing internal IT capacity in Egyptian organisations. Currently, business curricula at Egyptian universities, like most universities in developed countries, are generally delivered through courses associated with functional areas: accounting, finance, marketing, information systems, operations and management. As a result, there is a need for integrating ERP in the business school curriculum in order to change education delivery from a functional orientation to a business process orientation. This integration is essential in increasing the capacity to deal with ERP implementation and use in Egyptian organisations.

Furthermore, developing internal IT capacity in Egyptian organisations is a matter of 'life and death', especially, for ERP projects. The findings of case studies, especially in IMC and NEEASAE, showed that the excessive reliance on external ERP consultants could lead to the failure of ERP projects. In the long run, companies have to develop their own internal personnel that are capable of dealing with ERP problems. In this regard, organisations adopting ERP systems urgently need to have both internal training centre and MIS department to manage the change process properly. The availability of well-trained internal IT experts is essential for reducing the failure of ERP projects and the sustainability of the software development and use in the long run. Both education and training are necessary in order that the logic and validity of any ERP project are accepted, especially in the early stages of ERP implementation, and to provide examples of how organisations have benefited from the 'new' ERP systems.

Second, the case studies' results have shown that some IT projects, whether ERP or custom software, were not associated with proper planning. For example, the use of different programming languages and different IT developers led to difficulties in integrating various custom software systems introduced to support the budget reform in ESTD. NEEASAE faced similar problems when it started implementing an ERP project. For example, the company relied on at least four different ERP teams from the consulting company. This led to discontinuity and mistrust on the part of NEEASAE's members. However, it is difficult to completely accuse these organisations of the lack of planning. In this regard, Burnes (2004: 985) stated that '...any attempt to predict or identify a specific outcome from planned change is very difficult because of the complexity of the forces concerned'.

Third, the findings of the case studies revealed only minor changes in the roles and relationships of management accountants in some Egyptian organisations arising from the implementation and use of new IT. However, with the continuous trend towards the adoption of ERP systems, management accountants should expect to be involved in continuing education. Otherwise, they might lose their current positions as information providers. However, the Egyptian environment does not support the continuous learning, especially, for management accountants in practice. This can be due to the non-existence of a management accounting association, like CIMA in the UK and IMA in the USA, which sponsors these educational programmes. Therefore, it would be helpful to establish a professional management accounting association to complement the role of universities.

Fourth, the results of the case studies indicated many difficulties facing the implementation of ERP projects in highly regularised organisations (see next section). ERP projects are highly expected to fail because these organisations have to obey certain laws and regulations that are difficult to be built into the ERP software. Therefore, it is appropriate for this type of organisations to adopt custom developed software systems. Custom software could be totally customised to fit the information needs of these organisations as well as to be in conformity with local laws and regulations. In fact, the experiences of AQF and ESTD were very successful because of following this strategy.

Finally, the research findings revealed that the proper selection of the IT project team's members, especially the project manager and key users, is vital for the successful implementation of the project. For example, the ERP Project Manager in NEEASAE did not have even basic IT skills and was approaching retirement age. Taking this information into account, it was not a surprise that ERP failed in NEEASAE. The selection of key users is important as well. In ESTD, the key users actively participated in providing the information needs that the custom software, the GSTACS, should satisfy. However, the key users were senior managers who did not know what was going on in the day-to-day activities. As a result, the software faced much delay in implementation and many difficulties in use that led to several modifications to the software.

8.4 Research contributions to knowledge

This study has contributed to the emerging research on ERP and management accounting change by identifying the unique nature of IT (ERP vs. custom software) implementations in Egyptian organisations, particularly state-owned enterprises and government agencies. In particular, the major contributions of this study are related to providing empirical evidence on ERP implementations and management accounting change in highly regularised organisations in Egypt. To date, little research has been conducted in these types of organisations or in the Egyptian context. Compared with the experiences reported in previous studies conducted in developed countries, the experiences gained from Egyptian organisations have some similarities but many differences.

First, there was an apparent tendency towards customising ERP software in Egyptian organisations. The use of ERP customisation strategy to stabilise management accounting systems and practices in Egyptian organisations was different from other strategies observed in developed countries. For example, Scapens and Jazayeri (2003) conducted a case study in a large US-based manufacture of building materials. They found that the company had chosen ERP systems that replace existing accounting systems with other very similar systems. Another strategy observed in developed countries was the use of BoB systems, where different ERP modules from different ERP vendors are used in different functions to closely align the selected software with the business processes of the organisation (Themistocleous *et al.*, 2001).

The trend towards ERP customisation or the use of custom software in Egyptian organisations to reinforce existing local developed accounting systems, such as the Uniform Accounting System in NEEASAE and AQF, has shed light on the conflict between the globalisation and localisation of management accounting practices. It illustrated the resistance to global best practices built into ERP software or it might simply mean that there were alternative local best practices perceived by Egyptian organisations. This study has questioned the relevance of Anglo-American management acccunting techniques built into ERP software in developing countries and added a new dimension to this issue – the use of ERP to promote Anglo-American management accounting techniques.

Second, the conduct of this study in highly regularised organisations, government agencies and state-owned enterprises, revealed the unique institutional circumstances that prevented adopting any new management accounting techniques, which could be in conflict with existing laws and regulations. For example, one of the main reasons for ERP failure in NEEASAE was the tension between the new rules built into the ERP and established routines and institutions. ERP contradicted the Uniform Accounting System, which is closely monitored by the CAA and has been used by public sector enterprises since 1966, and local tax rules during encoding existing institutional principles into the new rules built into the ERP. Another interesting observation in NEEASAE, as a state-owned enterprise, was the bankruptcy of the ERP vendor rather than the company itself. It is usual that the implementation of ERP systems in companies working in developed countries may lead to business bankruptcy due to the large amount of investments required and the changes required in business operations. However, the bankruptcy of ERP vendor is not expected. This observation clearly demonstrates the unique nature of state-owned enterprises in which there is no notion of bankruptcy in the public sector.

Third, conducting research on ERP implementation in developing countries is a major contribution of this study. In this regard, Huang and Palvia (2001) point out that little research has been undertaken to compare ERP implementation in developed vs. developing countries. They argue that ERP projects faces additional challenges in developing countries related to economic, cultural and basic infrastructure issues. In fact, ERP implementations in Egyptian organisations faced many challenges. For example, various forces played a major role in limiting the widespread use of ERP in IMC such as:

- The failure to secure legitimacy for the ERP project due to the lack of financial support from the EU,
- The competing interests between accountants and IT specialists over managing IT facilities in IMC,
- Lack of capacity to deal with ERP on part of IT specialists and line managers due to the lack of training on using the ERP,
- Scarce financial resources due to the Iraq War and the transfer of part of IMC's budget to support the Egyptian government, and
- Scarce human resources (ERP experts) in ERP vendor that threatened the failure of ERP project in IMC.

Similar challenges faced the ERP implementation in NEEASAE. However, these challenges contributed to the ERP failure. Examples of these problems were:

- The new rules built into ERP software were incompatible with the established ways of thinking and the norms of behaviour embedded in the existing accounting routines,
- The lack of expertise on the part of both the ERP Project Manager and external IT consultants led to mistrust,
- The success in securing legitimacy for the ERP project but without financial or technical support from the holding company,
- Scarce financial resources due to continuous losses, and
- Lack of capacity to cope with ERP on the part of almost all organisational members at all levels due to the lack of training.

Finally, the findings of this study reported the experiences of Egyptian government units in adopting the performance-based budget. These results could be useful to both the World Bank and IMF, which normally recommend this type of budget reform to countries seeking to control their expenditures. This study has contributed to existing studies conducted in this area such as Diamond (2002), who examined budget system reform in transitional economics, especially the experience of Russia.

8.5   Limitations of research

The research process is a series of choices made by researchers. These choices include the selection of subject matter of the study, theoretical framework, research methodology, research method, data collection methods, and organisations under study. Researchers set limits to their research by making these selections that are based on researchers' knowledge and other resources available to them, including time, money, efforts, access to information and skills. In this regard, going down one road inevitably closes off the possibility of certain others. Therefore, research is constrained by researchers' choices that are shaped by researchers' resources and justifications. We can identify five limitations of this study and these are discussed as follows.

First, this research focused on one aspect of ERP's impacts on organisations, which is the impact of ERP on management accounting rules and routines and management accountants' role and relationships. However, ERP has other impacts and can be adopted in other functional areas such as human resources and logistics. For example, ERP implementation and use have effects on firm performance. A number of studies have begun to emerge in this area (e.g. Santhanam and Hartono, 2003; Nicolaou, 2004). The delimitation of the area of study is justifiable on the ground that it allows other researchers to make contributions by extending the selected area or exploring new areas of research (Scapens, 1990).

Second, the authors adopted structuration theory and its extensions in management accounting literature and IS literature. Structuration theory has its own shortcomings that have been discussed in detail in Chapter 3. However, the authors tried to overcome these limitations by adopting other complementary theories and frameworks. The theoretical framework for this research, which is based on structuration theory and its extensions, is only one possible framework from other available perspectives that could provide alternative or complementary interpretations for the phenomenon under study. Examples of these other perspectives are introduced in the next section.

Third, the empirical study in this book was conducted in highly regularised organisations, government units and state-owned enterprises, to address the lack of evidence in accounting literature in this area and to highlight the unique nature and circumstances surrounding these types of organisations, especially during the economic transition period in Egypt. However, there are still other types of organisations needed to be considered for research on ERP and management accounting change such as small and medium enterprises and universities. The implementation of ERP in universities is a promising area for research because of the role of universities in institutionalising, among others, accounting routines. There are some studies that have been conducted in universities but outside the accounting area (e.g. Scott and Wagner, 2003; Furumo and Pearson, 2004).

Fourth, the empirical study was conducted in companies that adopted Baan software. The selection of Baan software was based on the high level of assistance given by the ERP vendor, internationally and locally. This grateful assistance facilitated access to companies and information to compare between a failure case and a success case. In addition, unexpected circumstances, which have been explained in Chapter 5, have led to excluding another company, Coca-Cola Egypt Co., which has adopted Oracle software. However, one of the authors has visited other companies adopting Oracle software but their results have not been included in this book.

Finally, this study was based on the use of semi-structured interviews as the primary data collection method. This method has some limitations. It is a costly and time consuming method. Furthermore, there is a possible bias on the part of interviewees and interviewer in interpreting social reality (Silverman, 2001). However, this side effect has been avoided by collecting other types of evidence such as documentary evidence and articles to alleviate this perceived shortcoming of using semi-structured interviews.

8.6   Future research opportunities

In the light of research findings, recommendations and limitations, this book ends with suggesting some research opportunities to extend and improve the current work. A number of directions might be pursued to contribute to our understanding of management accounting change associated with IT implementation and use, in particular ERP implementation and use.

Firstly, the empirical evidence revealed the need for improving the education system in order to help developing the required IT skills to particularly implement and use ERP software in Egyptian organisations. Addressing the impact of technology on accounting education, Jordan (1999: 346) states that:

> An increased need for education results from advancements in technology. Accountants must be familiar with these new software programs, expert systems, and communications systems to utilize them efficiently.

However, ERP has another effect. It affects and is affected by existing accounting education at the same time. Although a significant gap between management accounting education and actual practice has been observed by a number of commentators over the last few decades (Otley, 1985; Chouldhury, 1986; Flint, 1988), none of the previous studies have tried to identify the impact of ERP on this gap. As discussed earlier, ERP systems support modern management accounting techniques and are business-process oriented. Knowledge contained in accounting textbooks forms a part of the professional institutions that influence management accounting practices. As such, it may support or hinder the implementation of ERP systems. For example, Scapens (1994) observes that the theoretical material contained in current textbooks was based largely on accounting research undertaken in the 1960s. In this regard, Mouritsen (1994) suggests that applying the technical-rational choice model in decision-making can hinder the development of accounting systems when textbook systems are

adopted. In addition, Johnson and Kaplan (1987) argue that accounting educators increasingly encouraged the use of financial accounting
information for managerial decision-making, and indoctrinated the mind-
set of future US business managers. Therefore, accounting education may
constrain management accounting change when it lags far behind best
business practices embedded in ERP systems. Future research should address
this issue.

Secondly, the conflict, caused by the implementation of ERP systems in
developing countries, between the globalisation and localisation of management accounting practices is worth of further investigations. However,
this conflict is not a unique phenomenon to developing countries. It has
been observed in developed countries as well. For example, Scapens *et al.*
(1998: 48) observed that '...the British subsidiary of a US multinational,
which was implementing SAP world-wide, found considerable difficulty in
adapting SAP to its operating needs... SAP was configured for the US operations and this led to inflexibility for the British subsidiary'. Research should
attempt to explore the relevance of best management accounting practices
built into ERP to other countries – developing or developed. In this regard,
undertaking comparative case studies from different countries would be of
great benefit and represents an avenue for future research.

Thirdly, this research focused on collecting empirical evidence from two
companies that implemented Baan software to compare between successful
and failure experiences in using this software. However, one of the authors
visited other companies that have adopted other ERP packages, especially
Oracle. Future research should consider comparing management accounting change associated with ERP software across different companies that
have implemented different ERP packages. This type of comparison is valuable in understanding management accounting change in widely differing
circumstances.

Fourthly, the empirical study was conducted in highly regularised organisations, state-owned enterprises and government units, to fill a serious gap
in management accounting literature and to shed light on the unique institutional circumstances in these organisations that could hinder management accounting change triggered by ERP systems. However, one of the
authors visited other private sector companies that implemented ERP projects. Future research on ERP and management accounting change should
focus on the experiences of private sector companies that face different
institutional contexts. In this regard, private sector companies could accept
best management accounting practices built into ERP software or follow
other strategies to stabilise management accounting systems and practices.

Fifthly, the empirical research collected evidence from two Egyptian
organisations that have adopted the performance-based budget. However,
different institutional pressures were behind the introduction of this type
of budgeting to the two organisations. In the IMC case, the EU was the

major force in that respect. In ESTD, the World Bank was behind the adoption of performance-based budget. As previously mentioned, the performance-based budget was adopted by other Egyptian government units. Further research should try to examine the experiences of these government units, which face the same institutional pressures, in the move from line-item budgeting to performance-based budgeting.

Sixthly, the findings presented in Chapter 6 indicated that Egyptian organisations face conflicting institutional demands due to the move from a centrally managed economy to a market economy. For example, AQF was partially privatised. It was registered in Egyptian Stock Exchange that requires the registered companies to adopt international accounting standards. However, the company still uses the Uniform Accounting System and traditional planning budgets as the majority of the company's shares are still owned by non-manufacturing state-owned enterprises. Other Egyptian organisations faced similar conflicting institutional demands. How have the organisations dealt with this conflict? Some researchers such as Meyer and Rowan (1977) and D' Aunno *et al.* (1991) gave some insights about this issue. However, there is no definite answer to this question. The response will depend on the circumstances of each organisation. Future research should further explore this issue.

Seventhly, the primary data collection method in this study was semi-structured interviews. In addition, other sources of evidence were used. Among these sources were direct and participant observations. However, the use of these methods was unplanned. These ethnographic methods have the advantages of spending more time on the research sites and repeating data collections over a long period over interviews to acquire tacit knowledge. However, the authors admit that these methods are time-consuming and require resources that were not available to the authors at this stage of research. Future research should address this limitation.

Finally, this study has used a theoretical framework which is based on the applications and extensions of structuration theory in IS literature and management accounting literature, to interpret the empirical evidence collected on IT implementation and use and management accounting change. However, there are other theoretical frameworks that could give different interpretations and useful insights about this phenomenon. As previously mentioned, the capacity to cope with ERP was a critical factor in the success/failure of ERP projects. In this regard, the use of learning theories such as the theory of organisational knowledge creation (Nonaka and Takeuchi, 1995), which has many similarities to structuration theory, would be useful in adding a complementary interpretation to structuration theory. This approach has been recently adopted by some researchers (Newell *et al.*, 2001; Ke *et al.*, 2003) and further research is needed.

Appendices

Appendix 1 – Interview Schedule for Management Accountants

IT adoption and implementation

1. What is the role of management accountants in IT (ERP vs. custom software) decisions?
2. What are the criteria used to evaluate IT (ERP vs. custom software) proposal?
3. Do you think that management accountants support IT (ERP vs. custom software) projects that tend to increase their power and oppose those that do not?
4. Has IT (ERP vs. custom software) allowed some management accountants to move into new functions linked to information systems?
5. Are the management accountants the custodians or managers of the organisation's IT (ERP vs. custom software) capacity?
6. Could you please describe the processes by which IT (ERP vs. custom software) project takes place? (i.e. the major steps or stages involved in implementing IT).
7. What are the contextual forces for IT (ERP vs. custom software) project and the reasons for introducing IT (ERP vs. custom software)?
8. Who supports for and resists IT (ERP vs. custom software) project? And why?
9. Which departments assist with the implementation of IT (ERP vs. custom software) project?
10. What problems (if any) did you encounter with the implementation of IT (ERP vs. custom software) project?
11. What types of problems are still being encountered?
12. How do you describe IT (ERP vs. custom software) project? Revolutionary systems changes or incremental changes within existing systems.
13. What is the impact of IT vendors on IT (ERP vs. custom software) implementation processes?
14. Who initiates IT (ERP vs. custom software) systems?
15. Who are the executive sponsors and managerial champions of IT (ERP vs. custom software) project?

Change in management accounting methods/procedures over time in the IT environment

Please express you view about each of the following matters in your organisation:
1. Could you please describe current management accounting systems (financial reporting systems, product costing systems and operational and strategic performance measurement systems) in your company?
2. To what degree are current management accounting systems computerised in your company?
3. What are the changes in management accounting systems that associated and/or have taken place since the introduction of IT projects?
4. Could you please express the role of IT in changing management accounting techniques?

5. Has your company introduced any modern management accounting techniques such as ABC, ABM, BSC...etc in the past few years? And whether IT availability influences the introduction of these techniques?
6. What are the difficulties you have encountered or might experience in introducing such modern techniques to your company?
7. Do you think that the availability of IT might contribute in overcoming some of these difficulties? And how?
8. What are the main reasons for changes in management accounting techniques and the circumstances that associated these changes?

The changing role and relationships of management accountants

Please express your opinion concerning each of the following issues:

1. Have the implementation and use of IT (ERP vs. custom software) reduced in the time spent on data recording, accuracy checking and reporting requirements within the accounting department?
2. Have the implementation and use of IT (ERP vs. custom software) improved the information related to routine tasks such as budgeting and simplified the operation of this information?
3. Have the implementation and use of IT (ERP vs. custom software) increased the comprehensiveness, accuracy, regularity and timeliness of management accounting information?
4. Do the implementation and use of IT (ERP vs. custom software) enable management accountants to provide more focused and tailored information for user managers, i.e. a creation of user-defined reports.
5. Have the implementation and use of IT (ERP vs. custom software) led to the collection and use of multi-dimensional data (financial vs. non-financial, *ex post* vs. *ex ante*, and internal vs. external) for decisions taken by user managers (decision-support)?
6. Have the implementation and use of IT (ERP vs. custom software) enabled more attention to decision-support and used to provide new approaches to decision-support?
7. Do you think that IT projects have led to increase your perceived power when managing or using the new IT software?
8. Does IT improve relationships between the management accountant and user managers in terms of increased respect for the former and reduced conflict?
9. How do you perceive the role of management accountants in your company? (e.g. historian-consultant-advisor-team member-watchdog-controller)
10. How do you describe changes that happened in the role and relationships between management accountants and user managers as the result of the introduction of IT?
11. Do the implementation and use of IT (ERP vs. custom software) result in user managers challenging management accounting reports and demanding more information?
12. Do the implementation and use of IT (ERP vs. custom software) enable the direct interrogation of management accounting systems by user managers?
13. Do you feel that the implementation and use of IT (ERP vs. custom software) increase the risk of user (non-accountant) managers misinterpreting management accounting information?
14. Do the implementation and use of IT (ERP vs. custom software) increase the visibility of user managers' activities?

15. Have the implementation and use of IT (ERP vs. custom software) led to data recording changes?
16. Do you perceive that the management accountants will lose control of some information and information systems as IT develops?
17. Do you think that IT projects have led to change in the distribution of power within your organisation? (i.e. the responsibility for meeting user managers' information requirements)

Management accounting education in the IT environment

Please express your opinion in the following issues concerning the relationship between university accounting education and practice in the IT (ERP vs. custom software) environment:

1. From what source have you known about modern management/accounting techniques such as ABC, ABM, TQM, TOC...etc.?
2. Do you believe that your university accounting education helps you/contributes in adopting, implementing and using modern management accounting techniques such as ABC, ABM, TQM, TOC...etc.?
3. Do you consider that university accounting education supports your role/work in the IT (ERP vs. custom software) environment?
4. In your opinion, how significant is the gap between management accounting education and practice in the IT environment? ...
5. What are the reasons for the education/practice gap? ...
6. In your opinion, how can the education/practice gap be filled? ...
7. Do you feel that the use of ERP, which contains best management accounting practices, could contribute in reducing the education/practice gap?
8. In your opinion, what qualifications/training should a management accountant have to cope with modern IT software such as ERP?
9. If you believe that university accounting education should be improved to support management accountants in the IT (ERP vs. custom software) environment, what changes do you suggest to current university accounting education?
10. In your view, should management accounting education become process and team-oriented to fit the requirements of modern management accounting techniques and modern IT software such as ERP?
11. Do you think that the costs spent on training programmes can be significantly reduced if graduate accountants are well trained on modern management accounting techniques and modern IT software in universities?
12. Do you believe that a professional management accounting association should be established to complement university accounting education?
13. How do you view the role/objectives of the management accounting association?

Appendix 2 – Interview Schedule for Line Managers

Please express your opinion concerning each of the following issues:
1. Have the implementation and use of IT (ERP vs. custom software) increased the comprehensiveness, accuracy, regularity and timeliness of management accounting information?
2. Do the implementation and use of IT (ERP vs. custom software) enable management accountants to provide more focused and tailored information for user managers, i.e. a creation of user-defined reports?

3. Have the implementation and use of IT (ERP vs. custom software) led to the collection and use of multi-dimensional data (financial vs. non-financial, *ex post* vs. *ex ante*, and internal vs. external) for decisions taken by user managers (decision-support)?

4. Have the implementation and use of IT (ERP vs. custom software) enabled more attention to decision-support and used to provide new approaches to decision-support?

5. Do you think that IT systems have led to increase your perceived power when managing or using the new IT software?

6. Does IT improve relationships between the management accountant and user managers in terms of increased respect for the former and reduced conflict?

7. How do you perceive the role of management accountants in your company? (e.g. historian-consultant-advisor-team member-watchdog-controller)

8. How do you describe changes that happened in the role and relationships between management accountants and user managers as the result of the introduction of IT?

9. Do the implementation and use of IT (ERP vs. custom software) result in user managers challenging management accounting reports and demanding more information?

10. Do the implementation and use of IT (ERP vs. custom software) enable the direct interrogation of management accounting systems by user managers?

11. Do you feel that the implementation and use of IT (ERP vs. custom software) increase the risk of user (non-accountant) managers misinterpreting management accounting information?

12. Do the implementation and use of IT (ERP vs. custom software) increase the visibility of user managers' activities?

13. Have the implementation and use of IT (ERP vs. custom software) led to data recording changes?

14. Do you perceive that the management accountants will lose control of some information and information systems as IT develops?

15. Do you think that IT systems have led to change in the distribution of power within your organisation? (i.e. the responsibility for meeting user managers' information requirements)

Appendix 3 – Interview Schedule for IT Specialists

1. Could you please describe the processes by which IT (ERP vs. custom software) project takes place? (i.e. the major steps or stages involved in implementing IT).

2. What are the contextual forces for IT (ERP vs. custom software) project and the reasons for introducing or changing IT?

3. Who supports for and resists IT (ERP vs. custom software) project? And why?

4. Which departments assist with the implementation of IT (ERP vs. custom software) project?

5. What problems (if any) did you encounter with the implementation of IT (ERP vs. custom software) project?

6. What types of problems are still being encountered?

7. How do you describe IT (ERP vs. custom software) project? Revolutionary systems changes or incremental changes within existing systems.

8. What is the impact of IT vendors on IT (ERP vs. custom software) implementation processes?
9. Who initiates IT (ERP vs. custom software) projects?
10. Who are the executive sponsors and managerial champions of IT (ERP vs. custom software) project?

Appendix 4 – Interviewees Background Information

Could you please answer the following questions about your positions, educational and professional qualifications, training and skills?

1. Name of interviewee: ....
2. Current position: ....
3. Previous positions: ....
4. Number of years with this organisation: ....
5. University education: ....
6. Professional qualifications (Certificates): ....
7. Internal and external training programmes obtained (with especial focus on accounting and IT training programmes): ....
8. Could you please briefly describe your IT skills (e.g. your ability to use the computing facilities and knowledge of hardware, software and programming): ....

Appendix 5 – Detailed Empirical Evidence Collected

Number and description of interviewees

Organisational members	Organisations adopted ERP systems		Organisations adopted custom software systems	
	IMC (government)	NEEASAE (state-owned)	ESTD (government)	AQF (state-owned)
Accountants	1. Ex-Financial Systems Manager (ERP Project Manager) 2. Current Financial Systems Manager (a member of ERP project team) 3. Financial Manager (a member of ERP project team) 4. Senior Accountant (a member of ERP project team)	1. General Manager of Budgeting and Costing (a key user in ERP project team) 2. A Cost Accountant (an end user in ERP project team) 3. General Manager of Financial Accounts (a key user in ERP project team)	1. General Manager of Costing Department (IT developer) 2. Financial Manager – East Region, Alexandria 3. General Manager of Revenues 4. General Manager of Budgeting and Encumbrances 5. Budget Accountant 6. Tax Official – Return Department – SIDY GABER	1. Head of Financial Sector 2. A cost accountant 3. A budget accountant 4. General Manager of Financial Accounts 5. General Manager of Cost Department 6. Another cost accountant
IT specialists	5. Current MIS Manager	4. General Manager of MIS (a key user in ERP project team) 5. A Computer Engineer (an end user in ERP project team)	7. General Manager of Database Administration 8. MIS Manager, East Region, Alexandria 9. MIS Manager, Duties Region, Alexandria 10. IT developer – Finance Department 11. IT developer – Planning Department	7. IT Specialist 8. General Manager of MIS

Number and description of interviewees – continued

Organisational members	Organisations adopted ERP systems		Organisations adopted custom software systems	
	IMC (government)	NEEASAE (state-owned)	ESTD (government)	AQF (state-owned)
			12. IT network specialist – Middle Region, Alexandria 13. IT specialist – Middle Region, Alexandria 14. IT specialist – Middle Region, Alexandria 15. IT specialist – Middle Region, Alexandria 16. IT specialist – Karmoz District, Alexandria	9. Head of Technical Sector (Factories)
Line managers	6. Component Manager – Financial Policy	17. Ex-Chairman and Managing Director (the sponsor of ERP project team) 18. General Manager of Production Planning (a key user in ERP project team)	17. General Manager of Karmoz District, Alexandria 18. General Manager of Duties Region, Alexandria 19. A Researcher in Planning Department 20. General Manager of Tax Research and Tax Operations	
Consultants	7. Technical Manager – Baan vendor in Egypt (a member of ERP project team)	–	21. Ministry of Finance Consultant 22. World Bank Consultant	
Total Interviews	7	7	22	9

Data Sources of the Egyptian Sales Tax Department (ESTD) – Other evidence and data sources

Data sources	Detailed descriptions
Documentary evidence	A number of documentary evidence has been collected. For example: • Organisational structure chart (the headquarter and the branches), • The full plan of the ESTD for 2000/2001, • The full programming-performance budgets of the ESTD for 2003/2004, • A number of reports prepared to help the general manager of each district in monitoring its tax operations (e.g. the influential companies in the district and the compliance rate of submitting the tax return), • A number of forms used by the public (i.e. the registrars) to deal with the ESTD (e.g. the tax return and a form for monthly purchases), • Some guidelines issued by the ESTD to help the registrars to handle their tax return, • A sample page from the general journal (i.e. form no. 224 'accounts') and another page from revenues and expenses journal (i.e. form no. 81 'accounts'), • A sample of the actual reports to implement the programming-performance budgets for the current year, • A sample report of revenues and expenses account (i.e. form no. 75 (general accounts)), • A number of forms that are internally used in collecting costing data, • A summary of the work plan that are going to be implemented to develop the central administration of financial and administrative affairs, • The GSTACS (custom software for managing tax operations) Documentation, and • The sales tax law no. 11 for 1991 and the general budget law for the government no. 53 for 1973.
CDs/Floppy disks	A floppy disk has been collected from the IT developer in planning department. This disk contains a full description of the software that has been developed to follow-up the programming-performance budgets.
E-mails	No.

Data Sources of the Egyptian Sales Tax Department (ESTD) – Other evidence and data sources – *continued*

Data sources	Detailed descriptions
Direct observations	The IT developer in the planning department has shown the researcher the use of the software developed for the programming-performance budgets. The researcher also observed the presentation prepared for the World Bank's representatives that will be presented on 22 of September 2004. The general manager of tax research and tax operations took the researcher's opinion in a calculation problem caused by the GSTACS system in computing the additional taxes. During the attendance of the two development committees mentioned below, the researcher observed a lot of conflicts that arose between different parties.
Web sites	The ESTD has a web site that contains a lot of information and articles about its activities. Its address is http://www.salestax.gov.eg.
Printed screens from software used	There are four types of printed screens: 1) Printed screens from the GSTACS system implemented by the ESTD to centrally manage the tax operations, 2) Printed screens from another custom software developed for collecting and calculating the costs of each department and activity, 3) Printed screens from the traditional government accounting system that has been computerised, and 4) Printed screens from another system that has been developed to follow-up the programming-performance budgets.
Meetings or committees attended	The researcher was invited to two development committees (the finance development committee and the IT development committee). These committees were headed by both the world bank consultant and the ministry of finance consultant. They discussed the achievements so far in computerising all the ESTD's systems and in implementing the programming-performance budgets in the ESTD. They also set the targets for the coming year.

Data Sources of the Egyptian Sales Tax Department (ESTD) – Other evidence and data sources – *Continued*

Data sources	Detailed descriptions
Publications	There are some publications: 1) Some articles have been published in Egyptian periodicals about the implementation of the programming-performance budgets in the ESTD and other governmental units, 2) The ESTD issues a magazine (called 'taxation culture') that has a lot of articles related to the ESTD's activities, and 3) Some papers are available on the web site of the ESTD.

Data Sources of Industrial Modernisation Centre (IMC) – Other evidence and data sources

Data sources	Detailed descriptions
Documentary evidence	A number of documentary evidence has been collected. For example: • Organisational structure chart (IMC Core Staff), • Budget reports (e.g. budget variance report), • A document explaining financial component's plan for 2004, • Handwriting papers used by IMC staff to give the researcher examples about some calculations and data entries, • BaanERP 5.0C Finance Documentation, and • A manual explaining IMC's activities.
CDs/Floppy disks	1) Two floppy disks have been collected from ERP Project Manager. These disks contain: • Business Process Manual • Business Process Summary-Document for Baan Finance Implementation • BaanERP 5.0C Finance Documentation (Accounts Receivable, Accounts Payable, Cash Management, Financial Budget System and Cost Accounting and General Ledger). 2) A CD has been collected from Technical Manager of Baan vendor in Egypt. This contains the full documentation of iBaan 5.0c modules.

Data Sources of Industrial Modernisation Centre (IMC) – Other evidence and data sources – *continued*

Data sources	Detailed descriptions
E-mails	A number of e-mails have been received from ERP Project Manager, MIS Managers and Technical Manager. These e-mails contain arrangements for meetings (e.g. Technical Manager's e-mails), some explanations about ERP project and IMC's activities (e.g. ERP Project Manager) and printed screens from software used (e.g. MIS Manager).
Direct observations	A Component Manager – Financial Policy has shown the researcher the use of his web site in managing his budget lines. He also explained the use of e-mail in communication about budget. Current Financial Systems Manager presented for the researcher the use of ERP systems in managing contracts and preparing trial balances.
Web sites	IMC has a web site that contains a lot of information and articles about the centre's activities. Its address is www.imc-egypt.org.
Printed screens from software used	There are two types of printed screens: 5) Printed screens from the ERP system implemented by IMC in finance department. 6) Printed screens from an alternative program (custom software) on the web (intranet – LAN) that is developed using Java language in MIS department.
Meetings or committees attended	No.
Publications	There are two types of publications:- 4) Articles are available on the web site of IMC. Other web sites administrated by the EU (European Union) present some articles that are useful, and 5) A book that evaluates the role of the Ministry of Industry in industrial development before the IMC is available (Handoussa, 2002).

Data Sources of El NASR Electric and Electronic Apparatus (NEEASAE) – Other evidence and data sources

Data sources	Detailed descriptions
Documentary evidence	A number of documentary evidence has been collected. For example: • Organisational structure chart, • The Planning Budgets for 1998/1999, • A document that is used to prepare budget estimates for raw materials, • Training materials prepared by Baan Senior Application Consultant for finance department and planning department, • A document that contains the full details about the ERP project team (steering committee) and their duties, the consulting company's team and their duties, a description of key users and end users, the project plan and implementation scheme (i.e. business modelling, simulation, training, data collection and transformation, installation and customisation), • BaanERP 5.0C Finance, Manufacturing and Distribution Documentation, and • A manual explaining NEEASAE's activities.
CDs/Floppy disks	No.
E-mails	No.
Direct observations	The researcher visited GLS bulbs factory and a cost accountant accompanied the researcher and explained the different stages of bulbs production. In addition, a computer engineer in the information centre has shown the researcher the current custom software used by the company in recording financial transactions. The researcher also observed the computers and network prepared by the company for the use of the ERP system.
Web sites	NEEASAE has a web site that contains some information about the company's activities. Its address is http://www.neeasae.com.eg.
Printed screens from software used	There are a lot of printed screens from the ERP system that the company tried to implement in finance department and planning department.
Meetings or committees attended	No.
Publications	The company issues a periodical magazine that has articles about topics related to its activities.

Appendix 6 – Important Evidence Related to ESTD

Programmes and Performance-Based Budget Models Issued by Ministry of Finance for 2004/2005

Budget _____

Government Unit _____

Current Expenditure Programmes

(Model No. 1 – Programmes)

Organisational Unit		
Programmes and Projects Analysis *		
Estimates for new fiscal year	Chapter (1)	
	Chapter (2)	
	Total	
Appropriations for current fiscal year	Chapter (1)	
	Chapter (2)	
	Total	
Change	Chapter (1)	
	Chapter (2)	
	Total	
Programmes' objectives		
Performance unit (measure)		
Performance units in current year	Units in-process	
	Added (new) units	
	Total	
Cost per unit		

* This column includes different programmes. In this respect, details are given for each programme, its projects, appropriations assigned to each project and the totals for projects and programmes.

Budget

Government Unit

Capital Expenditure Programmes

(Model No. 2 – Programmes)

Organisational Unit		
Programmes		
Total cost of each programme	Total	
Appropriations for new fiscal year assigned by plan segments	Segment	
	Segment	
	Segment	
	Segment	
	Segment	
	Segment	
	Total	

Continued

Appropriations for new fiscal year assigned by cash component	Local				
	Cash	Free			
		Agreements			
	Credit	Free			
		Agreements			
	Total				
Project implementation period					
Performance unit (measure) in the project					
The number of performance units in the project					
Cost per performance unit					
Project revenues in the new year					
Appropriations for current fiscal year					

Budget ———————————

Government Unit ———————————

Current Expenditure Programmes

(Model No. 3 – Programmes)

Organisational Unit	
Programmes	1. Long-term loan programme: • local loans • foreign loans 2. Long-term repayment programme: • local loans • external (foreign) loans 3. Financial investments programme 4. Other capital transfers programme
Loan amount	L.E.
Loan term	
Loan purpose	
Instalment in new fiscal year	L.E.
Instalment maturity date	
Loan provider	
Loan currency	

Form Used by the Central Costing Unit to Collect Cost Data from Various ESTD'S Regions

Ministry of Finance

Sales Tax Department

General Accounts Unit

Costing Unit

The monthly analysis for month ...... the fiscal year ...... / ...... Region ....

Account Code	Responsibility centre	Chapter 1	Chapter 2	Registrants' number	Employees' number
60422	Region				
5181	District...				
	Total				

Reports Prepared by the Revenues Department in ESTD to Monitor Sale Taxes Collected

Ministry of Finance

Sales Tax Department

A summarised report to be presented to the Commissioner:

R/D and G/S	Commodity 1	Commodity 2	...	Service 1	Service 2	...	Total
Region: District 1 District 2	Taxes collected	Taxes collected	..	Taxes collected	Taxes collected	...	Taxes collected
Total							Aggregated amount

Note: R/D refers to Regions and Districts. G/S refers to goods and services

Ministry of Finance

Sales Tax Department

A Report on Taxes collected at the Level of each District:

G/S	Encumbrances	Taxes collected to date			Achievement Percentage
		Imported	Local	Total	
Goods:					
....					
....					
Services:					
....					
....					
Total					

Note: G/S refers to goods and services

Ministry of Finance

Sales Tax Department

A Report on Taxes collected at the Level of each Region:

D/O	Encumbrances	Taxes collected to date										Total	Achievement Percentage
		Goods					Services						
Districts:		1	2	3	.	.	1	2	3	.	.		
....													
....													
Offices:													
....													
....													
Total													

Note: D/O refers to Districts and Offices

The Responsibilities of Committee Set to Reform Budget in ESTD

Committee	Responsibilities
Principal Committee (the steering committee)	1. Approving plans and work programmes of functional committees and periodically following up these committees that have been formed to implement performance-based budget, 2. Evaluating committees' results, and 3. Evaluating and implementing reform proposals, including performance evaluation systems and incentives systems that help in achieving efficiency and effectiveness in the ESTD.
Committee of Tax system	1. Targeting fairness, credibility, relevance, and flexibility to achieve total quality, 2. Recommending any developments in the tax system, 3. Proposing unified interpretations for sales tax problems, taking into account other tax systems, 4. Prioritising goods and services according to their effects on tax revenues and suggesting any necessary developments in the tax system, 5. Suggesting estimates of tax revenues in budget proposal and the role and programme of each responsibility centre in their achievement, 6. Suggesting necessary procedures that help in achieving annual estimated revenues as a minimum, 7. Recommending policies and necessary systems that could help in reducing tax disputes, and 8. Suggesting incentives systems that is related to performance and standards of productivity, efficiency, effectiveness and quality in the area of the committee's responsibilities, and
Committee of Budget Proposal Preparation	1. The preparation of current budget and capital budget proposals in accordance with performance-based budget, taking into consideration total quality, 2. Monitoring current budget and capital budget throughout the fiscal year, 3. Analysing variances' causes, and 4. Taking necessary procedures to adjust budgets according to implementation results.

The Responsibilities of Committee Set to Reform Budget in ESTD – *continued*

Committee	Responsibilities
Committee of Organisation, Human Resources and incentives	1. Proposing necessary developments in the organisational structure and achieving vertical and horizontal integration, 2. Introducing a good system for selecting and appointing labour, 3. Suggesting necessary procedures to achieve total quality in organisation and human resource area, 4. Proposing estimates on organisational structure, labour and training that are related to performance-based budget, and 5. Suggesting incentives systems that is related to performance and standards of productivity, efficiency, effectiveness and quality in the area of the committee's responsibilities, and
Committee of Administrative and Financial Affairs	1. Taking necessary procedures that ensure the immediate addition of tax receipts to the ESTD's bank account in the Central Bank, 2. Automating the government accounting system used in different accounts units, 3. Setting up a cost accounting system, 4. Setting up systems for managing the use of fixed assets and inventories and 5. Suggesting incentives systems that is related to performance and standards of productivity, efficiency, effectiveness and quality in the area of the committee's responsibilities, and
Committee of Information Systems	1. Integrating and developing existing databases in the ESTD to improve productivity, efficiency, effectiveness and quality, 2. Ensuring the flow of information among different databases and responsibility centres, 3. Following up the achievement of total quality in information so as to be comprehensive, timely and updated, 4. Achieving efficiency and effectiveness in using equipments and computer programmes to control the costs of information systems, 5. Maximising the benefits of available information and data in the Information Centres in other departments of the Ministry of Finance, 6. Suggesting incentives systems that is related to performance and standards of productivity, efficiency, effectiveness and quality in the area of the committee's responsibilities, and 7. Setting targets to achieve information systems integration in the performance-based budget reform.

The Responsibilities of Committee Set to Reform Budget in ESTD – *continued*

Committee	Responsibilities
Committee of Planing and Performance Budget	1. Suggesting objectives, strategies and methods; designing plan forms, measuring performance and and Evaluation determining performance indicators, including productivity, efficiency, effectiveness and quality; and determining achievement times of plans and work programmes for various responsibility centres in the ESTD, 2. Conducting economic studies on the impact of local and international economic phenomena on the GST, monitoring their effects and suggesting suitable solutions, 3. Predicting external variables affecting tax, investigating their causes and suggesting corrective actions, 4. Achieving total quality control in the committee's responsibilities, 5. Suggesting incentives systems that is related to performance and standards of productivity, efficiency, effectiveness and quality in the area of the committee's responsibilities, and 6. Preparing five-year plan, annual plan, work programmes and performance indicators for various responsibility centres, including tax estimated revenues.

The ESTD's Mission, Principles, Strategy, Policy and Methodology

Mission	The mission is to contribute in maximising the General State revenues by means of transparently implementing the General Sales Tax Law. This might contribute in achieving fiscal balance in the General State Budget.
Principles	Fairness, Credibility, Relevance, and Flexibility.
Strategy	• To elevate performance level and control costs, • To improve services provided to registrants, • To increase the rate of voluntary compliance by registrants, • To develop labour's skills and behaviours, and • To expand the use of modern technologies.
Policy	• To satisfy taxpayers and boost their confidence, • To support economic development, encourage investments, and support competitive efficiency of national economy, and • To increase labour's satisfaction and loyalty.
Methodology	• To achieve the total quality, • To implement the system of programs-and-performance-based budget, • To develop the internal work system in all districts to satisfy the registrants' needs at minimum cost and time, • To recruit trained qualified labour, and • To boost the registrants' confidence.

Appendix 7 – The Privatisation Programme and the Transformation of Extra-Organisational Institutions Governing Public Sector Enterprises

1   The birth of public sector in centrally planned economy era

The defining period of modern Egypt is still the revolutionary socialist regime under President Nasser (1952–1970). After the revolution of 1952, the Egyptian Government made a break with the past and moved the Egyptian economy from a free market-oriented economy to a massively state-controlled economy in few years. The nationalisation laws and expropriation of various private enterprises became the expression of change in Egypt after the July Revolution in 1952. A series of nationalisation decrees was issued in 1956, 1961, and 1963 to eliminate the dominant role of both foreign and large-scale, local private capital. In 1952, the private sector made about 76% of the total investment in the economy. The public sector very quickly established its dominance in the economy and for the next three decades was making between 80–90% of the investment in the economy and constituted around 37% of GDP annually (PCSU, 2002).

All nationalised State-Owned Enterprises (SOEs) were organised and categorised into groups according to the nature of their main products (Briston and El-Ashker, 1984). Each group was placed under the supervision of a 'Public Organisation', established specifically for this purpose. The groups were classified into sectors on the basis of supervision by a pertinent minister. Each minister was responsible for the public organisations, which were working under his/her supervision. However, the activities of these public organisations were co-ordinated and supervised by the Supreme Council of Public Organisations, which was headed by the President of the state.

In the late 1960s and the beginning 1970s, the Egyptian economy was centrally planned (Marie, 1969). Virtually all new investment decisions in the economy were made directly or indirectly through the Government. These investments were allocated to various sectors according to a five-year plan. Each General Organisation allocated its appropriated share of investments between its affiliated enterprises according to a predetermined scheme of priorities of investment projects and according to the position of each enterprise's planned projects in the scheme. Although investment in fixed capital was set by the government in the National Plan, investment in current capital was by and large decentralised. Each SOE drew its own production plans according to its available capacity and supply and demand conditions subject to the approval of the mother Organisation. It was independent in its decisions concerning intra-firm allocation and employment of economic resources, as long as they were not specifically appropriated to a given project by the Organisation, and as long as the firm observed the requirements of the law.

Labour and material markets were generally free with a minimum wage level imposed by the law and with a mixture of administered and free market prices of materials. Prices of the final products of public enterprises were generally administrated by the Government and set on the basis of cost plus a fair profit margin. Some commodities were priced at or below cost and subsidised by the Government for reasons of social relief or export market competition. Some commodities, as well as some materials, were rationed usually at a cost or below cost official-price (e.g. sugar, kerosene, cotton seed oil, and others) and those wanting to buy rationed goods in excess of their ration could do so at higher official prices.

In view of the state's dependence on accounting information to prepare the National Plan, the Uniform Accounting System was introduced by the Central

Agency for Accountancy (CAA) in 1966. It was compulsory for all SOEs in the public sector, with the exception of banks and insurance companies. In that accounting system, accounts were classified in homogeneous classes in a manner that assisted in preparing national accounts, as well as satisfying the needs of the traditional financial and cost accounting (for more details about the Uniform Accounting System, see, for example, Briston and El-Ashker, 1984). The next section addresses the performance crisis faced by SOEs and the initiation of privatisation programme.

2 Public sector crisis and the initiation of privatisation programme

The government of Egypt overextended itself in areas unsuited for public ownership as a result of nationalisation and centralised state control introduced between 1952 and 1974. The foundations of liberalisation were laid in 1974 with laws to open up the economy to foreign investment and protect investments against nationalisation and confiscation. However, little was done to weaken state control over the economy. The industries set up in the 1970s were highly protected, inward-looking and dependent on imported inputs. Since early 1980s there were a number of privatisation initiatives. But the public sector remained a dominant force in the economy constituting around 37% of GDP, was responsible for about 55% of the industrial production, controlled over 80% of import/export and about 90% of the banking and insurance sectors (PCSU, 2002).

Egyptian State-Owned Enterprises (SOEs) contributed to continual annual fiscal deficits because they were operating with soft budget and their deficits were financed by the Government's budget. They suffered from serious problems. The abundant data about the highly overstaffed and low labour productivity in Egyptian SOEs reflected only part of the problem. While SOEs were receiving the lion's share of the investment in the productive sectors of the economy, the return on the capital was gradually decreasing and by 1989 reached a low of 5.9%, while the average interest rate was 14% (PCSU, 2002). At the same time, the Government's continued policy and regulations aimed at protecting the SOEs resulted in the country's low economic growth by mid-1980s, thereby bringing about the vicious cycle of low growth in employment opportunities and no other choice but the Government further overstaffing the SOEs.

By 1989/90, the Egyptian economic performance had reached an untenable situation (Licari, 1997: 14):

1. The current account deficit was $1.3 billion in 1989;
2. At the end of 1989, Egypt was among the world's most heavily-indebted countries. Its foreign debt was $43.7 billion and servicing it costs the equivalent of 22% of Egypt's exports of goods and services;
3. The general government deficit, at the root of foreign indebtedness, stood at 7% of GDP in 1990;
4. Inflation, measured by the retail price index, averaged 18% a year between 1989 and 1992;
5. At the end of 1989, total reserves, apart from gold, stood at $1.5 billion.

Thus Egypt entered the 1990s with severe financial imbalance, high inflation and declining productivity, an unmanageable external debt and unsustainable current account deficit. The turnaround came in 1990/91. Following the Gulf War crisis, an agreement with the Paris Club led to the stabilisation of Egypt's external debt. This agreement was conditional on the IMF's certification that Egypt had sound policies leading towards macroeconomic stabilisation. In turn, the IMF required Egypt to adopt a comprehensive economic and structural adjustment programme, which led to economic progress. The Government of Egypt (GOE) accepted privatisation as part of the economic and structural adjustment programme agreed with the World Bank and the IMF in the early 1990s. The legal basis for privatisation was laid down in 1991 by the transfer of 314 SOEs from government ministries and their conversion into affiliates of 17 holding companies. This latter topic is discussed in more detail in the next section.

3   Public sector reform: Ministry of Public Sector, Law No. 203 of 1991 and holding companies

The privatisation programme was undertaken due to both the dissatisfaction of GOE with the failure and losses of public sector enterprises and the external pressures from international donors (World Bank and IMF) in favour of privatisation. The GOE launched the privatisation programme with the Public Enterprise Law No. 203 of 1991 and its regulations, establishing the legal framework for sale of 314 public enterprises that earmarked for privatisation. This law marked the start of public enterprise reform. It was designed to eliminate the difference in treatment between public and private enterprises. The law spells out clearly the new rules of the game for SOEs as follows:

- Profit maximisation is the primary objective for all SOEs,
- No subsidies for SOEs either directly *via* transfers to losing companies, or indirectly *via* subsidised inputs,
- Non-differential terms or special interest rates on loans to SOEs,
- SOE autonomy in all decisions pertaining to their operations, and
- SOEs are affiliated to public holding companies, which monitor SOE performance and can name or change SOE management according to criteria of profitability.

Public holding companies were established in 1991. The ownership and management of 314 public enterprises, subjected to Law 203 of 1991, were transferred from the various ministries to 17 holding companies, which are held accountable to the Ministry of Public Enterprises. Holding companies are primarily responsible for organising the sale of their constituent SOEs known as affiliated companies, with a mandate to maximise the present value of their affiliated companies on behalf of the state. SOEs affiliated to any holding company do not necessarily belong to the same line of activity to eliminate sectorial monopolies, to introduce competition, and to ensure that each holding company have an array of enterprises with differing profitability and sale potential. According to this organisation, all SOEs, including the 'newly' established holding companies, are subjected to one Minister for Public Enterprise, hence abolishing any means of intervention by government authorities in the companies' management.

The Ministry of Public Enterprise was given the mandate of achieving the long-term goal of complete implementation of Egypt's overall privatisation plan. It is responsible for all reform aspects of public enterprises, including privatisation, restructuring, labour and legal issues. The Public Enterprise Office (PEO) was established in 1991 to assist the Minister of Public Enterprise and to act as a co-ordinator for the privatisation and restructuring programmes. It is responsible for setting plans and monitoring the restructuring and privatisation programmes. It is also the link between the Government and the holding companies. The PEO has re-organised the entire structure of public sector by reassigning SOEs to the 'newly' formed public holding companies.

Law No. 203 of 1991 has solved several legal and institutional constraints that could have hindered the privatisation programme. Nonetheless, the legal and institutional frameworks were still incomplete even after Law No. 203 of 1991 was issued. The build up of the necessary legal and institutional frameworks demanded the enhancement of the capital market and its institutions. A 'new' Law No. 95 of 1992 was launched to introduce new types of institutions not known previously to the Egyptian capital market. The capital market reform is the topic of next section.

4 Capital market reform: Law No. 95 of 1992 and capital market authority

Historically, the Egyptian stock exchange has two locations: Alexandria and Cairo. The Alexandria Stock Exchange was officially established in 1888 followed by Cairo in 1903. The two stock exchanges were very active till the 1940s. However, the central planning and socialist policies, adopted since the 1950s, led to a drastic reduction in activity on the Egyptian stock exchanges for four decades. The Egyptian stock market till the late 1980s was not prepared to execute privatisation transactions. In the 1990s, capital market reform became mandatory with the move towards a free-market economy and the privatisation programme. The Capital Market Law No. 95 of 1992 was promulgated in 1992 and came into effect in 1993 through the issuance of its executive regulations.

Prior to enacting the Capital Market Law, there were several laws that regulated the securities market and hindered the development of a market-oriented market. The Law No. 95 of 1992 and its executive regulations were introduced to replace the multiplicity of existing laws in order to simplify and reform the legislative environment. The 'new' law was enacted to reorganise the primary and secondary financial markets, to encourage investment and private savings, and to stimulate the capital market through the establishment of mutual funds. This law is open-ended and, therefore, responsive to changes in market demand for any type of new instrument, institution or service.

The Law No. 95 of 1992 encourages establishing service institutions, intermediary companies such as brokerage companies, underwriters, portfolio managers and depositories. It also introduced the idea of Employee Shareholders Associations (ESA) for public and private enterprises. Furthermore, all restrictions, which hinder easy entry to the market of foreign investors, were removed. International investors can easily invest in securities without limitations on capital, no mobility or foreign exchange restrictions. Furthermore, the listing rules governing the exchange allow for foreign securities to be listed and traded, meeting the same requirements as applicable to local securities.

According to Law No. 95 of 1992, the Capital Market Authority (CMA) was given sole control over supervising the securities market, including Alexandria and Cairo Stock Exchanges. It is charged with market development, supervision of trading, broker licencing, and market surveillance. The CMA, a government organisation that reports to the Minister of Foreign Trade, was established in 1979. However, the Capital Market Law introduced new roles and functions for the CMA. These include monitoring the performance of exchanges and enforcement of listing and trading regulations. The CMA also monitors compliance by listed companies, and directs exchanges to de-list securities and to suspend listing or trading for non-compliance if the exchange fails to act promptly.

Listing on the stock exchange is optional and in accordance with clearly defined listing criteria. The Capital Market Law stipulates that listed companies comply with full disclosure of financial statements and all other relevant information requirements according to international accounting standards,[1] which were issued in September 1997. The law also requires that any prospectus must be approved by the CMA for both content and format prior to any public offering. In addition to the disclosure of information from the issuer's side, the stock exchange publishes daily bulletins containing market quotations, daily transactions, and other details of trading activities. The privatisation programme has stimulated the stock market activities. The privatisation progress is the topic of next section.

5 Progress on privatisation

The pace of privatisation up to 1993 was slow because time was needed to introduce the necessary legislative and regulatory arrangements. Also, the socio-economic culture of the country had not yet been ready to accept the concept of privatisation. First, the economy was suffering from a set of major price distortions and market imperfections. Second, the macroeconomic environment was unstable, with major imbalances in the structure of the economy. Third, the stabilisation policies adopted in the early phase of the 1991 reform programme produced a slowdown of the economy with some negative outcomes on the vulnerable classes of the population. Given these conditions, the government moved cautiously on the privatisation programme.

Once the enabling mechanisms were in place the privatisation programme gained momentum in the second half of 1990s, after a favourable ruling by the constitutional court upholding the Government's right to privatise the public sector. The period of *status quo* came to an end with the appointment of a new Cabinet at the beginning of 1996. The new Cabinet was empowered with a mandate to speed-up the privatisation programme and broaden the ownership structure by privatising the majority of SOEs. In May 1996, three Initial Public Offerings (IPOs) took place, two of which were pushed to be majority privatised for the first time via the stock market. In addition, two secondary floatations took place and another company offered 27.5% of its capital to an anchor investor (SIS, 2002). Both the local and international markets have welcomed the government's new stance and reacted positively to these privatisation efforts.

Early 1996, a list of 120 companies ripe for privatisation was published and two of 120 others were released in 1997 (Khattab, 2002). They covered a wide range of activities – cement, metallurgy, textiles, pharmaceuticals, food processing, maritime transport and tourism. By mid-1997, the government had sold stakes in 40 companies and, in the case of 11 others, sold a majority of shares to employees. In fiscal year 1996/97, privatisation drew portfolio investment of $1.3 billion and foreign direct investment of $800 million. However, since late 1997, a group of factors led to some difficulties in privatising SOEs, which in turn threatened the progress of privatisation programme. The economic crisis in East Asia, which hit first Thailand in July 1997 and spread later to several other parts of the world, and the terrorists' attack, which took place in Luxor (Upper Egypt) in November 1998, had negative effects on investment and the capital inflow to Egypt. For example, some of the public offerings of privatised companies failed to be fully subscribed.

Furthermore, by the late 1990s the fixed exchange rate peg to the US dollar ($1/L.E. 3.40) introduced in 1991 had become unsustainable in the face of insufficient competitiveness improvements. By mid-2000, when the fixed peg was abandoned, the real exchange rate had appreciated by about 30% and real interest rates on lending had risen to about 10%. After the 11th of September 2001's attack on the USA, the Egyptian economy suffered even further. Thus the privatisation programme of SOEs has made slow progress after the large divestitures of the 1990s for a number of reasons among them: difficult market conditions, political sensitivity to privatisation related to job losses and, to some degree, the nature of assets left for privatisation as well as the less attractive investment opportunities in the remaining companies in the Law 203 portfolio.

As of June 30, 2002, 189 public enterprises of the 314 Law 203 portfolio of companies have been sold through various methods, including anchor investor, asset sales, sales to ESA, asset liquidations as well as long-term leases. Nevertheless, the GOE has launched activities to support public enterprise reform, such as giving the management more flexibility in decision-making. In late 2002, the GOE asked for support from the World Bank to revive the privatisation process. It also offered for privatisation some assets in the strategic tourism sector. Emphasis has now moved from the initial batch of public companies identified under Law 203 of 1992 to state financial institutions and utilities, but in the context of privatisation programme that is perceived as losing its momentum.

Appendix 8 – Euro-Mediterranean Partnership, EU-Egypt Association, MEDA Programme and the Industrial Crisis in Egypt

1 Euro-Mediterranean Partnership

Since 1977, EU/Egypt bilateral relations have been governed by a Co-operation Agreement, which provides for economic co-operation between the parties and establishes provisions for non-reciprocal trade liberalisation and market access. In the framework of the economic co-operation under the Co-operation Agreement, four financial protocols have provided EC funding for programmes and projects in Egypt until the mid-90s. In 1995, it was decided to change the system to enable the EC and its Mediterranean partners to adapt their development co-operation activities more clearly to the goals set out in the Barcelona Declaration of 1995 and subsequently included in the Association Agreements signed with each partner country.

The Euro-Mediterranean Conference held in Barcelona on 27–28 November 1995 marked the starting point of the Euro-Mediterranean Partnership or what is called the Barcelona Process. The Barcelona Process is a wide framework of political, economic and social relations between the EU members and the southern Mediterranean's partners. It comprises two complementary frameworks, the bilateral and the regional. At the bilateral level, the EU negotiates Euro-Mediterranean Association Agreement with the Mediterranean partners individually taken. These agreements are governed by the new Euro-Mediterranean relationship's general principles, although each agreement contains characteristics specific to the relations between the EU and each Mediterranean partner. At the regional level, regional dialogue covers the regional co-operation in the political, economic and cultural fields.

The Euro-Mediterranean Partnership aims at achieving three main objectives (EC, 2000b):

1. Political and Security Dialogue: the definition of a common area of peace and stability through the reinforcement of political and security dialogue,
2. Economic Integration: the construction of a zone of shared prosperity through an economic and financial partnership and the gradual establishment of a free trade zone, and

3. Social and Cultural Co-operation: the rapprochement between peoples through a social, cultural and human partnership aimed at encouraging understanding between culture and exchanges between civil societies.

The next section is about the bilateral agreement between EU members and Egypt known as EU-Egypt Association.

2 The EU-Egypt Association Agreement

An essential instrument to implement the Euro-Mediterranean Partnership is the bilateral Association Agreements between the EU and each Mediterranean partner, which provide the contractual framework underpinning the three pillars of the partnership. Association Agreements have already been signed with eight of the Mediterranean countries, including Egypt. Negotiations between the EU and Egypt for the conclusion of an association started in 1995 and lasted four and a half years. Compromise was founded on the most sensitive chapters such as agriculture, tariff dismantling, rules of origin, human rights and social provisions.

In June 1999, negotiations were concluded and the EU General Affairs Council endorsed the negotiated text. Since then, an internal debate has taken place in Egypt on the content of the Association Agreement, finally leading to its initialling on January 2001. On 25 June 2001, the EU-Egypt Association Agreement was signed in Luxembourg. After approval by the EU Member States' Parliament and the Egyptian People's Assembly (ratification process), the EU-Egypt Association Agreement has entered into force. Following its signature in June 2001, the Association Agreement has been ratified by the Egyptian People's Assembly in April 2003. On the EU side, all EU Member States have ratified the Agreement that fully entered into force in summer 2004.

To implement and manage the EU-Egypt Association Agreement, Association Bodies have been established (see Figure (A8.1)). An Association Council is set up at ministerial level to provide the political guidance, make the main policy decisions and settle disputes on the implementation of the Agreement. It consists of EU Member States, the European Committee and representatives of Egypt. It meets once a year and is presided in turn by the rotating Presidency of the EU and Egypt. An Association Committee, with the same composition and working modalities, has been delegated powers for the implementation. It can take binding decisions for the management of the Agreement by consensus between the parties. Working Groups can be set up by the Association Council, if appropriate. In some 25 areas of the Agreement consultations are institutionally to take place in the above forums. On the Egyptian side, Egypt has set up a structure to follow implementation of Association under the Secretary General of the Permanent Secretariat for the implementation of the Association Agreement at the Ministry of Foreign Affairs. Moreover, in each Ministry (Ministry of Foreign Trade, Agriculture, etc.) there will be special units dealing with the implementation of the Association Agreement.

The next section examines the MEDA programme and its detailed sub-programmes that have been implemented in Egypt according to EU-Egypt Association Agreement.

3 MEDA programme

The MEDA programme, which was put in place in 1996, is the principal financial instrument of the EU for the implementation of the Euro-Mediterranean Partnership (EC, 2000a). The MEDA budget line of the general EU budget (B7-4100) entails by far the largest financial resources dedicated to the Barcelona Process. The programme offers technical and financial support measures to accompany the reform of economic and social structures in the Mediterranean partner countries. The first legal basis of the

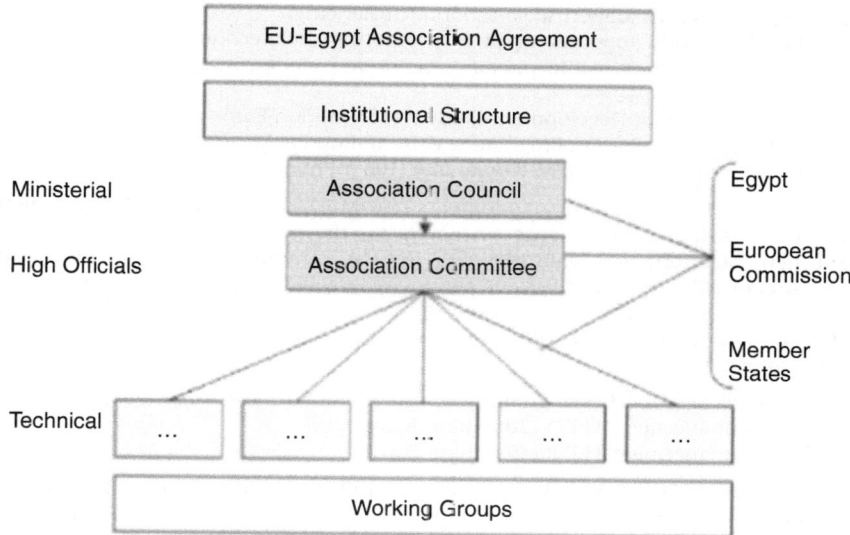

Figure A8.1 The EU-Egypt Association Bodies [*Source*: EC (2001a)]

MEDA programme was 1996 MEDA I Regulation (Council Regulation No. 1488/98) for the period of 1995–1999 where the programme accounted for 3,435 million Euros. On November 2000, a new improved regulation (No. 2698/2000) establishing MEDA II for the period 2000–2006 was adopted. The funding of the new programme amounts to 5.35 billion Euros. The main areas of intervention and objectives are directly derived from those of the 1995 Barcelona Declaration.

Some 88% of the resources to MEDA are channelled bilaterally to the partners. The other 12% are devoted to regional activities that all the partners are eligible to benefit from these activities. MEDA resources are subject to programming where three-year national indicative programmes are drawn up jointly for the bilateral channel and a regional indicative programme covers the multi-lateral activities. At the bilateral level, the priorities for MEDA resources are to support the economic transition and strengthen the socio-economic balance. At the regional level, the regional indicative programme complements and reinforces the bilateral indicative programmes and foresees the activities in the Barcelona Declaration.

Under MEDA I (1995–1999), total funds committed for Egypt as a bilateral assistance amounted to 686 million Euros (20% of the total MEDA I funds). The following major ongoing programmes are being financed in Egypt under MEDA I regulation (1995–1999) (EC, 2000c):

1. Programmes that support economic transition in Egypt:
   The EU supports economic transition in Egypt with four key programmes providing a total grant funding of about 350 million Euros, through:
   a) The Industrial Modernisation Programme (250 million Euros),
   b) Private Sector Development Programme (45 million Euros),
   c) Public Enterprise Reform and Privatisation Programme (3 million Euros), and
   d) Banking Sector Reform (11.7 million Euros).

2. Programmes that support socio-economic balancing:
   The EU actively supports Egypt in promoting socio-economic balancing and poverty alleviation while pursuing economic modernisation and free trade, through:
   a) Social Fund for Development-Phase II (155 million Euros),
   b) Health Sector Reform Programme (110 million Euros), and
   c) Education Enhancement Programme (100 million Euros)

In 2000, the European Council adopted a new MEDA regulation (MEDA II) which made available 5.4 billion Euros in grants for the period 2000–2006 for all the Southern Mediterranean countries (EC, 2001b). Commitments of the European Investment Bank (EIB) for the same period are targeted at 7.6 billion Euros. During the first Financial Perspective of the National Indicative Programme (2002–2004), the EU is committing 351 million Euros to Egypt to help finance the following programmes:

a) Technical and Vocational Training Reform (33 million Euros),
b) Trade Enhancement TEP-A (20 million Euros), and
c) Trade Enhancement TEP-B (40 million Euros).

Among these EU programmes, the focus is on Industrial Modernisation Programme as one of MEDA I programmes that support economic transition in Egypt. The main aims of this programme is to supply assistance in modernising Egyptian industry, especially the restructuring of the Ministry of Industry and Technological Development (MITD) as well as supplying proposals for policy reform regarding competition, customer protection and international trade. The next section examines the conditions which preceded the implementation of IMP and IMC, which represents the executive arm of this programme.

4   Industrial Crisis and the Role of MITD

During the 1960s, 1970s and 1980s, industrial policies in Egypt were typically characterised with protection, predominance of the public sector, favouring of specific sectors and limited attention to research and development. In 1991, the Egyptian government launched its economic reform and structural adjustment programme supported by both the International Monetary Fund and the World Bank. This programme aimed at achieving macroeconomic stability, transforming the Egyptian centrally planned economy into a free market economy, promoting private sector and stimulating export-based trade.

With the economic reform in 1991, the 1990s witnessed serious efforts to encourage more participation by the private sector, more exports and macroeconomic stability to encourage investment. These efforts, still continuing to date, have been translated into a package of industrial policies involving incentives to investors and exporters among others. Unfortunately, however, these policies have often been inconsistent and thus far from being effective. In fact, some times they even have a negative impact on industrial development (see Table A8.1). For example, the present education system cannot adequately support governmental efforts to encourage innovation, research and development, or technological improvement. On the one hand incentives to investors are given while extra taxes, complicated procedures and macroeconomic ambiguity discourage investors on the other hand. Similarly, calls for less bureaucracy and simplified procedures cannot be realised with the present characteristics of the civil servants especially those who are directly associated with the execution of laws and the interaction with people.

Egyptian industrial performance in the 1990s has suffered from several weaknesses. Examples of shortcomings were as follows (IMC, 2003):

- Limited contribution of industry to Gross Domestic Product (GDP) and GDP
  growth. For instance, although growth rates achieved by the industrial sector have
  averaged a high of 8.9% from 1975 to 1995, the sector's contribution to GDP has
  remained at only 17%, its growth having been superseded by that of petroleum,
  the utilities and services,
- Limited absorptive capacity for high technology by the Egyptian industrial system,
- Low wages and low productivity of labour,
- Limited integration among enterprises, and
- Low levels of manufactured exports and high cost of industrial growth in Egypt
  due to the significant contribution of fixed and working capital to growth in comparison to the limited contribution of productivity.

Table A8.1 Impediments to Industrial Development in Egypt

National Level	Sectoral Level	Enterprise Level
• Shortcomings in the educational and vocational training systems, • Shortcomings in the Egyptian quality system, • Bureaucratic obstacles related to import and export procedures, • High and multiple level of taxation, • Institutional weaknesses in the investment and operational environment, • Lack of attention to the environmental aspects of industrial operation, • Absence of strong links between national and research and development systems and the manufacturing sector, and • Problems of restructuring public sector enterprises, which suffer from accumulated losses, financial structure imbalances and surplus labour.	• Absence of a sufficiently developed and diversified financial sector, • The inadequate role played by business associations in serving the needs of their members, • Scare supply of sector-specific technical and marketing support services for industrial clusters, • Deficiency in quality and costs of goods from local suppliers for specific industry segments, and • Absence of a support policy for small and medium enterprises.	• Concentration of the product mixes in the low value-added segments of the market, • Inward orientation with little effort to enter new exports markets, • Poor managerial and organisational skills and the absence of strategic planning, • Minimal attention to technological innovation and progress, • Absence of regular training and retraining schemes for various skills, and • Inability to network internationally so as to secure co-operative agreements with large and small firms abroad in the realms of subcontracting, outsourcing and other forms of alliances.

Source: Based on Handoussa (2002: 89–103).

MITD's role is to orchestrate industrial development on various axes such as industrial planning, investment promotion for the industrial sector, supporting technological development for manufacturing enterprises and other services supporting industrial development. However, it, like other government agencies, suffers from a number of impediments. Examples of these shortcomings include an inadequate incentive system, low productivity, lack of a merit-base system of promotion, low wages and salaries, inadequate performance evaluation, lack of a competitive recruitment process, overlapping responsibilities and lack of communications' skills in workers and finally cumbersome structure of procedures and administrative requirements.

The organisational chart of MITD is shown in Figure A8.2. From the preliminary evaluation of this organisational structure, a number of remarks are put forward (Handoussa *et al.*, 2003). These remarks are related to the fact that some policy areas are left unattended such as industrial policy formulation, drivers of competitiveness analysis, technological development, technical training and human resource development and crisis management and exit policy for distressed sectors. In addition, it is not clear which division can be utilised to institute a built-in mechanism to review and monitor implementation of policies and adopt any needed corrective measures. Furthermore, there may be duplication in research activities as well as conducting technical and sectoral studies; there would also seem to be overlap between the activities of the Industrial Control Authority and the Egyptian Organisation for Standardisation and Quality Control.

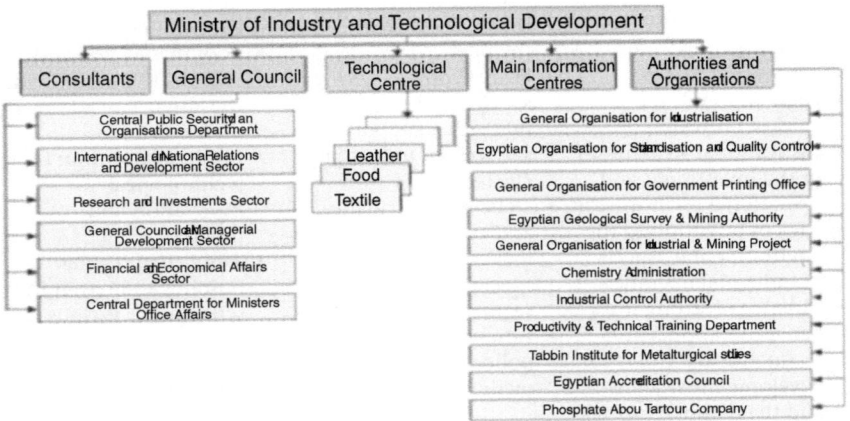

Figure A8.2 Current Organisational Structure of MITD

Appendix 9 – State Budget Reform Programmes and the Transformation of Extra-Organisational Institutions Governing Governmental Units

1   Egyptian Ministry of Finance

The Egyptian Ministry of Finance (MOF) was established in 1870s. It is mainly responsible for planning and implementing the Government's overall fiscal policy. In this reflection, the Ministry prepares the draft state budget to be approved by the People's Assembly, monitors implementation of the approved budget, and manages state revenues as well as collects direct and indirect taxes. It also manages the external and internal public debt and achieves integration between the fiscal policy and the monetary policy to serve the national economy through co-ordination and co-operation with the Central Bank of Egypt and other related public agencies. The following departments are currently linked to the MOF: Income Tax Department, Customs Department, Real Estate (Property) Tax Department, General Sales Tax Department, Governmental Services, Coinage Department, Treasury Central Department and Minister's Office.

The MOF is responsible for preparing the Government budget, governed by Law No. 53 of 1973, which was amended in 1980 by Law No. 104 of 1980, and managing all transactions, except new investments, which are the responsibility of the National Investment Bank founded in 1980. In budget preparation and approval, a number of MOF's sectors take part, including the Sector of General State Budgeting, Sector of Local Governments Budgeting, Sector of Economic Organisations and Units, State Treasury Department and Financing Sector. Until 1980, the budgetary procedures involved a complex accounting system with several budgets and special funds. Budget formats took a long time to standardise and the fiscal year was altered several times. In July 1980, budgetary procedures were simplified and the fiscal year was fixed between July 1 and June 30, instead of the previously used calendar year. The current budget still contains a number of special-purpose funds, such as subsidies and support for the armed forces, which were outside the main budget. Public sector enterprises and general organisations, such as the Suez Canal, have their separate budgets, although they are connected to the government budget through transfers to and from the latter.

In budget execution (budgetary accounting and budgetary reporting), the Government Accounting Act No. 27 of 1981 is followed to account for actual revenues and expenditures and to prepare final accounts. A number of MOF's sectors use this act in budget execution, monitoring and reporting, including the Sector of Accounts and Financial Directorates, Financing Sector and Sector of Final Accounts. Before April 1981, there was no legal framework for the government accounting in Egypt. The government accounting was subjected to the financial regulation of the budget and accounts. This regulation is a group of instructions and periodical books issued by the MOF during different periods. This regulation was not formulated in a form of law and, of course, did not have the power of law. As a result, the estimated revenues that should be collected during the budgetary year are delayed and the appropriations for the governmental units are not precisely followed and most of the governmental units have expended more than their appropriations. This, in turn, has led to an increase of the budget deficit. Therefore, there was an imperative for enacting the Government Accounting Act.

The MOF is also in charge of the enforcement of various tax laws *via* its independent tax departments. These departments are also involved in amending, designing and drafting tax laws, which are then submitted to the legislature for ratification. These departments are as follows:

- General Income Tax Department which is in charge of Unified Income Tax Law No. 187 of 1993, Stamp Duties Law No. 111 of 1980 and Development Fees Law,
- Customs Department which is responsible for Custom Duties Law No. 66 of 1963,
- Real Estate Tax Department which is in charge of the Agricultural Land Law No. 113 of 1939 and Building Tax Law No. 56 of 1954, and
- General Sales Tax Department which is in charge of the General Sales Tax Law No. 11 of 1991.

Egyptian Sales Tax Department (ESTD) is the second government agency under study. So the next sections present the fiscal crisis that led to the establishment of ESTD as one of the most important tax reform of the Egyptian tax system in the early 1990s. This revenue-side reform is followed by another reform that addresses the expenditure-side of the state budget, that is, the performance-based budgeting at the beginning of 2000. ESTD as one of the MOF's departments started implementing the performance-based budgeting. The introduction of performance-based budgeting was associated with automating almost all information systems in ESTD.

2 Fiscal crisis

Towards the latter part of the 1980s, Egyptian authorities were faced with the un-enviable convergence of major economic and fiscal imbalances, a growing budget deficit, high inflation, low savings, low investments, high debt and deteriorating local currency. At that time, the Egyptian economy was not in a good state. Economic growth had fallen sharply; the rate of inflation was high; and both the balance of payments deficit and the state budget deficit had expanded enormously. In 1986, for example, Egypt's debt to GDP ratio was one of the highest in the world and the consolidated budget deficit had reached 23% of GDP (Licari, 1997).

Efforts to reduce expenditure were being outstripped by the falling off in revenues. The tax to GDP ratio had fallen from 1981–82 through 1986–87 before settling at a level of around 15–16% (Ramos, 2002). The decline in tax to GDP had occurred primarily in income taxes and was for a time offset by an increase in the trade taxes and consumption taxes. But the structure and narrow base of the old Consumption Tax meant it lacked buoyancy while no country dependent on imports can seek to meet its fiscal requirements from trade taxes indefinitely. Despite repeated discretionary changes in tax rates and the introduction of a number of new levies, tax revenues grew only about half as fast as GDP, i.e., about half the desired rate.

This unfavourable fiscal picture was the result of the structural and administrative characteristics of the Egyptian tax system (Ramos, 2002). There was heavy reliance on the external sector, both in trade taxes and in corporate income tax revenues. At the same time, a large proportion of domestic taxes came from the consumption of imports. In addition, inflation adversely affected revenues because of the pro-longed time lag between the assessment and collection of taxes. Furthermore, the lack of application of penalties when taxes were not paid in a timely fashion further encouraged taxpayers to postpone as long as possible. Finally, the tax base was being gradually eroded by a combination of generous incentives, acute tax evasion, and government policies in areas such as price controls. The attempt to close the deficit by introducing a serious of discretionary taxes proved ineffective, but it did serve to complicate the tax code and to increase the compliance cost to both the tax admin-istration and the taxpayers. The next sub-section focuses on fiscal reforms.

3 Fiscal reforms

3.1 Revenue-side reform: the introduction of General Sales Tax

In 1991, the Egyptian government signed two economic reform and structural adjustment agreements with the World Bank and the International Monetary Fund (IMF) to stabilise the economy via a package of speedy-recovery reforms and guarantee fiscal sustainability by balancing public revenues and expenditures. A tax reform programme began in the early 1990s as part of the Economic Reform and Structural Adjustment Programme that emerged from discussions between 1987 and 1991 with IMF and also, in 1991, with the World Bank. A number of revenue-side reforms have been introduced.

Since the beginning of the 1990s, the USA Government has provided about $60 million in assistance to the Egyptian government to assist in reforming its tax system, strengthening its institutional capacity to administer taxes, and building analytic capacity for the design of fiscal, and especially tax policy (Ramos, 2002). From a policy perspective, two of the most important achievements have been the enactment of the General Sales Tax (GST) in 1991 and the Global Income Tax in 1993. Both led to transformations in the Egyptian tax system, and to the establishment of a new institution and the modernisation of the country's tax administration. However, this sub-section focuses only on one of these reforms: the GST.

The introduction of the GST with many characteristics of a Value Added Tax (VAT) was a major reform to the Egyptian tax system. Law No. 11 of 1991, levying sales tax, came into force as of 3 May 1991 to replace the old Consumption Tax. This law identifies persons assigned for tax supply and collection in all the stages of implementation. The first stage was limited to the manufacturers, service providers, importers and producers of taxable commodities with sales that go beyond the registration threshold set forth by law, i.e. annual turnover of L.E. 54,000. The second and third stages, implemented in 2001 according to Law No. 17 of 2001, applied to wholesale and retail merchants dealing in taxable products with an annual turnover of L.E. 150,000, representing a very important step toward implementing a full VAT system in Egypt.

Certainly, the GST played a strong role in restoring government revenues. GST, which formed 21.75% of total tax revenue in the fiscal year 1990/91 and 32.64% in the fiscal year 1999/2000,[2] has played an outstanding role in increasing tax revenue and consequently the budget deficit has declined considerably. A review of sales tax collections show that sales tax revenue almost doubled between 1991 and 1992 and increased by about 12% per annum through the remainder of the decade (Ramos, 2002). The sales tax was proved highly elastic, producing both a large initial increase in tax revenues and an increase in the rate of growth of indirect tax revenues over time. The tax, being broader based than the prior Consumption Tax, was more neutral in its impact on the economy and also significantly reduced tax cascading. Moreover, imported goods were taxed on a par with domestically produced goods, effectively eliminating the protectionist features of the previous tax. The next sub-section addresses the expenditure-side reform and the crisis that led to this reform.

3.2 Expenditure-side reform: performance-based budgeting

The reform programme adopted during the 1990s was successful. Despite the dwindling economic growth rates experienced in the early 1990s, macroeconomic stabilisation policies bore fruit towards the mid-1990s with the private sector becoming a partner in the development of the economy. The GDP growth rate was at 5.7% in

1997–98 and investments in industry grew at a higher rate than in agriculture and services. Furthermore, the growth rate of per capita income went up to around 3.5% in 1997–98 from 0% in 1990–91 (Dessus and Suwa-Eisenmann, 1998). However, with the termination of the economic reform and structural adjustment programmes towards the end of the 1990s, a lax attitude towards growth in many of the key economic sectors and activities was witnessed. This coincided with a series of internal and external shocks, such as the South East Asian crisis, that were an obstacle to progress and had multiple effects on overall performance and economic outlook.

A decline in both tourism and oil revenues negatively affected the trade balance. The capital account was also not far from the same trends due to an obvious correlation with foreign direct investment from Asian countries and Russia. Subsequently, the account incurred a deficit equivalent to $3.6 billion in 1999–2000 after realising a surplus of $1 billion in 1997–98. Similarly, the budget deficit grew from 1% of GDP in 1997–98 to 4.7% of GDP in 1999–2000 (Ramos, 2002). As a consequence, a number of expenditure-side reforms have been introduced. However, this subsection focuses only on one of these reforms: the performance-based budgeting.

Recently, the GOE has focused increasingly on not only economic reform but also public service reform in order to rationalise public expenditures without jeopardising operational requirements. Ministries and departments have been urged to improve their internal management. They are to experiment with new management techniques that can promote greater public service efficiency and effectiveness. Examples of the reforms, which the public service has put in place, are e-government, simplification of rules and regulations and budget reform. One aspect of budget reform is the introduction of performance-based budgeting. Performance-based budgeting is a system that the World Bank and the IMP recommend to countries seeking to reform their budget.

In September 2000, the World Bank introduced a budget reform programme to the GOE. It recommended replacing the current traditional line-item budgeting with a performance-based or results-oriented budgeting system. In November 2002, the Egyptian People's Assembly approved an agreement with the World Bank that seeks to design and implement a performance-based budgeting system for the purpose of fiscal reform, expenditure control and enhanced quality public service delivery. A Presidential Decree No. 275 of 2002 was issued to regulate the experimental application of performance-based budgeting in Egyptian governmental units. According to this decree, the GOE is experimenting with performance-based budgeting in five ministries – the Ministry of Finance, the Ministry of Planning, the Ministry of Industry and Technological Development, the Ministry of Electricity and Energy and the Ministry of information and Communication. This effort is among the first of its kind in the Arab world. Among the governmental units that achieved a good progress in implementing the performance-based budgeting is ESTD.

Notes

1 In 1996, the Central Agency for Accountancy issued another set of accounting standards as a complementary framework for the Uniform Accounting System. These standards are based on International Accounting Standards (IASs) and have to be applied by SOEs. In fact, there were many conflicting areas between the Uniform Accounting System and IASs (Kholeif, 1997).

2 Central Bank of Egypt statistics.

Bibliography

Abdel-Khalik, A. R. and Ajinkya, B. B. (1983) 'An Evaluation of "The Everyday Accountant and Researching His Reality"', *Accounting, Organisations and Society*, 8 (4): 375–384.

Aghazadeh, S.-M. (2003) 'MRP Contributes To A Company's Profitability', *Assembly Automation*, 23 (3): 257–265.

Ahmed, M. N. (1992) *A Critical Evaluation of the Methodological Underpinnings of Management Accounting Research: An Alternative Institutional Economics Framework*, Unpublished Ph.D. Dissertation, University of Manchester.

Ahmed, M. N. and Scapens, R. W. (2000) 'Cost Allocation in Britain: Toward an Institutional Analysis', *The European Accounting Review*, 9 (2): 159–204.

Al-Ahram Weekly (2002) 'Mobilising Modernisation', *Al-Ahram Weekly Online*, 4–10 April: 580. Available at: http://weekly.ahram.org.eg/2002/580/ec3.htm (accessed 10th April 2005).

Alam, M. (1997) 'Budgeting Process in Uncertain Contexts: A Study of State-owned Enterprises in Bangladesh', *Management Accounting Research*, 8: 147–167.

Amat, J., Carnona, S. and Roberts, H. (1994) 'Context and Change in Management Accounting Systems: A Spanish Case Study', *Management Accounting Research*, 5: 107–122.

Anderson, S. W. and Young, S. M. (1999) 'The Impact of Contextual and Process Factors on the Evaluation of Activity-Based Costing Systems', *Accounting, Organizations and Society*, 24: 525–559.

Angyal, A. (1941) 'Disgust and related aversions', *Journal of Abnormal and Social Psychology*, 36: 393–412.

Anthony, R. N. (1965) *Management Control: Case and Readings*, Homewood, Illinois: Richard D. Irwin.

Anthony, R. S. (1988) *The Management Control Function*, Boston, MA: Harvard Business School Press.

Archer, M. S. (1982) 'Morphogenesis Versus Structuration: On Combining Structure And Action', *British Journal of Sociology*, 33: 455–483.

Archer, M. S. (1990) 'Human Agency and Social Structure: A Critique of Giddens', in J. Clark, C. Modgil and J. Modgil (eds) *Anthony Giddens: Consensus and Controversy*, Brighton, UK: Falmer Press, 73–84.

Archer, M. S. (1995) *Realist Social Theory: The Morphogenetic Approach*, Cambridge: Cambridge University Press.

Argyris, C. and Kaplan, R. S. (1994) 'Implementing New Knowledge: The Case of Activity-Based Costing', *Accounting Horizon*, 8 (3): 83–105.

Armstrong, P. (1994) 'The Influence of Michel Foucault on Accounting Research', *Critical Perspectives on Accounting*, 5 (1): 25–55.

Atkinson, A., Balakrishnon, R., Booth, P., Cate, J. M., Groot, T., Malmi, T., Roberts, H., Uliana, E. and Wu, A. (1997) 'New Directions in Management Accounting Research', *Journal of Management Accounting Research*, Fall, 9: 79–108.

Bailey, K. D. (1994) *Methods of Social Research*, London: The Free Press.

Bancroft, N. H., Seip, H. and Sprengel, A. (1998) *Implementing SAP R/3: How to Introduce a Large System into a Large Organisation*, Greenwich, CT: Manning.

Barbalet, J. M. (1987) 'Power, Structural Resources and Agency', *Current Perspectives in Social Theory*, 8: 1–24.

Barley, S. R. and Tolbert, P. S. (1997) 'Institutionalization and Structuration: Studying the Links between Action and Institution', *Organization Studies*, 18 (1): 93–117.

Barley, S. R. (1986) 'Technology as an Occasion for Structuring Evidence from Observation of CT Scanners and the Social Order of Radiology Departments', *Administrative Science Quarterly*, 31 (1): 78–108.

Benbasat, I., Goldstein, D. K. and Mead, M. (1987) 'The Case Research Strategy in Studies of Information Systems', *MIS Quarterly*, 11: 369–386.

Bergen, A. and While, A. (2000) 'A Case for Case Studies: Exploring the Use of Case Study Design in Community Nursing Research', *Journal of Advanced Nursing*, 31 (4): 926–934.

Berger, P. L. and Luckmann, T. (1966) *The Social Construction of Reality: A Treatise in the Sociology of Knowledge*, Harmondsworth: Penguin University Books.

Bhimani, A. (1993) 'Indeterminacy and the Specificity of Accounting Change: Renault 1898–1938', *Accounting, Organizations and Society*, 18 (1): 1–39.

Bjornenak, T. and Olson, O. (1999) 'Unbundling Management Accounting Innovations', *Management Accounting Research*, 10: 325–338.

Bogt, H. J. and Helden, J. V. (2000) 'Accounting Change in Dutch Government: Exploring the Gap between Expectations and Realisation', *Management Accounting Research*, 11: 263–279.

Bonoma, T. V. (1985) 'Case Research in Marketing: Opportunities, Problems and A Process', *Journal of Marketing Research*, 22 (2): 199–208.

Booth, P., Matolcsy, Z. and Wieder, B. (2000) 'The Impacts of Enterprise Resource Planning Systems on Accounting Practices – The Australian Experience', *Australian Accounting Review*, 10 (3): 4–18.

Boslender, R. (1995) 'Critical Management Accounting', in D. Ashton, T. Hopper and R. W. Scapens (ed.) *Issues in Management Accounting*, pp. 65–86, London: Prentice Hall.

Bowring, M. A. (2000) 'De/Constructing Theory: A Look at the Institutional Theory that Positivism Built', *Journal of Management Inquiry*, September, 9 (3): 258–270.

Braverman, H. (1974) *Labour and Monopoly Capital: The Degradation of Work in the Twentieth Century*, New York: Monthly Review Press.

Briston, R. J. and El-Ashker, A. A. (1984) 'The Egyptian Accounting System: A Case Study in Western Influence', *International Journal of Accounting, Education and Research*, 19 (Fall): 129–155.

Bromwich, M. and Bhimani, A. (1989) *Management Accounting: Evolution not Revolution*, London: CIMA Publications, 1989.

Bruns, W. J. (1989) 'A Review of Robert K. Yin's Case Study Research: Design and Methods', *Journal of Management Accounting Research*, Fall: 157–163.

Bryant, C. and Jary, D. (eds) (1991) *Giddens' Theory of Structuration: A Critical Application*, London: Routledge.

Bryman, A. (1984) 'The Debate about Quantitative and Qualitative Research: A Question of Method or Epistemology?', *The British Journal of Sociology*, 35 (1): 75–92.

Buck-Emden, R. (2000) *The SAP R/3 System: An Introduction to ERP and Business Software Technology*, London: Addison-Wesley.

Burnes, B. (2004) 'Kurt Lewin and the Planned Approached to Change: A Reappraisal', *Journal of Management Studies*, 41 (6): 977–1002.

Burns, J. (1996) *The Routinization and Institutionalization of Accounting*, Unpublished PhD Thesis, the University of Manchester, the Faculty of Economics and Social Studies.

Burns, J. (2000) 'The Dynamics of Accounting Change: Interplay between New Practices, Routines, Institutions, Power and Politics', *Accounting, Auditing & Accountability Journal*, 13 (5): 566–596.

Burns, J. and Scapens, R. W. (2000) 'Conceptualising Management Accounting Change: An Institutional Framework', *Management Accounting Research*, 11: 3–25.

Burns, J., Ezzamel, M. and Scapens, R. (1999) 'Management Accounting Change in the UK', *Management Accounting*, March: 28–30.

Burns, J., Ezzamel, M. and Scapens, R. W. (2003) *The Challenge of Management Accounting Change: Behavioural and Cultural Aspects of Change Management*, London, UK: Elsevier Ltd.

Burrell, G. and Morgan, G. (1979) *Sociological Paradigms and Organisational Analysis: Elements of the Sociology of Corporate Life*, London: Heinemann.

Caglio, A. (2003) 'Enterprise Resource Planning Systems and Accountants: Towards Hybridization?', *The European Accounting Review*, 12 (1): 123–153.

Campbell, R. J. and Porcano, T. M. (1979) 'The Contributions of Materials Requirements Planning (MRP) to Budgeting and Cost Control', *Cost and Management*, January–February: 31–34.

Carr, J. G. (1985) *IT and the Accountant, Summary and Conclusions*, Aldershot: Gower Publishing Company Ltd/ACCA.

Carruthers, B. G. (1995) 'Accounting, Ambiguity, and the New Institutionalism', *Accounting, Organisations and Society*, 20: 313–328.

Chapman, C. and Chua, W.-F. (2000) 'Information Technology, Organisational Form, and Accounting', Proceedings of the *2nd Conference on New Directions in Management Accounting: Innovations in Practice and Research*, Brussels, Belgium, 14–16 December 2000, 193–211.

Chenhall, R. H. and Langfield-Smith, K. (1998a) 'Adoption and Benefits of Management Accounting Practices: An Australian Study', *Management Accounting Research*, 9: 1–19.

Chenhall, R. H. and Langfield-Smith, K. (1998b) 'The Relationship between Strategic Priorities, Management Techniques and Management Accounting: An Empirical investigation using a Systems Approach', *Accounting Organisations and Society*, 23 (3): 243–268.

Chouldhury, N. (1986) 'In Search of Relevance in Management Accounting Research', *Accounting and Business Research* (Winter): 21–32.

Chua, W. F. (1986) 'Radical Developments in Accounting Thought', *The Accounting Review*, LXI (4): 601–632.

Chung, S. H. and Snyder, C. A. (2000) 'ERP Adoption: A Technological Evolution Approach', *International Journal of Agile Management Systems*, 2/1: 24–32.

Coase, R. H. (1937) 'The Nature of the Firm', *Economica*, 3: 386–405.

Cobb, I., Christine, H. and Innes, J. (1995) 'Management Accounting Change in Bank', *Management Accounting Research*, 6: 155–175.

Collier, P. A. (1984) *The Impact of IT on Management Accountant*, London: ICMA.

Cooper, D. (1983) 'Tidiness, Muddle and Things: Commonalties and Divergences in Two Approaches to Management Accounting Research', *Accounting, Organisations and Society*, 8 (2/3): 269–286.

Cooper, D. J. and Sherer, M. J. (1984) 'The Value of Accounting Reports: Arguments for a Political Economy of Accounting', *Accounting, Organisations and Society*, 9 (3/4): 207–232.

Cooper, R. and Kaplan, R. S. (1992) 'Activity-Based Systems: Measuring the Costs of Resources Usage', *Accounting Horizon* (September): 1–13.

Cooper, R. and Kaplan, R. S. (1998) 'The Promise and Peril of Integrated Cost Systems', *Harvard Business Review* (July–August): 109–119.

Cooper, R. B. and Zmud, R. W. (1990) 'Information Technology Implementation Research: A Technological Diffusion Approach', *Management Science*, 16 (2): 123–139.

Covaleski, M. A., Dirsmith, M. W. and Samuel, S. (1996) 'Managerial Accounting Research: The Contributions of Organizational and Sociological Theories', *Journal of Management Accounting Research*, 8: 1–29.

Crosby, P. B. (1979) *Quality is Free*, New York: McGraw-Hill.

Cullen, A., Webster, M. and Muhlemann, A. (2001) 'Enterprise Resource Planning (ERP) Systems: Definitions, Functionality and the Contribution to Global Operations', Working Paper, the University of Bradford, Management Centre.

Cyert, R. M. and March, J. G. (1963) *A Behavioural Theory of the Firm*, Englewood Cliffs, NJ: Prentice Hall.

D'Aunno, T., Sutton, R. I. and Price, R. H. (1991) 'Isomorphism and External Support in Conflicting Institutional Environments: A Study of Drug Abuse Treatment Units', *The Academy of Management Journal*, 34 (3): 636–661.

Dacin, M. T., Goodstein, J. and Scott, W. R. (2002) 'Institutional Theory and Institutional Change: Introduction to the Special Research Forum', *The Academy of Management Journal*, 45 (1): 45–57.

Damanpour, F. and Evan, W. M. (1984) 'Organisational Innovations and Performance: The Problem of Organisational Lag', *Administrative Science Quarterly*, September, 29 (3): 392–409.

Daniel, S. J. and Reitsperger, W. D. (1992) 'Management Control Systems for Quality: An Empirical Comparison of the US and Japanese Electronics Industries', *Journal of Management Accounting Research*, Fall: 64–78.

Davenport, T. H. (1998) 'Putting the Enterprise into the Enterprise System', *Harvard Business Review*, July–August: 121–131.

Davenport, T. H. (2000) *Mission Critical: Realising the Promise of Enterprise Systems*, Boston, MA: Harvard Business School Press.

Deming, W. E. (1982) *Quality, Productivity, and Competitive Position*, M.I.T. Centre for Advanced Engineering Study.

Denzin, N. K. and Lincoln, Y. S. (1994) 'Introduction: Entering the Field of Qualitative Research', in N. K. Denzin and Y. S. Lincoln (eds) *Handbook of Qualitative Research*, London: Sage Publications.

DeSanctis, G. and Poole, M. S. (1994) 'Capturing the Complexity in Advanced Technology Use: Adaptive Structuration Theory', *Organization Science*, 5 (2): 121–147.

Dessus, S. and Suwa-Eisenmann, A. (1998) 'Trade Integration with Europe, Export Diversification and Economic Growth in Egypt', OECD Development Centre, Technical Paper No. 135, June: 6–18. Online. Available at: http://www.oecd.org/dataoecd/19/17/1922542.pdf (accessed on 10th April 2005).

Dewar, R. D. and Dutton, J. E. (1986) 'The Adoption of Radical and Incremental Innovations: An Empirical Analysis', *Management Science*, November, 32 (11): 1422–1433.

Diamond, J. (2002) 'Budget System Reform in Transitional Economics: The Experience of Russia', IMF Working Paper, WP/02/22, International Monetary Fund. Online. Available at: http://www.imf.org/external/pubs/ft/wp/2002/wp0222. pdf (accessed on 10th April 2005).

Dillard, J. F. and Yuthas, K. (1997) 'Fluid Structures: A Structuration Approach to Evaluating Information Technology', *Advances in Accounting Information Systems*, 5: 247–271.

DiMaggio, P. and Powell, W. (1983) 'The Iron Cage Revisited: Institutional Isomorphism and Collective Rationality in Organizational Fields', *American Sociological Review*, 48: 147–160.

Drury, C. (2000) *Management and Cost Accounting (5th edition)*, London: Thomson Business Books.

Dugdale, D. and Jones, C. (1995) 'The Theory of Constraints', *Accountancy*, September: 124.

Dunk, A. S. (1989) 'Management Accounting Lag', *Abacus*, 25 (2): 149–155.

Easterby-Smith, M., Thorp, R. and Lowe, A. (1991) *Management Research: An Introduction*, London: Sage.

EC (European Commission) (2000a) 'Euro-Mediterranean Partnership: Information Notes', Brussels, Belgium: European Commission. Online. Available at: http://europa.eu.int/comm/external_relations/euromed/brochures/infonotes_en.pdf (accessed on 10th April 2005).

EC (2000b) 'The Barcelona Process, Five Years On: 1995–2000', Brussels, Belgium: European Commission. Online. Available at: http://www.europa.eu.int/comm/external_relations/med_mideast/euro_med_partnership/brochures/barcelona-5yrs_en.pdf (accessed on 10th April 2005).

EC (2000c) 'Report from the Commission: Annual Report of the MEDA Programme 1999', Brussels, Belgium: European Commission. Online. Available at: http://europa.eu.int/comm/external_relations/euromed/meda/report1999_en.pdf (accessed on 10th April 2005).

EC (2001a) '25 Years and Beyond: European Union and Egypt in Partnership', Brussels, Belgium: European Commission. Online. Available at: http://europa.eu.int/comm/external_relations/euromed/brochures/barcelona-5yrs_en.pdf (accessed on 10th April 2005).

EC (2001b) 'Annual Report on the Implementation of the European Commission's External Assistance', Brussels, Belgium: European Commission. Online. Available at: http://europa.eu.int/comm/europeaid/reports/aidco_2001_big_annual_report_en.pdf (accessed on 10th April 2005).

Eisenhardt, K. M. (1988) 'Agency – and Institutional-Theory Explanations: The Case of Retail Sales Compensation', *The Academy of Management Journal*, 31 (3): 488–511.

Eisenhardt, K. M. (1989) 'Building Theories from Case Study Research', *The Academy of Management Review*, 14 (4): 532–550.

El Sayed, H. and Westrup, C. (2003) 'Egypt and ICTs: How ICTs Bring National Initiative, Global Organizations and Local Companies Together', *Information Technology and People*, 16 (1): 76–92.

Emmanuel, C., Otley, D. and Merchant, K. (1990) *Accounting for Management Control (2nd edition)*, London: Chapman and Hall.

ESTD (Egyptian Sales Tax Department) (2002a) 'Why Should the State Budget be Modernized Today?', *Tax Culture*, February: 38–39.

ESTD (2002b) 'A Meeting between Officials from the Sales Tax Department and the World Bank', *Tax Culture*, April: 40–44.

ESTD (2002c) 'A Press Interview with the Commissioner', *Tax Culture*, December: 24–25.

Ezzamel, M. (1994) 'Organizational Change and Accounting: Understanding the Budgeting System in its Organizational Context', *Organization Studies*, 15: 213–240.

Ezzamel, M., Hoskin, K. and Macve, R. (1990) 'Managing It All by Number: A Review of Johnson and Kaplan's "Relevance Lost"', *Accounting and Business Research*, 20 (78): 153–166.

Fahy, M. J. and Lynch, R. (1999) 'Enterprise Resource Planning (ERP) Systems and Strategic Management Accounting', Paper Presented at the *22nd Conference of the EAA*, Munich, Germany, 5–7 May.

Fisher, J. (1995) 'Contingency-Based Research on Management Control Systems: Categorisation by Level of Complexity', *Journal of Accounting Literature*, 14: 24–53.

Flint, D. (1988) 'Academic Research and Accounting Practice', *The Accountant's Magazine*, May: 29–30.

FMAC (Financial and Management Accounting Committee) (1994) *A View of Tomorrow: Management Accountancy in the year 2004*, New York: International Federation of Accountants.

Foster, G. and Young, S. M. (1997) 'Frontiers of Management Accounting Research', *Journal of Management Accounting Research*, 9 (Fall): 63–77.

Foucault, M. (1980) *Power/Knowledge: Selected Interviews and Other Writings, 1972–1977*, London: Harvester.

Freeman, R. J. and Shoulders, C. D. (1999) *Governmental and Non-profit Accounting: Theory and Practice – Sixth Edition*, London, UK: Prentice Hall International.

Furumo, K. and Pearson, J. (2004) 'A Case Study of ERP Implementation in Two Public Universities: Why Was One a Success and the Other a Failure?', Proceedings of the Tenth Americans Conference on Information Systems, August, New York.

Galloway, D. and Waldron, D. (1988) 'Throughput Accounting-I: The Need for A New Language for Manufacturing', *Management Accounting*, November: 34–35.

George, J. F. and King, J. L. (1991) 'Examining the Computing and Centralisation Debate', *The Communications of the ACM*, 34 (7): 63–72.

Giddens, A. (1976) *New Rules of Sociological Method: A Positive Critique of Interpretative Sociologies*, London, UK: Hutchinson.

Giddens, A. (1977) *Studies in Social and Political Theory*, London, UK: Hutchinson.

Giddens, A. (1979) *Central Problems in Social Theory*, Basingstoke, UK: Macmillan.

Giddens, A. (1982) 'Power, the Dialectic of Control and Class Structuration', in A. Giddens and G. Mackenzie (eds) *Social Class and the Division of Labour: Essays in Honour of Ilya Neustadt*, Cambridge: Cambridge University, 29–45.

Giddens, A. (1983) 'Comments on the Theory of Structuration', *Journal for the Theory of Social Behaviour*, 13 (1): 75–80.

Giddens, A. (1984) *The Constitution of Society*, Cambridge: Polity Press.

Giddens, A. (1989) 'A Reply to My Critics', in D. Held and J. B. Thompson (eds) *Social Theory of Modern Societies: Anthony Giddens and his Critics*, Cambridge, UK: Cambridge University Press, 249–301.

Giddens, A. (1991) *Modernity and Self-Identity: Self and Society in the Late Modern Age*, Cambridge, UK: Polity Press.

Giddens, A. and Pierson, C. (1998) *Conversations with Anthony Giddens: Making Sense of Modernity*, Cambridge, UK: Polity Press.

Goffman, E. (1983) 'The Interaction Order', *American Sociological Review*, 48: 1–17.

Goldratt, E. M. (2000) *Necessary but Not Sufficient: A Theory of Constraints Business Novel*, USA: The North River Press.

Goldratt, E. M. and Cox, J. (1984) *The Goal*, London: Gower.

Goldratt, E. M. and Cox, J. (1993) *The Goal: A Process of Ongoing Improvement* (2nd edition), London: Gower.

Gordon, L. A. (1998) *Managerial Accounting – Concepts and Empirical Evidence*, New York: The McGraw-Hill Companies, Inc. Primis Custom Publishing.

Gould, L. (1997) 'Planning and Scheduling Today's Automotive Enterprises', *Automotive Manufacturing and Production*, 109 (April): 62–66.

Granlund, M. and Malmi, T. (2002) Moderate Impact of ERPS on Management Accounting: A Lag or Permanent Outcome?, *Management Accounting Research*, 13: 299–321.

Granlund, M. (2001) 'Towards Explaining Stability in and Around Management Accounting Systems', *Management Accounting Research*, 12: 141–166.

Granlund, M. (2003) 'Management Accounting System Integration in Corporate Mergers: A Case Study', *Accounting, Auditing & Accountability Journal*, 16 (2): 208–243.

Granlund, M. and Lukka, K. (1998) 'It's a Small World of Management Accounting Practices', *Journal of Management Accounting Research*, 10: 153–179.

Granlund, M. and Mouritsen, J. (2003) 'Introduction: Problematizing the Relationship between Management Control and Information Technology', *The European Accounting Review*, 12 (1): 77–83.

Greenberg, L. (1996) 'The Most Common Business Re-Engineering Success Factors and Pitfalls', Online. Available at: http://www.earthrenewal.org/bprmist.htm (accessed on 10th April 2005).

Greenwood, R. and Hinings, C. R. (1996) 'Understanding Radical Organisational Change: Bringing Together the Old and New Institutionalism', *The Academy of Management Review*, 21: 1022–1054.

Greenwood, R., Suddaby, R. and Hinings, C. R. (2002) 'Theorising Change: The Role of Professional Associations in the Transformation of Institutionalised Fields', *The Academy of Management Journal*, 45 (1): 58–80.

Gupta, P. P., Dirsmith, M. W. and Fogarty, T. J. (1994) 'Co-ordination and Control in a Government Agency: Contingency and Institutional Perspectives on GAO Audits', *Administrative Science Quarterly*, 39: 264–284.

Gurd, B., Smith, M. and Swaffer, A. (2002) 'Factors Impacting on Accounting Lag: An Exploratory Study', *The British Accounting Review*, 34: 205–221.

Haldma, T. and Laats, K. (2002) 'Contingencies Influencing the Management Accounting Practices of Estonian Manufacturing Companies', *Management Accounting Research*, 13: 379–400.

Hambrick, D. and Lei, D. (1985) 'Toward an Empirical Prioritisation of Contingency Variables for Business Strategy', *The Academy of Management Journal*, December, 28 (4): 763–788.

Hamilton, W. H. (1932) 'Institution', in E. R. A. Seligman and A. Johnson (eds) *Encyclopaedia of Social Science*, 73 (4), 560–595.

Handoussa, H. (2002) 'A Balance Sheet of Reform in Two Decades', in N. El-Mikawy and H. Handoussa (eds) *Institutional Reform and Economic Development in Egypt*, Cairo, Egypt: AUC Press.

Handoussa, H., Nour El-Din, D. and Abou Shnief, H. (2003) 'The Future Structure and Role of the Ministry of Industry and Technological Development in Egypt: Lessons from International Experiences', Economic Research Forum for the Arab Countries, Iran and Turkey, Working Paper, July, Cairo, Egypt: IMC. Online. Available at: http://www.imc-egypt.org/download.asp?fileid=6C1706E406BB4D16858208055 AECF721 (accessed on 10th April 2005).

Hardy, C. (1996) 'Understanding Power: Bringing about Strategic Change', *The British Journal of Management*, 7: 3–16.

Hassanein, M. (2004) 'The Second Wave of Fiscal Reforms in Egypt', Paper Presentation at the Institute for International Economics, Washington, DC, 15 June. Online. Available at: http://www.iie.com/publications/papers/hassanein0604.pdf (accessed on 10th April 2005).

Hedberg, B. and Jonsson, S. (1978) 'Designing Semi-confusing Information Systems for Organisations in Changing Environments', *Accounting, Organisations and Society*, 3 (1): 47–64.

Hedges, A. (1985) 'Group Interviewing', in R. Walker (ed.) *Applied Qualitative Research*, UK: Gower Publishing Company Limited, 71–91.

Hofstede, G. H. (1968) *The Game of Budget Control*, London: Tavistock.

Hofstede, G. H. (1991) *Cultures and Organizations: Software of the Mind*, London: McGraw-Hill.

Hopper, T. and Armstrong, P. (1991) 'Cost Accounting, Controlling Labour and the Rise of Conglomerates', *Accounting, Organisations and Society*, 25: 405–438.

Hopper, T. M. and Powell, A. (1985) 'Making Sense of Research into Organisational and Social Aspects of Management Accounting: A Review of Its Underling Assumptions', *Journal of Management Studies*, 22 (5): 429–436.

Hopper, T., Storey, J. and Willmott, H. (1987) 'Accounting for Accounting: Towards the Development of A Dialectical View', *Accounting, Organisations and Society*, 12: 437–456.

Hopwood, A. (1983) 'On Trying to Study Accounting in Contexts in Which it Operates', *Accounting, Organisations and Society*, 8 (2/3): 287–305.

Hopwood, A. (1985) 'Editorial', *Accounting, Organisations and Society*, 10 (1): 1–2.

Hopwood, A. (1990) 'Accounting and Organization Change', *Accounting, Auditing & Accountability Journal*, 3: 7–17.

Hoque, Z. and Alam, M. (1999) 'TQM Adoption, Institutionalism and Changes in Management Accounting Systems: A Case Study', *Accounting and Business Research*, 29 (3): 199–210.

Hoque, Z. (2001) *Strategic Management Accounting: Concepts, Processes and Issues*, Oxford: Chandos Publishing.

Hoque, Z. and Hopper, T. (1997) 'Political and Industrial Relations Turbulence, Competition and Budgeting in the Nationalised Jute Mills of Bangladesh', *Accounting and Business Research*, 27 (2): 125–143.

Hove, M. R. (1989) 'The Inappropriate Uses of International Accounting Standards in Less Developed Countries: The Case of International Accounting Standards Number 24 – Related Party Disclosures Concerning Transfer Prices', *International Journal of Accounting*, 24: 165–179.

Howell, R. A. and Soucy, S. R. (1987) 'Cost Accounting in the New Manufacturing Environment', *Management Accounting*, August: 42–48.

Huang, Z. and Palvia, P. (2001) 'ERP Implementation Issues in Advanced and Developing Countries', *Business Process Management Journal*, 7 (3): 276–284.

Humphrey, C. and Scapens, R. (1996) 'Theories and Case Studies of Organisational Accounting Practices: Limitations or Liberations?', *Accounting, Auditing and Accountability Journal*: 86–106.

Hussey, J. and Hussey, R. (1997) *Business Research: A Practical Guide for Undergraduate and Postgraduate Students*, London: Macmillan Press Ltd.

Hyvonen, T. (2003) 'Management Accounting and Information Systems: ERP versus BOB', *European Accounting Review*, 12: 1, 155–173.

ICAEW (Institute of Chartered Accountants in England and Wales) (1997) 'Added-value Professionals: Chartered Accountants in 2005 – A Consultation Document', Online. Available at: http://www.icaew.co.uk/index.cfm?AUB=TB2I_2931,MNXI_2931 (accessed on 10th April 2005).

IFAC (International Federation of Accountants) (1998) *Management Accounting Concepts*, International Federation of Accountants, New York. Online. Available at: http://www.ifac.org/StandardsAndGuidance/FMAC/IMAP1.htm (accessed on 10th April 2005).

IMC (Industrial Modernisation Centre) (2003) 'Green Paper on Industrial Policy in Egypt', November, IMC, Cairo, Egypt. Online. Available at: http://www.imc-egypt.org/en/greenpaper/en/TOC.htm (accessed on 10th April 2005).

Innes, J. and Mitchell, F. (1990) 'The Process of Change in Management Accounting: Some Field Study Evidence', *Management Accounting Research*, 1: 3–19.

Ito, Y. (1995) 'Strategic Goals of Quality Costing in Japanese Companies', *Management Accounting Research*, 6: 183–397.

Ittner, C. D. and Larcker, D. F. (1995) 'Total Quality Management and the Choice of Information and Reward Systems', *Journal of Accounting Research*, 33 (Supplement): 1–34.

Ittner, C. D., Larcker, D. F. and Rajan, M. V. (1997) 'The Choice of Performance Measures in Annual Bonus Contracts', *The Accounting Review*, 72 (2): 231–255.

Johnson, H. T. and Kaplan, R. S. (1987) *Relevance Lost: The Rise and Fall of Management Accounting*, Boston: Harvard Business School Press.

Johnson, H. T. (1981) 'Toward a New Understanding of Nineteenth Century Cost Accounting', *The Accounting Review*, 56 (3): 510–518.

Johnson, H. T. (1983) 'The Search for Gain in Markets and Firms: A Review of the Historical Emergence of Management Accounting Systems', *Accounting, Organisations and Society*, 17: 139–146.

Johnson, H. T. (1988) 'Activity-Based Information: A Blueprint for World-Class Management Accounting', *Management Accounting (US)*, (June): 23–30.

Johnson, H. T. (1994) 'Relevance Regained: Total Quality Management and the Role of Management Accounting', *Critical Perspective on Accounting*, 5: 259–267.

Jones, C. S. (1985) 'An Empirical Study of the Evidence for Contingency Theories of Management Accounting Systems in Conditions of Rapid Change', *Accounting, Organisations and Society*, 10 (3): 303–328.

Jones, M. and Karsten, H. (2003) 'Review: Structuration Theory and Information Systems Research', Working Paper No. 2003/11, Cambridge, UK: University of Cambridge, the Judge Institute of Management. Online. Available at: http://www.jims.cam.ac.uk/research/working_papers/abstract_03/wp0311.pdf (accessed on 10th April 2005).

Jones, T. C. and Dugdale, D. (2002) 'The ABC Bandwagon and the Juggernaut of Modernity', *Accounting, Organisations and Society*, 27: 121–163.

Jordan, A. S. (1999) 'The Impact Technology is Having on the Accounting Profession', *Journal of Accounting Education*, 17: 341–348.

Kanter, R. M., Stein, B. A. and Jick, T. D. (1992) *The Challenge of Organisational Change: How Companies Experience It and Leaders Guide It*, New York: Free Press.

Kaplan, R. S. (1983) 'Measuring Manufacturing Performance: A New Challenge for Management Accounting Research', *The Accounting Review*, October, 58 (4): 686–705.

Kaplan, R. S. (1984) 'The Evolution of Management Accounting', *The Accounting Review*, July, 59 (3): 390–418.

Kaplan, R. S. (1986) 'Accounting Lag: The Obsolescence of Cost Accounting Systems', *California Management Review*, Winter, XXVIII (2): 174–199.

Kaplan, R. S. and Cooper, R. (1998) *Cost & Effect: Using Integrated Cost Systems to Drive Profitability and Performance*, Boston, Massachusetts: Harvard Business School Press.

Kaplan, R. S. and Norton, D. P. (1992) 'The Balanced Scorecard-Measures That Drive Performance', *Harvard Business Review*, Jan–Feb: 71–79.

Kasurinen, T. (2002) 'Exploring Management Accounting Change: The Case of Balanced Scorecard Implementation,' *Management Accounting Research*, 13: 323–343.

Ke, W., Wei, K., Chau, P. and Deng, Z. (2003) 'Organizational Learning in ERP implementation: An Exploratory Study of Strategic Renewal', Paper presented at Ninth American Conference Information Systems.

Keller, G. and Teufel, T. (1998) *SAP R/3 Process Oriented Implementation: Iterative Process Prototyping*, Boston, MA: Addison-Wesley Publishing.

Khattab, M. (2005) 'Constraints of Privatisation in the Egyptian Experience'. Online. Available at: http://www.worldbank.org/mdf/mdf2/papers/partnerships/khattab.pdf (accessed on 10ᵗʰ April 2005).

Kholeif, A. O. R. (1997) (in Arabic) *Studying and Evaluating International Accounting Standards and their Applicability to Practice in Egypt*, Unpublished MSc Thesis, Egypt: Alexandria University, Faculty of Commerce.

Kimberly, J. R. and Evanisko, M. D. (1981) 'Organisational Innovation: The Influence of Individual, Organisational and Contextual Factors on Hospital Adoption of Technological and Administrative Innovations', *The Academy of Management Journal*, December, 24 (4): 689–713.

King, M., Lee, R. A., Piper, J. A. and Whittaker, J. (1991) *Information Technology and the Management Accountant*, London: CIMA.

Kuhn, T. S. (1962) *The Structure of Scientific Revolutions*, Chicago: University of Chicago Press.

Laitinen, E. K. (2001) 'Management Accounting Change in Small Technology Companies: Towards a Mathematical Model of the Technology Firm', *Management Accounting Research*, 12: 507–541.

Larson, R. K. and Kenny, S. Y. (1995) 'An Empirical Analysis of International Accounting Standards, Equity Markets and Economic Growth in Developing Countries', *Journal of International Financial Management and Accounting*, 6 (2): 130–157.

Larson, R. K. (1993) 'International Accounting Standards and Economic Growth: An Empirical Investigation of their Relationship in Africa', *Research in Third World Accounting*, 2: 27–43.

Laughlin, R. (1987) 'Accounting Systems in Organisational Contexts: A Case for Critical Theory', *Accounting, Organisations and Society*, 12 (5): 479–502.

Laughlin, R. (1995) 'Empirical Research in Accounting Approaches and a Case of Middle-Range Thinking', *Accounting, Auditing and Accountability Journal*, 8 (1): 63–87.

Layder, D. (1985) 'Power, Structure and Agency', *Journal for the Theory of Social Behaviour*, 15 (2): 131–149.

Layder, D. (1987) 'Key Issues in Structuration Theory: Some Critical Remarks', *Current Perspectives in Social Theory*, 8: 25–46.

Lee, A. and Modell, S. (2000) 'The Coordinating Role of Budgetary Participation: Rationalistic and Institutional Perspectives', Unpublished Working Paper, Royal Institute of Technology.

Lee, A. S. (1991) 'Integrating Positivist and Interpretive Approaches to Organizational Research', *Organization Science*, November, 2 (4): 342–365.

Leong, S. M. (1985) 'Meta-theory and Meta-methodology in Marketing: A Lakatosian Reconstruction', *Journal of Marketing*, 49: 23–40.

Liao, J. (1996) 'Information Technology Investment: The Effect of Institutional Isomorphism', *The Journal of High Technology Management Research*, 7 (1): 37–52.

Libby, T. and Waterhouse, J. H. (1996) 'Predicting Change in Management Accounting Systems', *Journal of Management Accounting Research*, 8: 137–150.

Licari, J. (1997) 'Economic Reform in Egypt in a Changing Global Economy', OECD Development Centre, Technical Paper No. 129, December: 1–54. Online. Available at http://www.oecd.org/dataoecd/18/36/1922293.pdf (accessed on 10ᵗʰ April 2005).

Light, B., Holland, C. P. and Wills, K. (2001) 'ERP and Best of Breed: A Comparative Analysis', *Business Process Management Journal*, 7 (3): 216–224.

Longden, S., Luther, R. and Bowler, D. (2001) *Management Accounting in a Society Undergoing Structural Change: A Southern African Study*, London: CIMA.

Luft, J. A. (1997) 'Long-term Change in Management Accounting: Perspectives from Historical Research', *Journal of Management Accounting Research*, 8: 163–197.

Luther, R. G. and Longden, S. (2001) 'Management Accounting in Companies Adapting to Structural Change and Volatility in Transition Economies: A South African Study', *Management Accounting Research*, 12: 299–320.

Macintosh, N. B. and Scapens, R. W. (1990) 'Structuration Theory in Management Accounting', *Accounting, Organisations and Society*, 15 (5): 455–477.

Macintosh, N. B. (1994) *Management Accounting and Control Systems: An Organisational and Behavioural Approach*, New York, USA: John Wiley and Sons.

Mackey, J. and Thomas, M. (1995) 'Costing and the New Operations Management', in D. Ashton, T. Hopper and R. W. Scapens (ed.) *Issues in Management Accounting*, pp. 87–113, London: Prentice Hall.

Mangos, N. C. and Lewis, N. R. (1995) 'A Socio-Economic Paradigm for Analyzing Managers' Accounting Choice Behaviour', *Accounting, Auditing & Accountability Journal*, 8 (1): 38–62.

Manson, S., McCartney, S. and Sherer, M. (2001) 'Audit Automation as Control within Audit Firms', *Accounting, Auditing & Accountability Journal*, 14 (1): 109–130.

Marie, A. A. (1969) *A Critical Study of Asset Valuation and Income Determination under the New Uniform UAR (Egypt) Accounting System Relative to the Objectives of Economic Planning*, Unpublished PhD Thesis, Michigan State University.

Markus, M. L. and Tanis, C. (2000) 'The Enterprise Systems Experience – From Adoption to Success', in R. W. Zmud (eds) *Framing the Domains of IT Research: Glimpsing the Future through the Past*, Cincinnati, OH: Pinnaflex Educational Resources, Inc.

McCosh, A. M. (1986) 'Management Accountancy in the Information Technology Age', in M. Bromwich and A. G. Hopwood (eds) *Research and Current Issues in Management Accounting*, pp. 192–204, London: Pitman.

Mensah, Y. W. (1981) 'Financial Reporting Model for Dependent Market Economies', *Abacus*, 17: 161–170.

Meyer, J. W. and Rowan, B. (1977) 'Institutionalized Organization: Formal Structure as Myth and Ceremony', *American Journal of Sociology*, September, 83 (2): 340–363.

Mia, L. and Clarke, B. (1999) 'Market Competition, Management Accounting Systems and Business Unit Performance', *Management Accounting Research*, 10: 137–158.

Miles, M. B. and Huberman, A. M. (1994) *Qualitative Data Analysis: An Expanded Sourcebook*, 2nd ed., Sage: Thousand Oaks, CA.

Miles, R. and Snow, C. (1978) *Organisational Strategy, Structure and Process*, New York: McGraw Hill.

Miller, D. and Friesen, P. H. (1984) *Organisations: A Quantum View*, Englewood Cliffs, NJ: Prentice-Hall.

Miller, P. and Napier, C. (1993) 'Genealogies of Calculation', *Accounting, Organisations and Society*, 18 (7/8): 631–647.

Miltenburg, J. (2001) 'Computational Complexity of Algorithms for MRP And JIT Production Planning Problems in Enterprise Resource Planning Systems', *Production Planning and Control*, 12 (2): 198–209.

Modell, S. (2001) 'Performance Measurement and Institutional Processes A Study of Managerial Responses to Public Sector Reform', *Management Accounting Research*, 12: 437–464.

Modell, S. (2002) 'Institutional Perspectives on Cost Allocations: Integration and Extension', *The European Accounting Review*, 11 (4): 653–679.

Morgan, G. and Smircich, L. (1980) 'The Case of Qualitative Research', *The Academy of Management Review*, 5 (4): 491–500.

Morse, W. J., Roth, H. P. and Poston, K. M. (1987) *Measuring, Planning and Controlling Quality Costs*, New Jersey: Institute of Management Accountants.

Mostafa, M. (1989) *The Financial Planning and Control in the Airways and Egypt Air*, Unpublished PhD Thesis, University of Hull.

Mouck, T. (1990) 'Positive Accounting Theory as a Lakatosian Research Programme', *Accounting and Business Research*, Summer: 231–239.

Mouritsen, J. (1994) 'Rationality, Institutions and Decision-Making: Reflection on March and Olsen's Rediscovering Institutions', *Accounting, Organisations and Society*, 19 (2): 193–211.

Mouzelis, N. P. (1991) *Back to Sociological Theory: The Construction of Social Orders*, London, UK: Macmillan Academic and Professional Ltd.

Murphy, C., Currie, J., Donnelly, R. and Fahy, M. (1992) 'Decision Support Systems and Management Accounting', *Management Accounting*, February: 46–47, 54.

Napier, C. (1989) 'Research Directions in Accounting History', *British Accounting Review*, 21 (3): 237–254.

Ndubizu, G. A. (1984) 'Accounting Standards and Economic Development: The Third World in Perspective', *International Journal of Accounting*, 19: 181–196.

Neimark, M. and Tinker, T. (1986) 'The Social Construction of Management Control Systems', *Accounting, Organization and Society*, 11 (4/5): 369–395.

Nelson, R. R. and Winter, S. G. (1982) *An Evolutionary Theory of Economic Change*, Cambridge, Mass.: Belknap.

Neu, D. (1992) 'The Social Construction of Positive Choices', *Accounting, Organisations and Society*, 17 (3/4): 223–237.

Newell, S., Tansley, C. and Huang, J. (2001) 'Knowledge Creation in an ERP Project Team: The Unexpected Debilitating Impact of Social Capital', Paper presented at Seventh American Conference Information Systems.

Nicolaou, A. I. (2004) 'Firm Performance Effects on the Implementation and Use of Enterprise Resource Planning Systems', *Journal of Information Systems*, Fall, 18: 79–105.

Nonaka, I. and Takeuchi, H (1995) *The Knowledge-Creating Company*, Oxford: Oxford University Press, Inc.

Nour, A. M. (1969) *Accounting and Allocation of Production Processes and Resources in Underdeveloped Countries, With Special Reference to the United Arab Republic*, Unpublished PhD Thesis, University of Birmingham.

Oliver, C. (1991) 'Strategic Responses to Institutional Processes', *The Academy of Management Review*, 16 (1): 145–179.

Oliver, C. (1992) 'The Antecedents of De-Institutionalisation', *Organisation Studies*, 13: 563–588.

Orlikowski, W. J. (1992) 'The Duality of Technology: Rethinking the Concept of Technology in Organizations', *Organization Science*, 3 (3): 398–429.

Orlikowski, W. J. (2000) 'Using Technology and Constituting Structures: A Practice Lens for Studying Technology in Organizations', *Organization Science*, 11 (4): 404–428.

Otley, D. T. (1978) 'Budget Use and Managerial Performance', *Journal of Accounting Research*, 16 (1): 122–149.

Otley, D. T. (1980) 'The Contingency Theory of Management Accounting: Achievement and Prognosis', *Accounting, Organizations and Society*, 5 (4): 413–428.

Otley, D. T. (1985) 'Development in Management Accounting Research', *British Accounting Review*, Autumn, 17: 3–23.

Otley, D. (1995) 'Management Control, Organizational Design and Accounting Information Systems', in D. Ashton, T. Hopper and R. W. Scapens (ed.) *Issues in Management Accounting*, pp. 45–65, London: Prentice Hall.

Otley, D. T. and Berry, A. (1994) 'Case Study Research in Management Accounting and Control', *Management Accounting Research*, 5: 45–65.

Ouibrahim, N. and Scapens, R. (1989) 'Accounting and Financial Control in a Socialist Enterprise: A Case Study from Algeria', *Accounting, Auditing and Accountability Journal*, 2 (2): 7–28.

Parker, J. (2000) *Concepts in the Social Sciences: Structuration*, Buckingham, USA: Open University Press.

Parker, K. (1996) 'The Enterprise Endeavour', *Manufacturing Systems*, 14 (1): 14–20.

Patton, M. Q. (2002) *Qualitative Research and Evaluation Methods – 3rd Edition*, Thousand Oaks, Calif.: Sage Publications.

PCSU (Privatisation Coordination Support Unit) (2002) 'The Result and Impact of Egypt's Privatisation Program', *Privatisation in Egypt-Quarterly Review*, April–June, CARANA Corporation: Privatisation Coordination Support Unit. Online. Available at: http://www.carana.com/pcsu/monitor/Q2/Impacts%20and%20Results.pdf (accessed on 10th April 2005).

Perren, L. and Grant, P. (2000) 'The Evolution of Management Accounting Routines in Small Businesses: A Social Construction Perspective', *Management Accounting Research*, 11: 391–411.

Perry, C. (1998) 'Processes of a Case Study Methodology for Postgraduate Research in Marketing', *European Journal of Marketing*, 32 (9/10): 785–802.

Peteroff, J. N. (1993) *Handbook of MRPII and JIT*, Englewood Cliffs, N.J.: Prentice-Hall.

Porter, K. (2000) 'The Electronic Plughole', *Control*, 26 (3): 7–10.

Porter, M. E. (1985) *Competitive Advantage: Creating and Sustaining Superior Performance*, New York: Free Press.

Porter, M. E. and Miller, V. E. (1985) 'How Information Gives Competitive Advantage', *Harvard Business Review*, July–August: 149–159.

Prasad, P. (1997) 'System of Meaning: Ethnography as a Methodology for the Study of Information Technologies', in A. Lee, J. Liebenau and J. Degross (eds) *Information Systems and Qualitative Research*, London: Chapman & Hall, 1–33.

Puxty, A. G. (1993) *The Social and Organisational Context of Management Accounting*, London: Academic Press.

Ramos, F. (2002) 'Economic Implications of the Egyptian Tax Reform Program', Paper presented at *The Conference on Institutional and Policy Challenges Facing the Egyptian Economy*, May 26–27, Cairo, Egypt.

Robert, J. and Scapens, R. (1990) 'Accounting as Discipline', in D. J. Cooper and T. M. Hopper (eds) *Critical Accounts*, pp. 107–125, London: Macmillan Press.

Robert, K. and Scapens, R. (1985) 'Accounting Systems and Systems of Accountability – Understanding Accounting Practices in their Organisational Context', *Accounting, Organisations and Society*, 10 (4): 443–456.

Ross, J. and Vitale, M. R. (2000). 'The ERP Revolution: Surviving vs. Thriving', *Information Systems Frontiers*, 2 (2): 233–241.

Ryan, B., Scapens, R. W. and Theobald, M. (1992) *Research Method and Methodology in Finance and Accounting*, London: Academic Press.

Ryan, B., Scapens, R. W. and Theobald, M. (2002) *Research Method and Methodology in Finance and Accounting*, London: Academic Press.

Santhanam, R. and Hartono, E. (2003) 'Issues in Linking Information Technology Capacities to Firm Performance', *MIS Quarterly*, March, 27: 125–153.

Satzinger, J. W., Jackson, R. B. and Burd, S. D. (2002) *System Analysis and Design in a Changing World (2nd edition)*, Canada: Course Technology, Thomson Learning.

Saunders, M., Lewis, P. and Thornhill, A. (2003) *Research Methods for Business Students – Third Edition*, Harlow: Financial Times Prentice Hall.

Scapens, R. W. (1990) 'Researching Management Accounting Practice: The Role of Case Study Methods', *British Accounting Review*, 22: 259–281.

Scapens, R. W. (1994) 'Never Mind the Gape: Towards an Institutional Perspective on Management Accounting Practice', *Management Accounting Research*, 5: 301–321.

Scapens, R. W. and Jazayeri, M. (2003) 'ERP Systems and Management Accounting Change: Opportunities or Impacts? A Research Note', *The European Accounting Review*, 12 (1): 201–233.

Scapens, R. W. and Roberts, J. (1993) 'Accounting and Control: A Case Study of Resistance to Accounting Change', *Management Accounting Research*, 4: 1–32.

Scapens, R. W., Turley, S., Burns, J., Joseph, N., Lewis, L. and Southworth, A. (1996) *External Reporting and Management Decisions: A Study of their Interrelationship in UK Companies*, London: CIMA.

Scapens, R. W., Jazayeri, M. and Scapens, J. (1998) SAP: Integrated Information Systems and the Implications for Management Accountants, *Management Accounting (UK)*, September, 76 (8): 46–48.

Schneider, P. (1999) 'Wanted: ERPeople Skills', *CIO Magazine*, March, 1: 30–37. Online. Available at http://www.cio.com/archive/030199/erp.html (accessed on 10th April 2005).

Schniederjans, M. J. and Kim, G. C. (2003) 'Implementing Enterprise Resource Planning Systems with Total Quality Control and Business Process Re-Engineering: Survey Results', *International Journal of Operations & Production Management*, 23 (4): 418–429.

Scott, B. (1994) *Manufacturing Planning Systems*, London: McGraw-Hill International.

Scott, S. and Wagner, E. (2003) 'Networks, Negotiations, and New Times: The Implementation of Enterprise Resource Planning into an Academic Administration', *Information and Organisation*, 13: 285–313.

Scott, W. R. (1987) 'The Adolescence of Institutional Theory', *Administrative Science Quarterly*, 32: 493–511.

Scott, W. R. (2001) *Institutions and Organisations (2nd edition)*, London: Sage Publication.

Seal, W., Cullen, J., Dunlop, A., Berry, T. and Ahmed, M. (1999) 'Enacting a European Supply Chain: A Case Study on the Role of Management Accounting', *Management Accounting Research*, 10: 303–322.

Shank, J. K. and Govindarajan, V. (1992) 'Strategic Cost Management: The Value Chain Perspective', *Journal of Management Accounting Research*, 4: 179–197.

Shank, J. K. (1989) 'Strategic Cost Management: New Wine or Just New Bottles', *Journal of Management Accounting Research*, 1 (Fall): 47–65.

Sharma, R. (2000) 'From Relevance Lost to Relevance Regained: Management Practice in the New Millennium'. Online. Available at: http://www.ifac.org/Library/Speech Article.tmpl?NID=9762908175453 (accessed on 10th April 2005).

Shaw, R. (1998) 'ABC and ERP: Partners at Last?', *Management Accounting*, November: 56–58.

Shields, M. D. and Young, S. M. (1989) 'A Behavioural Model for Implementing Cost Management Systems', *Journal of Cost Management*, Winter, 17–27.

Shields, M. G. (2001) *E-Business and ERP: Rapid Implementation and Project Planning*, New York: John Wiley.

Sibanda-Ndiweni, E. (2002) *A Structuration Analysis of the Production and Re-production of Management Accounting and Quality Practices in a Volatile Socio-Political Environment*, Unpublished PhD Thesis, University of Essex, UK.

Silk, S. (1998) 'Automating The Balanced Scorecard', *Management Accounting*, May: 38–44.

Silverman, D. (2001) *Interpreting Qualitative Data: Methods for Analyzing Talk, Text and Interaction*, London: Sage Publications.

Simmonds, K. (1981) 'Strategic Management Accounting', *Management Accounting*, 59 (4): 26–29.

Simons, R. (1987) 'Accounting Control Systems and Business Strategy', *Accounting, Organisations and Society*, 12: 357–374.

SIS (State Information Service) (2002) 'Privatisation Update'. Online. Available at: http://www.sis.gov.eg/egyptinf/economy/html/eep/html/text45.htm (accessed on 10ᵗʰ April 2005).

Soin, K., Seal, W. and Cullen, J. (2002) 'ABC and Organizational Change: An Institutional Perspective', *Management Accounting Research*, 13: 249–271.

Spathis, C. and Constantinides, S. (2002) 'ERP Systems and Management Accounting Practice', *3ʳᵈ Conference on New Direction in Management Accounting: Innovations in Practice and Research*, 12–14 December 2002, Brussels.

Spicer, B. H. (1992) 'The Resurgence of Cost and Management Accounting: A Review of Some Recent Developments in Practice, Theories and Case Research Methods', *Management Accounting Research*, March, 3 (1): 1–37.

Stake, R. E. (1994) 'Case Studies', in N. K. Denzin and Y. S. Lincoln (eds) *Handbook of Qualitative Research*, London: Sage Publications.

Stenzel, J. and Stenzel, C. (2002) 'ERP System Opportunities and Limitations', *Cost Management*, 16 (2): 5–12.

Storper, M. (1985) 'The Spatial and Temporal Constitution of Social Action: A Critical Reading of Giddens', *Environment and Planning D: Society and Space*, 3 (4): 407–424.

Sulaiman, S. (2002) 'Management Accounting Change in Malaysian Manufacturing Organizations', Paper Presented in *3ʳᵈ Conference of CIMA on New Direction in Management Accounting*, London: CIMA.

Sutton, S. G. (2000) 'The Changing Face of Accounting in an Information Technology Dominated World', *International Journal of Accounting Information Systems*, 1 (1): 1–8.

Themistocleous, M. and Irani, Z. (2001) 'Benchmarking: the Benefits and Barriers of Application Integration', *Benchmarking: An International Journal*, 8 (4): 317–331.

Themistocleous, M., Irani, Z. and O'Keefe, R. M. (2001) 'ERP and Application Integration: Exploratory Survey', *Business Process Management Journal*, 7(3): 195–204.

Tiessen, P. and Waterhouse, J. H. (1983) 'Towards Descriptive Theory of Management Accounting', *Accounting, Organisations and Society*, 17: 251–268.

Tomkins, C. and Groves, R. (1983) 'The Everyday Accountant and Researching his Reality', *Accounting, Organisations and Society*, 8 (4): 361–374.

Uddin, S. and Hopper, T. (1999) 'Management Control, Ownership and Development: Illustrations from a Privatised Bangladeshi Enterprise', in M. Mavkintosh and R. Roy (eds) *Economic Decentralisation and Public Management Reform*, Cheltenham: Edward Elgar.

Uddin, S. and Hopper, T. (2001) 'A Bangladeshi Soap Opera: Privatisation, Accounting and Regimes of Control in a Less Developed Country', *Accounting, Organization and Society*, 26 (7/8): 643–672.

Vaivio, J. (1999) 'Exploring a "Non-Financial" Management Accounting Change', *Management Accounting Research*, 10: 409–437.

Vamosi, T. S. (2000) 'Continuity and Change: Management Accounting During Processes of Transition', *Management Accounting Research*, 11: 27–63.

Van de Ven, A. (1986) 'Central Problems in the Management of Innovation', *Management Science*, May, 32 (5): 590–607.

Venkatesan, R. (1992) 'Strategic Sourcing: To Make or Not to Make', *Harvard Business Review* (November–December): 98–107.

Volkoff, O. (2001) *A Grounded Process Model of Enterprise System Implementation*, Unpublished PhD Thesis, Faculty of Graduate Studies, The University of Western Ontario, London, Ontario.

Wallace, R. S. O. (1993) 'Development of Accounting Standards for Developing and Newly Industrialized Countries', *Research in Third World Accounting*, 2: 121–165.

Wallace, R. S. O. (1997) 'African Labor System, Maintenance Accounting and Agency Theory: Some Fundamental Questions', *Critical Perspective on Accounting*, 8: 393–407.

Washington, W. N. (2000) 'DoD Financial Management: More Reliable Information for Decision Makers', *PM (Program Manager)*, November–December: 38–41. Online. Available at: http://www.dau.mil/pubs/pm/pmpdf00/washn-d.pdf (accessed on 10th April 2005).

Weick, K. E. (1969) *The Social Psychology of Organising*, Reading, MA: Addison.

Williams, J. J. and Seaman, A. E. (2001) 'Predicting Change in Management Accounting Systems: National Culture and Industry Effect', *Accounting, Organizations and Society*, 26: 443–460.

Williamson, O. E. (1975) *Markets and Hierarchies: Analysis of Antitrust Implications: A Study in the Economics of Internal Organisation*, New York: Free Press.

Wilson, R. A. and Sangster, A. (1992) 'The Automation of Accounting Practice', *Journal of Information Technology*, 7: 65–75.

Yin, R. K. (1994) *Case Study Research, Design and Methods*, Beverly Hills: Sage Publications.

Index

[Page numbers appearing in **bold** denote those containing tables; page numbers appearing in *italics* denote those containing figures]